A Compendium of
Statements of the United
States Catholic Bishops on
the Political and Social
Order 1966–1980

QUEST FOR
JUSTICE

J. Brian Benestad and Francis J. Butler
Co-editors

NATIONAL CONFERENCE OF CATHOLIC BISHOPS
UNITED STATES CATHOLIC CONFERENCE

In the exercise of your ministry of truth, as bishops of the United States you have, through statements and pastoral letters, collectively offered the word of God to your people, showing its relevance to daily life, pointing to the power it has to uplift and heal. . . . In your pastoral interest for all your people in all their needs—including housing, education, health care, employment, and the administration of justice—you gave further witness to the fact that all aspects of human life are sacred. You were in effect proclaiming that the Church will never abandon man, nor his temporal needs, as she leads humanity to salvation and eternal life. . . .

John Paul II Address to the
bishops of the United States
October 5, 1979

Preface

The Catholic bishops of the United States are today organized nationally as the United States Catholic Conference (USCC) and the National Conference of Catholic Bishops (NCCB). Both organizations were established at the end of 1966, succeeding the National Catholic Welfare Conference (NCWC) which had served the Church at the national level for most of the previous half-century.

The NCCB is a canonical body established by Church law. Like other bishops' conferences around the world, the NCCB finds its basis in the Second Vatican Council's *Decree on the Bishops' Pastoral Office in the Church.* Its concerns are "ecclesiastical": for example, liturgy, ecumenism, education and ministry of priests, permanent deacons, canon law, and, in general, the pastoral responsibilities of bishops.

The USCC is a civil entity. Like the NCCB, its members are the bishops, but its policymaking structures include priests, religious, and lay people. USCC concerns are reflected in its organization into three major departments: Education, Communication, and Social Development and World Peace, along with specialized offices such as General Counsel and Government Liaison offices, and quasi-autonomous agencies like the Campaign for Human Development, a Church-sponsored anti-poverty program, and Catholic Relief Services, the overseas aid program of the Church in the U.S.

Bishops' statements on political and social issues most often emanate from the offices and committees of the USCC. However, the NCCB also issues statements that touch on political and social matters.

In recent years the bishops have taken public positions on numerous domestic and international issues and have articulated these positions not only in statements but in congressional testimony, meetings with government officials, and similar efforts. Yet relatively few Americans are aware of this activity. Typically, bishops' statements are published in pamphlet form and receive passing coverage in the secular press. Although the bishops' advocacy has been forthright and frequently effective, it is not too widely recognized.

This volume is intended as a record of the bishops' stands on social and political questions issued between 1966 and 1980. It contains statements on domestic and foreign policy by the USCC, the NCCB, the USCC Administrative Board, the NCCB/USCC Executive Committee, the USCC

Committee on Social Development and World Peace, and the USCC Department of Social Development and World Peace.

Appendices A and B provide a list of selected political and social statements made by Presidents of the NCCB/USCC, the General Secretary, individual bishops testifying on behalf of the USCC, staff members of the Department of Social Development and World Peace, and *ad hoc* committees. It is helpful, and even necessary in many cases, to consult such statements in order to understand more fully the nature and implications of the bishops' statements themselves. Appendix C contains a list of papal encyclicals and letters as well as conciliar documents. These must be consulted in order to understand the theological and philosophical foundations of the bishops' view of their own political responsibility.

There have been three previous volumes of statements by the bishops of the U.S.: *The National Pastorals of the American Hierarchy (1792-1919)*,[1] *Our Bishops Speak*,[2] and *Pastoral Letters of the American Hierarchy 1792-1970*.[3] *Our Bishops Speak*, which covers the period from 1919 to 1951, contains not only statements by the bishops but resolutions of episcopal committees and communications of the Administrative Board of the National Catholic Welfare Conference. The other two volumes contain only the bishops' statements and pastoral letters.

These previous volumes do not separate socio-political from other kinds of statements as this Compendium does. In this Compendium, the texts are arranged in three parts, under the headings "Political Responsibility," "Foreign Policy," and "Domestic Policy." "Foreign Policy" is divided into three sections: war and peace, development, and human rights. Statements under "Domestic Policy" are arranged alphabetically and touch on the following issues: abortion, birth control, Call to Action (The U.S. Bishops Bicentennial Consultation on Social Justice), crime and punishment, economic issues, family life, freedom of religion, housing, immigrants, labor disputes, minorities, race, rural America, and television.

Statements on such varied and complex issues require both moral insight and political and economic expertise. The bishops fully recognize that reasonable people may disagree with their application of principles to concrete situations.

> The principles of revelation do not provide specific solutions to many social problems, nor do they constitute a blueprint for organizing society. In proposing concrete policies in the social order, the Church is aware that often the more specific a proposal or program, the more room there may be for persons of sincere faith to disagree.[4]

---

[1] Monsignor Peter Guilday, ed. (Washington: NCWC, 1923).

[2] Very Reverend Raphael M. Huber (Milwaukee: Bruce Publishing Company, 1952).

[3] Hugh J. Nolan, ed. (Huntington, Indiana: Our Sunday Visitor, Inc., 1971).

[4] National Conference of Catholic Bishops, "The Bicentennial Consultation: A Response," in *A Call to Action* (Washington: United States Catholic Conference, 1977), p. 137.

The bishops are, however, happy if their statements prompt men and women to reflect more deeply on the complex political and economic problems facing the nation.

Bishop Thomas Kelly, O.P.
General Secretary
National Conference
of Catholic Bishops/
U.S. Catholic Conference

Table of Contents

Part III: Domestic Policy

Part I:
Political Responsibility

Political Responsibility

The initial section of this Compendium of statements of the bishops of the United States includes a lengthy reflection on political responsibility by the USCC's Administrative Board and resolutions on the same subject issued by the USCC in previous years. These appear before the bishops' statements on domestic and foreign policy because they explain why and how the Church intends to participate in the political process.

The USCC Board argues that the Gospel requires Christians not only to practice charity on an individual level, but also to promote human rights and social justice. The 1971 Synod of Bishops reaffirmed this latter obligation by declaring:

> ... the Church has the right, indeed the duty, to proclaim justice on the social, national and international level, and to denounce instances of injustice when the fundamental rights of man and his very salvation demand it.

To accomplish this task, individuals and organizations must get involved in the political process "since social injustice and the denial of human rights can often be remedied only through governmental action." In particular, members of the Church should do the following: explain the social teaching of the Church to the faithful, analyze public policy in the light of Gospel values, call attention to the moral and religious dimension of secular issues, show what changes are required by the Christian faith in order to bring about a just society, participate with other parties in debate over public policy, and speak out with courage in a comprehensive and consistent fashion on human rights, social justice, and the life of the Church in society.

The USCC Board also believes that the Constitution of the United States gives it the right not only to state principles but also to take positions on matters of public policy. The Board goes on to say that, when taking concrete positions on matters about which reasonable Christians may disagree, it does not impose its views by dint of authority. Hence, the bishops are not planning to form a religious voting bloc. They hope, instead, to move all citizens to take politics more seriously and to look at political issues from a moral and religious viewpoint:

> We seek to promote a greater understanding of the important link between faith and politics and to express our belief that our nation is enriched when its citizens and social groups approach public affairs from positions grounded in moral conviction and religious belief.

1

Also included in this introductory section is the bishops' 1976 pastoral let-
ter entitled To Live in Christ Jesus: A Pastoral Reflection on the Moral Life.
Its first part explains, in summary fashion, principles of the moral life; and
we include the pastoral letter at this point in the Compendium, because its
second part applies these moral principles to domestic and foreign policy
issues.

Political Responsibility: Choices for the 1980s

USCC, Administrative Board
October 26, 1979

The hallmark of a democratic nation is its ability to engage the voice of its
people in a broad range of public decisions. The United States, we fear, may
be losing this capacity.

Consider the evidence. Fewer of our citizens are registering to vote. Fewer
of the registrants are actually going to the polls. Our voting rolls have lost 15
million citizens in the last 10 years. For our national elections, the rate of
participation has been dropping for the last 20 years. Thus, the rate for the
1976 election was down sharply from the 1960 turnout and the rate for 1978
was the lowest for a national election since 1942. Our voter participation
rates are now among the lowest in the world.[1]

Clearly, fewer and fewer Americans believe it is worth their time and concern to follow campaigns, form positions on the candidates and issues, and
assert those positions at the polls. The result of this disaffection is also clear:
an erosion in the very foundations of American political life. Thus, we take
the eve of the national campaign year as the occasion to affirm again the importance of responsible political participation.

In 1976 we issued a statement calling for "a committed, informed citizenry
to revitalize our political life."[2] We now reiterate that call with a greater

---

[1] In the 1978 congressional elections, 37.9 percent of those eligible to vote actually did so. In
contrast, 46 percent voted in 1960. In the 1976 presidential elections, 54.4 percent of eligible
voters turned out as compared to 63.8 percent in 1960.

[2] "Political Responsibility: Reflections on an Election Year," Feb. 12, 1976.

sense of urgency and we ask all citizens to help restore our elections as the vital and popular forum they can and must be if our nation is to address democratically the crucial issues of the coming decade.

I. Public Responsibility and the Electoral Process

The reasons for the crisis in voter disaffection are many and complex, but we would like here to cite just three of its major causes.

First, large numbers of Americans evidently feel a sense of powerlessness. To a large degree, this feeling is justified by the evidence of our eyes and ears.

Some leaders of the political estate have done much in recent years to weaken it and even to discredit it. We know too well their abuses of power, evasions of responsibility and refusals to face up to tough choices. Many of our citizens have simply thrown up their hands and turned away from politics and government per se.

We can share some of these feelings without also condoning the withdrawal they have caused. It makes little sense to let these difficulties force us to abandon citizenship, since this only invites the problems to deepen and threaten to become a permanent feature of our political life. If this happens, what hope can there be? The sensible response is to return to citizenship with the will and dedication to breathe new life into it.

Second, as the patterns of our national life evolve, popular debate of issues becomes more complex and harder for the ordinary person to follow. Because of economic pressures and rapid social change, some of the traditional organizing principles of American politics no longer carry the force they once did—for example, the long-standing loyalties and identities of social institutions, geographic regions and political parties. At the same time, we have yet to see a fresh and vital set of organizing principles take shape either to renew or supplant the older ones.

The avenues of contemporary communications hold the promise of shaping new forums for popular debate, but we have yet to see compelling evidence that the mass media will fulfill this promise. They seem as likely to abet disaffection as to help to remedy it.

Finally, another cause of low participation is the persistent fact of widespread poverty in America. The poorer a person is, the less likely the person is to vote. Voting relies on a degree of hope, and there seems to be little reason for the people most in need to feel hopeful in this economy. Poverty shuts off the gates to the American mainstream and its institutions of influence and power. Thus, the poor have little concrete reason to see a stake in voting.

Consequently, unless we address America's social and economic inequities in the coming campaign and election, we will continue to weaken the franchise for millions of our people, run the risk of creating an insidious form of dual citizenship, and jeopardize the great democratic experiment we proudly call America.

We fear that some of the current popular reactions against the government and government programs reveal an excessive individualism and a decline in our commitment to the common good. It is important for all Americans to realize the extent to which we are all interdependent members of a national community. Increasingly, our problems are social in nature, demanding solutions that are likewise social. To fashion these solutions in a just and humane way requires the active and creative participation of all. It requires a renewed faith in the ability of the human community to cooperate in governmental structures that work for the common good. It requires, above all, a willingness to attack the root causes of the powerlessness and alienation that threaten our democracy.

All Christians have a call to citizenship and political life. In the words of Pope Paul VI: 'The Christian has the duty to take part in the organization and life of political society.'[3] Accordingly, we urge all citizens to use their franchise by registering to vote and going to the polls. Demand information from the campaigns themselves and from the media coverage of those campaigns. Make candidates declare their values, so you can compare those values with your own. Take stands on the candidates and the issues.

If the campaign year is to engage the values of the American people, the campaigners and voters alike must share the responsibility for making it happen. Become involved in the campaign or party of your choice. Finally, use the debates of the coming year to better understand the issues and inform your conscience.

II. The Church and the Political Order

It is appropriate in this context to offer our own reflections on the role of the church in the political order. Christians believe that Jesus' commandment to love one's neighbor should extend beyond individual relationships to infuse and transform all human relations from the family to the entire human community. Jesus came to "bring good news to the poor, to proclaim liberty to captives, new sight to the blind and to set the downtrodden free" (Lk. 4:18). He called us to feed the hungry, clothe the naked, care for the sick and afflicted and to comfort the victims of injustice (Mt. 25). His example and words require individual acts of charity and concern from each of us. Yet they also require understanding and action upon the broader dimensions of poverty, hunger and injustice which necessarily involve the institutions and structures of economy, society and politics.

The church, the people of God, is itself an expression of this love and is required by the Gospel and its long tradition to promote and defend human rights and human dignity.[4] In his recent encyclical, *Redemptor Hominis,* Pope John Paul II declares that the church "must be aware of the threats to

---

[3] Pope Paul VI, "A Call To Action," 1971, no. 24.
[4] 1974 Synod of Bishops, "Human Rights and Reconciliation."

(humanity) and of all that seems to oppose the endeavor 'to make human life ever more human' and make every element of life correspond to humanity's true dignity—in a word, (the church) must be aware of all that is opposed to that process."[5]

This view of the church's ministry and mission requires it to relate positively to the political order, since social injustice and the denial of human rights can often be remedied only through governmental action. In today's world, concern for social justice and human development necessarily requires persons and organizations to participate in the political process in accordance with their own responsibilities and roles.

The church's responsibility in the area of human rights includes two complementary pastoral actions: the affirmation and promotion of human rights, and the denunciation and condemnation of violations of these rights. In addition, it is the church's role to call attention to the moral and religious dimensions of secular issues, to keep alive the values of the Gospel as a norm for social and political life, and to point out the demands of the Christian faith for a just transformation of society. Such a ministry on the part of every Christian and the church inevitably involves political consequences and touches upon public affairs.

Christian social teaching demands that citizens and public officials alike give serious consideration in all matters to the common good, to the welfare of society as a whole, which must be protected and promoted if individual rights are to be encouraged and upheld.

In order to be credible and faithful to the Gospel and to our tradition, the church's concern for human rights and social justice should be comprehensive and consistent. It must be formulated with competence and an awareness of the complexity of issues. It should also be developed in dialogue with other concerned persons and respectful of the rights of all.[6]

The church's role in the political order includes the following:

• Education regarding the teachings of the church and the responsibilities of the faithful;

• Analysis of issues for their social and moral dimensions;

• Measuring public policy against gospel values;

• Participating with other concerned parties in debate over public policy; and

• Speaking out with courage, skill and concern on public issues involving human rights, social justice and the life of the church in society.

Unfortunately, our efforts in this area are sometimes misunderstood. The church's participation in public affairs is not a threat to the political process or to genuine pluralism, but an affirmation of their importance. The church

---

[5] Pope John Paul II, *Redemptor Hominis*, 1979, no. 14.

[6] "A Call to Action," op. cit., nos. 4, 50; Vatican Council II, "The Church in the Modern World," 1965, no. 43.

recognizes the legitimate autonomy of government and the right of all, including the church itself, to be heard in the formulation of public policy.

As Vatican II declared:

"By preaching the truth of the Gospel and shedding light on all areas of human activity through her teaching and the example of the faithful, she (the church) shows respect for the political freedom and responsibility of citizens and fosters these values. She also has the right to pass moral judgments, even on matters touching the political order, whenever basic personal rights or the salvation of souls make such judgments necessary."[7]

A proper understanding of the role of the church will not confuse its mission with that of government, but rather see its ministry as advocating the critical values of human rights and social justice.

It is the role of Christian communities to analyze the situation in their own country, to reflect upon the meaning of the Gospel, and to draw norms of judgment and plans of action from the teaching of the church and their own experience.[8]

In carrying out this pastoral activity in the social arena, we are confronted with complexity. As the 1971 Synod of Bishops pointed out: "It does not belong to the church, insofar as she is a religious and hierarchical community, to offer concrete solutions in the social, economic and political spheres for justice in the world."[9] At the same time, it is essential to recall the words of Pope John XXIII: "It must not be forgotten that the church has the right and duty not only to safeguard the principles of ethics and religion, but also to intervene authoritatively with her children in the temporal sphere when there is a question of judging the application of these principles to concrete cases."[10]

The application of gospel values to real situations is an essential work of the Christian community. Christians believe the Gospel is the measure of human realities. However, specific political proposals do not in themselves constitute the Gospel. Christians and Christian organizations must certainly participate in public debate over alternative policies and legislative proposals, yet it is critical that the nature of their participation not be misunderstood.

We specifically do not seek the formation of a religious voting bloc; nor do we wish to instruct persons on how they should vote by endorsing candidates. We urge citizens to avoid choosing candidates simply on the personal basis of self-interest. Rather, we hope that voters will examine the positions of candidates on the full range of issues as well as the person's integrity, philosophy and performance.

We seek to promote a greater understanding of the important link between

---

[7] "The Chuch in the Modern World," op. cit., no. 76.
[8] "A Call to Action," op. cit.
[9] 1971 Synod of Bishops, "Justice in the World."
[10] Pope John XXIII, *Pacem in Terris,* 1963, no. 160.

faith and politics and to express our belief that our nation is enriched when its citizens and social groups approach public affairs from positions grounded in moral conviction and religious belief. Our view is expressed very well by Pope Paul VI when he said:

"While recognizing the autonomy of the reality of politics, Christians who are invited to take up political activity should try to make their choices consistent with the Gospel and, in the framework of a legitimate plurality, to give both personal and collective witness to the seriousness of their faith by effective and disinterested service of (humanity)."[11]

The church's responsibility in this area falls on all its members. As citizens we are all called to become informed, active and responsible participants in the political process. The hierarchy has a responsibility as teachers and pastors to educate the faithful, support efforts to gain greater peace and justice and provide guidance and even leadership on occasion where human rights are in jeopardy. The laity has major responsibility for the renewal of the temporal order. Drawing on their own experience and exercising their distinctive roles within the Christian community, bishops, clergy, religious and laity should join together in common witness and effective action to bring about Pope John's vision of a well-ordered society based on truth, justice, charity and freedom.[12]

As religious leaders and pastors, our intention is to reflect our concern that politics receive its rightful importance and attention and that it become an effective forum for the achievement of the common good. For, in the words of John Paul II, "(humanity's) situation in the modern world seems indeed to be far removed from the objective demands of the moral order, from the requirements of justice, and even more of social love. ... We have before us here great drama that can leave nobody indifferent."[13]

III. Issues

Without reference to political candidates, parties or platforms, we wish to offer a listing of some issues which we believe are important in the national debate during 1980. These brief summaries are not intended to indicate in any depth the details of our positions in these matters. We refer the reader to fuller discussions of our point of view in the documents listed in the summary which appears below. We wish to point out that these issues are not the concerns of Catholics alone; in every case we have joined with others to advocate these positions. They represent a broad range of topics on which the bishops of the United States have already expressed themselves and are recalled here in alphabetical order to emphasize their relevance in a period of national debate and decision.

---

[11] "A Call to Action," op. cit., no. 46.
[12] *Pacem in Terris*, no. 35.
[13] *Redemptor Hominis*, 16.

A. Abortion

The right to life is a basic human right which should have the protection of law. Abortion is the deliberate destruction of an unborn human being and therefore violates this right. We reject the 1973 Supreme Court decisions on abortion which refuse appropriate legal protection to the unborn child. We support the passage of a constitutional amendment to restore the basic constitutional protection of the right to life for the unborn child. ("Documentation on the Right to Life and Abortion," 1974, 1976; "Pastoral Plan for Pro-Life Activities," 1975.)

B. Arms Control and Disarmament

The dangers of the arms race are a challenge and a concern to the whole human family. The primary moral imperative is that the arms race be stopped and the reduction of armaments achieved. With respect to nuclear weapons, at least those with a massive destructive capability, the first imperative is to prevent their use. As possessors of a vast nuclear arsenal, we must also be aware that not only is it wrong to attack civilian populations but it is also wrong to threaten to attack them as part of a strategy of deterrence. We urge the continued development and implementation of policies which seek to bring these weapons more securely under control, progressively reduce their presence in the world and ultimately remove them entirely. ("To Live in Christ Jesus," 1976; "The Gospel of Peace and the Danger of War," 1978.)

C. Capital Punishment

In view of our commitment to the value and dignity of human life, we oppose capital punishment. We believe that a return to the use of the death penalty can only lead to further erosion of respect for life in our society. We do not question society's right to punish the offender, but we believe that there are better approaches to protecting our people from violent crimes than resorting to executions. In its application, the death penalty has been discriminatory toward the poor, the indigent and racial minorities. Our society should reject the death penalty and seek methods of dealing with violent crime which are more consistent with the gospel vision of respect for life and Christ's message of healing love. ("Community and Crime," 1978.)

D. The Economy

Our national economic life must reflect broad values of social justice and human rights. Above all, the economy must serve the human needs of our people. It is important to call attention to the fact that millions of Americans are still poor, jobless, hungry and inadequately housed and that vast disparities of income and wealth remain within our nation. These conditions are intolerable and must be persistently challenged so that the economy will reflect a fundamental respect for the human dignity and basic needs of all.

We recognize that the present political atmosphere is characterized by a heavy emphasis on budget austerity, particularly with regard to federal spending. Some believe that the reduction of government spending for social programs is the most effective way of combating inflation.

There is no doubt that inflation is a serious national problem. It weakens the economic stability of our nation and erodes the economic security of our citizens. Moreover, its impact is most severe on the poor and those who live on fixed incomes. However, economic policies which attempt to reduce inflation by cutting back on human needs programs or by increasing unemployment are simply unacceptable.

Current levels of unemployment and the tremendous human costs which they represent are unnecessary and should not be tolerated. We support an effective national commitment to genuine full employment as the foundation of a just and responsible economic policy. We believe that all Americans who are willing and able to work have a right to useful and productive employment at fair wages. We also call for a decent income policy for those who cannot work and adequate assistance to those in need. ("The Economy: Human Dimensions," 1975).

E. Education

All persons of whatever race, condition or age, by virtue of their dignity as human beings, have an inalienable right to education. We advocate:

1. Sufficient public and private funding to make an adequate education available for all citizens and residents of the United States of America and to provide assistance for education in our nation's program of foreign aid.

2. Governmental and voluntary action to reduce inequalities of educational opportunity by improving the opportunities available to economically disadvantaged persons.

3. Orderly compliance with legal requirements for racially integrated schools.

4. Voluntary efforts to increase racial ethnic integration in public and non-public schools.

5. Equitable tax support for the education of pupils in public and non-public schools to implement parental freedom in the education of their children. ("Sharing the Light of Faith," 1979; "To Teach as Jesus Did," 1972.)

F. Family Life

The test of how we value the family is whether we are willing to foster, in government and business, in urban planning and farm policy, in education and health care, in the arts and sciences, in our total social and cultural environment, moral values which nourish the primary relationships of husbands, wives and children and make authentic family life possible.

Implicit government policy and explicit government planning and programs can contribute to an erosion of the health and vitality of the family. Comprehensive decisions of a national or regional scope must take into account their impact on family life. Families, especially those whose influence is lessened by poverty or social status, must be allowed their rightful input in those decisions which affect their daily lives. ("A Vision and Strategy: The Plan of Pastoral Action for Family Ministry," 1978.)

G. Food and Agricultural Policy

The right to eat flows directly from the right to life. We support a national policy aimed at securing the right to eat to all the world's people.

Internationally, U.S. food aid should effectively combat global hunger and malnutrition, be aimed primarily at the poorest countries and neediest peoples without regard to political considerations. In order to help stabilize prices and assure adequate supplies, the United States should join in a world grain reserve fair to both producers and consumers. Economic assistance should emphasize helping other nations move toward food self-sufficiency.

Domestically, nutrition programs should help meet the needs of hungry and malnourished Americans, especially children, the poor, the unemployed and the elderly. It is essential that the food-stamp program be funded at adequate levels. ("Food Policy and the Church: Specific Proposals," 1975.)

Through its income-support programs, its credit and research programs, its tax policies, its strategies for rural development and its foreign aid, the United States should support the maintenance of an agricultural system based on small and moderate-sized family farms both at home and abroad. ("The Family Farm," 1979).

H. Health Care

Adequate health care is an essential element in maintaining a decent standard of living. Yet the high costs of health care and uneven access to resources make it impossible for many in our society to meet their basic health needs. Therefore, we support the enactment of a national health insurance program. While endorsing no particular legislative proposal at this time, we have identified a set of principles which should govern the development of a national health plan. For example:

- Access to adequate health care is a basic human right.
- Coverage should be universal in scope.
- National standards for health services should be adopted.
- Benefits should be comprehensive, including preventive health care.
- The program should give consumers a reasonable choice of providers.
- Cost controls should be established and used to encourage provider ini-

tiative and lower the cost of service. ("USCC Statement on National Health Insurance," 1974.)

I. Housing

Decent housing is a basic human right. A greater commitment of will and resources is required to meet our national housing goal of a decent home for every American family. Housing policy must better meet the needs of low- and middle-income families, the elderly, rural areas and minorities. It should also promote reinvestment in central cities and equal housing opportunity. Preservation of existing housing stock and a renewed concern for neighborhoods are required. ("The Right to a Decent Home," 1975).

J. Human Rights

Human dignity requires the defense and promotion of human rights in global and domestic affairs. With respect to international human rights, there is a pressing need for the United States to pursue a double task: 1) to strengthen and expand international mechanisms by which human rights can be protected and promoted; and 2) to take seriously the human rights dimensions of U.S. foreign policy. Therefore, we support U.S. ratification of the international covenants on civil and political rights and on economic, social and cultural rights. Further, we support a policy which gives greater weight to the protection of human rights in the conduct of U.S. affairs. The pervasive presence of American power creates a responsiblity to use that power in the service of human rights. ("U.S. Foreign Policy: A Critique From Catholic Traditions," 1976.)

Domestically, human rights is also a subject of great importance. Discrimination based on sex, race, ethnicity or age continues to exist in our nation. Such discrimination constitutes a grave injustice and an affront to human dignity. It must be aggressively resisted by every individual and rooted out of every social institution and structure. ("To Do the Work of Justice," 1978.)

K. Mass Media

We are concerned that the communications media be truly responsive to the public interest and that future laws that govern the airwaves fully protect the common good. We strongly oppose government control over television-programming policy. At the same time, we deplore unilateral decision making by networks. We firmly believe that responsible licensing, use and programming of the public airwaves cannot be accomplished simply by relying on the forces of the marketplace. We recommend exploring ways to reduce the commercial orientation of the broadcasting industry to better serve the public. ("Statement on the Family Viewing Policy," 1975.)

L. Regional Conflict in the World

Three situations of regional conflict which are of significance for the whole international system, and where U.S. policy has a substantial, indeed a decisive influence, are South Africa, the Middle East and Central America.

We address ourselves particularly to South Africa not unmindful of the urgency of achieving majority rule in Rhodesia and the independence of Namibia. Nevertheless, South Africa is the object of substantial economic, political and military interest on the part of the United States. Both U.S. foreign policy and its influence on corporate activity in South Africa should be directed toward change of the racial policies of that government. Even more effective leverage would be achieved if the United States, as the leader of the Western nations, could develop a coordinated policy with them regarding South Africa. ("Southern Africa: Peace or War," 1976.)

In the Middle East, the quest for peace continues and the relevant parties bear distinct yet interdependent responsibilities. First, the international community, especially its principal diplomatic actors, inevitably influences the future of the Middle East. Second, the United Nations is a vital element in any Middle East negotiations, and its diplomatic and peacekeeping role will undoubtedly be crucial to a long-term resolution of the conflict. Third, the regional parties, whose conflicting claims of justice are the essence of the political and moral problem in the Middle East, are the key to peace.

Finally, the religious communities with roots in the Middle East must reflect the best of our traditions in supporting the movement for peace with justice for all the people of the region. We have a continuing concern for the protection of the basic rights, both civil and religious, of the Christian minorities in the Middle East, and we encourage the local churches there to continue their steadfast witness to the faith. ("The Middle East: The Pursuit of Peace With Justice," 1978.)

In Central America, challenges to long-standing patterns of injustice and domination by large sectors of the population have been met by brutal repression. Fundamental social, economic and political changes advocated by the church at the Puebla conference call us in the United States to examine how our policies of military assistance and economic investment are related to existing patterns of injustice. U.S. policy should be directed toward fostering peaceful but fundamental change designed to benefit the poor of Central America.

This is not an exclusive listing of the issues that concern us. As Pope John Paul II has said, "The church cannot remain insensible to whatever serves true human welfare any more than she can remain indifferent to whatever threatens it. . . ."[14] Thus we are also advocates for the civil and political rights of the elderly, the handicapped, immigrants and aliens. We oppose excessive government interference in religious affairs as well as any unjust bias

---

[14] Ibid., 13.

of government against religious institutions. We support measures to reform our criminal justice system. We are concerned about protection of the land and the environment as well as the monumental question of peace in the world.

IV. Conclusion

In summary, we believe that the church has a proper role and responsibility in public affairs flowing from its gospel mandate and its respect for the dignity of the human person. We hope these reflections will contribute to a renewed political vitality in our land, both in terms of citizen participation in the electoral process and the integrity and accountability of those who seek and hold public office.

We pray that Christians will provide courageous leadership in promoting a spirit of responsible political involvement. May they follow the example of Jesus in giving special concern for the poor, and may all their actions be guided by a deep love of God and neighbor.

For in the world of American politics, as in all human communities, the words of Pope John Paul II apply: "What is in question here is the human person. We are not dealing with the 'abstract' (human person) but the real, 'concrete,' 'historical' person. . . . Every person coming into the world on account of the mystery of the redemption is entrusted to the solicitude of the church. . . . The object of her care is (human persons) in their unique, unrepeatable human reality, which keeps intact the image and likeness of God himself. . . ."[15]

---

[15] Ibid.

Political Responsibility: Reflections on an Election Year

USCC, Administrative Board
February 12, 1976

This year marks the two hundredth anniversary of the founding of our republic with its remarkable system of representative democracy. It is also a year that will test the workings of this democracy. A national election is a time for decisions regarding the future of our nation and the selection of our representatives and political leaders. As pastors and teachers, we address this statement on political responsibility to all Americans in hopes that the upcoming elections will provide an opportunity for thoughtful and lively debate on the issues and challenges that face our country as well as decisions on the candidates who seek to lead us.

I. Public Responsibility And The Electoral Process

We call this year a test of our democratic institutions because increasing numbers of our fellow citizens regard our political institutions and electoral processes with indifference and even distrust. Two years ago only 36% of those eligible voted in the national Congressional elections; in contrast, 46% voted in 1962. In 1972 only half of the eligible citizens exercised their right to vote, down from a peak of 63% in 1960. This trend—and the alienation, disenchantment and indifference it represents—must be reversed if our government is to truly reflect the "consent of the governed."

Abuses of power and a lack of governmental accountability have contributed to declining public confidence, despite significant efforts to uncover and redress these problems. Equally important, government has sometimes failed to deal effectively with critical issues which affect the daily lives of its citizens. As a result, many persons caught in the web of poverty and injustice have little confidence in the responsiveness of our political institutions. This discouragement and feeling of powerlessness are not limited to the poor who feel these most intensely, but affect many social groups, most alarmingly the young and the elderly. This leads to a loss of human resources, talent and idealism which could be harnessed in the work of social and national progress.[1]

However, we believe that the abandonment of political participation is

---

[1] Joint Economic Committee Hearings, October 20, 1975; *New York Times*, February 1, 1976; *Wall Street Journal*, February 2, 1976.

neither an effective nor a responsible approach to the solution of these problems. We need a committed, informed, and involved citizenry to revitalize our political life, to require accountability from our political leaders and governmental institutions and to achieve the common good. We echo the words of Pope Paul VI who declared: "The Christian has the duty to take part in the organization and life of political society."[2] Accordingly, we would urge all citizens to register to vote, to become informed on the relevant issues, to become involved in the party or campaign of their choice, to vote freely according to their conscience, in a word, to participate fully in this critical arena of politics where national decisions are made.

Certain methods used in political campaigns sometimes have intensified this disaffection. We call on those seeking public office to concentrate on demonstrating their personal integrity, their specific view on issues and their experience in public service. We urge a positive presentation of their programs and leadership abilities. In this way, they can contribute to a campaign based on vital issues, personal competence and real choices which will help to restore confidence in our electoral process.

II. The Church And The Political Order

It is appropriate in this context to offer our own reflections on the role of the Church in the political order. Christians believe that Jesus' commandment to love one's neighbor should extend beyond individual relationships to infuse and transform all human relations from the family to the entire human community. Jesus came to "bring good news to the poor, to proclaim liberty to captives, new sight to the blind and to set the downtrodden free." (Luke 4:18). He called us to feed the hungry, clothe the naked, care for the sick and afflicted and to comfort the victims of injustice. (Matt. 25). His example and words require individual acts of charity and concern from each of us. Yet they also require understanding and action upon the broader dimensions of poverty, hunger and injustice which necessarily involve the institutions and structures of economy, society and politics.

The Church, the People of God, is itself an expression of this love, and is required by the Gospel and its long tradition to promote and defend human rights and human dignity.[3] The 1971 Synod of Bishops declared that action on behalf of justice is a "constitutive dimension" of the Church's ministry and that, "the Church has the right, indeed the duty, to proclaim justice on the social, national and international level, and to denounce instances of injustice, when the fundamental rights of man and his very salvation demand it."[4] This view of the Church's ministry and mission requires it to relate positively to the political order, since social injustice and the denial of human rights can often be remedied only through governmental action. In today's

---

[2] *A Call to Action*, Pope Paul VI, 24, 1971.
[3] *Human Rights and Reconciliation*, Synod of Bishops, 1974.

world, concern for social justice and human development necessarily require persons and organizations to participate in the political process in accordance with their own responsibilities and roles.

The Church's responsibility in the area of human rights includes two complementary pastoral actions: the affirmation and promotion of human rights and the denunciation and condemnation of violations of these rights. In addition, it is the Church's role to call attention to the moral and religious dimensions of secular issues, to keep alive the values of the Gospel as a norm for social and political life, and to point out the demands of the Christian faith for a just transformation of society.[5] Such a ministry on the part of every Christian and the Church inevitably involves political consequences and touches upon public affairs.

Christian social teaching demands that citizens and public officials alike give serious consideration in all matters to the common good, to the welfare of society as a whole, which must be protected and promoted if individual rights are to be encouraged and upheld.

In order to be credible and faithful to the Gospel and to our tradition, the Church's concern for human rights and social justice should be comprehensive and consistent. It must be formulated with competence and an awareness of the complexity of issues. It should also be developed in dialogue with other concerned persons and respectful of the rights of all.[6]

The Church's role in the political order includes the following:
• education regarding the teachings of the Church and the responsibilities of the faithful;
• analysis of issues for their social and moral dimensions;
• measuring public policy against Gospel values;
• participating with other concerned parties in debate over public policy;
• speaking out with courage, skill and concern on public issues involving human rights, social justice and the life of the Church in society.

Unfortunately, our efforts in this area are sometimes misunderstood. The Church's participation in public affairs is not a threat to the political process or to genuine pluralism, but an affirmation of their importance. The Church recognizes the legitimate autonomy of government and the right of all, including the Church itself, to be heard in the formulation of public policy. As Vatican II declared:

> By preaching the truth of the Gospel and shedding light on all areas of human activity through her teaching and the example of the faithful, she (the Church) shows respect for the political freedom and responsibility of citizens and fosters these values. She also has the right to pass moral

---

[4] *Justice in The World,* Synod of Bishops, 1971.
[5] *Justice in The World, ibid.*
[6] *A Call To Action, op, cit.,* 4, 50. *The Church In The Modern World,* Second Vatican Council, 43, 1965.

judgments, even on matters touching the political order, whenever basic personal rights or the salvation of souls make such judgments necessary.[7]

A proper understanding of the role of the Church will not confuse its mission with that of government, but rather see its ministry as advocating the critical values of human rights and social justice.

It is the role of Christian communities to analyze the situation in their own country, to reflect upon the meaning of the Gospel, and to draw norms of judgment and plans of action from the teaching of the Church and their own experience.[8] In carrying out this pastoral activity in the social arena we are confronted with complexity. As the 1971 Synod of Bishops pointed out: "It does not belong to the Church, *insofar as she is a religious and hierarchical community,* to offer concrete solutions in the social, economic and political spheres for justice in the world."[9] (Emphasis added.) At the same time, it is essential to recall the words of Pope John XXIII:

> ... it must not be forgotten that the Church has the right and duty not only to safeguard the principles of ethics and religion, but also to intervene authoritatively with her children in the temporal sphere when there is a question of judging the application of these principles of concrete cases.[10]

The application of Gospel values to real situations is an essential work of the Christian community. Christians believe the Gospel is the measure of human realities. However, specific political proposals do not in themselves constitute the Gospel. Christians and Christian organizations must certainly participate in public debate over alternative policies and legislative proposals, yet it is critical that the nature of their participation not be misunderstood.

We specifically do not seek the formation of a religious voting bloc; nor do we wish to instruct persons on how they should vote by endorsing candidates. We urge citizens to avoid choosing candidates simply on the personal basis of self-interest. Rather, we hope that voters will examine the positions of candidates on the full range of issues as well as the person's integrity, philosophy and performance. We seek to promote a greater understanding of the important link between faith and politics and to express our belief that our nation is enriched when its citizens and social groups approach public affairs from positions grounded in moral conviction and religious belief. Our view is expressed very well by Pope Paul VI when he said:

> While recognizing the autonomy of the reality of politics, Christians who are invited to take up political activity should try to make their choices consis-

---

[7] *The Church In The Modern World, op. cit.,* 76.
[8] *A Call To Action, op. cit.*
[9] *Justice In The World, op. cit.*
[10] *Pacem in Terris,* Pope John XXIII, 160, 1963.

tent with the Gospel and, in the framework of a legitimate plurality, to give both personal and collective witness to the seriousness of their faith by effective and disinterested service of men.[11]

The Church's responsibility in this area falls on all its members. As citizens we are all called to become informed, active and responsible participants in the political process. The hierarchy has a responsibility as teachers and pastors to educate the faithful, support efforts to gain greater peace and justice and provide guidance and even leadership on occasion where human rights are in jeopardy. The laity has major responsibility for the renewal of the temporal order. Drawing on their own experience and exercising their distinctive roles within the Christian community, bishops, clergy, religious and laity should join together in common witness and effective action to bring about Pope John's vision of a well ordered society based on truth, justice, charity and freedom.[12]

As religious leaders and pastors, our intention is to reflect our concern that politics—the forum for the achievement of the common good—receive its rightful importance and attention. For, as Pope Paul VI said, "politics are a demanding manner—but not the only one—of living the Christian commitment to the service of others."[13]

III. Issues

Without reference to political candidates, parties or platforms, we wish to offer a listing of some issues which we believe are central to the national debate this year. These brief summaries are not intended to indicate in any depth the details of our positions in these matters. We wish to refer the reader to fuller discussions of our point of view in the documents listed in the summary which appears below. We wish to point out that these issues are not the concerns of Catholics alone; in every case we have joined with others to advocate these concerns. They represent a broad range of topics on which the Bishops of the United States have already expressed themselves and are recalled here in alphabetical order to emphasize their relevance in a period of national debate and decision.

A. Abortion

The right to life is a basic human right which should have the protection of law. Abortion is the deliberate destruction of an unborn human being and therefore violates this right. We reject the 1973 Supreme Court decisions on abortion which refuse appropriate legal protection to the unborn child. We support the passage of a constitutional amendment to restore the basic con-

---

[11] *A Call To Action, op. cit.,* 46.
[12] *Pacem In Terris,* Pope John XXIII, 35, 1963.
[13] *A Call To Action, op. cit.*

stitutional protection of the right to life for the unborn child. (*Documentation on the Right to Life and Abortion, 1974; Pastoral Plan on Pro-Life Activities,* 1975).

B. The Economy

Our national economic life must reflect broad values of social justice and human rights. Current levels of unemployment are unacceptable and their tremendous human costs are intolerable. We support an effective national commitment to genuine full employment. Our strong support of this human right to meaningful employment is based not only on the income it provides, but also on the sense of worth and creativity a useful job provides for the individual. We also call for a decent income policy for those who cannot work and adequate assistance to those in need. Efforts to eliminate or curtail needed services and help in these difficult economic times must be strongly opposed. (*The Economy: Human Dimensions,* 1975).

C. Education

All persons of whatever race, condition, or age, by virtue of their dignity as human beings, have an inalienable right to education.

We advocate:

1. Sufficient public and private funding to make an adequate education available for all citizens and residents of the United States of America and to provide assistance for education in our nation's program of foreign aid.

2. Governmental and voluntary action to reduce inequalities of educational opportunity by improving the opportunities available to economically disadvantaged persons.

3. Orderly compliance with legal requirements for racially integrated schools.

4. Voluntary efforts to increase racial and ethnic integration in public and nonpublic schools.

5. Equitable tax support for the education of pupils in public and nonpublic schools to implement parental freedom in the education of their children. (*To Teach As Jesus Did,* Nov. 1972).

D. Food Policy

The "right to eat" is directly linked with the right to life. This right to eat is denied to countless numbers of people in the world. We support a national policy in which:

• U.S. world food aid seriously combats hunger and malnutrition on a global basis, separates food aid from other considerations, gives priority to the poorest nations, and joins in a global grain reserve.

• U.S. domestic food programs meet the needs of hungry and malnourished people here in America, provide strong support for food stamps to assist the needy, the unemployed, the elderly and the working poor, and strive to improve and to extend child nutrition programs.

• U.S. agricultural policy promotes full production and an adequate and just return for farmers. (*Food Policy and The Church: Specific Proposals, 1975*).

E. Housing

Decent housing is a basic human right. A greater commitment of will and resources is required to meet our national housing goal of a decent home for every American family. Housing policy must better meet the needs of low and middle income families, the elderly, rural areas and minorities. It should also promote reinvestment in central cities and equal housing opportunity. Preservation of existing housing stock and a renewed concern for neighborhoods are required. (*The Right To A Decent Home, 1975*).

F. Human Rights And U.S. Foreign Policy

Human dignity requires the defense and promotion of human rights. Many regimes, including communist countries and some U.S. allies, violate or deny their citizens human and civil rights, as well as religious liberty. Internationally, the pervasive presence of American power creates a responsibility to use that power in the service of human rights. In the face of regimes which use torture or detain political prisoners without legal recourse, we support a policy which gives greater weight to the protection of human rights in the conduct of U.S. affairs. (*Resolution On The 25th Anniversary of the U.N. Universal Declaration of Human Rights, 1973*).

G. Mass Media

We are concerned that the communications media be truly responsive to the public interest. We strongly oppose government control over television programming policy, but we deplore unilateral decision-making by networks. We urge that broadcasters, government, private business, and representatives of the viewing public seek effective ways to ensure accountability in the formulation and implementation of broadcast policy. We recommend exploring ways to reduce the commercial orientation of the broadcasting industry to better serve the public. (*Statement On The Family Viewing Policy, 1975*).

H. Military Expenditures

The arms race continues to threaten humanity with universal destruction. It is especially destructive because it violates the rights of the world's poor who are thereby deprived of essential needs and it creates the illusion of protecting human life and fostering peace. We support a policy of arms limitation as a necessary step to general disarmament which is a prerequisite to international peace and justice. (*U.S. Bishops on the Arms Race,* 1971 Synod).

This is not an exclusive listing of issues of concern to us. We are also concerned about issues involving the civil and political rights of racial and ethnic groups, women, the elderly and working families. We support measures to provide health care for all of our citizens and the reform of our criminal justice system. We are concerned about protection of the land and the environment as well as the monumental question of peace in the world.

IV. Conclusion

In summary, we believe the Church has a proper role and responsibility in public affairs flowing from its Gospel mandate and its concern for the human person and his or her rights. We hope these reflections will contribute to a renewed sense of political vitality in our land, both in terms of citizen participation in the electoral process and the integrity and accountability of those who hold and seek public office.

We pray that Christians will follow the call of Jesus to provide the "leaven" for society (Matt. 13:34; Luke 13:20), and heed the appeal of the Second Vatican Council:

> To enlighten one another through honest discussion, preserving mutual charity and caring above all for the common good ... to be witnesses to Christ in all things in the midst of human society.[14]

---

[14] *The Church In The Modern World, op. cit.,* 43.

Political Responsibility: A Resolution of the Catholic Bishops of the United States

USCC, May 6, 1976

The United States stands in the midst of an important national election year, a time for debate on national issues and decisions about our political leadership. We are deeply concerned that increasing numbers of voters seem to be choosing not to participate in this process out of distrust, apathy or indifference. Two years ago only 36% of those eligible voted in the national congressional elections, in contrast, 46% voted in 1962. In 1972, a presidential election year, only half of the eligible citizens exercised their right to vote, down from a peak of 63% in 1960. This trend—and the alienation, disenchantment and indifference it represents—must be reversed if our government is to reflect truly the "consent of the governed."

We therefore wish on this occasion to urge all citizens to participate fully in the political life of our country. We encourage them to register to vote, to become informed on the relevant issues, to become involved in the party or campaign of their choice and to vote freely according to their consciences.

As part of its mission, the Church, the People of God, is required by the Gospel and its long tradition to promote and defend human rights and dignity. This view of the Church's ministry and mission requires it to relate positively to the political order, since social injustice and the denial of human rights can often be remedied only through governmental action.

The Administrative Board of the American bishops at its February 1976 meeting, adopted an important statement, *Political Responsibility: Reflections On An Election Year*. In this statement, the Board discussed the responsibility of the Church toward political life, called for a "thoughtful and lively debate" on the issues that face our country and listed a broad range of issues central to that debate. In each case these are matters which we have already addressed in major policy positions, and we ask interested persons to examine these statements for our specific views. These issues as listed in our earlier statement include: abortion, the economy, education, food policy, housing, human rights and foreign policy, mass media and military expenditures.

As citizens we are all called to become informed, active and responsible participants in the political process. Drawing on their own experience and exercising their distinctive roles within the Christian community, bishops, clergy, religious and laity should join together in common witness and effective action to bring about a society based on truth, justice, charity and freedom. It is by participation of citizens in our democratic process that we can hope to move toward such a society.

To Live in Christ Jesus
A Pastoral Reflection
on the Moral Life

NCCB, November 11, 1976

I. Introduction

Dear Brothers and Sisters in Christ:

We wish to share our faith with you. We wish to speak of its power, of the great hope that is in us, of the Spirit that has been poured into human hearts. We wish to discuss some moral questions of our day which affect the dignity of human persons and to respond to them in accordance with what we have seen and heard concerning the word of life. "What we have seen and heard we proclaim in turn to you so that you may share life with us."[1] We also address these words in charity and respect to our fellow Christians and to others who, although they do not share our religious beliefs, may wish to know our vision of the moral life and our perception of many of the critical issues of our day.

Christ, Our Life

We believe the meaning and destiny of our lives are most fully revealed to us in Jesus of Nazareth, whom we acknowledge as Son of God made man, Savior and Lord of creation. In Him are revealed two great truths:

- who God is, and
- who we are.

---

[1] 1 Jn. 1:3

He tells us that God, whom we are to love and serve above all else,[2] loves us more than we can hope to understand and offers us His love irrevocably. As St. Paul says: "Neither death nor life, neither angels nor principalities, neither the present nor the future, nor powers, neither height nor depth nor any other creature, will be able to separate us from the Love of God that comes to us in Christ Jesus, our Lord."[3] Jesus Himself is the new covenant, the sacred and enduring bond, between God and ourselves.[4]

"Whatever came to be in Him, found life . . . any who did accept Him He empowered to become children of God."[5] Christ, in whom God and man are most perfectly one, manifests in the world God's hidden plan to share His life with us, to pour out His own Spirit upon all flesh,[6] so that we who were formed in His image should be called and be children of God,[7] addressing Him in truth as "our Father."

Christ also reveals the response which we are to make to our calling and gives us power to make it. This is the power of God's own Spirit. "All who are led by the Spirit of God are sons of God."[8] Jesus lived and was led by the Spirit as the dynamic force of His life.[9] As Son of God made man, He loves not only His Father but each human being. He teaches us that love of God and love of neighbor spring from the same Spirit and are inseparable.[10] "If anyone says, 'My love is fixed on God,' yet hates his brother, he is a liar."[11] We are to love all human beings, even our enemies, as we love ourselves;[12] even more, we are to obey Christ's new command to love all others as He has loved us.[13]

By this commandment Christ tells us something new
- about God,
- about love, and
- about ourselves.

His commandment to love is new not simply because of the scope and unselfishness of the love involved, but because it calls us to love with a divine love called charity, as the Father, Son and Spirit do. This call carries with it the inner gift of Their life and the power of Their love, for Christ does not command what is impossible.

Christ's life is one of total obedience to the Father in the Spirit. His obedience entailed hunger and thirst and weariness, obscurity and rejection, suf-

---

[2] Cf. Dt. 6:5; Mt. 22:37
[3] Rom. 8:38–39
[4] Cf. Words of Institution, Eucharistic Prayers
[5] Jn. 1:4–12
[6] Acts 2:17
[7] 1 Jn. 3:1; Ga. 4:5–7
[8] Rom. 8:14
[9] Cf. Lk. 4:14
[10] Cf. 1 Jn. 4:12; 20–21
[11] 1 Jn. 4:20
[12] Cf. Lv. 19:18; Mt. 5:44–48, 22:37–40; Lk. 10:25–28
[13] Jn. 13:34; 15:12–13

fering and death. Yet in accepting the suffering which came to Him as He walked the way of loving obedience, Jesus did not deny His humanity but realized it perfectly. In giving His Son the glorious victory over death, the Father showed His pleasure with the Son's loving obedience.[14]

His life challenges the lives we lead. He began His ministry by calling us to change our lives completely.[15] His very first word summons us to turn away from sin, turn toward God, and receive the gift of the Spirit.

Sin and Grace

We must recognize the brutal reality of sin. It is different from unavoidable failure or limitation. We all fail often through no fault of our own, and we all experience human limitations, among which the ultimate limitation is death. It is a sign of maturity to be able to accept our limitations and discover meaning in our failures.

Sin is different. It is a spirit of selfishness rooted in our hearts and wills which wages war against God's plan for our fulfillment. It is rejection, either partial or total, of one's role as a child of God and a member of His people, a rejection of the spirit of sonship, love and life. We sin first in our hearts, although often our sins are expressed in outward acts and their consequences.[16]

There is vast goodness in our world, yet sin's effects are also visible everywhere:

- in exploitative relationships,
- in loveless families,
- in unjust social structures and policies,
- in crimes by and against individuals and against God's creation.

Everywhere we encounter the suffering and destruction wrought by egoism and lack of community, by oppression of the weak and manipulation of the vulnerable; we experience explosive tensions among nations, ideological, racial, and religious groups, and social classes; we witness the scandalous gulf between those who waste goods and resources and those who live and die amid deprivation and underdevelopment—and all this in an atmosphere of wars and ceaseless preparations for war. Ours is a sinful world.

"But despite the increase of sin, grace has far surpassed it."[17] God remained faithful to His love for us, sending His own Son "in the likeness of sinful flesh"[18] into the midst of this sinful world. Jesus, "who was tempted in every way that we are, yet never sinned,"[19] accepted in Himself the full force of our sins, of the powers of darkness at large in the world, and of all the suf-

---

[14] Phil. 2:9–11
[15] Cf. Mk. 1:14–15
[16] Cf. Lk. 6:43–45
[17] Rom. 5:20
[18] Rom. 8:3
[19] Heb. 4:15

fering which fidelity to God entails. So that by His obedience many might be made righteous, [20] He was faithful unto death. This was His final, irrevocable act of absolute self-giving in love to God and to us.

Christ's offer of love and life is valid forever. Transcending space and time, He is present to all and offers to each the life that is in Him. It is freely offered, there for the taking, unless in our freedom we choose to reject His call and not to be united with Him.

Because of sin we are helpless if left to ourselves, unable even to do the good we know and truly wish to do.[21] But God, who loves us and is faithful to His promise, saves us from sin through Jesus.

- Through baptism we enter into Christ's saving death and are buried with Him;
  - through baptism we enter into His saving resurrection;
  - through baptism we are united to His body and share in His Spirit.

We who have been baptized in Christ are to consider ourselves "dead to sin but alive for God in Christ Jesus."[22] "Since we live by the Spirit, let us follow the Spirit's lead."[23]

Conversion

Even so, our final triumph over sin is a lifelong task. Christ's call to conversion is ever timely, for we still live in a sinful world and the power of sin is strong in us. "My inner self agrees with the law of God, but I see in my body's members another law at war with the law of my mind; this makes me the prisoner of the law of sin in my members."[24]

As disciples of Jesus who accept Him as our way and desire to love God and each other as we have been loved, we must acknowledge our sinfulness. We have to undergo conversion: "a profound change of the whole person by which one begins to consider, judge, and arrange his life according to the holiness and love of God."[25] In a special way we engage in a continuing process of conversion through the Sacrament of Penance, in which our sins are forgiven and we are reconciled with God and with the community of faith. We are to live the paschal mystery, which we proclaim at Mass: "Dying, He destroyed our death and, rising, He restored our life."[26] This paschal mystery is central to Christ's life and mission and to ours as His disciples.

Living in His spirit, we must deny ourselves, take up the cross each day, and follow in His steps.[27] Christ's atoning sacrifice is, in Cardinal Newman's

---

[20] Rom. 5:19
[21] Cf. Rom. 7:11–15
[22] Rom. 6:11
[23] Ga. 5:25
[24] Rom. 7:22–23
[25] *Paenitemini,* February 17, 1966
[26] Cf. Memorial Acclamation, Roman Sacramentary
[27] Cf. Lk. 9:23–24

words, "the vital principle in which the Christian lives, and without which Christianity is not."[28] As brothers and sisters of Jesus who are also His followers and members of His body, we must accept suffering and death as He did, and in so accepting them share His life. "If we have been united with Him through likeness to His death," so also "through a like resurrection" we shall be raised from the dead by the glory of the Father.[29] By our union with Christ we have already begun to share that risen life here on earth.

Fulfillment

All of us seek happiness: life, peace, joy, a wholeness and wholesomeness of being. The happiness we seek and for which we are fashioned is given to us in Jesus, God's supreme gift of love. He comes in the Father's name to bring the fulfillment promised to the Hebrew people and, through them, to all people everywhere. He is Himself our happiness and peace, our joy and beatitude.

Of old the divine pattern for human existence was set forth in the decalogue. And Jesus said: "He who obeys the commandments he has from Me is the man who loves Me; and he who loves Me will be loved by My Father."[30] In the beatitudes[31] Jesus, our brother, promises us the dignity of life as sons and daughters of God, and eternal enjoyment of a destiny which we now grasp imperfectly and which has yet to appear in its glorious fullness. Through these beatitudes, Jesus also teaches us values we must cherish and qualities we must cultivate if we are to follow Him.

Living these values by the grace of Christ, we possess in some measure even now the fulfillment promised to us. As God's reign takes root within us we become "gentle and humble of heart" like Jesus[32] through deeds done in holiness, and thus "a kingdom of justice, love and peace is furthered in this world."[33]

Guidance in Christ

God reveals to us in Jesus who we are and how we are to live. Yet He has made us free, able and obliged to decide how we shall respond to our calling. We must make concrete in the particular circumstances of our lives what the call to holiness and the commandment of love require. This is not easy. We know, too, that our decisions may not be arbitrary, for 'good' and 'bad,' 'right' and 'wrong' are not simply whatever we choose to make them. And so God gives us His guidance in manifold forms.

---

[28] *Parochial and Plain Sermons,* V, 7
[29] Rom. 6:4–5
[30] Jn. 14:21; cf. 15:14
[31] Mt. 5:3–12; Lk. 6:21–26
[32] Mt. 11:29
[33] Preface of Christ the King

The human heart is alive with desire for created goods. Behind this desire is our longing for God. "Athirst is my soul for God, the living God."[34] Our desire for created goods and our longing for the uncreated good are not in contradiction, since Christ came to perfect our nature, not to destroy it. He is the goal to whom all creatures tend, for whom all creatures long, in whom all hold together.[35] Everything good and worthwhile in the adventure of a human life is such because it shows forth in some way the glory of God and points back to Him. Created goods and loves are His gifts, and they tell us of their giver and His will for humanity. Though all other goods draw us in part to our perfection as individuals, members of human communities, and stewards of the world, union with God is the supreme and only perfect fulfillment. Those who follow Christ will value all that is truly human and be reminded by it of His call.

We rejoice in friends, in being alive, in being treated as persons rather than things, in knowing the truth. In this we are rejoicing in being ourselves, images of God called to be His children. Truth and life, love and peace, justice and friendship go into what it means to be human. Morality, then, is not simply something imposed on us from without, but is ingrained in our being; it is the way we accept our humanity as restored to us in Christ.

In giving us these goods and the desire for them, God wills that we be open to them and eager to foster them in ourselves and others. All these goods form a starting point for reflecting upon the meaning and purpose of our lives. In the life of every human person are reflected many elements of the "divine law—eternal, objective, and universal—whereby God orders, directs, and governs the entire universe and all the ways of the human community."[36] All these goods together bear witness to the existence of what is often called the natural moral law. No disciple of Christ will neglect these goods. We are not possessed of His Spirit, therefore, if we toss them aside with contempt, spurning the loving gifts of our Father; if we grasp at them selfishly and deny them to others; or if we make them, not their giver, the ultimate end and meaning of our lives.[37]

Conscience

Even when we have become conscious of these fundamental goods and have cultivated an attitude of cherishing them in ourselves and others, more remains to be done. We still must decide how to realize and affirm them in the concrete circumstances of our lives. Such decisions are called judgments

---

[34] Ps. 42:3
[35] Cf. Col. 1:15–20
[36] Vatican Council II, *Declaration on Religious Freedom,* 3. Cf. St. Thomas Aquinas, *Summa Theologiae,* 1-2, 91, 1 and 2; 94, 1
[37] Cf. Vatican Council II, *Pastoral Constitution on the Church in the Modern World,* 16

of conscience. In the final analysis, they take place in the "most secret core and sanctuary" of a person, where one "is alone with God."[38]

We live in good faith if we act in accord with conscience. Nevertheless our moral decisions still require much effort. We must make decisions of conscience based upon prayer, study, consultation and an understanding of the teachings of the Church. We must have a rightly informed conscience and follow it. But our judgments are human and can be mistaken; we may be blinded by the power of sin in our lives or misled by the strength of our desires. "Beloved, do not trust every spirit, but put the spirits to a test to see if they belong to God."[39]

Clearly, then, we must do everything in our power to see to it that our judgments of conscience are informed and in accord with the moral order of which God is creator. Common sense requires that conscientious people be open and humble, ready to learn from the experience and insight of others, willing to acknowledge prejudices and even change their judgments in light of better instruction.

Followers of Jesus will have a realistic approach to conscience. They will accept what Jesus taught and judge things as He judges them.

The Church

Where are we to look for the teachings of Jesus, hear His voice and discern His will?

In scripture, whose books were written under the inspiration of the Holy Spirit. In prayer, where we grow in knowledge and love of Christ and in commitment to His service. In the events of human life and history, where Christ and His Spirit are at work. In the Church, where all these things converge. This is why the Second Vatican Council said: "In the formation of their consciences, the Christian faithful ought carefully to attend to the sacred and certain doctrine of the Church."[40]

There are many instruments and agents of teaching in the Church. All have roles in drawing out the richness of Christ's message and proclaiming it, each according to his or her gift. Although we cannot discuss their role at length here, we wish in particular to acknowledge and encourage the contributions which theologians make to this effort.

The Holy Father and the bishops in communion with him have been anointed by the Holy Spirit to be the official and authentic teachers of Christian life. For Jesus "established His holy Church by sending forth the apostles as He Himself had been sent by the Father (cf. Jn. 20:21). He willed that their successors, namely the bishops, should be shepherds in His Church even to the consummation of the world."[41] It is their office and duty to ex-

---

[38] *Ibid.*
[39] 1 Jn. 4:1; cf. 1 Cor. 12:10
[40] *Declaration on Religious Freedom*, 14
[41] Vatican Council II, *Dogmatic Constitution on the Church*, 18

press the teaching of Christ on moral questions and matters of belief. This special teaching office within the Catholic Church is a gift of the Lord Jesus for the benefit of all His followers in their efforts to know what He teaches, value as He values, and live as free, responsible, loving, and holy persons. As Christ says, "He who hears you, hears Me."[42] The authoritative moral teachings of the Church enlighten personal conscience and are to be regarded as certain and binding norms of morality.

Following the teaching and example of Christ in the family of the Church, we become more like Him and more perfect as the Father's children and people. Christ brings us the life of the Father and fills our lives with His Spirit. So our best answer in face of the challenges we encounter in living the Christian life is this: "In Him who is the source of my strength, I have strength for everything."[43]

II. Moral Life in the Family, the Nation, and the Community of Nations

We turn now to three social clusters, three concentric communities, which provide the setting for human life and fulfillment in Christ:
- the family,
- the nation,
- and the community of nations.

In speaking of matters which bear upon these three communities today, we treat them as moral issues in light of the values given us by Jesus Christ and His Church, in whose name we proclaim them. We cannot here discuss every important issue. Moreover, we admit that in some cases the complexity of the problems does not permit ready, concrete solutions. Nevertheless, as teachers of morality we insist that even such complex problems must be resolved ultimately in terms of objective principles if the solutions are to be valid.[44]

Our point of focus is the human person. "The progress of the human person and the advance of society itself hinge on each other."[45] Every human being is of priceless value: made in God's image, redeemed by Christ, and called to an eternal destiny. That is why we are to recognize all human beings as our neighbors and love them with the love of Christ.

This love of neighbor, inseparably linked to love of God and indeed an expression and measure of it, is summoned forth first in regard to those closest to us—the members of our own families.

---

[42] Lk. 10:16

[43] Phil. 4:13

[44] Many of the matters treated here have been discussed in detail in papal and conciliar documents, documents of the Holy See and the Synods of Bishops, and statements of national episcopal conferences. The references which follow note a few of the sources.

[45] Vatican Council II, *The Church in the Modern World*, 25

THE FAMILY

Every human being has a need and right to be loved, to have a home where he or she can put down roots and grow. The family is the first and indispensable community in which this need is met. Today, when productivity, prestige or even physical attractiveness are regarded as the gauge of personal worth, the family has a special vocation to be a place where people are loved not for what they do or what they have but simply because they are.

A family begins when a man and woman publicly proclaim before the community their mutual commitment so that it is possible to speak of them as one body.[46] Christ teaches that God wills the union of man and woman in marriage to be lifelong, a sharing of life for the length of life itself.

The Old Testament takes the love between husband and wife as one of the most powerful symbols of God's love for His people: "I will espouse you to Me forever: I will espouse you in right and in justice, in love and in mercy: I will espouse you in fidelity, and you shall know the Lord."[47] So husband and wife espouse themselves, joined in a holy and loving covenant.

The New Testament continues this imagery: only now the union between husband and wife rises to the likeness of the union between Christ and His Church.[48] Jesus teaches that in marriage men and women are to pledge steadfast unconditional faithfulness which mirrors the faithfulness of the Son of God. Their marriages make His fidelity and love visible to the world. Christ raised marriage in the Lord to the level of a sacrament, whereby this union symbolizes and effects God's special love for the couple in their total domestic and social situation.

Jesus tells us that the Father can and will grant people the greatness of heart to keep such pledges of loving faithfulness.[49] The Church has always believed that in making and keeping noble promises of this sort people can through the grace of God grow beyond themselves—grow to the point of being able to love beyond their merely human capacity. Yet contemporary culture makes it difficult for many people to accept this view of marriage. Even some who admire it as an ideal doubt whether it is possible and consider it too risky to attempt. They believe it better to promise less at the start and so be able to escape from marital tragedy in order to promise once again.

But this outlook itself has increased marital tragedy. Only men and women bold enough to make promises for life, believing that with God's help they can be true to their word as He is to His, have the love and strength to surmount the inevitable challenges of marriage. Such unselfish love, rooted in faith, is ready to forgive when need arises and to make the sacrifices demanded if something as precious and holy as marriage is to be preserved. For

---

[46] Cf. Gn. 2:24
[47] Ho. 2:21–22
[48] Cf. Eph. 5:25–32
[49] Cf. Mt. 19:10–12

the family to be a place where human beings can grow with security, the love pledged by husband and wife must have as its model the selfless and enduring love of Christ for the Church. "Husbands, love your wives, as Christ loved the Church. He gave Himself up for her."[50]

Some say even sacramental marriages can deteriorate to such an extent that the marital union dies and the spouses are no longer obliged to keep their promise of lifelong fidelity. Some would even urge the Church to acknowledge such dissolution and allow the parties to enter new, more promising unions. We reject this view.[51] In reality it amounts to a proposal to forego Christian marriage at the outset and substitute something entirely different. It would weaken marriage further, while paying too little heed to Jesus' call to identify ourselves with His redeeming love, which endures all things. Its fundamental difficulty is that it cannot be reconciled with the Church's mission to be faithful to the word entrusted to it. The covenant beteen a man and woman joined in Christian marriage is as indissoluble and irrevocable as God's love for His people and Christ's love for His Church.

Since the following of Christ calls for so much dedication and sacrifice in the face of strong, contrary social pressures, Christ's Church has a serious obligation to help His followers live up to the challenge. In worship, pastoral care, education, and counseling we must assist husbands and wives who are striving to realize the ideal of Christ's love in their lives together and with their children. Young people and engaged couples must be taught the meaning of Christian marriage. Married couples must have the support and encouragement of the Christian community in their efforts to honor their commitments.

It remains a tragic fact that some marriages fail. We must approach those who suffer this agonizing experience with the compassion of Jesus Himself. In some cases romanticism or immaturity may have prevented them from entering into real Christian marriages.

But often enough "broken marriages" are sacramental, indissoluble unions. In this sensitive area the pastoral response of the Church is especially needed and especially difficult to formulate. We must seek ways by which the Church can mediate Christ's compassion to those who have suffered marital tragedy, but at the same time we may do nothing to undermine His teaching concerning the beauty and meaning of marriage and in particular His prophetic demands concerning the indissolubility of the unions of those who marry in the Lord. The Church must ever be faithful to the command to serve the truth in love.[52]

---

[50] Eph. 5:25
[51] Cf. Vatican Council II, *The Church in the Modern World,* 48
[52] Eph. 4:15

Children

The love of husband and wife finds its ideal fulfillment in their children, with whom they share their life and love. Children are really the supreme gift of marriage who in turn substantially enrich the lives of their parents.[53]

Openness to children is vitally linked to growth in marital and family love. Couples have a right to determine responsibly, in accord with God's law, how many children they should have, and they may also have valid reasons for not seeking children immediately. But in marrying with the intention of postponing children indefinitely, some appear simply to wish to enjoy one another's company without distraction or to achieve an arbitrary level of material comfort. This can mark a selfish entry into what should be an experience of generous giving. Even worse, children may come to be regarded as an intrusion and a burden instead of a gift. This may lead to a rejection of the children, particularly those who are disadvantaged, either before or after birth.

In order to reflect seriously upon the value they assign children, couples should begin by reflecting upon their understanding of marriage itself. Do they believe God is with them in this adventure to which they have committed themselves? If so, their love will reach confidently toward the future and provide a setting in which new life can be generously accepted, take root and grow. Openness to new life, founded on faith, in turn will strengthen their love. They will come to see how the love-giving and life-giving meanings of their love are joined in loving acts of marital intercourse, linked by a necessary relationship which exists not only on the biological level but on all levels of personality.

One need not always act to realize both of these values, but one may never deliberately suppress either of them. The love-giving and life-giving meanings of marital intercourse are real human values and aspects of human personhood. Because they are, it is wrong to act deliberately against either. In contraceptive intercourse the procreative or life-giving meaning of intercourse is deliberately separated from its love-giving meaning and rejected; the wrongness of such an act lies in the rejection of this value.[54]

Some distinguish between a so-called contraceptive mentality—a deep-seated attitude of selfish refusal to communicate life and love to a future generation—and particular contraceptive acts during a marriage otherwise generally open to the transmission of life. Though there is a difference, even in the latter case an act of contraceptive intercourse is wrong because it severs the link between the meanings of marital intercourse and rejects one of them.

We ask Catholics to reflect on the value at stake here. The Church is not engaged in a mere quibble over means of birth regulation; it is proclaiming the value of the life-giving meaning of marital intercourse, a value attacked,

---

[53] Vatican Council II, *The Church in the Modern World,* 50
[54] Cf. Humanae Vitae, 12,13

though in different ways, by both the ideology of contraception and by contraceptive acts.

Pastoral sensitivity requires that we be understanding toward those who
find it hard to accept this teaching, but it does not permit us to change or
suppress it. We recognize that couples face increasing pressure in family
planning. Contraceptive birth control results not only from selfishness and
improperly formed conscience but also from conflicts and pressures which
can mitigate moral culpability. Therefore, we ask our people not to lose heart
or turn away from the community of faith when they find themselves caught
in these conflicts. We urge them to seek appropriate and understanding
pastoral counsel, to make use of God's help in constant prayer and recourse
to the sacraments, and to investigate honestly such legitimate methods of
birth limitation as natural family planning.[55] At the same time we urge those
who dissent from this teaching of the Church to a prayerful and studied
reconsideration of their position.

Our Christian tradition holds the sexual union between husband and wife
in high honor, regarding it as a special expression of their convenanted love
which mirrors God's love for His people and Christ's love for the Church. But
like many things human, sex is ambivalent. It can be either creative or
destructive. Sexual intercourse is a moral and human good only within marriage; outside marriage it is wrong.[56]

Our society gives considerable encouragement to premarital and ex-
tramarital sexual relations as long as, it is said, 'no one gets hurt.' Such relations are not worthy of beings created in God's image and made God's
adopted children nor are they according to God's will.[57] The unconditional
love of Christian marriage is absent, for such relations are hedged around
with many conditions. Though tenderness and concern may sometimes be
present, there is an underlying tendency toward exploitation and self-
deception. Such relations trivialize sexuality and can erode the possibility of
making deep, lifelong commitments.

Some persons find themselves through no fault of their own to have a
homosexual orientation. Homosexuals, like everyone else, should not suffer
from prejudice against their basic human rights. They have a right to
respect, friendship and justice. They should have an active role in the Christian community. Homosexual activity, however, as distinguished from
homosexual orientation, is morally wrong. Like heterosexual persons,
homosexuals are called to give witness to chastity, avoiding, with God's
grace, behavior which is wrong for them, just as nonmarital sexual relations
are wrong for heterosexuals. Nonetheless, because heterosexuals can usually
look forward to marriage, and homosexuals, while their orientation con-

---

[55] Cf. Vatican Council II, *The Church in the Modern World,* 52; Humanae Vitae, 24

[56] Cf. Sacred Congregation for the Doctrine of the Faith, *Declaration on Certain Questions Concerning Sexual Ethics,* December 29, 1975

[57] Cf. 1 Cor. 6:9-10, 18

tinues, might not, the Christian community should provide them a special degree of pastoral understanding and care.

Though most people have two families, the one in which they are born and the one they help bring into being, the single and celibate have only the first. But from this experience they, too, know family values. Love and sacrifice, generosity and service have a real place in their lives. They are as much tempted as the married—sometimes more—to selfishness. They have as great a need for understanding and consolation. Family values may be expressed in different terms in their lives, but they are expressed.

The Aged

The adventure of marriage and family is a continuing one in which elderly people have important lessons to teach and learn. Contemporary American society tends to separate the aging from their families, isolating kin in ways that are more than physical, with the result that the wisdom of experience is often neither sought, imparted nor further developed.[58]

Families should see the story of loving reciprocity through life's closing chapters. Where possible, the elderly should be welcomed into their own families. Moreover, children have an obligation of human and Christian justice and love to keep closely in touch with aging parents and to do what lies in their power to care for them in their old age. "If anyone does not provide for his own relatives and especially for members of his immediate family, he has denied the faith; he is worse than an unbeliever."[59] The community should provide for those who lack families and, in doing so, attend to all their needs, not just physical ones. Here the Church has played and continues to play a special role. The elderly must be cherished, not merely tolerated, and the Church community, through parishes and other agencies, should seek to mediate to them the loving concern of Jesus and the Father.

Euthanasia or mercy killing is much discussed and increasingly advocated today, though the discussion is often confused by ambiguous use of the slogan 'death with dignity.' Whatever the word or term, it is a grave moral evil deliberately to kill persons who are terminally ill or deeply impaired. Such killing is incompatible with respect for human dignity and reverence for the sacredness of life.

Something different is involved, however, when the question is whether hopelessly ill and painfully afflicted people must be kept alive at all costs and with the use of every available medical technique.

Some seem to make no distinction between respecting the dying process and engaging in direct killing of the innocent. Morally there is all the difference in the world. While euthanasia or direct killing is gravely wrong, it

---

[58] Cf. United States Catholic Conference, *Society and the Aged: Toward Reconciliation,* May 5, 1976

[59] 1 Tm. 5:8

does not follow that there is an obligation to prolong the life of a dying person by extraordinary means. At times the effort to do so is of no help to the dying and may even be contrary to the compassion due them. People have a right to refuse treatment which offers no reasonable hope of recovery and imposes excessive burdens on them and perhaps also their families. At times it may even be morally imperative to discontinue particular medical treatments in order to give the dying the personal care and attention they really need as life ebbs. Since life is a gift of God we treat it with awesome respect. Since death is part and parcel of human life, indeed the gateway to eternal life and the return to the Father, it, too, we treat with awesome respect.

The Family and Society

Marriage and the family are deeply affected by social patterns and cultural values. How we structure society, its approach to education and work, the roles of men and women, public policy toward health care and care of the young and old, the tone and cast of our literature, arts and media—all these affect the family. The test of how we value the family is whether we are willing to foster, in government and business, in urban planning and farm policy, in education and health care, in the arts and sciences, in our total social and cultural environment, moral values which nourish the primary relationships of husbands, wives and children and make authentic family life possible.

THE NATION

Our nation is committed in principle to the inviolable dignity of the human person, to respect for religious faith and the free exercise of religion, to social and legal structures by which citizens can participate freely in the governmental process, and to procedures by which grievances can be adjudicated and wrongs can be righted. This commitment is a constant challenge, and at times we have failed to live up to its demands. Nevertheless, it remains possible to develop here a social order "founded on truth, built on justice, and animated by love."[60]

The Individual and the Nation

While the ultimate and most substantive values inhere in individuals, individuality and community are inseparable elements of the moral life. So, for instance, honesty, courage and hope, which abide only in individuals, can be fostered by freedom to learn, protection from violence, adequate income, and the availability of health care.

As followers of Jesus we are called to express love of neighbor in deeds

---

[60] Vatican Council II, *The Church in the Modern World,* 26

which help others realize their human potential. This, too, has consequences for the structures of society. Law and public policy do not substitute for the personal acts by which we express love of neighbor; but love of neighbor impels us to work for laws, policies and social structures which foster human goods in the lives of all persons.

Respect for the Unborn

It is therefore as ironic as it is tragic that, in a nation committed to human rights and dignity, the practice of legalized abortion is now widespread. Every human life is inviolable from its very beginning. While the unborn child may not be aware of itself and its rights, it is a human entity, a human being with potential, not a potential human being. Like the newborn, the unborn depend on others for life and the opportunity to share in human goods. Their dependence and vulnerability remind us of the social character of all human life: to live and thrive as a human being, each of us needs the help and support of others.[61]

To destroy these innocent unborn children is an unspeakable crime, a crime which subordinates weaker members of the human community to the interest of the stronger. God who calls us to Himself loves the helpless and weak; like him we should affirm the unborn in their being, not close our eyes to their humanity so that we may more easily destroy them. Their right to life must be recognized and fully protected by the law.

While many today seek abortion for frivolous and selfish reasons, there are women who see it as a tragic solution to agonizing problems. They deserve society's help in meeting and resolving these problems so that they will not feel a need to resort to the inhuman expedient of abortion. Recognition of the incomparable dignity of all human beings, including the unborn, obliges us to assume loving responsibility for all who are in need. The Church must take appropriate initiatives in providing support to women with problems during pregnancy or after, and in doing so bear witness to its belief in human dignity.[62]

Women in Society

As society has grown more sensitive to some new or newly recognized issues and needs (while at the same time growing tragically less sensitive to others), the movement to claim equal rights for women makes it clear that they must now assume their rightful place as partners in family, institutional, and public life. The development of these roles can and should be enriching for both women and men.

Even today some still consider women to be men's inferiors, almost their

---

[61] Cf. Vatican Council II, *The Church in the Modern World*, 51

[62] National Conference of Catholic Bishops, *Pastoral Plan for Pro-Life Activities*, November 20, 1975

property. It is un-Christian and inhuman for husbands to regard their wives this way; they ought instead to "love (them) as Christ loved the Church."[63] Such un-Christian and inhuman attitudes are expressed in a truly degraded manner when they take the form of exploiting women for pleasure and financial profit through prostitution and pornography.

Efforts to win recognition that women have the same dignity and fundamental rights as men are praiseworthy and good. But the same cannot be said of views which would ignore or deny significant differences between the sexes, undermine marriage and motherhood, and erode family life and the bases of society itself. Liberation does not lie in espousing new modes of dehumanization, nor in enslavement to an ideology which ignores the facts of human sexuality and the requirements of human dignity.

There is much to be done in the Church in identifying appropriate ways of recognizing women's equality and dignity. We have every reason and precedent for doing so, since our tradition has always honored the Mother of God and recognized Mary as the one in whom, next to Jesus Himself, human nature is expressed most perfectly. In canonizing so many women over the centuries, including our own country's St. Frances Xavier Cabrini and St. Elizabeth Seton, the Church has proposed them to both women and men as models of what it means to live the life of Christ. Thus we fully support constructive efforts to remove demeaning attitudes and customs with respect to women, however subtle and unconscious in origin they may be.

Respect for Racial and Ethnic Groups

The members of every racial and ethnic group are beings of incomparable worth; yet racial antagonism and discrimination are among the most persistent and destructive evils in our nation.[64] Those victims of discrimination of whom we are most conscious are Hispanic Americans, Black Americans, and American Indians. The Catholic community should be particularly sensitive to this form of injustice because it, too, has experienced prejudice and discrimination in America based on national origin and religion.

It is sometimes said to be pointless to lecture those who are not personally guilty of causing or directly contributing to racism and other ills of society. But the absence of personal fault for an evil does not absolve one of all responsibility. We must seek to resist and undo injustices we have not caused, lest we become bystanders who tacitly endorse evil and so share in guilt for it.

It is also wrong to say that those whose energy and motivation have been sapped by social injustices bear sole responsibility for bettering themselves.

---

[63] Eph. 5:25

[64] The National Conference of Catholic Bishops and its predecessor, the National Catholic Welfare Conference, have often spoken on racial justice. Cf., for example, *The National Crisis,* NCCB, April 25, 1968

Instead, the struggle for a just social order requires programs to undo the consequences of past injustices.

Law has an important role to play in the fight against racial discrimination. Just laws alert people that some deeds are forbidden and others are required if all members of society are to share equitably in its goods. Laws may not be able to change attitudes, but they can deter those who might otherwise seek to violate the rights of others. By protecting minority groups and also those who wish to respect them and their rights, laws at least can foster actions and institutions essential to racial justice. Finally, and especially at a time when many are confused about morality, good laws can contribute to educating people to know right from wrong.

Thanks in great part to law and the courts, we have made progress in recent years in removing some social, political, and cultural structures which supported racism. But we are far from final success. For example, the principles of legitimacy, proportionality and restraint have sometimes been violated in law enforcement within our nation. Racial justice in such areas as housing, education, health care, employment, and the administration of justice must be given high priority. The Church, too, must continue efforts to make its institutional structures models of racial justice while striving to eliminate racism from the hearts of believers by reminding them of what it means to be sons and daughters of God and brothers and sisters in Christ. "There is no Greek or Jew here, circumcised or uncircumcised, foreigner, Scythian, slave or freeman. Rather, Christ is everything in all of you."[65]

Employment

Chronic unemployment is a strong factor paralyzing some groups in our nation. "Minorities" are not its only victims. Women and young workers suffer disproportionately.

Behind the statistics of joblessness lie human tragedies. For example, the father who cannot feed his family, in desperation often lapses into a pattern of life whose effects spread in an ever widening circle: crime, the use of drugs, alcoholism, mental illness, family breakdown—all increase along with unemployment.

Blessed with God-given gifts that include creativity and imagination, the people of this affluent nation can and must find means by which everyone who is able to work can have gainful, productive employment. If we settle for less we are allowing ourselves to be ruled by our economy instead of ruling it.[66]

An injustice to which we have frequently drawn attention is the systematic

---

[65] Col. 3:11

[66] Cf. United States Catholic Conference, *The Economy: Human Dimensions.* November 20, 1975

exploitation of agricultural workers, many of them migrants.[67] These neighbors whose work puts food on our tables are often compelled to live without decent housing, schooling, health care and equal protection of the law. The economic risks of the industry they serve do not justify denying them the right to negotiate for their own protection and betterment. If exploitation is the cost of lower food prices, it is too high a price to pay.

Housing

In many American cities affluent and impoverished neighborhoods are divided mostly along racial lines. If this were a result simply of ethnic preference or the preservation of property values, we would still be concerned that genuine 'neighborhood' was being thwarted. But, in fact, the actions of government, banks and the real estate industry at times converge to deprive some racial groups of financing for housing and to manipulate real estate values for the profit of insiders, with the result that our cities remain divided and hostile. All Americans should be able to live where they wish and their means allow. Furthermore, while society must provide decent housing for the poor, public housing may not be used as a device for consistently isolating some groups from the rest of the community.[68]

In saying this, we wish also to note the many human values preserved in ethnic neighborhoods, where people are united by a common culture, common origin, and sometimes even a common language other than English. Only when their boundaries become barriers and their values are cherished in ways that exclude others from participation do such neighborhoods become elements in a larger pattern of social strife.

Clearly, though, it is not just Americans of moderate means, whether in or out of ethnic neighborhoods, who should bear the burden of achieving racial justice. This is a duty of the well-to-do as well as the less affluent, of suburbanites as well as city residents: in short, of all social and economic classes. We do not have answers to all the complex issues raised by specific measures for the desegregation of schools and neighborhoods, but we believe these reflections have a significant bearing on them.

Crime and Correction

People have a right and need to live in peace, yet one of the urgent issues in our country today is crime. Violent urban crime receives most of the attention, but the apparently growing amount of white collar criminal fraud and corruption is also ominous, for it indicates a collapse of respect for virtues such as truthfulness and honesty which hold society together.

---

[67] Cf., for example, National Conference of Catholic Bishops, *Resolution on Farm Labor,* November 16, 1973

[68] Cf. United States Catholic Conference, *The Right to a Decent Home,* November 20, 1975

In both categories, merely emphasizing sterner law enforcement while ignoring factors which occasion criminal acts will accomplish very little. Poverty and injustice, as well as our society's spirit of acquisitiveness, contribute to crime. Whatever improvements may be needed in law enforcement and the administration of justice, society will not come to grips with the crime crisis until it seriously addresses these underlying problems.

Ironically, our penal system itself is sometimes a cause of increased crime. Long delay of trial and unequal application of the law are unjust and a source of increase in crimes. Often enough imprisonment only confirms inmates in criminal attitudes and practices. Sometimes prisons are also settings for gross violations of prisoners' rights. Prisoners, like the rest of us, are beings of transcendent value, and incarcerating them in prisons which dehumanize is a form of brutality. They have a right to protection against assault and against threats to their lives and well being. They have a right to proper food, health care and recreation, and to opportunities to pursue other human goods such as education and the cultivation of their skills. Reform of our nation's penal system in light of these and the other human rights of prisoners is urgent and long overdue.[69]

The Nation and the Individual

We have spoken often of the need for just laws and wholesome public policies, for all that government can do to create a setting in which fundamental values are protected and can flourish in human lives. Among the other contributions which government should make to the creation of a more wholesome society are responsible, constitutional steps to stem the flood of pornography, violence and immorality in the entertainment media. Yet we are aware of the limitations of government and the risk of seeming to suggest that it is all-important. Just laws and policies, taxes and programs, are necessary but they will not by themselves secure justice and peace. Such values must be built upon the foundations of good and dedicated individual human lives.

THE COMMUNITY OF NATIONS

Our allegiance must extend beyond the family and the nation to the entire human family. In Christ we are brothers and sisters of people whose customs are unfamiliar to us, but whose Father is our Father.

Human interdependence is constantly increasing in today's world, so that many issues which pertain to human dignity call for the collaboration of a true community of nations.[70] Perhaps the central global issue of our day is

---

[69] Cf. United States Catholic Conference, *The Reform of Correctional Institutions in the 1970s,* November 14, 1973

[70] Cf. Vatican Council II, *The Church in the Modern World,* 26

how to create such a community out of a world of states. Pope John grasped the meaning of this challenge when he described the structural defect in the present situation: the lack of authority and institutions adequate to address the problems humanity faces.[71] Most people agree about the problems and their seriousness: hunger, environmental pollution, population growth, glaring disparities of wealth, and the persistent danger of war, to mention only a few. But agreement is lacking on ways to cooperate in dealing with them.

Believing that the human family is called to live in unity, we speak of two goals for the community of nations which will also help bring it into being: the development of peoples and peace on earth. From the perspective of the United States, both are best addressed in the context of power. Our nation's enormous military and economic power make it essential that we understand how power should be used in the pursuit of these goals.

The Development of Peoples

All power is from God[72] and is an expression of His being. God uses His power on our behalf: by creating us and sustaining us in existence, by bestowing His gifts upon us, by enabling us to grow in likeness to Him. As His creatures and children, we are to use the power He grants us for the good of others.

Power may never be used to attack the dignity of persons, to subjugate them, to prevent them from seeking and realizing the goods to which their humanity gives them a claim. Beyond this, the powerful have a duty to work positively for the empowerment of the weak and powerless: to help others gain control over their own lives, so that as free and responsible persons they can participate in a self-determining manner in the goods proper to human beings.

The powerful must therefore work for the liberation of the oppressed and powerless. Though liberation in the fullest sense is what "Christ Himself announced and gave to man by His sacrifice," it is not possible to foster such liberation in oneself and others without also "promoting in justice and peace the true, authentic advancement" of humankind.[73]

Our nation's power, wealth, and position of leadership in the world impose special obligations upon us. Americans have always responded generously to foreign crises involving immediate human suffering: to floods and droughts, earthquakes and famines and the ravages of war. This is to our credit. But the obligations of which we now speak extend further. We must work creatively for a just international order based on recognition of interdependence. We must live by the principle that all nations and peoples are en-

---

[71] *Pacem in Terris,* 132–135
[72] Cf. Jn. 19:11; Rom. 13:1
[73] Pope Paul VI, *Evangelii Nuntiandi,* 38, 31

titled to an equitable share of the world's goods as well as respect for their right of self-determination.

The values which comprise the international common good are threatened by existing patterns of international political and economic relations. Our lives, policies, and patterns of consumption and production should be examined in light of their impact on other nations and peoples. Pope Paul has urged such examination: When so many people are hungry, so many families are destitute, so many enchained by ignorance, so many schools, hospitals and homes worthy of the name have yet to be built, all public or private squandering of wealth, all expenditure prompted by national or personal ostentation, and the exhausting arms race become intolerable scandals.[74]

The discussion of international justice and of institutions for its realization has become more specific as a result of the call at the United Nations for a New International Economic Order. Its significance lies in its effort to change the language of the debate from that of aid and charity to that of obligation and justice. The traditional question about foreign aid has been how much we of the industrial nations would choose to give others within the framework of the existing international order. By contrast, a discussion cast in terms of justice would examine the rules by which the system works—such things as trade treaties, commodity prices, corporate practices and monetary agreements—with a view to making them more just. New rules would clarify obligations among the parties. Politically, they would be designed to improve the bargaining position of the developing nations in relation to the industrialized countries.

Such discussion of rules for relationships and the distribution of power on the international level may be new to us as Americans but the themes are familiar to our experience. The American tradition emphasizes that rules of fairness are central to a just political system. The developing countries argue that it is precisely rules of fairness in economic relations which do not now exist. Similarly, quest for a new and more equitable form of bargaining power in relation to us echoes the drive for bargaining power by American workers over the last century.

Peace

We are also obliged as Americans and especially as Christians to reflect profoundly upon war and, more importantly, upon peace and the means of building it.[75]

The Church has traditionally recognized that, under stringent conditions, engaging in war can be a form of legitimate defense.[76] But modern warfare,

---

[74] *Populorum Progressio,* 53
[75] Cf. National Conference of Catholic Bishops, *Human Life in Our Day, II,* November 15, 1968
[76] Cf. Vatican Council II, *The Church in the Modern World,* 79

in both its technology and in its execution, is so savage that one must ask whether war as it is actually waged today can be morally justified.

At the very least all nations have a duty to work to curb the savagery of war and seek the peaceful settlement of disputes. The right of legitimate defense is not a moral justification for unleashing every form of destruction. For example, acts of war deliberately directed against innocent noncombatants are gravely wrong, and no one may participate in such an act.[77] In weighing the morality of warfare today, one must also take into consideration not only its immediate impact but also its potential for harm to future generations: for instance, through pollution of the soil or the atmosphere or damage to the human gene pool.

A citizen entering the military service is fulfilling a conscientious duty to his or her country. He or she may not casually disregard the nation's conscientious decision to go to war in self-defense. At the same time, no nation, our own included, may demand blind obedience. No members of the armed forces, above all no Christians who bear arms as "agents of security and freedom,"[78] can rightfully carry out orders or policies requiring direct force against noncombatants or the violation of some other moral norm. The right to object conscientiously to war in general and the right of selective conscientious objection to a particular war should be acknowledged by government and protected by law.[79]

With respect to nuclear weapons, at least those with massive destructive capability, the first imperative is to prevent their use. As possessors of a vast nuclear arsenal, we must also be aware that not only is it wrong to attack civilian populations but it is also wrong to threaten to attack them as part of a strategy of deterrence. We urge the continued development and implementation of policies which seek to bring these weapons more securely under control, progressively reduce their presence in the world, and ultimately remove them entirely.

The experience of the last fifteen years shows clearly that it is not only nuclear weapons which pose grave dangers and dilemmas. We must learn from the moral and political costs, to ourselves and others, of conventional war as it was waged in Vietnam. With much of the world undergoing or approaching a period of deep and sometimes drastic change, there is need for restraint and for clear reflection about the purposes which can justify the use of force. The moral reasons and political purposes said to call for even conventional force of arms, besides being valid, must be clear and convincing before any commitment is made to a policy of force.

Today, however, the human family longs for peace which is more than the mere absence of war, peace rooted in justice and brought alive by charity.

---

[77] Cf. *ibid.*, 80

[78] *Ibid.*, 79

[79] Cf. United States Catholic Conference, *Declaration on Conscientious Objection and Selective Conscientious Objection*, October 21, 1971

Such peace truly reflects Christ's vision of human life. Why is it so difficult to achieve?

Peace depends upon both the policies of states and the attitudes of peoples. A policy of peace can only be conceived and supported where a commitment to peace prevails. Cultivating this commitment and carrying forward this policy are intricate, delicate tasks. It is not that some among us desire war, but that those who speak of the risks of weakness are likely to dominate public debate. So the race to accumulate ever more destructive weapons continues in this and other nations.

Human Rights

There are considerable differences between what is required internationally and what is required domestically to preserve peace and promote justice. On another broad issue, however, the protection and promotion of human rights,[80] the values sought in our domestic political life and our foreign policy converge.

This nation's traditional commitment to human rights may be its most significant contribution to world politics. Today, when rights are violated on the left and the right of the international political spectrum, the pervasive presence of our nation's political power and influence in the world provides a further opportunity and obligation to promote human rights. How this should be done will vary from case to case; at the very least, however, national policy and our personal consciences are challenged when not only enemies but close allies use torture, imprisonment, and systematic repression as measures of governance.

The issue of human rights in foreign policy is ultimately a question of values. There is a direct, decisive bond between the values we espouse in our nation and the world we seek to build internationally. When human rights are violated anywhere without protest, they are threatened everywhere. Our own rights are less secure if we condone or contribute even by passive silence to the repression of human rights in other countries.

III. Conclusion

Many institutions of society have roles to play in realizing the vision we have attempted to sketch here. In a pluralistic society, religiously neutral public institutions and structures cannot be expected to embody the beliefs of any one religious group, nor indeed should they reflect an anti-religious view of life. They can and should help create the conditions in which values flourish in human lives and persons committed to Christian goals can pursue them without hindrance, without surrendering their rights, and with full opportunity to transmit their principles to future generations.

---

[80] Cf. Second General Assembly of the Synod of Bishops, 1971, *Justice in the World*

The obligation of creating these conditions rests in different ways upon different elements in society:

Upon Government

- to infringe upon the authentic rights of none;
- to create through the instruments of law and public policy conditions for the fullest possible flowering of the rights of all, with particular attention to family values and family needs;
- to seek a true community of nations with international structures able to address the real problems of today's world and work for the common good of all nations and peoples.

Upon Business and Industry, Labor and the Professions:

- to define their roles not in relation to narrow self-interest but in relation to the well being of all members of this society, especially the poor and the vulnerable;
- to seek for all a good life encompassing a broad spectrum of values in addition to economic ones;
- to show by responsible actions that the common good can be realized in our nation without intrusion by the state into ever more areas of life.

Upon the Media, Education, and All Who Transmit Information and Help Form Attitudes:

- to be deeply committed to the truth;
- to be respectful of persons and scrupulous to avoid advocating or inculcating false and corrosive values;
- to be eager to foster such community-building values as justice, charity, and the understanding that all human beings have a claim upon the goods of human life.

Upon Churches and Religious Groups:

- to be teachers of holiness and justice;
- to give witness to their teaching through policies and practices which seek to further the realization of human goods in the lives of all, those who are not their members as well as those who are;
- to exercise a prophetic role in society by calling individuals, groups, and institutions to be ever more mindful and supportive of authentic values.

With all this said, however, the most important thing is still unsaid. The values proclaimed by Jesus Christ are not expressed by structures and institutions if they are not lived by men and women. Jesus is not the way, the truth, and the life for corporate abstractions like 'government,' 'business,' and 'religious groups' but for human beings.[81] Yet people live in and depend upon communities and social structures of many kinds; and so the reason for cherishing moral values in families, nations, and the community of nations, and the test of how well they are fostered there, are individual human lives lived according to God's will for us made manifest in Jesus Christ. For Christians the goal is holiness.

Because we have been made holy in Jesus, we are, He teaches us, also to be "made perfect . . . as your heavenly Father is perfect."[82] All of us are to be perfectly what we really are: living temples of the holy God. "All the faithful of Christ of whatever rank or status are called to the fullness of the Christian life and to the perfection of charity."[83] We are all challenged to grow in holiness according to our "own personal gifts and duties," and above all by loving service, which guides and energizes all the paths of holiness.[84] To do this requires self-discipline and self-sacrifice. But it is possible in the strength of Christ and His Spirit which we share. Recognizing its possibility is a step toward making it real. We, your bishops, pray that these reflections will help bring this possibility more alive in our lives and the lives of many, will help open our hearts and yours, our brothers and sisters in Christ, to God's immeasurable love for us all.

St. John of the Cross tells us that at life's nightfall "we will be examined in love."[85] A life of faith is one measured constantly throughout its course in light of the love and life of Christ in us. When we come to die, much we have cherished will seem worthless, many things deemed urgent and attractive now will appear useless or worse. What will matter then is how much we love now and how we live in response to our Father's love for us.

The cross of Jesus Christ shows us the deficiency of other value systems. Jesus yielded up His life for us in perfect loving union with the Father's will, and this is the meaning of His life which also gives meaning to our lives as His followers. If we can acknowledge selfishness as folly and self-sacrifice as victory, if we can love enemies, be vulnerable to injustice and, in being so, still say that we have triumphed, then we shall have learned to live in Christ Jesus.

---

[81] Jn. 14:6
[82] Mt. 5:48
[83] Vatican Council II, *Constitution on the Church*, 40
[84] *Ibid.*, 41, cf. 39–42
[85] *Spiritual Sentences and Maxims*, 57

Part II:
Foreign Policy

War and Peace

The American bishops have not hesitated to take positions on some very controversial and complex issues. In the areas of war and peace, these include the Vietnam war, the Middle East problem, conscientious and selective conscientious objection, amnesty, and nuclear weapons.

In 1971, the bishops called upon the United States to withdraw military forces from Vietnam. They no longer believed that the United States could morally justify its presence there.

> *At this point in history, it seems clear that whatever good we hope to achieve through continued involvement in the war is now outweighed by the destruction of human life and of moral values which it inflicts.*

Five years earlier, in 1966, the bishops had issued a statement entitled Peace and Vietnam *in which they argued that, in the light of the facts known to them, U.S. presence in Vietnam was morally justified.*

About a year-and-a-half after calling for an end to the Vietnam War, the bishops spoke out forcefully against U.S. bombing operations in Cambodia. The Committee on Social Development and World Peace of the USCC argued that the government was relying on dubious authority to carry out the bombing. It questioned the utility of shoring up an ineffectual government and, most important, condemned the bombing as immoral.

The bishops have issued two major statements on the Middle East, one in 1973, and the other in 1978. Both call, among other things, for a comprehensive political solution involving the following policies:

(1) recognition of the right of Israel to exist as a sovereign state with secure boundaries;

(2) recognition of the rights of the Palestinian Arabs, especially the refugees (this involves inclusion of them as partners in any negotiations, acceptance of their right to a state, and compensation for past losses to be paid not only by Israel but also by other members of the international community responsible for the 1948 partition plan);

(3) acceptance, as the basis for negotiations by all parties to the conflict, of the stipulations set forth in the United Nations Security Council Resolution 242 of 22 November 1967.

In Human Life in Our Day, *(1968) the bishops made their first call for modification of the U.S. Selective Service Act. The proposed change would allow selective conscientious objectors to refuse with impunity to participate in wars they consider unjust or in branches of service (e.g., the strategic nuclear forces) that would force them to perform actions contrary to deeply held moral convictions about indiscriminate killing. Instead, these objectors would be allowed to perform a morally acceptable service for the human community. This plea for the legalization of selective conscientious objection was reiterated in 1969 by the Justice and Peace Division of the USCC and in 1971 by the USCC. The 1971 statement asserts the right of Catholics to be conscientious objectors as well as selective conscientious objectors:*

> *In the light of the Gospel and from an analysis of the Church's teaching on conscience, it is clear that a Catholic can be a conscientious objector to war in general or to a particular war because of religious training and belief.*

In 1971, the bishops presented their stand on amnesty. On two occasions they urged civil officials to grant amnesty to those in prison as conscientious objectors to the Vietnam war, and to consider giving those who emigrated from the U.S. a chance to return with the understanding that sincere conscientious objectors should remain subject, in principle, to some form of service to the community. Toward the end of 1972, the NCCB repeated this call for amnesty.

Peace and Vietnam

NCCB, November 18, 1966

1. Our common humanity demands that all people live in peace and harmony with one another. This peace will exist only if the right order established by God is observed, an order which is based on the requirements of human dignity. Everyone, therefore, must be vitally and personally concerned about correcting the grave disorders which today threaten peace. As Catholics, we are members of the Church that Pope Paul has called a "messenger of peace."

2. We, the Catholic Bishops of the United States, consider it our duty to help magnify the moral voice of our nation. This voice, fortunately, is becoming louder and clearer because it is the voice of all faiths. To the strong words of the National Council of Churches, the Synagogue Council of America, and other religious bodies, we add our own plea for peace. Our approaches may at times differ, but our starting point (justice) and our goal (peace) do not.

3. While we cannot resolve all the issues involved in the Vietnam conflict, it is clearly our duty to insist that they be kept under constant moral scrutiny.

No one is free to evade his personal responsibility by leaving it entirely to others to make moral judgments. In this connection, the Vatican Council warns that "men should take heed not to entrust themselves only to the efforts of others, while remaining careless about their own attitudes. For government officials, who must simultaneously guarantee the good of their own people and promote the universal good, depend on public opinion and feeling to the greatest possible extent."[1]

Peace and Modern Warfare

4. While it is not possible in this brief statement to give a detailed analysis of the Church's total teaching on war and peace, it seems necessary to review certain basic principles if the present crisis is to be put in its proper moral perspectives.

5. We reaffirmed at the Council the legitimate role of patriotism for the well-being of a nation, but a clear distinction was made between *true* and *false* patriotism: "Citizens should develop a generous and loyal devotion to their country, but without any narrowing of mind. In other words, they must always look simultaneously to the welfare of the whole human family, which is tied together by the manifold bonds linking races, peoples and nations."[2]

6. But these limits on patriotism do not rule out a country's right to legitimate self-defense. While making it clear that all means short of force must first be used, the Council restated the traditional teaching regarding the right of self-defense: "As long as the danger of war remains and there is no competent and sufficiently powerful authority at the international level, government cannot be denied the right to legitimate defense."[3] And what a nation can do to defend itself, it may do to help another in its struggle against aggression.

7. In the conduct of any war, there must be moral limits: "Any act of war aimed indiscriminately at the destruction of entire cities or of extensive areas along with their population is a crime against God and man himself. It merits univocal and unhesitating condemnation."[4] Moreover, as the Council also reminded us, the fact that a war of self-defense has unhappily begun does not mean that any and all means may be employed by the warring parties.

8. While the stockpiling of scientific weapons serves, for the present, as a deterrent to aggression, the Council has warned us that "the arms race in which so many countries are engaged is not a safe way to preserve a steady peace."[5] Indeed, it is a "treacherous trap for humanity." Far from pro-

---

[1] *Pastoral Constitution on the Church in the Modern World* Part II, Chapter V, Section 1 (*The Documents of Vatican II,* Guild Press, New York, p. 296)

[2] Ibid, Part II, Chapter IV, p. 286

[3] Ibid, Part II, Chapter V, Section 1, p. 293

[4] Ibid, Part II, Chapter V, Section 1, p. 294

[5] Ibid, Part II, Chapter V, Section 1, p. 295

moting a sure and authentic peace, it actually fosters war by diverting resources which could be better used to alleviate the human misery which causes war. In their urgent plea for disarmament, however, the Council Fathers understood that it will be effective only if it is universal and if there are adequate means of enforcing it.

9. The Council commended those citizens who defend their nation against aggression. They are "instruments of security and freedom on behalf of their people. As long as they fulfill this role properly, they are making a genuine contribution to the establishment of peace."[6]

At the same time, however, it pointed out that some provision should be made for those who conscientiously object to bearing arms: "It seems right that laws make humane provisions for the care of those who for reasons of conscience refuse to bear arms; provided, however, that they accept some other form of service to the human community."[7]

Principles Put to Work

10. In the light of these principles, how are we as Americans to judge the involvement of the United States in Vietnam? What can we do to promote peace?

11. Americans can have confidence in the sincerity of their leaders as long as they work for a just peace in Vietnam. Their efforts to find a solution to the present impasse are well known. We realize that citizens of all faiths and of differing political loyalties honestly differ among themselves over the moral issues involved in this tragic conflict. While we do not claim to be able to resolve these issues authoritatively, in the light of the facts as they are known to us, it is reasonable to argue that our presence in Vietnam is justified. We share the anguish of our government officials in their awesome responsibility of making life-and-death decisions about our national policy in Vietnam. We commend the valor of our men in the armed forces, and we express to them our debt of gratitude. In our time, thousands of men have given their lives in war. To those who loved them, we express our sorrow at their loss and promise our constant prayer.

12. But we cannot stop here. While we can conscientiously support the position of our country in the present circumstances, it is the duty of everyone to search for other alternatives. And everyone—government leaders and citizens alike—must be prepared to change our course whenever a change in circumstances warrants it.

13. This can be done effectively only if we know the facts and issues involved. Within the limits imposed by our national security, therefore, we must always insist that these facts and issues be made known to the public so that they can be considered in their moral context.

---

[6] Ibid, Part II, Chapter V, Section 1, p. 293
[7] Ibid, Part II, Chapter V, Section 1, p. 293

14. On the basis of our knowledge and understanding of the current situation, we are also bound always to make sure that our Government does, in fact, pursue every possibility which offers even the slightest hope of a peaceful settlement. And we must clearly protest whenever there is a danger that the conflict will be escalated beyond morally acceptable limits.

15. On a broader level, we must support our government in its efforts to negotiate a workable formula for disarmament. What we seek is not unilateral disarmament, but one proceeding, in the words of the Council, "at an equal pace according to agreement, and backed up by authentic and workable safeguards."[8] We commend the officials of our country and others for their contribution to the proposed Treaty against Nuclear Proliferation which, hopefully, will soon become a reality.

16. Moreover, we must use every resource available, as a nation, to help alleviate the basic causes of war. If the God-given human dignity of the people of poorer nations is not to become an illusion, these nations must be able to provide for the spiritual and material needs of their citizens. We must help them do this. The economically developed nations of the world, as Pope John insisted in his great encyclical, *Pacem in Terris*, must come to the aid of those which are in the process of developing so that every man, woman and child in the world may be able "to live in conditions more in keeping with their human dignity."[9]

'The Second Mile'

17. There is a grave danger that the circumstances of the present war in Vietnam may, in time, diminish our moral sensitivity to its evils. Every means at our disposal, therefore, must be used to create a climate of peace. In this climate, prayer, personal example, study, discussion and lectures can strengthen the will for peace. We must advocate what we believe are the best methods of promoting peace: mutual agreements, safeguards and inspection; the creation of an international public authority to negotiate toward peace. Above all, in its peace-making efforts, we must support the work of the United Nations which, in the words of Pope Paul, marks "a stage in the development of mankind, from which retreat must never be admitted, but from which it is necessary that advance be made."[10]

18. We ask every person of good will to support with prayer the Holy Father's plea for a Christmas cease-fire. May it open the way to lasting peace. In the spirit of Christ, the Christian must be the persistent seeker in the Gospel, the man willing to walk the second mile (cf. Matt. 5:42). He

---

[8] Ibid, Part II, Chapter V, Section 1, p. 296
[9] *Pacem in Terris* (NCWC, Washington, D.C., pp. 28, 29)
[10] *Address to the United Nations Assembly*, Oct. 4, 1965 (*Pope Paul VI in New York*, NCWC, Washington, D.C., p. 77)

walks prudently, but he walks generously and he asks that all men do the same.

19. As Catholics, we walk in good company. Pope Paul, in his recent encyclical on peace, cried out, in God's name, to stop war. We pray God that the sacrifices of us all, our prayers as well as our faltering efforts toward peace, will hasten the day when the whole world will echo Pope Paul's historic words: "No more war, war never again!"[11]

War in the Middle East

NCCB, Cardinal John Dearden, President
June 8, 1967

In the name of the bishops of the United States, Archbishop John F. Dearden of Detroit wrote this letter setting Sunday, June 11, 1967 as a Day of Prayer for Peace throughout the United States.

1. The outbreak of the war in the Middle East is a tragic event, one fraught with consequences that are truly frightening. War in itself is deplorable, but this present conflict carries with it the additional danger that it might spread and indeed result in a world holocaust. We cannot forget the warning "given" to mankind by Vatican Council II, less than two years ago:

2. "Enmities and hatred must be put away, and firm, honest agreements concerning world peace reached in the future. Otherwise, for all its marvelous knowledge, humanity, which is already in the middle of a grave crisis, will perhaps be brought to that mournful hour in which it will experience no peace other than the dreadful peace of death." (The Church in the Modern World, No. 82.)

3. In this hour of crisis, we, the Catholic bishops of the United States, unite with the Holy Father in his fervent hope that the United Nations Organization will be successful in halting the conflict. We pray that arms will

---

[11] Ibid., p. 9. Since the formation of the National Conference of Catholic Bishops in 1966 their Statements have not been signed. Where the title would not make the subject completely clear an introductory sentence was usually used by the bishops to explain the topic. This original format is followed in this volume.

be laid down and that an honorable accord will be concluded, so that this conflict may be resolved, not on the battlefield, but in the forum of the United Nations and before the International Court of Justice.

4. We ask our Catholic faithful and all who believe in God to join in a crusade of prayer for peace throughout the world. Particularly, we set aside next Sunday, June 11, as a day of prayer in all our churches and chapels. Let us pray for immediate peace in the Middle East and ask God's guidance upon the leaders of nations, so that they may mediate this dispute quickly and permanently.

Most Rev. John F. Dearden,
President
National Conference of
Catholic Bishops

On Peace

NCCB, November 16, 1967

1. The National Conference of Catholic Bishops, meeting in Washington last year, said in their Statement on Peace issued on Nov. 18, 1966: "There is a grave danger that the circumstances of the present war in Vietnam may in time diminish our moral sensitivity to its evils." The intervening time and the reactions of responsible segments of our society have proved that the moral sensitivity of the American people has not diminished but in fact increased and intensified. We interpret this as a witness of the ever-deepening yearning of the American people for peace and an increasing horror of the evils of war.

2. This longing for peace has been expressed in extreme reactions for and against our presence in Vietnam. This has resulted in considerable division among our people. Our deep concern for our people on the battlefield as well as on the home front forces us to plead for more rational debate and greater solicitude for mutual understanding. In the longing for peace we ought not to forget our moral and civic responsibilities. We embrace with great compassion the peoples of the lands who suffer the hardships of prolonged war.

3. We acknowledge gratefully the repeated efforts of our government to negotiate a termination of conflict. Despite the rebuffs to these efforts, our government is urged to continue with even greater determination and action

in the cause of negotiation. We extend this plea to the governments of the world and urge them to join earnestly in the search for a just and lasting peace.

4. We wish it understood that we are not pleading for peace at any price—we are pleading and praying for that peace recently described by Pope Paul as "never to be separated from justice for nations nor from freedom for citizens and peoples."

Human Life in Our Day
Chapter II, "The Family of Nations"

NCCB, November 15, 1968

93. We share the deep concern of thoughtful people in our times, a concern voiced by the Vatican Council, that "the whole human family has reached an hour of supreme crisis" (*Gaudium et Spes*, 77). The crisis can ultimately offer great promise for a more abundant human life, but at the moment it portends grave threats to all life. The threats to life depend on urgent and difficult decisions concerning war and peace. In considering these we share the conviction of Vatican Council II that the horror and perversity of technological warfare "compel us to undertake an evaluation of war *with an entirely new attitude*" (n. 80, emphasis added).

94. This compelling obligation is the greater in our case since we are citizens of a nation in many ways the most powerful in the world. The responsibility of moral leadership is the greater in the local Church of a nation whose arsenals contain the greatest nuclear potential for both the harm that we would wish to impede or the help it is our obligation to encourage. We are acutely aware that our moral posture and comportment in this hour of supreme crisis will be assessed by the judgment of history and of God.

95. We renew the affirmation by the Council that "the loftier strivings and aspirations of the human race are in harmony with the message of the Gospel" (n. 77). We speak as witnesses to that Gospel, aware that the issues of war and peace test the relevancy of its message for our generation, particularly in terms of the service of life and its dignity. We seek to speak in the spirit of that Gospel message, which is at heart a doctrine of non-violence

rather than violence, of peace understood as Jesus proclaimed it (cf. Jn. 14:27).

96. We call upon American Catholics to evaluate war with that "entirely new attitude" for which the Council appealed and which may rightly be expected of all who, calling themselves Christians, proclaim their identity with the Prince of Peace. We share with all men of good will the conviction that a more humane society will not come "unless each person devotes himself with renewed determination to the cause of peace" (n. 77). We appeal to policy makers and statesmen to reflect soberly on the Council teaching concerning peace and war, and vigorously to pursue the search for means by which at all times to limit and eventually to outlaw the destructiveness of war.

97. The Vatican Council noted that "war continues to produce daily devastation in one or another part of the world" (n. 79). The observation has lost none of its truth in the period since the Council ended; indeed, there have been further grievous outbreaks of war and aggression.

98. Of one mind with the Council, we condemn without qualification wars of aggression however their true character may sometimes be veiled. Whatever case there may have seemed to exist in other times for wars fought for the domination of another nation, such a case can no longer be imagined given the circumstances of modern warfare, the heightened sense of international mutuality and the increasingly available humane means to the realization of that mutuality.

99. We join wholeheartedly in the Council's condemnation of wars fought without limitation. We recognize the right of legitimate self-defense and, in a world society still unorganized, the necessity for recourse to armed defense and to collective security action in the absence of a competent authority on the international level and once peaceful means have been exhausted. But we seek to limit warfare and to humanize it, where it remains a last resort, in the maximum degree possible. Most of all, we urge the enlisting of the energies of all men of good will in forging the instruments of peace, to the end that war may at long last be outlawed.

100. Meanwhile, we are gratefully conscious that "those who are pledged to the service of their country as members of its armed forces should regard themselves as agents of security and freedom on behalf of their people. As long as they fulfill this role properly, they are making a genuine contribution to the establishment of peace" (*Gaudium et Spes*, 79).

101. In the Christian message peace is not merely the absence of war. Ultimately, of course, it presupposes that presence within and among men of a positive principle of life and unity which is none other than the divine life to which the Church bears witness, of which Christ in His Church is the source. The soul, then, of a peaceful society is divine charity. But justice, the great concern of the well-ordered state and the justification for its existence, is the foundation of the organized society.

102. Therefore, peace cannot be reduced solely to the maintenance of a

balance of power between enemies; nor is it to be brought about by dictatorship, whether this be the imposition of the sheer will of a ruler, a party or even a majority. It is an enterprise of justice and must be built up ceaselessly in seeking to satisfy the all-embracing demands of the common good. This is the point of Pope Paul's positive, dynamic concept of peace: the modern word for peace is development. Peace therefore presupposes the fraternal confidence which manifests itself in a firm determination to respect other persons and peoples, above all their human dignity, and to collaborate with them in the pursuit of the shared hopes of mankind.

Arms Control

103. It is in nuclear warfare, even in its "cold" phase or form, that mankind confronts the moral issue of modern war in its extreme case. This has become a situation in which two adversaries possess and deploy weapons which, if used against each other, could annihilate their respective civilizations and even threaten the survival of the human race. Nothing more dramatically suggests the anti-life direction of technological warfare than the neutron bomb; one philosopher declares that the manner in which it would leave entire cities intact, but totally without life, makes it, perhaps, the symbol of our civilization. It would be perverse indeed if the Christian conscience were to be unconcerned or mute in the face of the multiple moral aspects of these awesome prospects.

104. It is now a quarter century since Pope Pius XII summoned that conscience to a "War on War." He pointed out World War II's "unspeakable atrocities," the "image of a hell upon which anyone who nourishes humane sentiments in his heart can have no more ardent wish than to close the door forever." He warned against the further progress of "human inventions . . . directed to destruction," and pleaded that to the recognition of the immorality of wars of aggression there be added "the threat of a judicial intervention of the nations and of a punishment inflicted on the aggressor by the United Nations, so that war may always feel itself proscribed, always under the watchful guard of preventive action." He argued that then "humanity, issuing from the dark night in which it has been submerged for so great a length of time, will be able to greet the dawn of a new and better era in its history" (Christmas broadcast, 1944).

105. The Second Vatican Council, in a solemn declaration, endorsed "the condemnation of total warfare issued by recent popes" and stated: "Every act of war directed to the indiscriminate destruction of whole cities or vast areas with their inhabitants is a crime against God and man which merits firm and unequivocal condemnation" (*Gaudium et Spes,* 80).

106. The Council explicitly condemned the use of weapons of mass destruction, but abstained from condemning the *possession* of such weapons to deter "possible enemy attack" (n. 81). Though not passing direct judg-

ment on this strategy of deterrence, the Council did declare that "men should be convinced that the arms race in which so many countries are engaged is not a safe way to preserve a steady peace. Nor is the so-called 'balance' resulting from this race a pure and authentic peace. Rather than being eliminated thereby, the causes of war threaten to grow gradually stronger. ... Therefore it must be said again: the arms race is an utterly treacherous trap for humanity, and one which ensnares the poor to an intolerable degree" (n. 81).

107. The Council did not call for unilateral disarmament; Christian morality is not lacking in realism. But it did call for reciprocal or collective disarmament "proceeding at an equal pace according to agreement and backed up by authentic and workable safeguards" (n. 82). There are hopeful signs that such a formula may be strengthened by the Partial Test Ban Treaty and that the commitment under the Non-Proliferation Treaty to proceed to a negotiation of balanced reductions of nuclear weapons—at the same time extending the use of nuclear power for peaceful development of the needy nations under adequate inspection safeguards—may provide a positive, sane pattern for the future. We earnestly pray so, commending the furtherance of these hopes to responsible political leaders and to the support of all citizens.

108. Meanwhile, it is greatly to be desired that such prospects not be dashed by irrational resolves to keep ahead in "assured destruction" capability. Rather it is to be hoped that the early ratification by the Senate of the Non-Proliferation Treaty—which in essence is a Treaty between the USSR and the US and other nations—will hasten discussion of across-the-board reductions by the big powers. Despite, and even because of, the provocations in Eastern Europe and elsewhere, the United States should continue steps to create a better climate for these dicussions, such as taking the lead in inviting the UN Atomic Energy Commission and other organizations and foreign states to visit its nuclear facilities, and scrupulously reviewing all commitments for the sale, loan or lease of armaments.

109. The Council's position on the arms race was clear. To recall it: "Therefore, we declare once again: the arms race is an utterly treacherous trap for humanity. ... It is much to be feared that if this race persists, it will eventually spawn all the lethal ruin whose path it is now making ready" (n. 81).

110. Nonetheless, the nuclear race goes on. The latest act in the continuing nuclear arms race is no doubt the US decision to build a "thin" anti-ballistic missile system to defend against possible nuclear attack by another world power. This decision has been widely interpreted as the prelude to a "thick" ABM system to defend against possible nuclear attack.

111. In themselves, such anti-ballistic missiles are purely defensive, designed to limit the damage to the United States from nuclear attack. Nevertheless, by upsetting the present strategic balance, the so-called balance of terror, there is grave danger that a United States ABM system will

incite other nations to increase their offensive nuclear forces with the seeming excuse of a need to restore the balance.

112. Despite the danger of triggering an expanded escalation of the arms race the pressures for a "thick" ABM deployment persist.

113. We seriously question, whether the present policy of maintaining nuclear superiority is meaningful for security. There is no advantage to be gained by nuclear superiority, however it is computed, when each side is admittedly capable of inflicting overwhelming damage on the other, even after being attacked first. Such effective parity has been operative for some years. Any effort to achieve superiority only leads to ever-higher levels of armaments as it forces the side with the lesser capability to seek to maintain its superiority. In the wake of this action-reaction phenomenon comes a decrease in both stability and security.

114. The National Conference of Catholic Bishops pledges its united effort toward forming a climate of public opinion for peace, mindful of the Council's advice that "government officials ... depend on public opinion and feeling to the greatest possible extent" (n. 82). We will therefore, through existing and improved agencies, support national programs of education for Catholic Americans and for all Americans in collaboration with all religious groups and other organizations.

115. With *Gaudium et Spes,* we commend the arduous and unceasing efforts of statesmen and specialists in the field of arms control and disarmament, and add our own encouragement of systematic studies in this field. As the Council appealed to Catholic scholars throughout the world to participate more fully in such studies, so we call upon intellectuals in the Church in our land to bring scholarly competence and their powers of persuasion to that "war on war" which the modern Popes have without exception pleaded that we wage.

116. We urge Catholics, and indeed all our countrymen, to make a ceaseless vigil of prayers for peace and for all those who are charged with the delicate and difficult negotiations of disarmament. Such prayers provide the most obvious and appropriate occasion for ecumenical services bringing together all in our communities who cherish the blessed vision of peace heralded by the Hebrew prophets and preached by Christ and His Apostles. We cannot but question the depth of the commitment to peace of people of religious background who no longer pray for peace. But those who only pray for peace, leaving to others the arduous work for peace, the dialogue for peace, have a defective theology concerning the relation between human action and the accomplishment of that will of God in which is our peace. So, too, those who, neglectful of the part of prayer, rely only on their own power, or on the pooling of merely human resources on intelligence, energy and even good will, forget the wisdom of Scripture: "If the Lord does not build the house, in vain the masons toil; if the Lord does not guard the city, in vain the sentries watch" (Ps. 127, 1–2).

The International Community

117. The Council Fathers recognized that not even ending the nuclear arms race, which itself cannot be accomplished without the full cooperation of the international community, would ensure the permanent removal of the awesome threat of modern war. Nor would disarmament alone, even assuming it to be complete and across the board, remove the causes of war. "This goal undoubtedly requires the establishment of some universal public authority acknowledged as such by all, and endowed with effective power to safeguard, on the behalf of all, security, regard for justice and respect for rights" (n. 82).

118. Such an authority, furthermore, is required by the growing, ever more explicit interdependence of all men and nations as a result of which the common good "today takes on an increasingly universal complexion and consequently involves rights and duties with respect to the whole human race" (n. 26).

119. Therefore political leaders should "... extend their thoughts and their spirit beyond the confines of their own nation, put aside national selfishness and ambition to dominate other nations, and nourish a profound reverence for the whole of humanity, which is already making its way so laboriously toward greater unity" (n. 82).

120. We commend the efforts of world statesmen, particularly those of our own nation, who seek to extend the spirit and practice of cooperation in international agencies and regional associations of nations, with the object not only of terminating or preventing war, and of building up a body of international law, but also of removing the causes of war through positive programs.

121. Since war remains a melancholy fact of life today, we believe the United States not only should insist on adherence to and the application by all nations of existing international conventions or treaties on the laws of war, such as the revised Geneva Convention relative to the treatment of prisoners of war, but should take the lead in seeking to update them. Certain forms of warfare, new and old, should be outlawed, and practices dealing with civilian populations, prisoners of war and refugees are always in need of review and reform.

122. Here, too, our dependence on responsible writers, informed speakers and competent critics is crucial to the cause of peace. Hence we encourage Catholic scholars to undertake systematic studies of new developments, theories and practices in warfare, including guerilla warfare, revolution and "wars of liberation." Changing political patterns, improved techniques of communication, new methods of remote controls and of surveillance of individuals and communities alike made possible by science, as well as shifting ethical standards, make it the vocation of devout intellectuals, both as citizens of their own nations and servants of the common good of mankind,

to bring informed competence to the illumination, discussion and resolution of the complex issues, many of them moral, arising from all these.

123. A Catholic position of opposition to compulsory peacetime military service, first formulated on the level of the Holy See by Pope Benedict XV, has had for its premise the fact that such service has been a contributing cause of the breeding of actual wars, a part of the "great armaments" and "armed peace" security concept, and, in the words of Cardinal Gasparri in a letter to Lloyd George, the cause of such great evils for more than a century that the cure of these evils can only be found in the suppression of this system. In the spirit of this position, we welcome the voices lifted up among our political leaders which ask for a total review of the draft system and the establishment of voluntary military service in a professional army with democratic safeguards and for clear purposes of adequate defense. Our call for the end of any draft system at home which, in practice, amounts at times to compulsory peacetime military service is in direct line with previous resolutions of the hierarchy of the United States on compulsory military training (cf. *Our Bishops Speak,* pp. 234, 237).

124. Apart from the question of war itself, we deem it opportune here to reiterate the Council's condemnation of genocide, the methodical extermination of an entire people, nation or ethnic minority for reasons connected with race, religion or status such as that undertaken by the Nazis against the Jews among their own citizens and later against all the Jewish people, as well as so-called "gypsies." We would urge United States ratification of the United Nations Convention on this subject and of every other sound implementing instrument by which the United Nations Declaration of Human Rights can be translated from the level of ideals to that of actuality. Furthermore, we urge increased support by our own countrymen and citizens of all nations of all international programs consistent with the protection and promotion of the sanctity of human life and the dignity of the human person in times of war and peace.

125. We earnestly appeal to our own government and to all governments to give the elimination of the present international "war system" a priority consistent with the damaging effect of massive armament programs on all the objectives of the good society to which enlightened governments give priorities: education, public health, a true sense of security, prosperity, maximum liberty, the flourishing of the humane arts and sciences, in a word the service of life itself. Thus can we strive to move away, as reason and religion demand, from the "war system" to an international system in which unilateral recourse to force is increasingly restricted.

126. This will require international peace-making and peace-keeping machinery. To this end we urge all to support efforts for a stronger and more effective United Nations that it may become a true instrument of peace and justice among nations. In this respect the peace motivation of Pope Paul's public support of the United Nations by his moral authority and teaching of-

fice at the time of his visit to that body on its anniversary should be normative for Catholics.

127. We would welcome in official pronouncements of our own and other governments, as well as in the increased support given to the United Nations and associated agencies by the citizens of all nations, a greater interest in and direction toward the establishment of that universal public authority which the Council Fathers urged.

128. We recognize that any use of police action by such an international authority, or, in the meantime, by the UN as presently constituted, or by duly constituted regional agencies, must be carefully subject to covenants openly arrived at and freely accepted, covenants spelling out clear norms such as that of proportionate force; here, again, the work of qualified and conscientious specialists is indispensable.

129. Turning to the more positive aspects of the building of an international community and the duties of us as Americans in this matter, we deplore the lack of a stable, persevering national concern for the promotion of the international common good. This is reflected in the fickleness of public interest in and Congressional support of foreign aid. It is reflected also in a seeming insensitivity to the importance of trade agreements beneficial to developing nations. A like lack of generosity, dangerous to the fully human common good, is present in the increasingly bold linking of contraceptive programs, even when superficially voluntary, to needed aid programs. Future aid and trade assistance programs should become increasingly multilateral; they should never merely serve national self-interest except to the extent that national interest is genuinely part and parcel of the general good of the human community.

130. Because of the war in Vietnam, and the growing preoccupation with the social problems of our cities, there is the peril of an upsurge of exaggerated forms of nationalism and isolationism which the teachings of all Churches reprove and the experiences of World War II, had, we hoped, forever discredited.

131. It is the duty of our political leadership, of citizens and especially of believers who acknowledge the brotherhood of man, to promote and develop the spirit of international concern, cooperation and understanding.

132. As the Council noted, ". . . there arises a surpassing need for renewed education of attitudes and for new inspiration in the area of public opinion. Those who are dedicated to the work of education, particularly of the young, or who mold public opinion should regard as their most weighty task the effort to instruct all in fresh sentiments of peace" (n. 82).

133. To assist the agencies and institutions of the Catholic Church in the United States in their response to this "most weighty task," the Catholic Bishops have recently established a Division of World Justice and Peace, corresponding to the newly established Vatican Commission. It is our desire that the Division will stimulate renewed efforts in this field, and coordinate

whenever possible such efforts with those of other Christian bodies in an ecumenical framework. We call upon all men of conscience, all public spirited citizens, to dedicate themselves with fresh energy to this work.

134. We believe that the talents and resources of our land are so abundant that we may promote the common good of nations at no expense to the vitally necessary works of urban and rural reconstruction in our own country. The latter are the first order of domestic policy, just as the former should be the first order of foreign policy. Neither should be neglected, both being equally urgent; in the contemporary and developing world order their fortunes are intertwined.

Vietnam

135. In a previous statement we ventured a tentative judgment that, on balance, the U.S. presence in Vietnam was useful and justified.

136. Since then American Catholics have entered vigorously into the national debate on this question, which, explicitly or implicitly, is going deeply into the moral aspects of our involvement in Vietnam. In this debate, opinions among Catholics appear as varied as in our society as a whole; one cannot accuse Catholics of either being partisans of any one point of view or of being unconcerned. In our democratic system the fundamental right of political dissent cannot be denied, nor is rational debate on public policy decisions of government in the light of moral and political principles to be discouraged. It is the duty of the governed to analyze responsibly the concrete issues of public policy.

137. In assessing our country's involvement in Vietnam we must ask: Have we already reached, or passed, the point where the principle of proportionality becomes decisive? How much more of our resources in men and money should we commit to this struggle, assuming an acceptable cause or intention? Has the conflict in Vietnam provoked inhuman dimensions of suffering? Would not an untimely withdrawal be equally disastrous?

138. Granted that financial considerations are necessarily subordinate to ethical values in any moral question, nonetheless many wonder if perhaps a measure of the proportions in this, as in any modern war, may be reflected in the amounts inevitably lost to education, poverty-relief and positive works of social justice at home and abroad (including Southeast Asia) as a result of the mounting budgets for this and like military operations. This point has frequently been raised by the Popes, notably by Pope Pius XII who invoked the principle of proportionality in his analysis of the morality even of defensive wars, particularly when these involve A.B.C. elements (atomic, biological, chemical) and losses disproportionate to the "injustice tolerated" (Address to Military Doctors, Oct. 19, 1953).

139. While it would be beyond our competence to propose any technical

formulas for bringing the Vietnam War to an end, we welcome the bombing halt and pray for the success of the negotiations now underway.

140. Meanwhile there are moral lessons to be learned from our involvement in Vietnam that will apply to future cases. One might be that military power and technology do not suffice, even with the strongest resolve, to restore order or accomplish peace. As a rule internal political conflicts are too complicated to be solved by the external application of force and technology.

141. Another might be the realization that some evils existing in the world, evils such as undernutrition, economic frustration, social stagnation and political injustices, may be more readily attacked and corrected through non-military means, than by military efforts to counteract the subversive forces bent on their exploitation.

142. In addition, may we not hope that violence will be universally discredited as a means of remedying human ills, and that the spirit of love "may overcome the barriers that divide, cherish the bonds of mutual charity, understand others and pardon those who have done them wrong"? (*Pacem in Terris*, Article 171).

The Role of Conscience

143. The war in Vietnam typifies the issues which present and future generations will be less willing to leave entirely to the normal political and bureaucratic processes of national decision-making. It is not surprising that those who are most critical, even intemperate in their discussion of war as an instrument of national policy or as a ready means to the settling even of wrongs, are among the young; the burden of killing and dying falls principally on them.

144. There is sometimes ground for question as to whether the attitudes of some toward military duty do not spring from cowardice. In this problem, as in all crises which test generosity and heroism, cases of moral as well as physical cowardice doubtless occur. But a blanket charge of this kind would be unfair to those young people who are clearly willing to suffer social ostracism and even prison terms because of their opposition to a particular war. One must conclude that for many of our youthful protesters, the motives spring honestly from a principled opposition to a given war as pointless or immoral.

145. Nor can it be said that such conscientious objection to war, as war is waged in our times, is entirely the result of subjective considerations and without reference to the message of the Gospel and the teaching of the Church; quite the contrary, frequently conscientious dissent reflects the influence of the principles which inform modern papal teaching, the Pastoral Constitution and a classical tradition of moral doctrine in the Church, in-

cluding, in fact, the norms for the moral evaluation of a theoretically just war.

146. The enthusiasm of many young people for new programs of service to fellow humans in need may be proof that some traditional forms of patriotism are in process of being supplemented by a new spirit of dedication to humanity and to the moral prestige of one's own nation. This new spirit must be taken seriously; it may not always match the heroism of the missionaries and the full measure of the life of faith, but it is not contradictory to these and may open up new forms of Christian apostolate.

147. As witnesses to a spiritual tradition which accepts enlightened conscience, even when honestly mistaken, as the immediate arbiter of moral decisions, we can only feel reassured by this evidence of individual responsibility and the decline of uncritical conformism to patterns some of which included strong moral elements, to be sure, but also included political, social, cultural and like controls not necessarily in conformity with the mind and heart of the Church.

148. If war is ever to be outlawed, and replaced by more humane and enlightened institutions to regulate conflicts among nations, institutions rooted in the notion of universal common good, it will be because the citizens of this and other nations have rejected the tenets of exaggerated nationalism and insisted on principles of non-violent political and civic action in both the domestic and international spheres.

149. We therefore join with the Council Fathers in praising "those who renounce the use of violence in the vindication of their rights and who resort to methods of defense which are otherwise available to weaker parties, provided that this can be done without injury to the rights and duties of others or of the community itself" (n. 78).

150. It is in this light that we seek to interpret and apply to our own situation the advice of the Vatican Council on the treatment of conscientious objectors. The Council endorsed laws that "make humane provision and for the care of those who for reasons of conscience refuse to bear arms, provided, however, that they accept some other form of service to the human community" (n. 79).

151. The present laws of this country, however, provide only for those whose reasons of conscience are grounded in a total rejection of the use of military force. This form of conscientious objection deserves the legal provision made for it, but we consider that the time has come to urge that similar consideration be given those whose reasons of conscience are more personal and specific.

152. We therefore recommend a modification of the Selective Service Act making it possible, although not easy, for so-called selective conscientious objectors to refuse—without fear of imprisonment or loss of citizenship—to serve in wars which they consider unjust or in branches of service (e.g., the strategic nuclear forces) which would subject them to the performance of ac-

tions contrary to deeply held moral convictions about indiscriminate killing. Some other form of service to the human community should be required of those so exempted.

153. Whether or not such modifications in our laws are in fact made, we continue to hope that, in the all-important issue of war and peace, all men will follow their consciences. We can do no better than to recall, as did the Vatican Council, "the permanent binding force of universal natural law and its all embracing principles," to which "man's conscience itself gives ever more emphatic voice."

154. In calling so persistently in this Pastoral for studies on the application of sound moral principles to new dimensions of changes in the problems of war and peace, we are mindful of our own responsibility to proclaim the Gospel of peace and to teach the precepts of both natural and revealed divine law concerning the establishing of peace everywhere on earth (n. 79). We therefore make our own the Council's judgment on "the deeper causes of war," sins like envy, mistrust and egoism. We echo the warning given by Pope Paul at the United Nations: "Today as never before, in an era marked by such human progress, there is need for an appeal to the moral conscience of man. For the danger comes not from progress, nor from science—on the contrary, if properly utilized these could resolve many of the grave problems which beset mankind. The real danger comes from man himself, who has at his disposal ever more powerful instruments, which can be used as well for destruction as for the loftiest conquests."

155. The hour has indeed struck for "conversion," for personal transformation, for interior renewal. We must once again begin to think of man in a new way, and of human life with a new appreciation of its worth, its dignity and its call to elevation to the level of the life of God Himself. All this requires that, with refreshed purpose and deepened faith we follow the urging of St. Paul that we "put on the new man, which has been created according to God in justice and holiness of truth" (Eph. 4:23).

Conclusion

156. Christians believe God to be the "source of life" (cf. Jn. 5, 26) and of love since "love comes from God" (cf. 1 Jn. 4, 7). "God is love" (1 Jn. 4, 8) and man has been made in His image and likeness (Genesis 1, 26). Thus, man is most himself when he honors life and lives by love. Then he is most like to God.

157. The doctrine and defense of life require a renewed spirituality in the Church. Such a spirituality will reaffirm the sacred character of married love through which life is begun, the dignity of the family within which love brings life to maturity, and the blessed vision of peace in which life is shared by men and nations in a world community of love.

158. These themes, all of which touch on life, we have explored in terms of

the family, the commonwealth of nations and some of the anti-life forces which threaten these.

159. In her defense of human life the Church in our day makes her own, as did Moses, the words by which God Himself reduces our perplexities to a clear, inescapable choice: "I call heaven and earth to witness against you this day, that I have set before you life and death ... therefore, choose life that you and your descendants may live ..." (Deut. 30, 19).

Prisoners of War

NCCB, November 14, 1969

A statement on prisoners of war adopted by the National Conference of Catholic Bishops at its semi-annual meeting in Washington, D.C., November 14, 1969.

1. Every war involves tragedy, for those who direct it, for those who must fight it and not least for those who must wait and hope at home in the most painful anguish of uncertainty about the return of their loved ones and those who fall into the hands of those who, in all charity, are temporarily called "enemies."

2. This bitter fact is now sharply dramatized in the plight of the American and other prisoners of war in Southeast Asia, and in the suffering of their families and friends at home.

3. We have a responsibility, before God, because of those families, the prisoners and the prospects for a decent world of peace, to help solve this problem. We wish, therefore, to add our voices to those already raised in this cause.

4. The United States government and other governments and international organizations are to be commended for their efforts on behalf of the prisoners of war and their relatives and friends. They should continue to place such efforts among their priorities now and in the future.

5. Among the objectives to be sought by the United States government and other governments and international agencies should be the release of the names of captured personnel, exchange of the sick and wounded, impar-

tial inspection of prisoners of war facilities, and proper treatment of and regular communication with all prisoners of war.

6. The families and friends of prisoners of war have our admiration for their courage and our prayerful sympathy in their suffering. Proper treatment of all prisoners of war in all wars must be the continuing concern of the individual Christian conscience and of governments until, hopefully, all wars can be eradicated.

Human Solidarity

NCCB, April 1970

Statement on the Twenty-Fifth Anniversary of the United Nations by the National Conference of Catholic Bishops

1. Twenty-five years ago this month, while World War II was still an agonizing reality, representatives of 51 nations gathered in San Francisco. In the name of "the Peoples of the United Nations," they pledged to unite their strength within a comprehensive new juridical and political world organization "to save succeeding generations from the scourge of war" in accordance with principles of justice and international law.

2. The American Bishops declared a few months later that our country acted wisely in deciding to participate in this world organization. Concerned that the great powers were placed in a position "above the law" in matters relating to the maintenance of peace and security, they expressed the hope that a sound institution would develop from the recognition of the rights and duties of international society.

3. As the American Bishops meet now in 1970 in San Francisco, a city which bears the name of the patron of peace, we deem it appropriate to welcome the twenty-fifth anniversary year of the United Nations. Even more important, however, this is a fitting occasion for an examination of conscience and a renewed resolve to unite, as both the Gospel and the times demand, to banish war and to make of the earth a peaceable kingdom.

4. We call upon American Catholics to join with us in appreciation of the noble purposes of the United Nations and of its innovative efforts and achievements in behalf of human solidarity, human development and peace, and we urge them to increase their knowledge and understanding of these ef-

forts and achievements. At the same time we recognize, as the United Nations itself is doing, how far it still is from meeting contemporary threats to and demands for that peace, justice and true human progress which are the theme of the anniversary year.

Achievements

5. Common endeavors of the Member States of the United Nations, harmonizing national interests, have indeed deepened and broadened awareness of the reciprocal rights and obligations of states in international life. Some conflicts have been averted, contained or halted by its efforts. The horrendous character of nuclear, chemical and biological warfare has been universally acknowledged, and treaties to limit or abolish the respective weapons have been concluded or initiated. Numerous new states, formerly under colonial rule, have been assisted in the transition to independence and the new responsibilities thereof, and they have been welcomed to United Nations membership on terms of juridical equality. The dignity and fundamental equality of all members of the human family, without regard to sex, race, color, religion or any other distinction, have been repeatedly affirmed and enhanced through formal declarations and treaties, through various educational campaigns and through positive action of a social nature. Worldwide technical cooperation and other forms of mutual assistance are feeding the hungry, healing the sick, instructing the ignorant and sheltering the homeless. A body of international law to cover existing and expanding relations in international life, which otherwise might lead to conflict, is being progressively developed. Agreements to preserve outer space, the ocean bed and an uncontaminated environment as the peaceful patrimony of all mankind have been concluded or are in the making.

Possibilities

6. There can be no doubt that the United Nations could move to that higher dimension of community and authority demanded by the contemporary crises of peoples, which are, in fact, world crises, if men and states would take seriously the injunction of Pope Paul to the United Nations: "We must get used to thinking of man in a new way, of men's life in common in a new way, in a new way, too, of the paths of history and the destiny of the world." In a world made one by the evolution of communications and transportation, this new way requires States to emerge from the anachronistic structures which enshrine old concepts of unlimited national sovereignty.

7. As Christians and as American citizens, we have a special responsibility to cherish and protect the life of men in community and to assist the United Nations to help us do so. As Americans we must acknowledge the reality of our massive power and take the lead in sharing it through strengthening the world organization. This calls for acceleration in the delicate exchange in

which the United States and other nations experience a limitation of the power to act unilaterally and an expansion of the obligation to share the responsibility of global peace and development.

8. This limitation of unilateral power occurs notably in the area of arms control which can effectively curb the power of any State to make war and the concomitant establishment of a UN peacekeeping system capable of speedy action to guarantee security. The success of the Strategic Arms Limitation Talks between the United States and the USSR is a first and necessary step.

9. As to possibilities of peacekeeping, without which there will be no real or lasting arms control, in the words of Charles Yost, U.S. Ambassador to the United Nations: "We have only to glance at some of the key provisions of the Charter to see how far we have fallen short of making them living realities, how substantially we have failed to develop the institution and the sort of international society which the authors of the Charter had in mind. . . . The United Nations is still waiting for its members to give it the authority to settle disputes and to live up to its promise of peace."

10. The United States should not only take the lead in the new efforts to institutionalize a standby UN peacekeeping force and to set up fact finding, arbitration, mediation and conciliation mechanisms for settling political disputes, it should also take bold steps to substitute for the rule of force a rule of law. In the light of changed world conditions we encourage and shall promote wide public discussion of greater use by the United States of the long established but practically unemployed International Court of Justice for the settlement of disputes.

11. The compelling needs of mankind no less than the growing dangers to peace are an indictment of the untrammeled pursuit of national self-interest. There is evidence that our great country and its generous people hold not the first but the eleventh place among the nations in percentage of our gross national product allotted to help in the development of poorer nations and peoples. We welcome the new directions, outlined by the President's Task Force on International Development, which call for the reversal of the downward trend of such contributions and for greater use of international rather than national channels in distributing such aid. Only in this way can we share effectively in the promotion of global solidarity and increase the common stake of all nations in a strengthened United Nations. Sympathetic exploration in the United Nations of an International Volunteer Corps should be given every encouragement.

12. The patterns and practices of international trade in which we are engaged also call for a serious assessment in light of the present needs and the future well-being of the world. Our country should provide a far more adequate response to those nations which suffer from the injustices of the present system in which we play a powerful role; the structures which support these injustices must be examined with a view to change.

13. All of our strivings for true human progress will be frustrated if we

cannot honestly regard each of our brothers as another self, whose true vocation, like ours, is to love and to seek and embrace the good and the true, and thus attain that higher level of life which is his destiny. This regard must be expressed also in laws and institutions. Of the many Conventions drafted since 1945 by the United Nations with the object of securing reciprocal commitment by all nations to protect and promote particular human rights, the United States has ratified but one. We urge again, as we did in 1968, U.S. ratification of the Convention on Genocide and pledge ourselves to assist in the promotion of wide public dialogue, not only on those Conventions which have already been submitted to Congress, *e.g.*, on forced labor and women's political rights, but also on others which should be so submitted, including those on racial discrimination and discrimination in education.

14. In any global approach to the problems of peace and human welfare, the real and potential magnitude of the People's Republic of China cannot be ignored. We commend the present Administration for continuing the efforts to develop workable relationships with the people of mainland China and encourage wide public discussion of this subject.

15. Informed and conscientious participation in forming national policies is the surest way to promote change looking to greater international cooperation. The exercise of this right and duty should be ensured by continuing education. We must ask ourselves whether our schools, organizations and institutions are ministering to the formation of a global mentality or whether they are reinforcing outmoded nationalistic, and even chauvinistic, attitudes of the past.

16. In the development of a world public opinion, we would urge study of the possibilities inherent in the common interests and actions of the many international non-governmental organizations. Their experience is a contribution to the growth of world community and is so recognized in the consultative status granted to many of them by the UN Economic and Social Council.

17. In concluding, we recall the words of Pope Paul VI to the General Assembly of the United Nations in 1965: "This Organization represents the obligatory path of modern civilization and of world peace ... Go forward." The path is obligatory because the world can no longer afford the luxury of completely autonomous and self-sustaining nation states. In the United Nations, therefore, we see the beginnings of a new international order to replace the jealous sovereignty of States and the fragmenting forces of nationalism—a new international order in which mutual cooperation and respect for rights and duties will lead to that human solidarity which may be said to reflect the plan of the Creator who made mankind one that they might seek Him.[1]

---

[1] This Statement was approved by the bishops assembled in San Francisco April, 1970 to be published at a later suitable date.

Declaration on Conscientious Objection and Selective Conscientious Objection

USCC, October 21, 1971

For many of our Catholic people, especially the young, the question of participation in military service has become a serious moral problem. They properly look to their spiritual leaders for guidance in this area of moral decision and for support when they judge their sentiments to be in keeping with Catholic Christian tradition. For this reason, we wish to express ourselves on the following principles.

The traditional teaching of the Church regarding the importance of individual conscience is crucial in this issue of conscientious objection and selective conscientious objection. The obligation to seek the truth in order to form right and true judgments of conscience and the obligation to follow conscience was put in positive terms by Pope Paul VI and the Fathers at the Second Vatican Council:

> Further light is shed on the subject if one considers that the highest norm of human life is the divine law—eternal, objective, and universal—whereby God orders, directs, and governs the entire universe and all the ways of the human community, by a plan conceived in wisdom and love. Man has been made by God to participate in this law, with the result that, under the gentle disposition of divine Providence, he can come to perceive ever increasingly the unchanging truth. Hence every man has the duty, and therefore the right to seek the truth in matters religious, in order that he may with prudence form for himself right and true judgments of conscience, with the use of all suitable means.

> Truth, however, is to be sought after in a manner proper to the dignity of the human person and his social nature. The inquiry is to be free, carried on with the aid of teaching or instruction, communication, and dialogue. In the course of these, men explain to one another the truth they have discovered, or think they have discovered, in order thus to assist one another in the quest for truth. Moreover, as the truth is discovered, it is by a personal assent that men are to adhere to it.

> On his part, man perceives and acknowledges the imperatives of the divine law through the mediation of conscience. In all his activity a man is bound to follow his conscience faithfully, in order that he may come to God, for whom he was created. ("Declaration on Religious Freedom," n. 3)

74

Addressing the question in the "Pastoral Constitution on the Church in the Modern World," Our Holy Father and the Bishops at the Second Vatican Council wrote:

> In the depths of his conscience, man detects a law which he does not impose upon himself, but which holds him to obedience. Always summoning him to love good and avoid evil, the voice of conscience can when necessary speak to his heart more specifically: do this, shun that. For man has in his heart a law written by God. To obey it is the very dignity of man; according to it he will be judged.

> Conscience is the most secret core and sanctuary of a man. There he is alone with God, whose voice echoes in his depths. In a wonderful way conscience reveals that law which is fulfilled by love of God and neighbor. In fidelity to conscience, Christians are joined with the rest of men in the search for truth, and for the genuine solution to the numerous problems which arise in the life of individuals and from social relationships.

> Hence the more that a correct conscience holds sway, the more persons and groups turn aside from blind choice and strive to be guided by objective norms of morality. ("The Church in the Modern World," n. 16)

In addition, the Church has always affirmed the obligation of individuals to contribute to the common good and the general welfare of the larger community. This is the basis for the participation of Christians in the legitimate defense of their nation.

The Council Fathers, recognizing the absence of adequate authority at the international level to resolve all disputes among nations, acknowledged that "governments cannot be denied the right to legitimate defense once every means of peaceful settlement has been exhausted." (The Church in the Modern World," n. 79)

When survival of the wider community has been threatened by external force, the Church has traditionally upheld the obligation of Christians to serve in military defensive forces. Such community-oriented service, that is, soldiers devoted to the authentic purposes of securing peace and justice, has merited the Church's commendation.

The Catholic Bishops of the United States are gratefully conscious of the sacrifices and valor of those men who are serving and who have served in the armed forces and especially those who have given their lives in service to their country. Their courage in the defense of the common good must not be underestimated or forgotten. In the words of the Second Vatican Council, "As long as they (members of the armed forces) fulfill this role properly, they are making a genuine contribution to the establishment of peace." ("The Church in the Modern World," n. 79)

It was also recognized by the Second Vatican Council that the common good is also served by the conscientious choice of those who renounce violence and war, choosing the means of nonviolence instead:

> ... we cannot fail to praise those who renounce the use of violence in the vindication of their rights and who resort to methods of defense which are otherwise available to weaker parties too, provided that this can be done without injury to the rights and duties of others or of the community itself. ("The Church in the Modern World," n. 78)

Furthermore, the Council Fathers, addressing themselves more specifically to the rights of the conscientious objector to war, stated:

> ... it seems right that laws make humane provisions for those who for reasons of conscience refuse to bear arms, provided however, that they accept some other form of service to the human community. ("The Church in the Modern World," n. 79)

Although a Catholic may take advantage of the law providing exemption from military service because of conscientious opposition to all war, there often arises a practical problem at the local level when those who exercise civil authority are of the opinion that a Catholic cannot under any circumstances be a conscientious objector because of religious training and belief. This confusion, in some cases, is the result of a mistaken notion that a person cannot be a conscientious objector unless the individual is a member of one of the traditional pacifist churches (for example, a Quaker).

In the light of the Gospel and from an analysis of the Church's teaching on conscience, it is clear that a Catholic can be a conscientious objector to war in general or to a particular war "because of religious training and belief." It is not enough, however, simply to declare that a Catholic can be a conscientious objector or a selective conscientious objector. Efforts must be made to help Catholics form a correct conscience in the matter, to discuss with them the duties of citizenship, and to provide them with adequate draft counseling and information services in order to give them the full advantage of the law protecting their rights. Catholic organizations which could qualify as alternative service agencies should be encouraged to support and provide meaningful employment for the conscientious objector. As we hold individuals in high esteem who conscientiously serve in the armed forces, so also we should regard conscientious objection and selective conscientious objection as positive indicators within the Church of a sound moral awareness and respect for human life.

The status of the selective conscientious objector is complicated by the fact that the present law does not provide an exemption for this type of conscientious objection. We recognize the very complex procedural problems which selective conscientious objection poses for the civil community; we call upon moralists, lawyers and civil servants to work cooperatively toward a policy which can reconcile the demands of the moral and civic order concerning this issue. We reaffirm the recommendation on this subject contained in our November 1968 pastoral letter, "Human Life in Our Day":

> 1) a modification of the Selective Service Act making it possible for selective conscientious objectors to refuse to serve in wars they consider unjust, without fear of imprisonment or loss of citizenship, provided they perform some other service to the human community; and
> 2) an end to peacetime conscription.

In restating these recommendations, we are aware that a number of young men have left the country or have been imprisoned because of their opposition to compulsory military conscription. It is possible that in some cases this was done for unworthy motives, but in general we must presume sincere objections of conscience, especially on the part of those ready to suffer for their convictions. Since we have a pastoral concern for their welfare, we urge civil officials in revising the law to consider granting amnesty to those who have been imprisoned as selective conscientious objectors, and giving those who have emigrated an opportunity to return to the country to show responsibility for their conduct and to be ready to serve in other ways to show that they are sincere objectors.

Resolution on Southeast Asia

NCCB, November 1971

In the light of the urgent appeal for justice in the world pronounced by the recent Synod in Rome, we Bishops of the United States address ourselves again to the agonizing issue of the American involvement in Southeast Asia. And we feel compelled to make some positive recommendations concerning the long journey ahead to peace with justice in our world.

I. The American Involvement in Southeast Asia

Three years ago, in our Pastoral Letter "Human Life in Our Day," we raised some basic moral questions concerning the Vietnam War:

> In assessing our country's involvement in Vietnam we must ask: Have we already reached, or passed, the point where the principle of proportionality becomes decisive? How much more of our resources of men and money

should we commit to this struggle, assuming an acceptable cause and intention? Has the conflict in Vietnam provoked inhuman dimensions of suffering?

At this point in history it seems clear to us that whatever good we hope to
achieve through continued involvement in this war is now outweighed by the
destruction of human life and of moral values which it inflicts. It is our firm
conviction, therefore, that the speedy ending of this war is a moral imperative
of the highest priority. Hence, we feel a moral obligation to appeal urgently
to our nation's leaders and indeed to the leaders of all the nations involved in
this tragic conflict to bring the war to an end with no further delay.

II. The Journey Ahead to Peace With Justice in Our World

It is our prayerful hope that we in America will have learned from the
tragedy of Vietnam important lessons for reconstructing a world with justice
and a world at peace.

First, we must be determined as never before to "undertake an evaluation
of war with an entirely new attitude" (Vatican II, Pastoral Constitution on
the Church in the World, No. 80). And we reach this new attitude by attending more carefully to the spirit of the Gospel and by heeding the pleas of recent Popes: "Nothing is lost by peace; everything may be lost by war" (Pius
XII, Radio Broadcast of 24 August 1939); "In this age of ours which prides
itself on atomic power, it is irrational to believe that war is still an apt means
of vindicating violated rights" (John XXIII, Pacem in Terris, No. 127); "No
more war, war never again" (Paul VI, Address to the United Nations, 4 October 1965).

Secondly, we realize that "peace is not merely the absence of war, but an
enterprise of justice" (Vatican II, Past. Const. on the Church in the World,
No. 78). In this vein we recognize our nation's moral obligation, together
with other nations, to contribute mightily to the restoration and development
of Southeast Asia. After World War II our country launched an unprecedented program of economic assistance and social reconstruction of
war-torn countries. Certainly we can do no less now.

Thirdly, we are convinced that the United Nations must become more effective in the promotion of world justice and peace. In saying this, we echo
the words of Pope Paul VI that "the people of the earth turn to the United
Nations as the last hope of concord and peace," and we recognize with the
Holy Father that the United Nations "must be perfected and made equal to
the needs which world history will present" (Address to the United Nations, 4
October 1965). Only by strengthening the United Nations as an international
forum for peace and as a multilateral instrument for peace-keeping can
future Vietnams be averted.

Finally, we recognize a clear need at this point in history to urge upon all
Americans a spirit of forgiveness and reconciliation. We recall that at a simi-

larly critical moment in American history, Abraham Lincoln urged his countrymen to act "with malice towards none, with charity towards all." We invite our fellow Americans to let these words guide new efforts to heal wounds in our divided society and to unite our country in the years after the war in Southeast Asia.

We speak with special concern for those who have borne the heaviest burden of this war: the young men who chose conscientiously to serve in the Armed Forces, many of whom lost life or limb in this conflict. We wish to express our profound sympathy to the wives and families of the soldiers who have died in Southeast Asia. We express our profound concern for our prisoners of war and their families and promise our prayers for the prisoners' welfare and release. And on behalf of the returning veterans we urge strongly that the Government increase the present benefits and educational opportunities afforded by the G.I. Bill, and that it create new programs of drug rehabilitation, vocational training and job placement wherever necessary.

Those who in good conscience resisted this war are also subjects of our genuine pastoral concern. They too must be reintegrated as fully as possible into our society and invited to share the opportunities and responsibilities of building a better nation. Hence we repeat our plea of October 21, 1971 that the civil authorities grant generous pardon of convictions incurred under the Selective Service Act, with the understanding that sincere conscientious objectors should remain open in principle to some form of service to the community. Surely a country which showed compassion by offering amnesty after the Civil War will want to exercise no less compassion today.

Conclusion

In setting forth our position at this time, we realize that the task of constructing a just social order and a world genuinely at peace will never be an easy one. But we must reaffirm that followers of Christ and all men of good will must redouble their efforts to achieve this task so worthy of our best efforts.

> Otherwise, for all its marvelous knowledge, humanity, which is already in the middle of a grave crisis, will perhaps be brought to that mournful hour in which it will experience no peace other than the dreadful peace of death. But while we say this, the Church of Christ takes her stand in the midst of the anxiety of this age, and does not cease to hope with the utmost confidence. She intends to propose to our age over and over again, in season and out of season this apostolic message: "Behold, now is the acceptable time" for a change of heart; "Behold, now is the day of salvation!" (Vatican II, Pastoral Constitution on the Church in the World, No. 82).

Resolution on Imperatives of Peace

NCCB, November 16, 1972

This is a critical moment in the history of the Vietnam war. Intensive efforts on the part of our government as well as other parties involved appear to be refining the final details of a settlement which will end the fighting. Recalling our exhortation a year ago to our nation's leaders and to leaders of all nations to "bring the war to an end with no further delay," we pray earnestly to Christ, the Prince of Peace, for a successful outcome of the present negotiations: that is, for a just and lasting peace with stability and freedom for all the nations and peoples of Southeast Asia. We couple this prayer with a plea to both sides for an end to bombing and terrorism which are causing such loss of civilian life and destruction of the land itself. Indeed, a particularly anguishing and, in many cases, immoral aspect of this war has been the suffering and death inflicted on non-combatants.

It is vitally important that Americans now turn their attention to the task of reconciliation not only in Southeast Asia but also in our country. This war can well leave a residue of bitterness which could poison our national life for years to come. This must not be allowed to happen. We must instead seek to resolve our differences in a spirit of mutual understanding and respect.

Special attention must be given to the young people of our nation whom the war has profoundly affected in so many ways, material, psychological, and spiritual. Our returning veterans and especially the wounded and the prisoners of war, must be given every possible consideration and assistance to enable them to reintegrate their personal and professional lives into civilian society. Our sincere compassion should be extended to the families of men killed in the fighting. The dead, the maimed, and the missing in action should have constant remembrance in our prayers. Those who continue to serve in the military should also receive the moral and material support of the nation.

In a spirit of reconciliation, all possible consideration must be given to those young men who, because of sincere conscientious belief, refused to participate in the war. A year ago, we urged "that the civil authorities grant generous pardon of convictions incurred under the Selective Service Act, with the understanding that sincere conscientious objectors should remain open in principle to some form of service to the community." (*Resolution on Southeast Asia, National Conference of Catholic Bishops,* November, 1971). We again urge government officials and all Americans to respond in this spirit to the conspicuous need to find a solution to the problems of these men.

Generosity represents the best of the American tradition and should characterize our response to this urgent challenge.

Generosity must also mark our participation in efforts to rebuild the war-torn nations and societies of Southeast Asia. There can be no doubt that the people of North and South Vietnam, Laos and Cambodia have suffered a tragedy far greater than ours. The dramatic and successful programs of aid and reconstruction carried out by the United States following World War II provide a model for what is demanded of us now. We must be unstinting in the expending of our moral, material and technical resources and skills on behalf of the people of Southeast Asia who have suffered so grievously.

Finally, we believe that the imperatives of peace now demand intensive study of many complex and pressing moral issues. The return of peace should not cause a slackening of attention to these matters. The experience of recent years amply illustrates the fact that grave ethical and moral questions regarding warfare remain unresolved. While recognizing the right of self-defense, we are nevertheless convinced that war is not an apt means of settling disputes. The quest for viable means of preventing war and for effective alternative methods of resolving conflicts—through such agencies as the United Nations—is an urgent imperative. Technological skill in the science of war must not outstrip humane skill in the arts of peace. Church agencies, including the United States Catholic Conference, Catholic educational institutions, diocesan offices for justice and peace and organizations of the laity should in the months and years to come take a leading role in the effort to work for international justice and to find ways to ensure that peace—which, God willing, is returning to Southeast Asia and also to the United States—will be the permanent condition of human life in all nations and for all time.

Statement on U.S. Bombing Operations in Cambodia

*USCC, Committee on Social
Development and World Peace
July 5, 1973*

The general climate in the United States of uncertainty about moral issues
leaves the vacuum wherein military and political decisions become the moral
judgment of the moment. The Social Development and World Peace Committee feels the gradual increase of military operation in Cambodia presents
to the conscience of the American people such a situation. Therefore, the
Committee makes these observations:

First of all, the authority by which the bombing is being carried out is
dubious. The repeal of the Tonkin Gulf resolution, and the return of the
prisoners of war has terminated any Congressional granting authority for the
present operation. In fact, the sense of the Congress against such bombing
was manifested recently in votes in both the House of Representatives and the
Senate aimed at cutting off such bombing.

Secondly, we question the utility of continuing to use a massive military
power to shore up a shaky and ineffectual government.

In 1970, Secretary of State Rogers said: "We don't intend to become involved militarily in the support of the Lon Nol government, or any other
(Cambodian) government." About three years later (May 8, 1973) he said:
"The choice before us today is whether to allow a military takeover of Cambodia by North Vietnam and its allies, or insist on observation of a negotiated
peace."

From February through April of this year, we have dropped over 80,000
tons of bombs at a cost of $160 million and still there has been little or no
progress toward stability in Cambodia. It is apparent that the opposite is
true. The situation continues to deteriorate.

Thirdly, and most importantly, we question the moral basis for such
bombing. According to traditional Christian principles, weapons may not be
used which are indiscriminate in their effects. It appears to us that the carpet
bombing techniques used in Cambodia violate this principle in that it is difficult or impossible in practice to discriminate between combatants and non-
combatants.

The Committee condemns the bombing in Cambodia and feels that the
moral issue of massive and carpet bombing must be clearly faced.

Statement on President Ford's Conditional Amnesty Plan

USCC, Executive Committee
September 16, 1974

The action of President Ford to provide a clemency review board to grant conditional amnesty for the young men who refused to participate in the Vietnam War is greatly welcomed.

We are all aware of the serious effect that the war has continued to have on Americans, especially those young men whose consciences led them to resist military service and who now find themselves ostracized and alienated from our society. We are also reminded of the words of Pope Paul VI when he proclaimed the Holy Year of 1975, with its theme of reconciliation. He expressed the desire that

> ... The proper authorities of the different nations should consider the possibility of wisely granting an amnesty to prisoners, as a witness to clemency and equity, especially to those who have given sufficient proof of moral and civic rehabilitation, or who may have been caught up in political and social upheavals too immense for them to be held fully responsible.

We therefore urge that the board be generous in granting pardon to these individuals.

Furthermore, we recognize that in certain cases some form of service to the community will be expected of these young men. We again urge that all Americans respond in a generous spirit to the conspicuous need to find a solution to the problems of these young men, and to provide a variety of options of service wherein the young men's talents and capabilities can be appropriately applied. Alternative service to the community is not to be a punitive measure, but rather, an opportunity in fact to serve the common good. In this regard, we encourage Catholic agencies throughout the nation—in a spirit of generosity and in the name of justice—to volunteer their facilities to the appropriate authorities as sites for alternative service. Among such Catholic institutions and agencies are hospitals, homes for the aged, social service agencies and youth centers.

Since generosity represents the best of the American tradition, it should characterize the nation's response to this urgent challenge.

The Gospel of Peace
and the Danger of War

USCC, Administrative Board
February 15, 1978

In his Day of Peace Message for 1978, Pope Paul VI again called upon the community of the Church and the entire human community to reflect upon the meaning of peace in a world still marked by multiple forms of violence. Among these the spectre of technological warfare is the unique menace of the age. Listen to the Holy Father:

> We would like to be able to dispel this threatening and terrible nightmare by proclaiming at the top of our voice the absurdity of modern war and the absolute necessity of Peace—Peace not founded on the power of arms that today are endowed with an infernal destructive capacity (let us recall the tragedy of Japan), nor founded on the structural violence of some political regimes, but founded on the patient, rational and loyal method of justice and freedom, such as the great international institutions of today are promoting and defending. We trust that the magisterial teachings of our great predecessors Pius XII and John XXIII will continue to inspire on this fundamental theme the wisdom of modern teachers and contemporary politicians. (Paul VI, *No to Violence, Yes to Peace,* January 1, 1978).

As teachers in the Church these words of Pope Paul speak to us with a special resonance. His annual messages on the Day of Peace constitute a striking fulfillment of the mandate of Vatican Council II: "to undertake an evaluation of war with an entirely new attitude." (*Gaudium et Spes,* para. 80) Such a new attitude was clearly evident in the 1976 intervention of The Holy See at the United Nations when it said that the arms race is "to be condemned unreservedly" as a danger, an injustice and a mistake. ("A Plea for Disarmament," *Osservatore Romano,* June, 1976).

The dangers of the arms race are a concern and a challenge to the whole human family. Moreover, all the members of the universal Church are called to witness to the Gospel of Peace. For the Church in the United States, however, the prophetic words of the Holy Father have a special significance. No nation has a more critical role in determining the delicate balance between the dangers of war and the possibilities of peace. It is an illusion to think the U.S. bears this responsibility alone; but is a more dangerous deception not to recognize the potential for peace that our position in the world offers to us.

In 1978 two events will highlight the U.S. role and responsibility in the arms race. The first is the forthcoming VIII Special Session of the United

Nations on Disarmament. The second is the continuing debate in the U.S. about a SALT II agreement with the Soviet Union designed to place new limits on nuclear weapons. It is not our purpose in this statement to engage in a detailed analysis of either of these topics, but to identify them as two instances of political debate in which the moral issues of the arms race can be articulated along with its technical dimensions.

The primary moral imperative is that the arms race must be stopped and the reduction of armaments must be achieved. ("A Plea for Disarmament"). In pursuit of these objectives several specific choices must be made to bring the superpower arms race under control quantitatively and qualitatively, to restrain the proliferation of nuclear weapons, and to place restrictions on the rapid growth of conventional arms sales in the world.

Each of these complex issues requires separate treatment so that the relationship of moral and technical factors can be articulated and weighed. The evaluation must occur within the policy process and in the wider ambit of informed public discussion. Catholic teaching on the morality of war has traditionally been designed to speak to both of these audiences. The teaching seeks to establish a moral framework for policy debate and to provide pastoral guidance for individuals. It is incumbent upon us as bishops and other members of the Church, especially lay Catholics with particular competencies relevant to preserving peace, to fulfill this task today.

The contemporary resources of Catholic teaching on war and peace are rich. The doctrine of *Pacem in Terris* (1963) and *Gaudium et Spes* (1965) supplies new and fresh religious and moral perspectives to support those who in conscience choose the way of nonviolence as a witness to the Gospel. These same documents affirm, as Catholic teaching traditionally has acknowledged, that some uses of force in defense of the common good are legitimate. Both of these moral positions are rooted in the Gospel and provide for Catholics and others a reasonable and sound means of evaluating questions of war and peace in the modern world. In an effort to contribute to the policy and public debate in the months to come, we will draw from both of these moral positions to speak to specific issues in the arms debate.

Beyond this important task of moral analysis, however, the Church has another role. The Church must be a prophetic voice for peace. In the tradition of the last three popes the Church in our land must explain the meaning of peace, call people and governments to pursue peace and stand against those forces and elements which prevent the coming of true peace. To pursue peace in the political process requires courage; at times it means taking risks for peace. The Church in a competent and careful manner must encourage reasonable risks for peace. To risk requires a degree of faith and faith in turn is based on the hope that comes from prayer. As the Church in this nation we seek to be a moral voice placing restraints on war, a prophetic voice calling for peace and a prayerful community which has the courage to work for peace.

Resolution Towards Peace in the Middle East

NCCB, November 1973

The conflict in the Middle East is a complex fusion of political, military, economic and religious factors. As bishops of the Catholic Church in the United States, we speak to the issue as pastors concerned for the parties immediately involved, seeking to offer guidance to American Catholics on the issue, and eager to do what we can, even from this distance, to contribute to a just, peaceful and lasting resolution of this painful tragedy.

Faced with a problem which has frustrated the efforts of statesmen for years, we offer our reflections with no pretensions of formulating a definitive solution. We seek instead to highlight factors which we believe point the way toward reconciliation, peace and justice in the Middle East. The problem must be viewed at a global and a regional level.

First, we are impelled to observe the grave dangers of this conflict. Because of the strategic significance of this area of the world and the relationships of major nuclear powers to the parties involved, this conflict contains the potential of wider war, even of nuclear war. Such a war must be avoided at all costs. We believe that we voice the sentiments of people everywhere when we recall Pope John's words that in such a situation, "it is hardly possible to imagine that in the atomic era war could be used as an instrument of justice." (*Peace on Earth*, n. 127)

Second, the roots of the conflict reside in the region; these causes must be removed if the Middle East is to have peace and the world is to be secure from a greater war. The history of this region is one of claims and counterclaims which may never be perfectly adjudicated. We hope that the parties can transcend this troubled and complex past and move toward a new beginning for all the peoples of the Middle East. We believe all parties possess certain just claims, probably none of which can be perfectly fulfilled, all of which can be partially realized.

Rather than rehearse the past, we would point to the significance of the present moment: A convergence of international and regional forces has produced the situation in which all parties appear ready to make some concessions, to test alternatives and to take steps which offer hope for a reasonable settlement.

The road to such a settlement is still long, dangerous and complex; we have no illusions about the difficulties of the task ahead for all concerned.

Yet we find in the history of the region and in previous attempts at a peaceful solution certain factors which we believe are essential to future progress. We wish to call attention to these elements in this resolution, making the following plea to the parties concerned.

We call for a comprehensive political solution involving the following:

1. Recognition of the right of Israel to exist as a sovereign state with secure boundaries;

2. Recognition of the rights of the Palestinian Arabs especially the refugees: this involves, in our view, inclusion of them as partners in any negotiations, acceptance of their right to a state and compensation for past losses to be paid not only by Israel but also by other members of the international community responsible for the 1948 partition plan;

3. Acceptance as the basis for negotiations by all parties to the conflict of the stipulations set forth in the United Nations Security Council Resolution 242 of 22 November 1967;

4. Recognition of the need for continued restraint and continuing responsible diplomatic involvement by the Soviet Union and the United States; we believe this can be most effectively achieved if superpower actions are mutually coordinated with U.N. activities in the region;

5. Continuing reliance on the United Nations diplomatically and through its peacekeeping machinery;

6. Given recognition of the unique status of the city of Jerusalem and its religious significance which transcends the interests of any one tradition, we believe it necessary to insure access to the city through a form of international guarantee. Moreover, the character of the city as a religiously pluralist community, with equal protection of the religious and civil rights of all citizens must be guaranteed in the name of justice.

In proposing these reflections we seek to fulfill our ministry of justice and peace. We ask men and women of good will to consider them in the spirit in which they are offered, as a contribution to reconciliation in the Middle East and peace in the world. We pray that the Prince of Peace will bless our efforts and those peoples and governments who labor as peacemakers.

Statement on the Middle East

USCC, November 16, 1978

The challenge of achieving peace with justice in the Middle East confronts the conscience of the international community. As bishops of the Catholic Church in the United States we feel a dual responsibility to respond to the moral and religious dimensions of this challenge. On the one hand, we are bound to the Middle East by ties of history, tradition and faith. On the other hand, we are citizens of a nation which plays a direct and continuing role in the Middle East.

We address this problem as pastors whose pastoral ministry involves a constant concern for protecting human life and dignity by fostering justice and peace at every level of society. We are vividly aware of the complexity of the political, legal, religious and moral problems of the Middle East, and we acknowledge with respect and gratitude the multiple efforts of political leaders who have labored to resolve this tragic conflict. We wish in the first place to encourage them and to give voice to the silent hopes of all people everywhere who long for a common effort for peace in one of the world's most dangerous political areas.

We seek in this statement to bring the problem of the Middle East before the Catholic community in the United States, so that this universal challenge to conscience may be in their thoughts and prayers. We seek also to make a constructive contribution to the public debate in a nation whose impact on the Middle East is recognized throughout the world. We realize that the specific technical questions at the heart of the Middle East conflict must be resolved in the diplomatic arena, but it is our conviction that on an issue at once so politically and emotionally significant, public opinion in a society shapes the atmosphere for political choices. In accord with this conviction we offer the following:

I. 1973–1978

In our 1973 statement "Toward Peace in the Middle East" we specified a series of principles which should be part of an effective political solution. While acknowledging the process of continuous change that marks the life of that region, we believe the central elements of our 1973 statement to be still valid and useful guidelines for a comprehensive approach to peace and justice in the Middle East. Therefore, we again call for a comprehensive political solution involving the following:

• *The rights of Israel:* to existence as a sovereign state within secure and recognized boundaries;

• *The rights of the Palestinian Arabs:* to participate in negotiations affecting their destiny, and to a homeland of their own;

• *Compensation:* just compensation should be provided for all parties concerned, of whatever national origin, deprived of home and property by the three decades of conflict;

• *The status of Jerusalem:* recognition of its unique religious significance which should be preserved through an international guarantee of access to the holy places and through the preservation of a religiously pluralist citizenry;

• *U.N. Resolution 242:* its continuing utility as a basis for a just settlement in the region.

These elements set a framework for understanding the key issues of justice and peace in the Middle East. The problems posed by them persist in spite of multiple efforts to resolve them. In seeking to address these continuing dimensions of the issue two other developments must be considered: the tragedy of Lebanon and the event of Camp David.

II. Lebanon

Since the outbreak of civil war in Lebanon, where almost one-third of the population (750,000) have become refugees, its fate has been directly tied to the question of a regional settlement in the Middle East. On the one hand, it is clear that Lebanon is highly vulnerable to a multiplicity of regional and international forces which directly influence its domestic life. On the other hand the fate and future of the Palestinians, whose refugee status evokes our sympathy, join the internal problem of Lebanon to the regional problems of the Middle East. While a regional peace is a *de facto* condition for peace in Lebanon, it is not a sufficient condition. The internal dimensions of the Lebanese problem—political, social, economic and religious—must be addressed with a blend of political wisdom and moral courage as a first step toward peace. The value of Lebanon to the Middle East, to Christianity and the world is a truth we cannot forget. The independence of Lebanon and its fabric of political and religious pluralism must be preserved. We call upon our government to have a special concern for all these elements.

The dimensions of the Lebanese problems are so great that a grave responsibility for assistance lies not only with a group of nations, but requires the interest, care and action of the international community especially the continuing involvement of the United Nations. The urgent needs of the nation are that the cease-fire be preserved, that the Lebanese army be rebuilt to provide for the internal security of the country, that discussions among local parties be fostered to establish a new constitution safeguarding the human rights and religious liberty of all inhabitants in Lebanon, and that the sovereignty of Lebanon be securely preserved.

The neutrality of Lebanon must be guaranteed and preserved in order to keep the country independent and sovereign. The Lebanese must be the principal agents of their destiny, but they may rightly expect from the United States and other key actors in the international community both diplomatic assistance and the significant economic aid which rehabilitation in Lebanon will require. We commend the efforts of the Catholic Relief Services, the Catholic Near East Welfare Association and the Pontifical Mission for Palestine in alleviating the suffering of the victims of the conflict in Lebanon and we urge the continued support of their endeavors.

III. Camp David

The Camp David agreements involving Egypt, Israel and the United States already have earned a unique status in the modern history of the Middle East. The contents of the agreements and their ultimate impact on the region are complex issues which do not yield to a simple standard of judgment. To evaluate it adequately, Camp David ought to be seen as part of a process of peacemaking in the Middle East.

In our view the Camp David accords have an intrinsic value which ought to be praised and supported, and they have limitations which need to be acknowledged and amended. The symbolic and substantive value of a peace treaty which now seems possible between two principal states in the Middle East conflict is an achievement of the highest importance. It not only reorients the political process away from conflict and toward peace for Egypt and Israel, it provides hope that progress is possible in the Middle East. It is of the essence of diplomatic greatness to act boldly and courageously in the face of complexity and ambiguity. Camp David is such an action and deserves our support.

At the same time it is necessary to recognize that if Camp David is part of a process, the diplomatic initiatives taken there must be broadened. The limitations of the Camp David accords involve both the scope and terms of the agreements. One form of limitation is evidenced by the need to bring other key actors in the Middle East into the peacemaking process. This in turn is related to the terms of the agreements: It is partially due to some dimensions of the accords that key parties are unwilling to participate in the process. Two issues which exemplify the substantive limits of the accords, and which the principles of this statement make us particularly concerned about, are the status of Jerusalem and the fate of the Palestinians, those living in the occupied territories and in the region of the Middle East. The question of Palestinian sovereignty remains unresolved by the accords and calls for further negotiations. What has been initiated at Camp David must be extended with the same boldness and vision.

IV. Beyond Camp David

The Middle East problem is now set in the context of new signs of hope mixed with continuing elements of danger. Aware of the conflicted and tragic history of the recent past, we are cautious but choose to emphasize the signs of hope: Peace is possible. In transforming the possibility into a reality we see the same basic dimensions of the problem at work which structured our 1973 statement.

First, the international community, especially its principal diplomatic actors, inevitably influences the future of the Middle East; all those who touch the problem have an enormous responsibility to act with wisdom and vision.

Second, the United Nations is a vital element in any Middle East negotiations, and its diplomatic and peacekeeping role will undoubtedly be crucial to a long-term resolution of the conflict.

Third, the regional parties, whose conflicting claims of justice are the essence of the political and moral problem in the Middle East, are the key to peace. In their political vision, moral courage and will for peace lie our hopes for a peaceful future.

Finally, the religious communities with roots in the Middle East must reflect the best of our traditions in supporting the movement for peace with justice for all the people of the region. We have a continuing concern for the protection of the basic rights, both civil and religious, of the Christian minorities in the Middle East and we encourage the local churches there to continue their steadfast witness to the faith.

We call upon the inhabitants of the Holy Land to renew and intensify their efforts to build a spirit of peace, by drawing upon the rich resources of the three great religious traditions which venerate the Holy Land as a sacred place. We pray that the Prince of Peace who lived and taught and prayed in the Middle East will bless the efforts of all who hope and strive for justice and peace in the land which is still called holy.

Development

The American hierarchy has made a concentrated effort to obtain food for the hungry of the world. Between November 1974 and February 1976, the American bishops and the staff at the USCC issued several different statements on the food crisis.

The bishops' first major statement, published on November 21, 1974, recommends a change in U.S. public policy and presents a pastoral plan of action. From the government, the bishops request immediate emergency aid to prevent starvation throughout the world and long-range programs to render the underdeveloped countries capable of increasing their food production. The NCCB offers Congress several guidelines for legislative action.

The bishops also propose a plan of action for themselves and their people. They intend to keep the food issue before the public, in both its factual and moral dimensions. For example, they suggest three ways to promote the Church's concern for human development at the level of pastoral ministry. First, to use liturgy to make people aware of the food crisis. Second, to encourage people to adopt a sparing life style and to avoid wasting food and energy; they specifically urge Catholics to fast two days a week. Third, to encourage Catholics not only to support Catholic relief agencies but to locate the poor and minister to them.

The bishops remind American Catholics that problems of world hunger and malnutrition present the whole Church with the opportunity "to experience an essential dimension of its mission, acting on behalf of justice and participating in the transformation of the world."

In the summer of 1974, the USCC's Department of Social Development and World Peace published a special-issue booklet entitled Development-Dependency: The Role of Multinational Corporations. In the booklet, the USCC asserts that "concentrated power in the hands of a relatively few multinational corporations and banks inhibits international development and deters the process of achieving justice here and abroad." The booklet puts forth the belief that the practices of multinational corporations and the foreign policy of the U.S. serve jointly to keep Third World countries in a state of dependency and underdevelopment.

A Statement on the Missions is included here because it discusses development from the perspective that, while development is important, man does not live by bread alone:

It is imperative in the missionary effort "to keep modern man ... from becoming a stranger to things divine." This is an urgent need for the "developed" as well as the "underdeveloped" peoples. Too many in both worlds look to science and technology as the only avenues to liberation.

Statement on the Missions

NCCB, December 1971

Vatican II reminds us that "the pilgrim Church is missionary by her very nature.[1] It recalls that all bishops "are consecrated not just for some one diocese, but for the salvation of the entire world."[2] To accomplish this we, the Catholic Bishops of the United States, need the help of everyone in this country who shares with us the life and mission of the Church.

Like her divine Founder, the Church must continually share "the good news" of salvation with all men of every race and nation, even in the most remote corner of the earth.[3] Jesus came to save all men without exception. This He did by His suffering, death and resurrection.

This "good news" He wants proclaimed to all creation. He promises salvation to all who hear, believe and live the message of This Gospel.[4] We continue His mission by our lives within the community served by His Church.

Salvation for some today means meeting people's needs in the temporal order. For others it cannot be found this side of eternity. The meeting of these two points of view constitutes the alleged conflict as to which is primary in the missionary effort, the development or the evangelization of people.

Some who emphasize the development of people in the temporal order disagree as to the proper means to this end. There are those who feel violence must be done to existing social structures in order to free people from the tyranny of the past. Others would stop short of violence. Still others see liberation as a peaceful evolution under the guidance of the Gospel.

For those who carefully follow the social teachings of Pope Paul and his beloved predecessor, Pope John, the resolution of these questions should be clear. "There is no true humanism, but that which is open to the Absolute, and is conscious of a vocation which gives human life its true meaning."[5]

There can be little spiritual growth for people unless temporal needs are first satisfied. There can be no lasting spiritual growth for them unless sights are fixed firmly on God and an eventual union with Him. Missionaries generally were and are aware of these priorities.[6]

Unfortunately, modern man too often forgets this necessary balance. It is

---

[1] *Ad Gentes,* 2 "The conditions of this age lend special urgency to the Church's task of bringing all men to full union with Christ, since mankind today is joined together more closely than ever before by social, technical, and cultural bonds." *Lumen Gentium,* 1

[2] *Ad Gentes,* 38

[3] *Revelation,* 14:6

[4] Mark, 16

[5] *Populorum Progressio,* 42

[6] *Idem,* 12

imperative in the missionary effort "to keep modern man . . . from becoming a stranger to things divine."[7] This is an urgent need for the "developed" as well as the "underdeveloped" peoples. Too many in both worlds look to science and technology as the only avenues to liberation.

We clearly hear the anguished cry of people everywhere for a life of dignity, firmly based on this missionary preaching. We sense urgency in the Council's stress upon "reverence for man"[8] and upon the universal human desire to be recognized individually as a human person. We understand this desire to share justly in the good things of the earth, so essential to this life of dignity.

We affirm the right of every individual to this sharing, regardless of race, color, national origin or religious convictions. This is a right born of the inalienable demands of justice, for things produced are for "the service of man."[9] Its realization is assured only in a society which honestly recognizes a mutual and unselfish love among all people. It is the message of the missionary that it is realistically attained only in a society built on this sort of trust, understanding and love.

Every Christian, every Christian community, and indeed the entire Christian Church must by their very nature retain this missionary sense. As true disciples of Christ, we have the obligation to teach constantly this concept of man and his destiny with God both in time and in eternity.[10] There is no other way to true happiness.

We must prepare the way for the faith, and proclaim the Gospel message which is informed by a living faith. We must pray, make continuing sacrifices, and become personally involved in ministering to the needs of our less fortunate neighbors, wherever in this world they may live, whatever might be their need. In what other way can wars, racism, exaggerated nationalism, violence and injustice, as well as the hunger, disease, ignorance and misery they engender, be conquered?

This missionary obligation of preaching the Gospel message is shared by every member of this pilgrim Church.[11] This obligation naturally differs according to our respective roles in the Church. Whether bishops, priests, religious or lay people, however, we must constantly recognize our common obligation to those who neither know nor feel the impact of Christ and His love and peace in their lives.

Conscious of this shared responsibility, we remind all the faithful of the need to support the missionary effort of the Church. We urge a renewed

---

[7] *Ad Gentes*, 11

[8] *Gaudium et Spes*, 27

[9] "The fundamental purpose of this productivity must not be the mere multiplication of products. It must not be profit or domination. Rather, it must be the service of man, and indeed of the whole man, viewed in terms of his material needs and the demands of his intellectual, moral, spiritual, and religious life. And when we say men, we mean every man whatsoever and every group of men, of whatever race and from whatever part of the world." *Idem*, 64

[10] Matthew, 28:19-20

[11] *Ad Gentes*, 36

awareness of the missions and missionary activity in every Catholic parish and institution in our country. We rejoice in our people's constant concern for the continuing needs of poor missionary churches on every horizon of the world at home and abroad. This concern is a ray of hope to suffering millions floundering in a world without God.

In a very special way we wish to encourage every legitimate effort to stir this sense of mission in all our priests, religious and laity. In particular we reaffirm our commitment to promote in every diocese and parish in this country the Society for the Propagation of the Faith and the Association of the Holy Childhood, as urged by Vatican II.[12] We are especially grateful for the support given the national and diocesan directors of these societies, whose effort helps us meet our grave responsibility to the churches which need our special help.

Both of these societies, approved by the Holy See, involved the laity in their origin. They were concerned about providing concrete help for early missionary evangelization in America, among other places in the world. From the very outset their approach was first of all *spiritual,* emphasizing prayer and personal sacrifice as indispensable in helping the missions. In addition it was *universal,* sharing sacrifices with *all* the missionaries of the world.

The Society for the Propagation of the Faith and the Association of the Holy Childhood retain this universal view. The Society for the Propagation of the Faith, for example, provides basic support for more than 819 Catholic missions in Asia, Africa, Oceania and every other quarter of the world. Over 135,000 missionary priests, brothers and sisters, and associates from the laity, look to the Society to sustain and develop their mission of mercy to the underprivileged of the world. With special joy we note in this blessed company some 8,373 native Americans among our world missionaries. This number includes 3,490 priests, 666 brothers, 90 scholastics, 3,824 sisters and 303 members of the laity.[13]

We salute in a very special way the men and women religious who constitute the bulk of this heroic missionary army overseas. We recognize with gratitude the substantial help they have received in recent years from the involvement of diocesan priests and the laity in their work. Over the years, however, it was the prayer, the sweat and the toil of these religious, committed to the missions by their religious profession and their loyalty to the Holy Father, which made unmistakably clear the sensitivity of the American Church to the problems which plague millions everywhere.[14]

Symbolic and truly representative of these sterling men and women religious is our venerable brother, Bishop James Edward Walsh. We salute his admirable example of Christian patience and fortitude in the face of trials which missionaries are often called to bear. In him are personified the mis-

---

[12] *Idem,* 38
[13] Statistics provided by the Society for the Propagation of the Faith
[14] *Ad Gentes,* 27

sionaries who make themselves one with their people in every joy and sorrow which comprise the daily human experience. We thank him and all who give witness by their lives and work that the Church in America, like the Church in other lands, does seriously accept its missionary responsibility to the world.

Urgently we ask young Americans to recognize the missionary vocation as their own. Signs of their commendable concern for relieving the needs of people, particularly the deprived whether young or old, are visible daily. In praising their efforts to find positive solutions to the problems of war, poverty and prejudice, we also express the hope that many more of these young people will personally close ranks with missionaries by seeking solutions to such problems in preaching, by word and example, the Gospel message of salvation.

We are proud of our part in establishing the United States Catholic Mission Council. Together with the priests, religious and laity with whom we worked, we hope it will achieve its clear purpose. This Council is intended to "provide a forum and organ for the evaluation, co-ordination and fostering, in the United States, of the worldwide missionary effort of the Catholic Church."[15]

The recent statement of the Catholic Mission Council, "The Whole Missionary Church," succinctly reviews the teaching of Vatican II on the missions and urges ways to implement that teaching. The plans embodied there hold great hope for the growth of mission awareness among all American Catholics.

Of particular interest and importance are the mission committees at the diocesan level. These committees can be instruments for uniting priests, religious and laity in the service of the missions. They already exist in a number of dioceses; and in every diocese the appointed director of the papal mission-aid societies is already guiding many of the undertakings proposed for the committee. To avoid duplication of structures it is desirable that the diocesan committees develop in close collaboration with the diocesan director.

We bishops are grateful for the support our people have given the missions in the past. We see this support as another evidence of their generous response to people in need anywhere and everywhere in the world. This help must continue, so that together we can meet our collegial responsibility to the whole missionary Church. Through this response we trust we will in fact be neighbors, as Jesus says, "to the least of these brothers of mine."[16]

---

[15] Preamble to the By-Laws of the United States Catholic Mission Council
[16] Luke, 10:29–31; Matthew, 25:31–46

Statement on Population

NCCB, November 12, 1973

The United Nations has designated 1974 as U.N. Population Year, and has invited member nations to initiate programs of population education and to work toward the development of population policies throughout the year and beyond. At this point we take a positive attitude toward the U.N. Population Year. We hope that those conducting and participating in the public discussion will do so with objectivity, humility and honesty.

Population questions must be considered within the larger context of man's total relationship to the entire human family, that is, in terms of his relationship to the human and social environment of our world. The population discussion must include a recognition of moral and ethical principles, convictions about human rights and the good of society and a determination to preserve the true values of marriage and family life. The population discussion cannot be reduced to a simple discussion of demographic facts, economics or patterns of social organization. We must remember that our ability to make accurate predictions about the distant future is limited, and the picture can be seriously distorted unless equal attention is given to man's ability to solve social problems, to discover or invent new resources, and to change patterns of consumption.

We believe that the Church can make a valuable contribution to the discussion of population by calling attention to the Gospel message and to her social teaching which applies the Gospel to the changing situations of man's life on earth. Indeed, as Pope Paul has stated in the encyclical *On the Development of Peoples,* "A renewed consciousness of the demands of the Gospel makes it the Church's duty to put herself at the service of all men, to help them grasp their serious problem in all its dimensions, and to convince them that solidarity in action at this turning point in human history is a matter of urgency."[1]

The Church, in unfolding her social teaching, focuses on the dignity of man, the need for worldwide equality and social justice, and the pressing urgency for a new unity among nations. Existing in this world and taking her place in human history, the Church must "foster the human progress of the nations to which she brings faith in Christ."[2] Such progress demands that all men attain a decent standard of living, which includes the availability of employment and educational opportunities, adequate nutrition, health care and housing facilities. But the fulfillment of human desires also demands an

---

[1] *On the Development of Peoples,* Paul VI, March 27, 1967, #1.
[2] *On the Development of Peoples,* #12.

97

"acknowledgement by men of supreme values, and of God—their source and their end."[3] Indeed, this acknowledgement is the most important aspect of human development. For "faith, a gift of God accepted by the good will of man"[4] creates an attitude toward the problems of daily living and relates this present life to the life of complete unity with God in heaven.

In proposing solutions to the various aspects of the population question, Christians must emphasize the need for human solidarity, for social justice, and for universal charity.[5] Men and women must come to realize that we are our brother's keepers, that we hold a common responsibility to increase the access to the banquet of life and to assure all persons an equitable share in the goods provided there.[6]

In light of these considerations and in anticipation of the activities of U.N. Population Year, we wish to make some basic observations and to restate some principles that contribute to understanding the population issue and the formulation of population policies.

Observations

The following facts provide a context in which to approach population questions.

1. The population challenge does not affect all nations in the same way. Some nations have a high and uneven rate of growth that complicates or inhibits the development process. Other nations need an increase of population to enhance development. In some nations, the relocation of population resulting from urbanization creates a special problem. Most of the developed nations, and particularly the United States, do not have the problem of *rapid population growth*. In fact, the United States birth rate has continually declined over the past 10 to 15 years, resulting in a low rate of population growth.

2. Population growth must be analyzed in the larger context of concern for the development of peoples. It must take into account the care and improvement of the human and physical environment.

3. Population projections must be based on an accurate presentation of demographic factors. They must include sound projections of resource development and of the discovery of new natural resources or synthetic materials.

4. Migration policies can help solve some of the problems resulting from a maldistribution of population. Thus, international and national migration policies should be examined and perhaps changed in light of population concerns.

---

[3] *On the Development of Peoples,* #21.
[4] *On the Development of Peoples,* #21.
[5] cf. *On the Development of Peoples,* #44.
[6] cf. *Address of Paul VI to UN General Assembly,* October 4, 1965.

5. In many nations, shortages of food, housing, schools and jobs generate extraordinary pressure on governments trying to develop dignified and equitable living standards for their people. *Rapid population growth* may gravely aggravate these pressures. However, population control alone is not the proper solution. Each situation should be met with specific policies and programs which favor human and social development.

6. Developing nations will hardly be able to reach their potential without the aid and cooperation of the already developed nations. This is not simply a matter of sending food, medicine, clothing and financial assistance, but also of granting access to world markets, enabling these nations to draw credit in the financial centers of the world, assisting them in the education and training of their people, entering into partnership in helping them tap their own resources and encouraging imports of necessary but absent raw materials.

7. National resources, especially the precious resources of air and water, and the delicate biosphere of life on earth are not infinite. They must be preserved, protected and used as a unique patrimony belonging to all mankind.[7]

Principles

In order to provide a moral perspective, we affirm the following principles derived from the social teaching of the Church.

1. Within the limits of their own competence, government officials have rights and duties with regard to the population problems of their own nations—for instance, in the matter of social legislation as it affects families, of migration to cities, of information relative to the conditions and needs of the nation. Government's positive role is to help bring about those conditions in which married couples, without undue material, physical or psychological pressure, may exercise responsible freedom in determining family size.[8]

2. Decisions about family size and the frequency of births belong to the parents and cannot be left to public authorities.[9] Such decisions depend on a rightly formed conscience which respects the divine law and takes into consideration the circumstances of the places and the time. In forming their consciences, parents should take into account their responsibilities toward God, themselves, the children they have already brought into the world and the community to which they belong, "following the dictates of their conscience instructed about the divine law authentically interpreted and strengthened by confidence in God."[10]

3. Public authorities can provide information and recommend policies

[7] cf. *Justice in the World,* Report of World Synod of Bishops, 1971.
[8] cf. Statement of NCWC Administrative Board, November, 1966.
[9] cf. *Constitution on the Church in the Modern World,* December 7, 1965, # 50, 87; *On the Development of Peoples,* #37,
[10] *On the Development of Peoples,* #37.

regarding population, provided these are in conformity with moral law and respect the rightful freedom of married couples.[11]

4. Men and women should be informed of scientific advances of methods of family planning whose safety has been well proven and which are in accord with the moral law.[12]

5. Abortion, directly willed and procured, even if for therapeutic reasons, is to be absolutely excluded as a licit means of regulating births.[13]

Conclusions

We strongly urge our Catholic people to take a positive approach to the question of population. We encourage research and education efforts in Catholic educational institutions, in order that discussions of population and social development may be carried on in light of a value system rooted in sound ethical and moral principles. To this purpose, intensive discussion of the central themes of the U.N. Population Year—family, development, environment and human rights—should be carried on with the dignity of the family and social justice as the focal points.

Finally, we urge the United States Government to increase foreign assistance programs to the developing nations, especially to those nations where population problems are complicating economic and social development. We must all realize that policy decisions governing the activity of the United States government agencies at home and abroad will be the focus of attention throughout 1974 and beyond. We have rights and responsibilities as citizens and as Christians to contribute to the creation of government policies which respect human dignity and the moral law.

---

[11] cf. *Constitution on the Church in the Modern World*, #87; *On the Development of Peoples*, #37; *On the Regulation of Birth (Humanae Vitae)*, #23.

[12] cf. *Constitution on the Church in the Modern World*, #87.

[13] *On the Regulation of Birth*, #14.

Statement on Global Food Crisis

USCC, Executive Committee
October 1974

In the face of a global food crisis, we wish to highlight certain moral implications.

The right to eat flows directly from the right to life. Food, therefore, is a unique commodity. To be in the U.S. position as prime exporter of foodstuffs is an awesome responsibility: we are literally involved in judging who will live or die.

As a nation, we must treat our food resource as a sacred trust, not simply a matter of money and markets. In the past, we have helped to feed others from our surplus; today, we are asked to share our scarcity. Where once we shared in charity, we must now share in justice. The law of the market, like every human creation, has its moral limits. When it denies food to starving people, it must be modified.

We urgently appeal to our government to bring a broadly conceived and just policy to November's World Food Conference. We encourage those in our government who would support:

• First, an international food reserve to provide a permanent supply to meet global emergencies;

• Second, an increase in short-term emergency relief to areas threatened with starvation;

• Third, technical assistance for developing nations to increase their food-producing capacity.

Meeting our international responsibilities will have domestic implications. We appeal to our government to see that those Americans least able to pay do not bear the brunt of our policy: specifically, the independent farmer, often the most vulnerable person in the chain of food production, processing and sales, and the consumer from the middle and lower income categories.

The American food policy must be characterized by justice as we share our scarcity with those whose right to eat is now in our hands as a trust and responsibility.

Statement on the World Food Crisis: A Pastoral Plan of Action

NCCB, November 21, 1974

The world food crisis is part of the larger pattern of global interdependence. The crisis is linked directly and systemically with questions of environment, population, economic relationships, political and military power.

World hunger and malnutrition are part of this complex pattern. They must be attacked on two levels: immediate assistance programs to prevent starvation in many regions in the world; and a long range program to increase food production, especially in the less industrialized nations.

The long range program must strike at the root problem of underdevelopment which plagues the people of many nations. Plans for agricultural development require the cooperation of the U.S. government, the poorer nations, the FAO, and voluntary agencies including religious organizations such as our own Catholic Relief Services.

It is not enough, however, that such development merely foster economic growth. Development must significantly reach the "little farmer" and so-called marginal people, and reduce the gap between the wealthy and the poor. Christian missionaries have effective contacts with the poor sectors of these societies and have demonstrated the capacity to assist materially in their agricultural development. Efforts by these missionaries merit increased support by the American religious community.

Moreover, the food crisis poses for the United States both domestic and international implications. An appropriate pastoral response for the Church must include a series of interrelated activities at the level of public policy/legislative program, community information and education, and pastoral practice.

A. Public Policy/Legislative Program

The bishops, acting through the United States Catholic Conference and its General Secretary, propose a program of public discussion directed toward influencing appropriate executive and legislative action which, in a systematic and organized way, will seek to achieve national policies effectively dealing with the food issue, internationally and domestically.

The fundamental premise of the program is that food is a unique commodity and a sacred resource. The guidelines for legislative initiatives meriting USCC support are the following:

First, increase genuine agricultural development overseas; technical assistance and development programs must be expanded to promote greater food production in the less industrialized nations;

Second, increase funding for Food for Peace (PL 480); as an immediate step, increase substantially food allocations through Title II of Food for Peace (humanitarian aid), and resist efforts to use food as a political and strategic weapon;

Third, modify U.S. trade policies to lower trade barriers and to provide just prices for imports from poor countries. Special trade preferences for these nations' exports and substantially increased adjustment assistance for adversely affected U.S. workers and industries must be part of this revised trade policy;

Fourth, assure American farmers of a fair return for their capital and labor. The productivity and viability of American agriculture must be maintained. Serious disruption of this sector of the economy could adversely affect the world food crisis;

Fifth, promote more equitable distribution of resources in the United States. Areas of legislation in this regard are the following: expanding programs of food stamps and school lunches, providing special assistance to the elderly, the unemployed and the poor, revising income tax burdens, and restructuring land use policies;

Sixth, protect both family farmers who are often subject to severe economic pressures in the agricultural chain of food production, processing and sales, and also consumers in middle and lower income categories;

Seventh, modify the operation of the free market system, especially the impact of the large corporation, when it stands in the way of justice.

B. Community Information and Education

Since the food crisis is a long term problem as well as one of immediate concern, it will be necessary to keep the structural dimensions of the issue, both in its factual and moral aspects, before the public. The Church has means of doing this through already funded programs which merit implementation at the national, diocesan and parish level. Among them are the following:

First, its educational system for adults, youth and children;

Second, its access to the public through the secular and religious media of press, radio and television;

Third, workshops, special days of reflection and study for priests, religious communities and laity.

C. Pastoral Care

The most direct, universal and concrete contact the Church has with its people is at the level of pastoral ministry. Unique opportunities are available to promote the Church's deep concern about human development.

1. Liturgy: The themes of life, bread, community, solidarity, and responsiblility flow through the symbol and substance of the liturgical life of the Church. These can be woven into teaching, worshiping and prayer experiences which address the food crisis to the whole community. Liturgical seasons of the Church's year are especially appropriate, for example, Advent, Lent, rogation days, the Holy Year. Particularly to be encouraged are parish and diocesan programs of worship, fasting and abstinence on appointed days. The funds from such fasting would be directed toward efforts ministering to the needs of others.

2. Lifestyle: A major pressure on food supply is the pattern of consumption. Especially evident in our consumer-oriented way of life are the waste of food and the excessive consumption of energy. Appeals to Christian conscience of responsible stewardship highlighting the practice of days of fast and abstinence, flow from the deepest roots of our biblical and ecclesiastical traditions. We urge the whole Catholic community—priests, religious and laity—to join with us in observing at least two days a week as days of fast. We also urge resistance to advertising and other forms of social pressure which promote affluent and wasteful eating habits.

3. Locating and feeding the hungry: In this time of food scarcity, inflation, economic recession and rising unemployment, methods of pastoral care require renewal and adaption. First, awareness must be heightened about the condition of many members of our society, and efforts by priests, religious and laity must be intensified to locate and minister to those suffering severe hardships in our dioceses, parishes and local communities. Commanding attention, in particular, are the aged on limited fixed incomes, the working poor and the unemployed, and families and individuals on welfare and other public assistance programs.

Second, support for increased activities must be given to such agencies as Catholic Charities, Catholic Relief Services, the Campaign for Human Development and others. This will enable them to intensify their efforts to provide immediate short term relief and to work for long term structural changes for human development.

Conclusion

In this pastoral response to the food crisis the American Catholic community is called to address a broad agenda of issues. World hunger and malnutrition present Church agencies, diocesan offices, parishes, educational systems, the bishops, priests, religious and laity, that is, the whole Church, with an opportunity to experience an essential dimension of its mission: acting on behalf of justice and participating in the transformation of the world. This should be done in the context of a broad ecumenical effort, working with other Christians, Jews, those of other faiths and all men and women of good will.

The goals outlined here for the Church are only a beginning. No document could possibly embrace the many activities and programs which will be required to respond to the cries of the hungry and to what Pope Paul has called this "crisis of civilization and solidarity."

Development-Dependency: The Role of Multinational Corporations

USCC, Department of Social Development and World Peace August 1974

Preface

Pope Paul VI in his encyclical *Populorum Progressio* praised the process of industrialization as a necessity for economic growth and human development. But he also said that, unfortunately, in industrialized society:

> A system has been constructed which considers profit as the key motive for economic progress, competition as the supreme law of economics and private ownership of the means of production as an absolute right that has no limits and carries no corresponding social obligations. This unchecked liberalism leads to dictatorship rightly denounced by Pius XI as producing "the international imperialism of money." One cannot condemn such abuses too strongly, solemnly recalling once again that the economy is at the service of man.

U.S. citizens may be unaware either of the encyclical or of the response of the *Wall Street Journal* and other similar interests in the United States who rejected the encyclical as "warmed-over Marxism." And yet, the concern for human dignity and justice reflected in the encyclical is only one link in the chain of the Church's traditional regard for social justice.

It is also relevant to note that, in his Apostolic Letter *A Call to Action*,

Pope Paul VI treated a number of new currents of thought concerning socio-
economic ideologies and systems. His treatment of "liberal ideology,"
prompted Msgr. George Higgins, in his Commentary on the Apostolic Letter, to note that many conservative Americans "will be disappointed to learn
that the Holy Father takes a dim view of (unbridled economic individualism)
and goes out of his way to warn Christians that, like the ideology of Marxism,
the liberal ideology likewise calls for careful discernment on their part."
Similarly, in its document *Justice in the World*, the 1971 Roman Synod
treated world conditions from two rather different diagnoses. As Rev. Philip
Land of the Pontifical Commission Justice and Peace noted, these two
analyses have distinctly different perspectives. The first view emphasizes the
need to harness modern technology, while the latter, "in origin, Marxist, is
widely endorsed in the Third World and receives healthy, if qualified, support from a wide spectrum of non-Marxist authorities."

From Leo XIII's *Rerum Novarum* in 1891 to Vatican II's *Gaudium et Spes*
and the 1971 Synod of Bishops document *Justice in the World*, the Church
has consistently raised a prophetic voice to defend the integrity and dignity of
those people who suffer injustice. In doing so, the Church follows the gospel
message of Jesus Christ and his concern for his chosen people—the poor.

In the past decade, Latin American bishops and priests have expressed
themselves with increasing frequency on the root causes of poverty in their
homelands. Their pastoral letters have often been directed to their northern
neighbors in the Americas because it is the system of capitalism of Western
Europe and the United States that many believe is a contributing cause of
continual poverty in Latin America. For example, the Second General Conference of the Latin American Episcopate in Medellin, Colombia, declared in
1968:

> Another feature of this economic situation is our subjection to capital in-
> terests in foreign lands. In many cases, these foreign interests exercise un-
> checked control, their power continues to grow, and they have no permanent
> interest in the countries of Latin America. Moreover, Latin American trade
> is jeopardized by its heavy dependence on the developed countries. They buy
> raw materials from Latin America at a cheap price, and then sell manufac-
> tured products to Latin America at ever higher prices; and these manufac-
> tured goods are necessary for Latin America's continuing development.

When American citizens read the words of Pope Paul VI and the bishops
and other leaders in Latin America, they often only partially see the truth
stated because they are looking through the shaded glasses of the social and
economic culture of capitalism. To apply a phrase from Msgr. Higgin's Commentary, "we are a people so deeply committed in theory, if not in practice,
to the philosophy or the ideology of free enterprise in the old fashioned sense
of the word."

It behooves us as citizens of the United States to sharpen our vision in these times when the maldistribution of the earth's resources and the concentration of the world's wealth are so blatant. This enlightened vision is a prerequisite to a more truly Christian response.

Bishop John J. Dougherty, Chairman
USCC Committee on Social
Development and World Peace

DEVELOPMENT-DEPENDENCY:
THE ROLE OF MULTINATIONAL CORPORATIONS

In the Spring of 1974, an historically significant drama occurred at the United Nations. For the first time in its history, delegates of the 135 member nations were called to a special session of the General Assembly to listen specifically to the complaints of the Third World nations about the inadequacies of the international economic system. U.N. Secretary General Kurt Waldheim said of the session: "We know in the history of mankind that the present economic system isn't workable anymore. We have to work out a new economic system for the world."

The issue of economic development is central to an examination of the relationship of the international economic system and the Third World. In recent years, the debate about development and dependency has engaged government officials, economists, international investors and scholars, and at an increasing rate, leadership in various national Catholic hierarchies. The presence of Catholic episcopal leaders in this debate is understandable in view of the explicit papal writings on the issue, beginning in 1931 with Pope Pius XI's *Quadragesimo Anno*.[1] The development-dependency theme was also evident in the Second Vatican Council's *Gaudium et Spes*.[2] The same theme dominated the 1971 Roman Synod document *Justice in the World*.

The national hierarchies in Latin America which have entered the debate, identify excessive dependency upon North American interests as a contributing factor in Latin America's underdevelopment. In doing so, they

---

[1] Pope Pius XI, *Quadragesimo Anno*, esp. nn. 105, 109: "It is obvious that not only is wealth concentrated, but immense power ... is consolidated in the hands of a few." And as to international relations, two phenomena are evident: "On the one hand, economic nationalism or even economic imperialism; on the other, international imperialism whose country is where profit is." Pope Paul VI in 1967 (*Populorum Progressio* n. 26), and again in 1971 (*A Call To Action*, n. 44), reiterated Pius XI's condemnation of economic concentration.

[2] Vatican II, *Gaudium et Spes*, n. 85: "The developing nations will be unable to procure the necessary material assistance unless the practices of the modern business world undergo a profound change."

reinforce the position taken by the Latin American Episcopate at Medellin, Colombia, in 1968: "the principal guilt for economic dependence of our countries rests with powers inspired by uncontrolled desire for gain, which leads to economic dictatorship and 'the international imperialism of money' condemned by Pius XI in *Quadragesimo Anno* and by Paul VI in *Populorum Progressio*.[3] In addition to the statements of Latin American bishops, a number of lay, religious and clerical groups in Latin America have also pinpointed the influence of foreign businesses, governments and cultures as a cause of much of the poverty and social ills of the Third World.[4]

The impact of U.S. policies on the lives of millions of people in less developed countries, particularly in Latin America, where traditionally our nation's ties and that of our Church are most evident, compels us to reflect on our role as members of a universal church and as citizens of the United States. This reflection is especially prompted by the recent statement of the U.S. bishops in which they said: "Internationally, the pervasive presence of American power creates a responsibility of using that power in the service of human rights."[5]

Impact in Latin America

Evidence is mounting that the concentrated power in the hands of a relatively few multinational corporations and banks inhibits international development and deters the process of achieving justice here and abroad.[6] Realization is growing that so-called economic development and the resultant growth in Gross National Product (GNP) does not assure the amelioration of the harsh living conditions of the vast majority of people of the Third World.[7]

The oppressive conditions of poverty and marginality frequently result

---

[3] Second General Conference of Latin American Bishops, *The Church in the Present-Day Transformation of Latin America in the Light of the Council,* 1968. (Hereafter: Medellin).

[4] Various statements, e.g., ONIS (Peru), Golconda (Colombia), Christians for Socialism (Chile), Priests for the People (Mexico), Third World Priests Movement (Argentina). Also, the 1972 "Letter from Chile" from the U.S. Missioners in Latin America.

[5] Cf. "Resolution on the 25th Anniversary of the Universal Declaration of Human Rights," United States Catholic Conference, November 1973.

[6] Ronald Müller, "The Multinational Corporation: Asset or Impediment to World Justice," in *Poverty, Environment and Power—CICOP 1973.* (Available from the Division of Latin America, United States Catholic Conference.) Also, Müller and Barnet, *Global Reach: The Power of the Multinational Corporations* (New York: Simon and Shuster, 1974). Also, "Implications of Multinational Firms for World Trade and Investment and for U.S. Trade and Labor." Report of the Subcommittee on International Trade of the U.S. Senate Finance Committee, February 1973. Also, "Investigations of Conglomerate Corporations." Staff report of the Antitrust Subcommittee of the House Judiciary Committee, June 1971. Also, U.N. Economic and Social Affairs Department, Special Inquiry, "The Group of Eminent Persons," 1972-73.

[7] Cf. Robert S. McNamara, Address to UNCTAD, April 14, 1972 (Santiago, Chile).

from the influx of foreign private capital.[8] The fact that concentrated economic power results in enriching 30% of a population in Latin America at the expense of the other 70% indicts it as a major impediment to world justice.[9]

Such concentrated power, motivated by the worldwide maximization of profits, leads to the development and control of an international market strategy which is of primary benefit to the controlling power and not to the development of peoples. The recent disclosures about the activities of I.T.T. in Nazi Germany[10] and in Chile along with Kennecott; and Ford and General Motors in Nazi Germany,[11] accentuate the boldness of this strategy. This evidence lends credence to Pope Paul's charge that "multinational enterprises . . . can conduct autonomous strategies which are largely independent of the national political powers and therefore not subject to control from the point of view of the common good."[12]

It is necessary for us to acknowledge that a real dilemma exists. On one level, as Christians we are committed to the ideal that nations have the right of self-determination and economic development.[13] On another level, our nation is committed to protect our national self-interests narrowly defined in economic and political terms.[14]

Since U.S. government policy tends to equate the free enterprise system with our political system, one of the primary tasks of American foreign policy

---

[8] The inadequacy of the development strategies of the industrialized nations is underscored in *Partners in Development,* edited by Lester B. Pearson, 1969. The report acknowledged on the one hand that foreign capital is "simply not available to finance many of the investments which are a prime need in developing countries—schools, roads, hospitals, irrigation." On the other hand, foreign aid programs are seriously misleading: "It is not uncommon to hear the total flow of resources to developing countries referred to as something which the rich countries 'give' to the poor. Nothing could be further from the truth, or more misleading . . . The flow of private capital . . . undertaken for commercial reason (has) no more the character of 'aid' when (it flows) to developing countries than when (it flows) between industrialized countries."

[9] In the period between 1950 and 1965, U.S. private corporations invested $3.8 billion in Latin America. Part of the profits were retained in Latin America to increase the total investment of the companies concerned; part of the profits were remitted to the United States. From this investment of $3.8 billion, no less that $11.3 billion in profits were remitted home to the United States, while the profits retained locally increased the investment of $3.8 billion to $10.3 billion. (Cf. "Balance of Payments Statistical Supplement," Revised Edition, Department of Commerce, Washington, D.C., 1963. Also, *Survey of Current Business* issues, 1962–65. It is important to note with respect to the concentration of profits in the hands of a few corporations (which in turn are controlled by a few people) that in 1966—the end of the period referred to above—more than one half of American profits from abroad went to but 16 firms. Arthur MacEwan, "Comment on Imperialism," *American Economic Review,* May 1970, p. 246.

[10] Anthony Sampson, *The Sovereign State of I.T.T.* (New York: Stein & Day, 1973).

[11] "American Ground Transport." Study submitted to the Subcommittee on Antitrust and Monopoly of the U.S. Senate Judiciary Committee, February 1974, pp. 16–23.

[12] Pope Paul VI, *A Call to Action,* 1971, no. 44.

[13] This proposition was initially stated in Pope Pius XII's Christmas Message of 1941, and cited again by Pope John XXIII in *Pacem in Terris,* n. 124.

[14] President Richard M. Nixon's State of the Union Address, 1972: "We will act to defend our interests whenever and wherever they are threatened, any place in the world."

is to provide a favorable climate overseas for U.S. private investments and to protect that interest.[15] However, for Latin Americans, this U.S. practice tends to perpetrate a condition of dependency and underdevelopment.[16] This dependency is reinforced, as the Latin American bishops noted, by a small wealthy elite within each of the continent's countries, who only too willingly cooperate with foreign business interests.[17]

Impact in the United States

It is important for us in the United States to recognize that multinational business interests which play such a dominant role in the less developed countries of Latin America also dominate, to a great extent, our own domestic economy.[18] The recent accounts of tax write-offs, increasing monopoly activity, political lobbying, machinations of the oil industry during the "energy crisis" provide grim testimony to the detrimental effect on U.S. citizens of the concentration of economic power. The American bishops expressed their deep concern about this concentration, specifically in the field of agriculture, where they observed that "agricultural conglomerates are expanding, raising the possibility of taking over virtually all farming in the United States."[19]

In our system of political economy, the presumption is that concentrations of power are to be guarded against, and governmental agencies are designed

---

[15] Secretary of State Dean Rusk told the Senate Foreign Relations Committee that ". . . our influence is used whenever it can be and persistently through our aid discussion and in direct aid negotiations to underline the importance of private investment." U.S. Senate Hearings on the Foreign Assistance Act, 1962.

[16] Cf. Peruvian Bishops' Conference, "La Justicia en el Mundo," 1969: "Like other nations of the Third World, we are the victims of systems that exploit our natural resources, control our political decisions, and impose on us the cultural dominations of their values and consumer civilization. . . . The more we try to change, the stronger the forces of domination become. Foreign interests increase their repressive measures by means of economic sanctions in the international markets and by control of loans and other types of aid. News agencies and the communications media, which are controlled by the powerful, do not express the rights of the weak; they distort reality by filtering information in accord with their vested interests." Cf. Mexican Bishops' Conference, Pre-Synod Paper, 1969: "By its past and present superiority in technology, in the socio-political area, and in business and finance, the United States exercises a big-power dominance over Mexico that makes us, as a bordering and overshadowed neighbor, an extension of its own system." Cf. Chilean Bishops' Conference, Pre-Synod Paper, 1971: "We see that nationalization presents many new moral problems because it involves a poor country facing companies that have their headquarters in one of the richest and most developed countries. . . . This is a problem that touches not only economic morality but world peace because of the reaction, in this case, of spokesmen of the United States Government, who have threatened measures that could affect many countries."

[17] CELAM Document on Peace, "Tensions Between Classes and Internal Colonialism," Medellin, 1968.

[18] Recognition of the interrelatedness of U.S. domestic and international policies is a major theme of Bishop James S. Rausch's "Statement on Proposed Reforms of U.S. Overseas Investment and Trade Policies for the 1970's," presented to the Ways and Means Committee of the U.S. House of Representatives, June 1973.

[19] "Where Shall the People Live?" United States Catholic Conference, 1972.

to prevent these concentrations. The facts are, however, that most of these regulatory agencies, underbudgeted and understaffed, are no match for the corporations' batteries of lawyers and networks of information. In addition, the corporations exercise such strong political power that the agencies are often captives of those they are supposed to regulate.[20]

Furthermore, as most citizens face constantly rising prices, lack of school funds, inadequate public transportation, and sky-rocketing medical and legal costs, many feel the economic crunch of cutbacks or elimination of federal funds to programs servicing the aged, homeless, jobless and poorer classes of our society.

At the same time, recent studies disclose that the wealth and power of a relatively small percentage of the population have in fact increased. As our GNP has risen from about $200 billion in 1940 to its present level of more than $1 trillion, "there is a startling and continuing inequality in the distribution of income in the U.S., and the overall pattern has remained virtually unchanged since World War II."[21] The concentration of ownership of the nation's wealth (stocks, bonds, real property, etc.) presents an even more depressing picture. The top 20% of wealth holders in the country own over three-fourths of all personal wealth. The top 1% alone holds between 20-30% of all personal wealth and have done so for decades.[22] The U.S. Bishops' Campaign for Human Development points out, in its publication "Poverty Profile," that 80% of the state and local bonds are owned by less than 5% of the citizens.[23]

The implications of concentrated financial power are underscored by the recent U.S. Senate report "Disclosure of Corporate Ownership." The report notes that information needed by government agencies to monitor adequately "the several levers of corporate control is held by a few institutional investors, principally six superbanks headquartered in New York."[24] The impact of this control on both domestic and international policy is highlighted in the report:

> ... the portfolio companies in which a few banks have substantial influence make many decisions affecting public policy. Oil companies deal with foreign nations regarding oil supply and cost. Pipeline companies deal with

---

[20] Mark J. Green, *et al.* Ralph Nader's Study Group, *The Closed Enterprise System* (New York: Grossman, 1972). Also, Morton Mintz and Jerry Cohen, *America, Inc.,* (New York: Dial Press, 1971).

[21] Letitia Upton and Nancy Lyons, "Basic Facts: Distribution of Personal Income and Wealth in the United States" (Cambridge Institute, 1878 Massachusetts Avenue, Cambridge, MA 02140).

[22] Upton and Lyons, *op. cit.*

[23] Campaign for Human Development, "Poverty Profile," United States Catholic Conference, 1972.

[24] "Disclosure of Corporate Ownership." Report of the Subcommittees on Intergovernmental Relations, and Budgeting, Management; and Expenditures, U.S. Senate Committee on Government Operations, March 1974, p. 10.

the Soviet Union for natural gas. Utilities exercise the right of eminent domain. Milling companies and the Soviet Union arrange grain sales which sharply affect domestic price, supply, transportation, and storage. These are momentous public issues in which Federal officials play a minor role, much of it after basic decisions have been agreed upon by American companies and foreign governments.[25]

The Role of the Church

A growing number of Catholics are beginning to share Pope Paul VI's concern about the emerging power of multinational corporations.[26] Church people, both here and in the Third World, are becoming increasingly aware that many U.S. domestic and international policies are linked together to serve the interests of these transnational business enterprises. The time is at hand for us not only to question the enormous power wielded by so few people and institutions, but in a more fundamental way, to question the underlying motivation behind such unbridled power. For the motivation continually to increase profit emerges from values which promote excessive individualism, unnecessary consumption, and disregard for the quality of human life, all of which are contrary to the deepest values of the Judeo-Christian tradition.[27]

Even the Church's traditional role in education is exposed to serious reevaluation because of this power concentration. The 1971 Roman Synod reminded the Church's educators that:

> the method of education very frequently still in use today encourages narrow individualism. Part of the human family lives immersed in a mentality which exalts possessions. The school and the communications media, which are often obstructed by the established order, allow the formation only of the man desired by that order, that is to say, man in its image, not a new man but a copy of man as he is.[28]

In the Third World, most people have the daily experience of powerlessness in the face of the relative few who own and control most of the wealth and income, land, industry, political and military power. In our country, there is a growing sense among working people as well as minority groups that power belongs only to those few who hold enormous wealth. As Catholics, we must continue to rediscover our own distinct identity as a religious, prophetic people who stand apart from the powers which possess dominant control in society. In such a process, we can learn much from the Church in the Third World. Together in our preaching and actions, we are moved to pronounce God's judgment on the side of powerless life whether of the unborn child, of the elderly without care or security, of the overtaxed citizen, or of the poor in the barrios of Latin America.

---

[25] *Ibid.*, p. 11.
[26] Pope Paul VI, *op. cit.*
[27] Pope Paul VI, *Populorum Progressio*, n. 26.
[28] Roman Synod of Bishops, *Justice in the World*, 1971.

Food Policy and the Church: Specific Proposals

USCC, Administrative Board
September 11, 1975

In October 1974, the Fourth International Synod of Bishops described "the right to eat" as fundamental to human dignity. In November 1974, the National Conference of Catholic Bishops adopted a Pastoral Plan of Action designed to mobilize the Catholic community in the United States in an effort to realize the right to eat for millions threatened last year by starvation and malnutrition.

One year later it is evident that "the right to eat" is still denied to many in our own country and to many more throughout the globe. Although the threat of starvation has been reduced significantly during the past year, the presence of hunger and malnutrition continue to stalk many lives in several regions of the globe; at home many of the unemployed, the elderly and the poor are forced to subsist on inadequate diets.

In the past year, however, many helpful steps were taken in the religious communities and in the wider society. Perhaps the most significant was the meeting of the World Food Conference held in Rome last November. Throughout the United States, programs were conducted in our dioceses, parishes and schools, and policies and practices adopted by individuals, Catholic families, priests' senates and religious communities to help alleviate the problem of global and domestic hunger. The media used its powers of persuasion and education to publicize the issue of hunger. Finally, in the Congress and in parts of the Administration initial efforts have been made to shape a coherent, just and generous food policy.

All these actions are significant, but public policy has a unique importance. Personal, voluntary efforts are essential, but they will prove inadequate to the scope of the hunger question if they are not encompassed in a broader public policy which links them to a systematic program of action. In this statement, continuing the effort of policy debate, public education and pastoral leadership we began last year, we seek to address the national policy issues which are needed to make a more just food policy a reality in our country.

A. Food and Foreign Policy

The World Food Conference produced a series of proposals for combatting hunger and malnutrition on a global basis. The unique position which the

United States holds as the largest food exporting nation in the world means that our response to these proposals has supreme importance for the hungry of the world.

Since the Food Conference, a serious and sustained debate has been carried on in the Congress and within the Administration about our food policy. Some of the fruits of the debate are now taking the form of specific legislative proposals. We believe the following ideas contained in some of these proposals deserve serious public consideration and support.

I. Food Aid

The restructuring of U.S. food aid policy should include: 1) clear policy guidelines separating food aid from strategic and political considerations; 2) a specific policy commitment to give priority in food aid to the U.N.-designated "most severely affected nations"; this commitment should be specified in the language of the law; 3) the establishment of a guaranteed minimum of food aid to be provided each year; 4) the establishment of a guaranteed minimum of food aid to be provided on a donation basis through non-governmental agencies rather than through concessional sales.

II. Grain Reserve

The World Food Conference proposal for an international system of national grain reserves needs the continued support and leadership of our government and should receive whatever legislative support is needed to allow the United States to participate in the system.

III. International Fund for Agricultural Development

Our government's pledge to contribute 200 million dollars to the Fund is most welcome; this pledge should receive Congressional support and implementation.

IV. Foreign Assistance

The foreign assistance program presently being debated in Congress should include several of the elements which have been proposed: 1) the separation of economic from military aid; 2) the support for multilateral aid programs; 3) the focusing of U.S. aid programs on the needs of the small farmer and the rural poor.

B. Domestic Food Policy

Many Americans face the reality of hunger and malnutrition intensified by high levels of unemployment, inflated food prices and persistent poverty.

Two federal programs are now under governmental review: food stamps and child nutrition programs.

I. Food Stamps

We support a major review of the food stamp program. Yet, we are concerned that reform efforts not lead to a diminished commitment to assist poor and working poor families. True reform seeks to make adequate assistance available where it is needed, but protects against abuses and excesses.

Unfortunately, the current debate over the value of the food stamp program is clouded by misunderstandings. Opponents maintain that the program is growing at uncontrollable rates and that affluent families and students are taking advantage of it. Some problems and abuses do exist; however, the evidence does not support these sweeping indictments.

a. Growth of the Program   The growth of food stamps is the result of three factors: the introduction of food stamps to additional counties, the conversion of many counties from food commodities programs to food stamps, and the increase in unemployment. Begun as a pilot program in 1961, food stamps or food commodities were available in virtually every county in the nation by 1971. Between that year and mid-1974, the number of participants in the two programs remained at 14.9 million. In the last year, however, the serious rise in unemployment brought participants to a level of 19.5 million. Since April the number of people receiving stamps has declined, and the USDA projects a lower level of participants and costs by 1980. These figures indicate that the program is not out of control, but is responding to the severe economic stress of the last year.

b. Income of Participants   According to USDA, 87 percent of all food stamp participants have family incomes of less than $6,000 after taxes and the average cash income of a family of four on food stamps is $3,456 a year. Congress has already acted to prohibit the eligibility of students who are dependents of affluent families, and this provision will take full effect this month. The evidence suggests that food stamps continue to offer nutritional assistance to the poor and near-poor who are least able to afford a nutritional diet.

c. Policy Reform   The food stamp program must be maintained and improved. We oppose drastic cuts and attempts to eliminate the working poor or unemployed from its coverage.

We support measures that will tighten up administration, improve responsiveness, and reduce certification errors. We do not support modifications that will penalize the working poor and result in disincentives for participants to work.

Any changes in the family asset limitations should not require the elderly or recently unemployed to sell their automobile, necessary household goods and personal effects in order to become eligible for food stamps.

We have opposed and will continue to oppose increases in food stamp prices that will have an adverse impact on the ability of needy families to obtain adequate nutrition.

Although the evidence indicates there are very few non-needy families on food stamps, we would support a reasonable gross income limit that would disqualify affluent families from receiving food stamps under any circumstances. We would oppose efforts to set this limit so low that it would eliminate families actually in need.

Ultimately, the future of food stamps is linked to reform of the welfare system. Fundamentally, our nation must provide jobs for those who can and should work and an adequate income for those who cannot. Until such a policy is implemented, the food stamp program deserves the support of our country's public officials and citizens.

II. Child Nutrition

We have consistently supported efforts to improve and extend the Child Nutrition programs, including the School Lunch and Breakfast, the Special Supplemental Feeding Program for Women, Infants and Small Children, and the Special Milk Program. These programs provide particularly important health and education benefits for children in public and non-public schools. We support recent Congressional efforts to strengthen these programs. We urge Congress to act swiftly and the President to sign this legislation into law.

Concluding Remarks

Enlightened government food policies and individual generosity are necessary to alleviate the world food problem, but they alone are not sufficient. Christians believe that despite the most inventive programs and the best of intentions, there remains an extra measure beyond human power, that is, God's active presence in the world. Christians also believe that prayer can solicit God's presence. The complexities of the food problem tax human ingenuity and invite Christians' efficacious prayers. Our Lord's belief in the power of prayer is enlightening and consoling; he instructed us to pray for our daily bread with confidence in the knowledge that when we ask our heavenly Father, he will give us neither a stone for bread nor a serpent for fish.

Human Rights

In 1973, U.S. bishops, as one body, began to address issues of human rights on the international level. The USCC issued a resolution on the twenty-fifth anniversary of the Universal Declaration of Human Rights, endorsing the Declaration and the United Nations itself. (It underlines the importance to the "global family" of the Declaration's endorsement of the right to life, the right to emigrate, the right to religious freedom, and parents' prior right to decide on the education of their children.) The bishops declared that all the ideas and ideals found in the Declaration are consonant with their own teaching on the socio-political order. They added this strong assertion:

> The rights of men and women which the Declaration seeks to define and fulfill are rooted in the idea of the dignity of the human person. ... To respect and realize the rights of the human person is to contribute to the fulfillment of God's design for the human community; it is not a peripheral but a pivotal responsibility for all Christians. Catholics should be in the forefront of those speaking in defense of and acting for the fulfillment of the rights of men and women at the local, national and international level.

The bishops addressed human rights questions in particular geographical areas: Chile and Brazil (1974); Panama (1975 and 1976); Southern Africa (1976); Eastern Europe (1977).

The USCC Administrative Board urged the U.S. government to withhold financial and military aid from Chile until human and civil rights were restored. It requested also that pressure be brought to bear on Brazilian authorities to cease such reported violations as arrest without identification of agents, without communication with judges, and without sentencing; physical and psychological torture to obtain confessions; and suppression of dissent. The bishops encouraged policymakers in multinational corporations and financial institutions "to assess the social consequences of their present or contemplated investments in Brazil," and they urged stockholders to exert moral influence on corporation policies.

The debate over the Panama Canal Treaty brought two statements from the American bishops, one from the Board and another from the USCC. Both argued that it was a moral imperative and a matter of social justice for the U.S. to negotiate a new treaty with Panama. Every nation has a right to be the primary agent of its own development. This principle, elaborated in Pacem In Terris, is flouted, say the bishops, by the terms of the 1903 Treaty, which "deprives the nation of a substantial part of its territory, income, and capacity for planning the integral development of its people." By restricting Panama's sovereignty, the Treaty injures Panama's sense of national dignity;

117

Panama has no control over the Zone and must tolerate the presence of a substantial American military force.

In the spring of 1976, Bishop James Rausch, then General Secretary of the USCC, wrote an open letter to Secretary of State Kissinger in which he suggested five measures the Administration should include immediately in its African policy. These measures were endorsed by both the USCC's Committee on Social Development and World Peace in its statement Southern Africa: Peace or War, *and by the Executive Committee of the NCCB in a statement of support for Donal Lamont, the Catholic bishop of Umtali, Rhodesia, who had been charged by the Rhodesian government with aiding black terrorists.*

In the spring of 1977, the bishops moved their human rights campaign to Eastern Europe. A USCC statement entitled Religious Liberty in Eastern Europe: A Test Case for Human Rights, *strongly criticizes Eastern European governments for engaging in religious persecution. It accuses all Eastern European countries of using the state to support atheism and specifically mentions oppressive conditions in the Ukraine, Albania, Poland, and Czechoslovakia. The USCC calls upon the U.S. government to find ways to promote religious freedom in Eastern Europe. The bishops are fully aware that the U.S. has not previously challenged the repressive policies of Eastern European governments for fear of provoking the Soviet Union. Now, however, the U.S. may be in a position to influence these governments, because it interacts with all of them on so many levels.*

In issuing these statements, the bishops emphasize their right and solemn duty to speak out on human rights: "We recall that the 1974 Roman Synod of Bishops affirmed that the promotion of human rights is required by the Gospel and is central to the Church's ministry."

Statement on East Pakistani Refugees

USCC, Administrative Board
September 1971

In an age that has witnessed more than its share of tragedies that have darkened the lives of thousands upon thousands of people, there is probably none more tragic than the plight of the millions of refugees from East Pakistan who have fled into India to save, if possible, the lives of themselves and their families. No one can offer an exact figure on the number of refugees who have already fled, but it is now being variously estimated at between seven to ten million, and there is no end to the exodus. It is said that even at this moment, 25 to 40 thousand refugees cross the border each day. In its concern for the East Pakistani refugees, the world must not lose sight of the fact also that many thousands of their fellow-countrymen are still suffering from the cyclone which devastated their land late last year. Efforts to come to their assistance, more particularly to provide for their rehabilitation, were more or less suspended at the outset of the present tragedy and it is only recently that they have been partially resumed.

It is almost impossible for the news media to adequately portray the plight of the refugees. Having arrived with barely the clothes on their backs, without food or shelter, they have found their way into hundreds of refugee camps. The Indian Government, with funds from a number of other governments, including our own United States, and the assistance of international and national governmental and private agencies, is feeding some hundreds of thousands on a minimum sustaining diet and is providing them with at least make-shift shelter from the heat and rain. Nevertheless, there are literally thousands, who because of lack of transportation facilities and the relative scarcity of supplies, for whom death seems to be the only escape from their suffering. One relief worker, when asked what they needed most, replied without hesitation, "Crematoria." It seems almost miraculous that a plague has not already destroyed hundreds of thousands of others.

It is agreed amongst all who represent the agencies which are struggling to meet this situation that, unless a relief effort is mounted on a more gigantic scale than that which is presently going on, no hope whatever can be held out for hundreds of thousands of those who are already suffering so tragically.

The Bishops who comprise the Administrative Board of the United States Catholic Conference, conscious of the gravity of the situation through the relief program of Catholics in the U.S. which is carried on under the auspices of their Catholic Relief Services, are keenly aware and deeply disturbed by the gravity of the situation. Meeting this week in our nation's capitol, they urge our President, the Administrative branch of our government and our Congress to take the leadership in promoting a much broader international relief program.

Our government should ask the United Nations and the more favored nations of the world to mount a program of relief, to be administered by the United Nations, that would have a value of at least one billion dollars to which the United States would set an example by pledging at least $300 million. These monies would be added to those already pledged by the United States Government and others to make available the ships and airplanes needed to get food and medical supplies to those parts of India where refugees are temporarily settled and to East Pakistan. Nothing should be spared and no political considerations should stand in the way of getting aid to both of these groups.

The Administrative Board of the United States Catholic Conference appeals to the Bishops of the countries of western Europe in particular to use their influence as religious leaders to have their governments join in this kind of an international project.

Statement on Father Francois Jentel

*USCC, Committee on Social
Development and World Peace
October 19, 1973*

When Father Francois Jentel, a disciple of Charles de Foucauld, left France nearly twenty years ago for one of the most remote regions of Brazil's Mato Grosso, he expected to live out his life in the same obscurity as the Indians and displaced peasants who barely eke out their subsistence in that desperately poor area. Today his name appears in the press of many countries. The case of Father Jentel, and that of his heroic bishop, Dom Pedro Casaldaliga, of the priests and religious of the Sao Felix Prelature and of a dozen or more dedicated lay workers—all of whom have been harrassed, threatened and arrested at one time or another and some of whom are still being held incommunicado—has become a *cause celebre* in Europe, North America and many parts of Latin America.

On May 28 of this year Father Jentel began serving a ten-year prison sentence, having been convicted of charges of subversion so patently false and absurd that his bishop has offered to be jailed in his stead. The one civilian judge on the five-man military tribunal which handed down the judgment declared in his dissenting opinion that Father Jentel should be rewarded, not imprisoned, for his actions.

What Father Jentel and the others have done is assist the people in their legitimate struggle to continue farming their land and to resist the forceful encroachment of powerful, monied interests from outside the region. Every legal and non-violent means has been employed by Father Jentel and two successive bishops, going as far as a personal request to the presidency of the republic in 1967, but the monied interests, together with the military, have continued to deprive the people of Sao Felix of their basic rights. And they have now deprived the people of their friend, the priest of Santa Terezinha.

Systematic violation of the rights of individuals (such as Father Jentel, Bishop Casaldaliga and their co-workers), communities (such as Santa Terezinha) and entire ethnic groups (such as the Tapirape Indians of the region) are still tragically common in this 25th anniversary year of the Universal Declaration of Human Rights. Comparable situations, affecting especially native peoples of the Americas, have occurred recently in other parts of the hemisphere. It is time for all who have eyes to see and a conscience to guide them to speak out against such injustice.

Therefore, we, the Committee on Social Development and World Peace of the USCC, join in the protest already filed with the Inter-American Commission on Human Rights by the USCC Division for Latin America. We also urge others to express their concern to the Inter-American Commission and we especially urge the National Conference of Catholic Bishops to address itself specifically to the issue of human rights in Brazil during their annual fall meeting. The Church in the United States cannot ignore the sufferings of its sister Church in Brazil and must strive to find ever more effective ways of expressing love and solidarity with the bishops, priests and people of Brazil.

Resolution of the United States Catholic Conference on the Twenty-Fifth Anniversary of the Universal Declaration of Human Rights

USCC, November 13, 1973

On December 10, 1973, we will commemorate the twenty-fifth anniversary of the United Nations' Universal Declaration of Human Rights. As bishops entrusted with the social teaching of the Church and as leaders of the Catholic community in the United States we wish to express our strong endorsement for the Declaration and for the institution of the United Nations.

The Universal Declaration of Human Rights deserves our support because it is a testament of vital importance to the global family. This is especially the case in view of the Declaration's explicit endorsement of such critical rights as respect for human life, the right to emigrate, the right to religious freedom, and parents' prior right to choose the kind of education that shall be given their children. The significance of the Declaration derives from the ideas in which it is rooted and the ideals which it seeks to achieve. Speaking from within the Roman Catholic tradition we find both the ideas and the ideals of the Declaration consonant with those of our own teaching on the socio-political order. The rights of men and women which the Declaration seeks to define and fulfill are rooted in the idea of the dignity of the human person. At Vatican II we joined with all our brother bishops to assert our belief that "the root reason for human dignity lies in man's call to communion with God." (*Gaudium et Spes,* para. 19) To respect and realize the rights of the human person is to contribute to the fulfillment of God's design for the human community; it is not a peripheral but a pivotal responsibility for all Christians. Catholics should be in the forefront of those speaking in defense of and acting for the fulfillment of the rights of men and women at the local, national and international level. Our commitment to these goals should be expressed personally and institutionally in the policies and programs the Church sponsors and supports in society.

We are mindful on this occasion that within our own religious community we are also celebrating the tenth anniversary of Pope John's encyclical *Pacem In Terris.* In this document John XXIII enumerated the spectrum of rights—political, cultural, economic—which are necessary if people are to live in accord with human dignity. That catalogue stands before us today as an unfinished agenda. In our own country recent events demonstrate the need to be creative and vigilant in protecting and fostering political rights. Similarly, in our own land thoughtful observers are commenting on the need for an examination of our protection of economic rights in terms of tax reform, protection for the elderly, the needs of all our citizens for health care and the special needs of the very poor and working poor for a basic minimum income. Internationally, the pervasive presence of American power creates a responsibility of using that power in the service of human rights. The link between our economic assistance and regimes which utilize torture, deny legal protection to citizens and detain political prisoners without due process clearly is a question of conscience for our government and for each of us as citizens in a democracy.

The teaching of *Pacem In Terris* and the content of the Universal Declaration of Human Rights converge to direct our attention and spur our action toward this unfinished agenda of human rights questions.

Finally, we take this opportunity to offer our endorsement and encouragement to the institution of the United Nations. It is not perfect but we believe it is indispensable in an imperfectly organized world. It is a first step toward realizing that juridical-political organization of the world community for which the last three Popes have incessantly called. We earnestly hope that the United Nations and its Declaration of Human Rights receive from Catholics and all people of good will the support they both deserve.

Statement of Solidarity on Human Rights: Chile and Brazil

USCC, Administrative Board
February 14, 1974

Human Rights Violations in Chile

In our resolution celebrating the twenty-fifth anniversary of the United Nations' Universal Declaration of Human Rights, we noted that moral principles must be applied to foreign policy:

> ... the pervasive presence of American power creates a responsibility of using that power in the service of human rights. ... The link between our

economic assistance and regimes which utilize torture, deny legal protection to citizens and detain political prisoners without due process clearly is a question of conscience for our government and for each of us as citizens in a democracy.

We are deeply distressed by the violations of human rights taking place in Chile. We associate ourselves in solidarity with the Church in Chile during these troubled times. We are also concerned that in the face of these violations our government is escalating its financial aid to the Chilean junta.

Therefore, with the exception of humanitarian aid, we urge the United States Government to condition its financial aid and military assistance to Chile upon the demonstration that human and civil rights have been restored in that country.

On Human Rights in Brazil

The Holy Father's address to the Cardinals of Rome last December dealt with particular insight with the issue of human rights. In his remarks, Pope Paul said:

> For as long as, within the individual national communities, those in power do not nobly respect the rights and legitimate freedoms of the citizens, tranquility and order (even though they can be maintained by force) remain nothing but a deceptive and insecure sham, no longer worthy of a society of civilized beings.

The American bishops' statement last November on the twenty-fifth Anniversary of the Universal Declaration of Human Rights was especially sensitive to the United States' international activities. It specifically highlighted the moral question of American economic assistance supporting regimes which seriously suppress the human rights of their citizens.

It is precisely to the international level, and more specifically, to the relations of the United States and Brazil that we address ourselves at this time.

We are compelled to focus attention on Brazil because of the level to which respect for human rights has deteriorated in that country, and also because continuous efforts have been made there to eliminate sources of dissent in the public sector—in youth groups, political parties, labor unions, peasant associations.

One of the last remaining organized voices in Brazil's society with power to speak in opposition to repressive government tactics is the Church and this obviously places it in a most vulnerable position.

The policies of the government must be seen in the context of the supposed economic "miracle" taking place in Brazil. Although Brazil's economy is growing at a remarkable annual rate, Robert S. McNamara, President of the World Bank, has pointed out that Brazil's development in the 1960s was severely distorted: "The very rich did very well. But throughout the decade the poorest 40% of the population benefited only marginally."

McNamara's general observations are also especially relevant to Brazil: "When the distribution of land, income, and opportunity becomes distorted to the point of desperation, what political leaders must often weigh is the risk of unpopular (among the rich) but necessary social reform—against the risk of social rebellion." The Brazilian regime, rather than effecting necessary social reforms, seems to favor measures, which suppress all sources of opposition and thereby hopes to eliminate "the risk of social rebellion."

In view of the oppressive conditions in Brazil, the March 1973 statement on the Universal Declaration of Human Rights, made by the National Conference of the Catholic Bishops of Brazil on the occasion of their annual assembly, is remarkably courageous and timely. The bishops stated that the Church in Brazil must inform public opinion of instances of violations of human rights, "and must be ready to accept the consequences of this action."

We associate ourselves in solidarity with the Brazilian bishops in their call for greater respect for human rights, as illustrated by the recent statement of the bishops of the Southern region of Brazil. Faced with severe violations of human dignity, they publicly chastised the government:

> It is not lawful for you to arrest people the way you do, without identification of agents, without communication to judges, without sentencing. Many of the arrests are kidnappings. It is not lawful for you to submit people to physical, psychological or moral torture in order to obtain confessions, even more so when this leads to permanent damage to the health, psychological breakdowns, mutilations and even death.

We also associate ourselves with the Brazilian Episcopal Conference in their call for the establishment of an international juridical body "on human dignity, whose function would be to judge, from an ethical point of view, the regimes which violate the basic rights of the human person, taking as a fundamental criterion for their judgements the United Nations' Declaration of Human Rights."

We also join with others in the protests already filed with the Inter-American Commission on Human Rights of the Organization of American States, concerning violation of human rights in Brazil. We pledge ourselves to search for ever more effective ways of expressing our solidarity with the Church in Brazil.

Our government must examine closely its programs of financial and military assistance to be certain they are not used in the denial of human rights. Further, the U.S. government must examine its trade and tariff policies to insure that they do not foster the repression of human rights. The U.S. government, along with other governments, must continue to scrutinize Brazilian affairs closely and bring pressure to bear on the Brazilian authorities for the restoration of human rights, especially through various international agencies such as the United Nations, as well as those bilateral United States-Brazilian programs.

In the private sector, we encourage policy makers in multinational corporations and financial institutions to assess the social consequences of their present or contemplated investments in Brazil. And further, since stock ownership entails a moral responsibility, stockholders are encouraged to use their influence to effect corporations' policies.

Americans, in general, should inform themselves about human rights conditons in Brazil, and assess their social responsibility in rectifying injustices.

Panama-U.S. Relations

USCC, Administrative Board
February 24, 1975

The United States and the Republic of Panama are currently engaged in active negotiations regarding a treaty involving the Panama Canal. It is a moral imperative—a matter of elemental social justice—that a new and a more just treaty be negotiated.

The history of these negotiations spans a seventy-year period, beginning with the original Treaty of 1903 by which the United States assumed virtually sovereign and perpetual control over the heartland of the Panamanian Isthmus. More recently, in February 1974, the two nations signed the Kissinger-Tack Agreement on Principles, which provides a significant basis for a new treaty.

Why is a new treaty imperative? In the first place, the 1903 treaty is, in itself, of dubious moral validity, drafted as it was when international affairs were frequently determined by precepts of power. Since that time, and despite the seventy years that have passed in this century in which other peoples have achieved their independence or have established functional control over their territory, this treaty has remained essentially unchanged at the insistence of the more powerful of the two parties.

In the second place, a more fundamental issue is the right of every nation to utilize its natural resources for the development of its people. In his 1963 encyclical *Pacem In Terris,* Pope John XXIII emphasized this basic principle of international justice which had been strongly affirmed in the previous year's declaration of the U.N. General Assembly (Resolution 1803, XXVII, December 14, 1962). Nations, the Holy Father stressed, "have the right to play the leading part in the process of their own development" and "no country may unjustly oppress others or unduly meddle in their affairs."

The principal natural resource of Panama is and always has been its geographic location and its configuration. The treaty of 1903 established a monopoly, "in perpetuity," in favor of another government over the principal natural resource of the Republic of Panama.

The question, therefore, lies in whether or not we accept the fact that Panama is a free and independent nation. As such, her claims over the Canal area are a simple consequence of her basic right. In other words, if we accept the rights of Panama over her territory, then instead of Panama negotiating with the United States to obtain for herself some compensation for the use of the Canal and the Canal Zone, it might be reasoned that negotiations should be the other way around. The main benefits from the Canal should accrue to Panama, as a nation with principal control over its natural resources, and a fair compensation should accrue to the United States for its investment in Panama.

Besides the political, social and cultural consequences of the 1903 treaty that argue strongly for a fundamental revision of U.S.-Panamanian relations, economic considerations are also considerable. It is worth reviewing, in this regard, some of the main benefits that accrue to each side as recently cited by the Archbishop of Panama, Marcos McGrath, C.S.C.:

• The Canal Zone, which measures roughly 10 by 50 miles in area, is the heartland, the most valuable economic area of Panama. Present use represents a significant waste of this natural resource: only 3.6% of the land is occupied by Canal installations; some 25% is not utilized at all, and 68% is designated for military use. For this entire territory, including 14 military bases established without any negotiations with Panama as to their location, the United States pays an annual $1.9 million, as contrasted, for example, to the $20 million paid annually for three bases in Spain.

• Since 70% of the goods that transit the Canal come from or go to U.S. ports, the non-commercial fees, frozen until this year at the 1914 level, have represented an annual saving to U.S. commerce of $700 million. In this way, Panama, a poor nation, is subsidizing the richest nation of the world and world commerce in general.

• The savings to the U.S. Armed Forces in the use of the Canal in the sixty years since its inauguration are calculated in excess of $11 billion.

• The U.S. military investment in the Canal Zone is more than double the total civil investment, an expense that goes far beyond any notion of mere defense of the Canal. In fact, the U.S. Southern Command, located in the Canal Zone, is a training center for military from all over Latin America and a nerve center of military contact throughout the continent. Surely military bases established within a nation should be the object of negotiation.

• Nearly 20% of the gross national income of the Republic of Panama derives from the Canal Zone economy, mostly in indirect form, through salaries and sales. The rise and fall of this income according to fluctuations in building and other operations within the Canal Zone, factors beyond the control of the Republic, has a strongly distorting effect upon the Panamanian economy.

• Since property and income in the Canal Zone are exempted from Panamanian taxes, the government of Panama is denied a major source of revenue. As a result, it has not been fully able to undertake programs of economic infrastructures and socio-economic development, particularly for the impoverished rural areas.

While these observations do not attempt to treat all questions relating to the Panama Canal issue, they do serve to place the question within an overall context of international social justice.

For peace in the world, which can come only with justice in the world, it is essential that we citizens of the United States, including our elected representatives, approach the Panama Canal issue with the same moral sensitivity we would apply to issues of justice within our own society.

Our national response to the new treaty will be a significant test of that sensitivity. Not only the rest of the Americas, but the whole world will be watching. The fundamental rights of the people of Panama, as well as the high ideals and long-range interests of the United States, require a new and just treaty. It can become a sign of and a significant contribution toward world peace based upon justice and fraternity between peoples.

Southern Africa: Peace or War?

*USCC, Committee on Social
Development and World Peace
July 7, 1976*

In 1967, Pope Paul VI wrote, in his encyclical letter on Africa:

> The equality of all men is based, as is well known, on their common origin
> and destiny as members of the human family ... This equality demands an
> ever more explicit recognition in civil society of every human being's essen-
> tial rights, even though this equality does not cancel but rather
> acknowledges and brings into harmony personal differences and the diver-
> sity of function in the community. Consequently, the aspirations of all men
> desiring to enjoy those rights which flow from their dignity as human persons
> are wholly legitimate.

Paul VI, *Ad Afros* par 19
Gremillion, p. 422–3

American awareness of the African continent has been heightened in the
past two years by several events: the independence of Mozambique and
Angola, and especially the internal struggle in the latter nation, and the participation of the U.S.A., Cuba, and the U.S.S.R. in that struggle; the recent
and initial visit of Secretary of State Henry Kissinger to Africa and his
belated pronouncements of U.S. African policy.

Shortly before the Secretary's journey, Bishop James S. Rausch, General
Secretary of the U.S. Catholic Conference, addressed an open letter to him in
which several important suggestions were made regarding United States
policy and actions in Africa. We fully endorse what Bishop Rausch said
therein and make it our own.

In this statement we wish to speak especially about the Republic of South
Africa (RSA), to address some of the urgent moral issues raised there, and to
comment on the responsiblility of the American people and their government
in dealing with that nation. We address ourselves particularly to the RSA not
unmindful of the urgency of achieving majority rule in Rhodesia and the independence of Namibia. Nevertheless, South Africa is clearly the most
developed, most influential nation in the southern part of the African continent, and is the object of economic, political, and military interest on the
part of the United States. The United States should conduct its foreign policy
toward the RSA, and influence business activity there to change its racial
policies, both to establish justice within that nation, and to avoid interna-

tional conflict. Even more effective leverage would be achieved if the United States, as the leader of the western nations, could develop a coordinated policy with them regarding the RSA.

For Black Africans, "South Africa is an obsession," said Bishop James D. Sangu, Chairman of the Tanzanian Catholic Bishops' Conference. He explained that assertion in these words:

> Its crude racialism is a continuous insult to black Africans. It not only keeps the races apart, as it claims, but it shouts from the rooftops the superiority of the White Race and the inferiority of the Black Race. As long as this situation continues, there is really little chance that the Black Africans will ever live in brotherhood with White Europeans.

Secretary Kissinger himself described South Africa's apartheid system by which he said "racial discrimination has been institutionalized, enshrined in law, and made all-pervasive." But Bishop Sangu maintains:

> Notwithstanding the half-hearted denunciation of racialism by the Western countries, South Africa feels strong because she is convinced of the backing she receives from the Western countries, and because of the strong economic ties she has with these countries. As Christians we must fight for justice for the oppressed, not for financial gain and economic interests.

This analysis is borne out by the contrast between the Secretary's severe condemnation of Rhodesia and stern demands for internal reforms and, on the other hand, his relatively mild strictures against South Africa. He seemed even to weaken the former U.S. position on South Africa's illegal occupation of Namibia. He did not call for majority rule in South Africa, as he did in Rhodesia, but for "a clear evolution toward equality of opportunity and basic human rights for all South Africans." The difference may seem to be merely a subtlety, but in light of Kissinger's former African policy, which included support for the white minority regimes, anything less than a forthright denunciation of apartheid and minority government is suspected of support and collusion.

Implicated here is not only the question of justice for black Rhodesians and South Africans; but world peace itself. The existence of the racist societies of the two nations (and Namibia, occupied and controlled by South Africa), since it is "an obsession" with black Africans, promises increased internal disorder, and activity of guerilla freedom-fighters. This, in turn, raises the possibility of external intervention by other African nations, by the superpowers, or others.

Such intervention would be translated either into racial terms—black against white—or ideological terms—communist against non-communist. Africa's black leaders of nations and liberation movements reject such a view. Many of them have benefitted from Christian education and are themselves Christians. Their vision is of multi-racial societies in which the human dignity of each person is respected. Their leaning toward the U.S.A. and the West, or toward the U.S.S.R. or China, is not so much an ideological stance as an expression of their need for assistance as they attempt to establish such societies, or to promote the development of the nations they represent.

South Africa, in contrast, plans to create bantustans, "independent nations" within its territory; all black persons will be assigned to one of these, on the basis of tribal ancestry, regardless of whether the person has even lived there. In South Africa, where most blacks must necessarily go to work, regardless of which bantustan he or she is technically a citizen, citizenship will be withdrawn, under the fiction that the individual is a citizen of the black nation. Racial segregation, in short, is so important that the nation will be dismembered to preserve it; economic superiority is so important that the territories assigned to blacks will comprise only 13% of the land, and are the least productive areas.

The only course of policy and action for Americans to take is one consistent with our national tradition of personal freedom and the Christian principle of universal love, directed especially to those who most need it. With such a policy, implemented by substantial and realistic action, the United States and the American people would win the admiration of the African people; considerations of economic and strategic interests would then fall into perspective, both for us and for them.

It is not enough to state such principles and policy; they must be translated into positive action. Hence, without attempting to draw up an exhaustive listing, we suggest the following:

1. that the U.S. raise for discussion in the U.N. Security Council the threat to world peace created by the Republic of South Africa by its internal policy of apartheid and its occupation of Namibia (South West Africa), with a view to imposing international economic sanctions against that nation until substantial changes have been made.

2. that the U.S. use every available means to restrict and discourage U.S. business and investment in the RSA, Namibia, and Rhodesia; particularly, that exceptions, licenses, or mitigations in favor of these nations not be granted.

3. that the U.S. recognize and enforce the decree of the U.N. Council for Namibia for the protection of the natural resources of Namibia against exploitation by South Africa during its illegal occupation of that territory. According to that decree, approved by the U.N. General Assembly in 1974, "any animal, mineral, or other natural resource produced in or emanating from the Territory of Namibia," taken without license granted by the Council for Namibia, may be seized, along with the vehicle or ship carrying it, "forfeited to the benefit of the Council, and held in trust by them for the benefit of the people of Namibia."

4. that the U.S. Congress give substance to Secretary Kissinger's promises

by assisting those frontier nations which may experience hardship because of their compliance with the U.N. sanctions against Rhodesia.

We suggest these actions not for political, economic, or strategic reasons, but because they would give assurance to the government of South Africa, to its black citizens, and to the rest of the world, that the United States still believes that liberty and equality are unalienable rights of every person; and that recognition of these rights in practice in southern Africa will be conducive to peace and prosperity in that part of the world.

The Drama of Rhodesia
Statement on Bishop Donal Lamont

USCC, Executive Committee
September 14, 1976

We wish to call the attention of the American press and public as well as the U.S. government and the American business community to the recent statement of Bishop Donal Lamont of Umtali, Rhodesia. Bishop Lamont, an Irish missionary for 30 years in Rhodesia and president of the Bishops' Justice and Peace Commission, has been a strong and consistent voice for racial, political and economic justice in Rhodesia for many years.

Bishop Lamont has patiently tried, against great odds, to encourage change within the system, using his persuasive powers of reason to call upon the white minority in Rhodesia to recognize the political and moral bankruptcy of existing laws and institutions.

He has pleaded with no less force and eloquence for the Western nations to bring their powers of political persuasion and economic influence to bear upon the Smith regime, either to evoke or to compel a change in national policy. His most recent statement of this kind was made in February 1976 at one of the public hearings sponsored by the American bishops in the "Liberty and Justice for All" programs.

On August 11, 1976, Bishop Lamont addressed the Rhodesian government. In his letter, he illuminates with piercing clarity the gravity and urgency of the present moment in Rhodesia. In terms drawn from Catholic political thought, he has called into question the political legitimacy of the Rhodesian government. He has implied that the forces opposing the Smith regime have a moral right to the resources and ministry of the church in their struggle for justice. He has encouraged Rhodesians, black and white, to evaluate whether the Smith regime deserves their support, obedience or loyalty.

It comes as no surprise that Bishop Lamont now stands accused by that government of having followed out his convictions by failing to report the presence of men thought to be guerrillas, and by encouraging others not to report them. Under Rhodesian law, these are crimes which may be severely punished.

The content of Bishop Lamont's letter should be given serious consideration in our country. The policy of the United States is being carefully watched in Africa. The tensions and grievances built up over decades in the white-dominated societies of Rhodesia and South Africa have reached a new level of intensity. As the future of these societies is being contested and determined, the future of the U.S. position in Africa is simultaneously being decided.

Bishop Lamont's courageous moral appeal to the people of Rhodesia to examine their relationship with their government also points to our need to examine our relationship to the drama being played out in Rhodesia. The speech of Secretary Kissinger at Lusaka in April has raised some expectations in Africa and in the United States. The test of the speech will be the specific form our actions take. Relevant measures, proposed in Bishop James S. Rausch's open letter to Secretary Kissinger (April 7, 1976), include the following:

• The Congress can and should repeal the Byrd amendment which presently allows the United States to subvert U.S. economic sanctions against the Smith regime;

• The administration should provide unequivocal assurances to Rhodesia and the Republic of South Africa that no U.S. assistance, military, political or financial, will be forthcoming to support or sustain the existing system of government; any aid will be contingent upon bringing black majorities into full participation in the respective governments;

• All available means, public and private, political and moral, should be used to restrict and discourage U.S. business and investment in Rhodesia, Namibia and South Africa;

• U.S. corporations operating in Rhodesia and South Africa have a responsibility to evaluate their presence in more than economic terms; a moral responsibility exists to assess the role they play in sustaining systems which stand indicted and ostracized in the international community.

Speaking in our capacity as the executive committee of the National Conference of Catholic Bishops and the U.S. Catholic Conference, we wish to affirm solidarity with and support for Bishop Lamont. Displays of moral courage and leadership of this type deserve support from other members of the church, especially from those in the episcopacy. In pledging him this support, we wish to extend it through him to all who struggle for justice, equality, human dignity and peace in Rhodesia.

U.S.-Panama Relations

USCC, November 10, 1976

The United States and the Republic of Panama are presently engaged in negotiations about the future of the Panama Canal. These negotiations have been in progress since 1964 and have been advanced significantly since the Statement of Principles formulated by the two governments in 1974.

The Administrative Board of the U.S. Catholic Conference issued a policy statement in February 1975 which affirmed that: "It is a moral imperative—a matter of elemental social justice—that a new and more just treaty be negotiated." (Panama-U.S. Relations, 1975) We continue to believe that the moral imperative exists to fashion a new treaty which respects the territorial integrity and sovereignty of Panama, and dissolves the vestiges of a relationship which more closely resembles the colonial politics of the nineteenth century than the realities of an interdependent world of sovereign and equal states.

Since 1975 there has been extensive debate in the United States about the treaty negotiations. Issues of a political, strategic and economic nature have been raised. In addition, the status of U.S. citizens living in the Canal Zone is a matter of concern for U.S. policy. Our purpose in this statement is to reaffirm our stance in favor of a new treaty by specifying major issues which we believe should be in the forefront of the public debate and policy decision-making in the United States.

Speaking as bishops of the Catholic Church, our perspective on the treaty negotiations is set by a text from Pope John XXIII's *Pacem in Terris*. In his discussion of relations between states, the Pope said: "Each of them, accordingly, is vested with the right to existence, to self-development and the means fitting to its attainment, and to be the one primarily responsible for this self-development." (para. 86) It is this principle which is at stake in the treaty negotiations: the fundamental question is the need to acknowledge in principle and in fact Panamanian sovereignty over its own territory. The terms of the 1903 Treaty acknowledge the principle of Panamanian sovereignty, but prevent its exercise in any form in the Canal Zone. Without rehearsing the history or the terms of the treaty, we simply would affirm that the moral, legal and political realities of international life today render the 1903 Treaty an anachronism.

The terms of the Treaty make it impossible for Panama to be the primary agent of its own development, because it deprives the nation of a substantial part of its territory, income and capacity for planning the integral development of its people. Finally, by restricting sovereignty in this way, the present relationship strikes directly at the national dignity and sense of respect which any nation needs for free and independent existence. To quote Pope John again, "Nor must it be forgotten, in this connection, that peoples can be highly sensitive, and with good reason, in matters touching their dignity and honor." (para. 89)

Because the issue of sovereignty is so closely tied to the freedom and self-determination of a nation, it has become an issue of dignity and honor for the Panamanians. Given our political history, the world has a right to expect that Americans will be especially sensitive to another nation's claims for freedom, dignity and self-determination.

The implications of the sovereignty issue for Panama can be illustrated with two examples: First, as we indicated in our 1975 statement, the inability of Panama to integrate the Canal and the territory comprising the Canal Zone into its national planning has significant economic consequences ranging from urban congestion in Panama City to the amount of revenue which can be garnered from operating the Canal. Second, through a process of unilateral actions, the Untied States has developed in the Canal Zone a very substantial military presence which goes far beyond the requirements for defending the Canal. The existence there of the U.S. Southern Command implies a U.S. military presence throughout Latin America. It is a continuing political problem, casting reflection on the independence of Panama, for its government to be so closely tied, without choice, to the military policy of the United States in Latin America. Without a new treaty the Panamanians have no possibility of addressing either of these issues.

We support a new treaty, therefore, because we see it as a requirement of justice between our nations. As we consider this larger question of justice, however, we wish also to express our pastoral concern and public support for a negotiated treaty which will protect the welfare of the people living and working in the Canal Zone. We especially call attention to the need for an agreement which will provide for the economic security of Americans presently employed in the Canal Zone. This too is a requirement of justice which rests upon both the United States and Panamanian governments.

The issues involved between our two countries are complex; they are also emotionally volatile. The need in both countries is for reasoned discussion, a sense of the other's point of view and a commitment to a fair resolution which will lay the basis for a long-term relationship of respect and cooperation between our governments and our peoples. It is to achieve these objectives that we commit ourselves to a continued program of public education and discussion in the United States.

Religious Liberty in Eastern Europe: A Test Case for Human Rights

USCC, May 4, 1977

The protection of human rights continues to be a major preoccupation among those who pursue peace, and with just cause. As Christians, we have become increasingly aware that the defense and promotion of human rights is a central task of the ministry of the Church. As Pope Paul VI in his 1977 Peace message has indicated: "where human rights are truly professed and publicly recognized and defended, Peace becomes the joyful and operative atmosphere of life in society."

Today, human rights in many places in the world are severely restricted. While no nation is faultless in the defense and promotion of human rights, we are obliged to note two recent statements by Episcopal Conferences—the bishops of West Germany and of Poland—deploring the denial of the human right to religious liberty in Eastern Europe.

We feel all the more obliged because so many American Catholics have their ancestral roots in these countries or are themselves refugees from the oppressive regimes of Eastern Europe. The denial of religious freedom in the countries from the Baltic Sea in the north to the Black Sea in the south is a tragic episode in humanity's efforts to defend and promote human rights. Churches and individual religious believers are continually hindered by governments in the practice of their religion. In some cases, they are subjected to outright persecution, and, in others, as in the instance of Eastern Catholic churches, they have been forcibly suppressed. No religion is spared:

Christians, Jews, and Moslems all suffer. The intensity and the scale of the suppression of religion is vigorous and comprehensive.

Attacks on the churches vary from country to country in Eastern Europe, reflecting the diversity of cultural traditions in each country, the depth and variety of religious conviction among the people, and the degree of tenacity and pragmatism of the Communist party leadership. Despite the differences in degree, a general pattern of religious oppression is clearly evident.

It is especially at the level of the individual believer that the infringement of the person's human right to practice his or her religion is most insidious, since in all of the Eastern European countries atheism is supported by the full apparatus of the state. For example, membership in a Christian community disqualifies one from becoming a teacher, a civil servant or an official in the government. In some situations, even visits to the sick and the administration of the sacraments to the dying require prior official permits. Conditions are especially severe in Lithuania where the church is subjected to constant and intense persecutions. In the Ukraine, no churches of the Ukrainian Catholic Rite and the Ruthenian Rite, are permitted or open, while in Albania there exists perhaps the most systematic repression of the Church in all of Eastern Europe.

Religious instruction is constantly hindered by a variety of intimidating measures taken against students and their parents by state officials. This process of violations of human rights was the subject of a recent courageous pastoral letter of the Polish bishops (September 1976). While Catholics in Poland have displayed remarkable resilience in the face of persistent and official suppression, the bishops said that the Church is now being subjected to a sophisticated program of atheization: existing building regulations are used to restrict the construction of needed churches in expanding urban centers; employment opportunities are reserved to persons who declare themselves to be non-believers or at least non-practicing Catholics; and admission to some schools is made dependent upon a declaration of non-belief. Similar practices are common throughout the Eastern European bloc.

In Czechoslovakia, the regime is under the control of the most hardened Stalinists. More than half of the Catholic dioceses do not have bishops because the intransigent government refuses to acknowledge the Holy See's nominees and refuses even to dialogue on the issue. The clergy are under severe repression as are the seminaries. The very existence of the religious orders of women is especially precarious. The law forbids women from joining religious orders, and the indications are that, due to the regime's restrictions, the women's orders may be virtually extinct within 25 years.

In summary, the lives of individual believers and the existence of the Christian community in Eastern Europe are both in serious jeopardy. Both are subject to the capricious whims of state bureaucrats, the intellectual abuse of ideologues and the continuous harassment—with the ultimate goal of extinction—by the state apparatus.

Since World War II, the political fate of Eastern Europeans has depended heavily upon relations between the United States and the Soviet Union. This relationship has been dominated by U.S. fears that provocation in Eastern Europe might precipitate a nuclear holocaust. This grim prospect has inhibited U.S. relations with the East.

The resulting U.S. policy of non-interference in the affairs of Eastern European nations has prevented the United States from making any form of effective protest against Communist oppression. Advocates for the defense of human rights, including courageous dissenters in the East, have earnestly appealed to the West to apply multiple kinds of pressures against regimes in Eastern Europe, including the Soviet Union.

A series of recent developments—the signing of the Helsinki Accords, an increase in the volume of commercial and cultural exchanges between the United States and the Eastern European nations, and a growing sense of independence within the bloc itself—may have given the United States a potentially greater measure of influence with Communist governments in the region. The real question is whether and how we can use that influence to protect one of humanity's most precious rights: the individual's religious freedom.

While we do not have any illusions about the political realities of international affairs, it does appear to us that circumstances and events suggest that new opportunities are present for the United States, which, if utilized, may contribute to the defense of human rights in Eastern Europe. We therefore urge the U.S. policymakers to give respect for religious freedom a more prominent role in the conduct of our relationship with these nations. We take note of the Congress' efforts to protect human rights and encourage it to expand on these efforts.

Specifically, we encourage the new Administration to engage seriously in the preparations for the follow-up to the Helsinki Accords scheduled for 1977. These include the establishment of an appropriate monitoring system to measure the compliance of nations—ours as well as the Eastern Europeans—in implementing the Helsinki Accords. We also encourage U.S. trade officials, businessmen, intellectuals, performing artists, technicians, and scientists to introduce the issue of religious liberty, as well as other human rights, into their relationships with individuals and groups in Eastern Europe. And, further, advocates of corporate responsibility are encouraged to apply to Eastern Europe the same norms for evaluating the appropriateness of U.S. business presence and activities there as they do in the Third World.

We recall that the 1974 Roman Synod of Bishops affirmed that the promotion of human rights is required by the gospel and is central to the Church's ministry. However, in some countries, members of the Church cannot speak up about human rights, while in others, they can do so only at great peril. We, in the United States, are not hampered in this regard. Therefore, we pledge ourselves to continue to make the public advocacy of human rights a matter of our prime concern.

We associate ourselves in solidarity with the persecuted Church in those regions around the world where the human right of religious freedom is severely restrained by overt acts of suppression or by subtle intimidations. We especially ally ourselves with the bishops of Eastern Europe in their suffering and their ministry to their oppressed peoples. We recognize that the best efforts of nations, private groups and concerned individuals will not necessarily thwart those who "persecute believers and speak all kinds of slander ..." (Mt. 5:11–12) While pledging ourselves to support these efforts, we pray that those who suffer will recall Jesus' assurance that public persecution bears witness to his name and contributes to the evangelization of the world. (Mk. 13:9–13)

We also acknowledge that there is a power beyond that of policymakers and politicians. Therefore, as we pray for the persecuted Church throughout the world, we also pray for its persecutors. In this way, we trust that God's wisdom and grace may provide what is lacking in our own efforts.

Statement on Small-Boat Refugees in Southeast Asia

NCCB, Administrative Committee
February 16, 1978

We urge the President and Congress to respond in a more forceful and humane manner to the anguished cries of the men, women, and children who, seeking a new life of freedom, are fleeing Southeast Asia by land and in small boats.

The number of these refugees, 60% of them children, has grown in recent months due to oppressive actions by new Communist regimes in some nations in Southeast Asia which are forcing families to undertake an almost suicidal endeavor in search of asylum.

As is generally the case in large-scale refugee movements in hostile circumstances, some do not reach their goal and there is a corresponding loss of life.

In the Southeast Asian turmoil there are firsthand reports of the terrors of the overland march from Laos and Cambodia and of the loss of life of an estimated 50% in the almost suicidal small-boat movement from Vietnam. For every two persons who start out, only one survives.

In Thailand there are approximately 100,000 refugees from Vietnam, Laos, and Cambodia. They have found a highly temporary asylum in 13 separate refugee compounds controlled by the government of Thailand. Approximately 5,000 new refugees are entering Thailand each month, around 1,500 by small boat from Vietnam and more than 3,000 overland from Cambodia and Laos. Despite traditional kindness founded in national history and religion, the Thai government is in a most precarious position from internal and diplomatic points of view, since the country is surrounded by well-armed Communist nations.

There is no way of knowing how many refugees have been turned back at the borders by local Thai officials. The United States press reported some months ago that a group of 29 had been returned to Cambodia and immediately executed.

Among the tragic aspects of this refugee movement is the reluctance of larger vessels plying the South China Sea to pick up those in distress in small boats. Past experience has taught the masters of these vessels that to do so can involve them and their shipping companies in many complications. Some countries, learning that refugees are aboard a vessel, will not permit even the crew to disembark. No landing rights are given to refugees, and the ship must keep them on board while hoping to reach a port that will grant temporary asylum. In some instances ships have sailed nearly around the world, dropping off refugees in South Africa, Kuwait, Italy, and other places.

It is an appalling fact that, after braving the terrors of the sea, refugees find that what awaits them is not really asylum. A proliferation of reports indicate that their boats are often driven off shore or towed back to the open sea. These refugees have no alternative but to seek haven in other countries bordering the South China Sea (the Philippines, Korea, Macao, Hong Kong, and Taiwan) or, in desperation, to set sail in their small, unseaworthy craft for Australia, over 3,000 miles away.

On August 11, 1977, the U.S. government authorized the admission of 7,000 boat cases and 8,000 land-based refugees. On January 25 of this year, the Attorney General authorized the admission of 7,000 additional boat refugees. These admissions are stopgap measures. Some type of established admission procedure is needed to avoid unimaginable disaster.

The government of France has instituted a humane procedure and is accepting approximately 1,000 refugees each month as it has done for some time. The governments of Australia, Canada, and some nations of Europe have made more limited commitments.

In appealing to the President and Congress to respond in a more humane and forceful manner to the tragic situation of the small-boat refugees in

Southeast Asia, we are not unmindful of the responsibility of the business world and of the Church itself in this matter. The business world, particularly the shipping interests of the United States, must not abandon these men, women and children to the perils of the sea. The ancient tradition of rendering aid to the occupants of boats and ships in distress on the high seas must be continued by American ship masters and crews, and indeed by the masters and crews of the ships of all nations.

As for the Church, we renew our commitment to aid the refugees of any nation, regardless of religion and political ideology. We call on the dioceses, parishes, and individual Catholics of the U.S. to expand their works of mercy through sponsoring and resettling those refugees who will come to our shores. We are mindful of the words of Pope Paul VI: "The pastoral care of migrants has always attracted the motherly attention and the solicitude of the Church. In fact, it has never ceased throughout the centuries to help in every way those who, like Christ in exile in Egypt with the family of Nazareth, were compelled to emigrate to lands far away from their country." (*Pastoralis Migratorum Cura*)

Part III:
Domestic Policy

Abortion

Between 1968 and 1976, the American bishops issued many declarations and statements against abortion. The 1974 testimony before the Senate Judiciary Committee began by clearly indicating the grounds on which the USCC opposes abortion.

1. The right to life is a basic human right which should be protected by law.

2. Abortion, the deliberate destruction of an unborn human being, is contrary to the law of God and is a morally evil act.

The first argument implies that human reason unaided by revelation can discover the right to life as a human or natural right, which has standing whether or not it is supported by positive law. The second argument indicates that Catholic moral teaching also appeals to revelation as a standard by which to judge the morality of abortion. This is confirmed by the bishops' statement in reaction to the Supreme Court's 1973 decision legalizing abortion: "Human life is valuable from conception to death because God is the Creator of each human being, and because mankind has been redeemed by Jesus Christ." The USCC's opposition to abortion, then, is based on philosophical, theological, and legal grounds.

On November 20, 1975, the NCCB issued a Pastoral Plan for Pro-life Activities, *outlining the Catholic Church's plan to undertake three major efforts in defense of life. The first is a public information and education program. The Church plans to inform the general public of the threat to human dignity posed by a permissive abortion policy, and of the need to establish legal safeguards for the protection of life. A more intensive and long-range aspect of this educational effort is to present scientific information on the humanity of the unborn child; to make medical, sociological, legal, and especially moral and theological arguments in favor of societal protection of the child at every stage of its existence; and to point out the problems women face during pregnancy as well as humane and morally acceptable solutions to these problems.*

The Church's second major effort to support life is in the area of pastoral care. The Church intends to provide a moral perspective on abortion, which includes "accurate information regarding the nature of the act, its effects and far-reaching consequences, and [evidence] that abortion is a violation of God's laws of charity and justice." A further aspect of pastoral care is the establishment of programs and care for pregnant women.

The third major effort concerns public policy. The legislative program of the Church includes the following elements:

a. Passage of a constitutional amendment providing protection for the unborn child to the maximum degree possible.

b. Passage of federal and state laws and adoption of administrative policies that will restrict the practice of abortion as much as possible.

c. Continual research into and refinement and precise interpretation of *Roe* and *Doe* and subsequent court decisions.

d. Support for legislation that provides alternatives to abortion.

Excerpt from
Human Life in Our Day
Pastoral Letter

NCCB, November 15, 1968

Further Threats to Life

At this tense moment in our history when external wars and internal violence make us so conscious of death, an affirmation of the sanctity of human life by renewed attention to the family is imperative. Let society always be on the side of life. Let it never dictate, directly or indirectly, recourse to the prevention of life or to its destruction in any of its phases; neither let it require as a condition of economic assistance that any family yield conscientious determination of the number of its children to the decision of persons or agencies outside the family.

Stepped-up pressures for moral and legal acceptance of directly procured abortion make necessary pointed reference to this threat to the right to life. Reverence for life demands freedom from direct interruption of life once it is conceived. Conception initiates a process whose purpose is the realization of human personality. A human person, nothing more and nothing less, is always at issue once conception has taken place. We expressly repudiate any contradictory suggestion as contrary to Judaeo-Christian traditions inspired by love for life, and Anglo-Saxon legal traditions protective of life and the person.

Abortion brings to an end with irreversible finality both the existence and the destiny of the developing human person. Conscious of the inviolability of life, the Vatican Council II teaches:

> "God, the Lord of life, has conferred on man the surpassing ministry of safeguarding life, a ministry which must be fulfilled in a manner that is worthy of man. Therefore, from the moment of its conception life must be guarded with the greatest care while abortion and infanticide are unspeakable crimes" (*Gaudium et Spes*, 51).

The judgment of the Church on the evil of terminating life derives from the Christian awareness that men are not the masters but the ministers of life. Hence, the Council declares:

> ". . . whatever is opposed to life itself, such as any type of murder, genocide, abortion, euthanasia, or wilful self-destruction, whatever violates the integrity of the human person . . . all these things and others of their like are infamies indeed. They poison human society but they do more harm to those who practice them than those who suffer from the injury. Moreover, they are a supreme dishonor to the Creator" (*Gaudium et Spes*, 27).

Statement on Abortion

NCCB, April 17, 1969

In recent years there has been a growing concern for the dignity of human life. The crisis of conscience that has gripped the country over the war in Vietnam, the re-examination of the question of capital punishment, the ethical questions raised by newly developed skills in the transplantation of vital organs are all indications that our people continue to place a high value on human life. Moreover, our society recognizes that it must increasingly guarantee the basic rights of every person, particularly of those who are least able to defend themselves.

At the same time, we face a widespread effort to "liberalize" the present laws that generally prohibit abortion. Initial efforts to liberalize these laws focused on specific problem situations—some of which have already become less problematical due to scientific discovery and advance. During the past year the emphasis has begun to change, and we are now facing a determined effort to repeal totally all abortion laws—thereby resulting in abortion-on-demand.

In previous statements on this question we have drawn upon our Judaeo-Christian heritage of concern for the person and have stressed the intrinsic value of human life—a value that bridges the gap between man's temporal existence and his eternal destiny.

In a pastoral letter on Human Life in Our Day (November, 1968) we urged that "society always be on the side of life," that "it never dictate, directly or indirectly, recourse to the prevention of life or to its destruction in any of its phases." Our concern is heightened by the awareness that one of the dangers of a technological society is a tendency to adopt a limited view of man, to see man only for what he does or produces, and to overlook the source of man's dignity, the fact that he is made in the image of God, and that from the moment of his conception he is worthy of the full support of the human family of which he is a member.

Consequently, we have frequently affirmed as our own the teaching of the Second Vatican Council, that "whatever is opposed to life itself, such as any type of murder, genocide, abortion, euthanasia or wilful self-destruction, whatever violates the integrity of the human person . . . all these things and others of their like are infamies indeed. They poison human society but they do more harm to those who practice them than those who suffer from the injury. Moreover, they are a supreme dishonor to the Creator." (Pastoral Constitution on the Church in the Modern World, no. 27) At the same time, we have emphasized that society has an obligation to safeguard the life of every person from the very beginning of that life, and to perfect a legal-political system that assures protection to the individual and the well-being of the community.

We restate with strong conviction and growing concern our opposition to abortion. In so doing, we do not urge one ethical conviction as the sole basis of public policy, but we articulate the concerns that are also held by persons of other faiths and by specialists in the fields of medicine, law and the social sciences.

Fully aware of problem situations that may exist at times, such as illegitimacy, great emotional stress, possible disadvantage for the child after birth, we find no evidence that easy abortion laws will solve these problems. In fact, the termination of life in these particular situations violates our whole legal heritage, one that has always protected the right to life. Moreover, it allows for an extension of the principle that may well endanger the lives of persons who are senile, incurably ill, or unable fully to exercise all their faculties.

We strongly urge a renewed positive attitude toward life and a new commitment to its protection and support. We affirm our social responsibility, together with all society, to bring encouragement, understanding and support to the victims of rape, to intensify our scientific investigation into the causes and cures of maternal disease and fetal abnormality, and to provide to all women adequate education and material sustenance to choose motherhood responsibly and freely in accord with our basic commitment to the sanctity of life.

We are certain that respect for human dignity and the reverence for human life are such widely shared values in our society that the discussion by lawyers, doctors, ethicians, social scientists and all concerned citizens of ethical questions like abortion will lead to a deeper understanding of the eminent value and inviolability of human life.

Statement on Abortion

NCCB, April 22, 1970

Last year, we stated our strong opposition to ongoing efforts to strike down laws prohibiting abortion. Our defense of human life is rooted in the biblical prohibition, "Thou shalt not kill." Regrettably, there has been a radical turn of events during this past year, and a new effort has been directed to the total repeal of all such laws. At the same time, an effort has been mounted in the courts to have such laws declared unconstitutional.

Therefore we speak again on this important issue of public policy, addressing ourselves to the Catholic community and to all our fellow citizens. For the question of abortion is a moral problem transcending any particular sectarian approach. Our opposition to abortion derives from our conviction that whatever is opposed to life is a violation of man's inherent rights, a position that has a strong basis in the history of American law. The U.S. Bill of Rights guarantees the right to life to every American, and the U.N. Declaration on the Rights of the Child, which our nation endorses, affirms that the child, because of his dependent status, should be accorded a special protection under the law before as well as after birth. (U.N. General Assembly, November 20, 1959)

In light of the attempts to remove all prohibition of abortion from our legal system, the life of the innocent unborn child is no longer given universal protection in the laws of our land. Moreover, the absence of all legal restraint promotes the acceptance of abortion as a convenient way for a woman to terminate the life of her child and the responsibilities that she has as its mother.

The implications of this proposed change in legal philosophy are enormous. Once we allow the taking of innocent human life in the earliest stages of its development for the sake of convenience, how can we logically protect human life at any other point, once that life becomes a burden?

The assertion is made that a woman has a right not to be forced to bear a child against her will, but when a woman is already pregnant, this right must be considered in light of the child's right to life, the woman's responsibilities as its mother, and the rights and responsibilities of the child's father. The life of the unborn child is a human life. The destruction of any human life is not a private matter, but the concern of every responsible citizen.

We remain convinced that human life is a priceless gift, and our pastoral duty prompts us to reaffirm that "God, the Lord of life, has conferred on men the surpassing ministry of safeguarding life, a ministry which must be fulfilled in a manner which is worthy of man. Therefore from the moment of its conception life must be guarded with the greatest care, while abortion and infanticide are unspeakable crimes." (Pastoral Constitution on the Church in the Modern World, no. 51)

Once again, we declare our determination to seek solutions to the problems that lead some women to consider abortion. We pledge our efforts to do all that is possible to remove the social stigma that is visited on the woman who is pregnant out of wedlock, as well as on her child. We also pledge the facilities and the efforts of our Church agencies to provide counseling and understanding to the woman who faces a difficult pregnancy. At the same time, we are encouraged by the scientific advance of recent decades that has already provided us with ways to support and maintain the life and health of the mother and the development of the child in the womb.

Finally, we are aware that the value of human life is not exclusively a Catholic concern. Many Americans agonize over the loss of life involved in modern warfare, the serious ethical questions raised by recent scientific and surgical advances, the implications of pollution on our environment and the long-range effects of drug use. But safeguarding the life of all men requires safeguarding the life of every individual, for our hold on life itself is only as strong as the weakest link in our system of law.

Declaration on Abortion

NCCB, November 18, 1970

In fulfillment of our teaching responsibility as bishops, once again, we speak of the grave evil of abortion. Since the first centuries of the Church's existence abortion has been considered the destruction of human life. Nothing permits us to judge it differently now. Scientists tell us that, from the moment of conception, the child is a complex and rapidly-growing being, endowed with the characteristics of human life. Although dependent on a privileged environment for development, the child in the womb has a life of its own.

The fundamental principle has been solemnly recalled by the Second Vatican Council:

> "For God, the Lord of life, has conferred on men the surpassing ministry of safeguarding life—a ministry which must be fulfilled in a manner worthy of man. Therefore from the moment of its conception life must be guarded with the greatest care, while abortion and infanticide are unspeakable crimes." (Pastoral Constitution on the Church in the Modern World, no. 51.)

The function of law is to support and protect the rights of every person. The unborn child's civil rights have consistently been recognized by American law. Proposed liberalization of the present abortion laws ignores the most basic of these rights, the right to life itself.

The child in the womb is human. Abortion is an unjust destruction of a human life and morally that is murder. Society has no right to destroy this life. Even the expectant mother has no such right. The law must establish every possible protection for the child before and after birth.

We remind Catholic physicians and nurses that regardless of changing laws, direct abortion is always morally wrong. Catholic hospitals and their staffs must witness to the sanctity of life by respecting and defending human life, before birth as well as afterwards. Theirs ought to be the highest standards possible in the total care both of mother and child.

The evil of abortion is not exclusively the responsibility of one person. Society is also often guilty of a lack of compassion and justice for the expectant mother. In fulfillment of its responsibility, society should do all that is possible to provide necessary medical and other assistance. We urge government and all voluntary agencies including church-sponsored institutions to intensify and broaden counseling and care for expectant mothers who otherwise may be tempted to resort to solutions contrary to God's law.

Population and the American Future: A Response

NCCB, April 13, 1972

The Commission on Population Growth and the American Future has recently issued a report in which it makes recommendations for limiting further population growth in the United States.[1] As religious leaders—but also as concerned Americans—we wish to record our objections to this report.

Population growth is more than a matter of statistics. In fact, population decisions reflect society's total view of man. We repeat our concern that "one of the dangers of a technological society is a tendency to adopt a limited view of man, to see man only for what he does or produces and to overlook the source of man's dignity, the fact that he is made in the image of God, and that from the moment of conception, he is worthy of the full support of the human family of which he is a member."[2] The Commission's preoccupation with limiting population growth has led to a confined view of the inherent value of every person, and a narrow vision of man's ability to live in peace, justice and charity with his fellow man.

We take serious exception to the general approach taken by this Commission—that is, to equate quality of life simply with a lower rate of population growth, on the grounds that a smaller number of people will result in greater affluence and material comfort for all. Experience has already taught us that our social problems—poverty, disease, injustice and violence—are not solved merely by population decrease, but require a change of heart and a re-ordering of priorities for the entire nation.

Population growth and distribution are serious topics. They deserve careful study and discussion by all Americans. In order to safeguard human rights and the dignity of man, we reaffirm the following principles.

1. "The well-being of the individual person and of human and Christian society is intimately linked with the healthy condition of that community produced by marriage and the family."[3]

2. "It is for the parents to decide, with full knowledge of the matter, on the number of their children, taking into account their responsibilities towards

---

[1] *Population and the American Future,* 1972, U.S. Govt. Printing Office, Washington, D.C. (The Commission on Population Growth and the American Future was established by Congress in March, 1970, to conduct a two-year study of population growth in the United States and its foreseeable social consequences. The Commission completed its work in March, 1972, with the issuance of its final report.)

[2] NCCB Statement on Abortion, April 17, 1969

God, themselves, the children they have already brought into the world, and the community to which they belong."[4]

3. "It is certain that public authorities can intervene, within the limit of their competence, by favoring the availability of appropriate information and by adopting suitable measures, provided that these be in conformity with the moral law and that they respect the rightful freedom of married couples."[5]

4. "Abortion, directly willed and procured, even if for therapeutic reasons, is to be absolutely excluded as a licit means of regulating births."[6]

Many of the recommendations of the Commission cannot be harmonized with our moral convictions, nor with the values and beliefs of many of our fellow Americans. Without attempting a comprehensive analysis of the Commission's Report, we cite the following instances.

The Commission recommends nationwide abortion-on-demand as a means of eliminating the unwanted child, "particularly when the child's prospects for a life of dignity and self-fulfillment are limited." This is an immoral and dangerous principle. What constitutes self-fulfillment? How does one arrive at the conclusion that another person's prospects for a life of dignity and self-fulfillment are in fact limited? Who is to make such decisions, and on what basis, especially when the conclusion leads to the death of the child? Furthermore, if this thinking is extended to other persons whose prospects for a life of dignity and self-fulfillment are limited, the lives of the aged, the sick, and the mentally or physically disadvantaged are thereby endangered. This argument—drawn to its ultimate conclusions—could also be used to discriminate against racial and social minorities.

We re-state our teaching that "from the moment of its conception life must be guarded with the greatest care, while abortion and infanticide are unspeakable crimes."[7] We are opposed to the continuing efforts in our society to deprive the unborn child of legal protection for his or her right to life. We also reject the reasoning of some courts that have decided that the right to privacy outweighs the child's right to life.

The Commission makes a series of recommendations that lead to a population policy. However, policies affecting population—as well as the administrative guidelines of government agencies—must always respect the well-being and stability of the family unit, the free and voluntary decision-making power of parents, and the good of society. In point of fact, a population policy may be only a positive part of a broader policy that is calculated to

---

[3] *Constitution on the Church in the Modern World,* #47
[4] *On the Development of Peoples,* Paul VI, # 37, Cf also, *Constitution on the Church in the Modern World,* #87
[5] *On the Development of Peoples,* Paul VI, #37
[6] *Of Human Life,* Paul VI, #14
[7] *Constitution on the Church in the Modern World,* #51

support and strengthen family life. We find that the report of the Commission on Population Growth and the American Future is beset with inconsistencies, as the conscientious dissent of individual Commission members records.

Because of continuing efforts to deprive the unborn child of legal protection for the right to life, we propose a Week of Prayer and Study focusing on the sanctity of human life, and the many threats to human life in our world, including war, violence, hunger and poverty. This Week will be held during October 1972, in all dioceses in the United States, and it will be initiated by the Sunday liturgy. Throughout that Week we will urge that educational programs be conducted on the dignity of human life and the responsibility of society to protect all its members—the unborn child, and also the aged, sick and disadvantaged. In this endeavor we will seek the counsel and advice of scientists and legal scholars, and we will invite the participation and cooperation of all concerned Americans, especially those who have demonstrated deep ethical convictions concerning the sacredness of human life and the good of society.

Pastoral Message of the Administrative Committee

NCCB, February 13, 1973

Almighty God, the Creator of the world, has imprinted in the heart of man a law which calls him to do good and avoid evil. To obey this law is the dignity of man, according to it he will be judged (cf. *Constitution on the Church in the Modern World*, no. 16). In the encyclical letter, *Peace on Earth*, Pope John XXIII spoke of how nations can achieve justice and order by adhering to God's law:

> Any human society, if it is to be well-ordered and productive, must lay down as a foundation this principle, namely, that every human being is a person, that is, his nature is endowed with intelligence and free will. By virtue of this, he has rights and duties of his own, flowing directly and simultaneously from his very nature. These rights are therefore universal, inviolable and inalienable (*Peace on Earth*, no. 9).

... Every man has the right to life, to bodily integrity, and to the means
which are necessary and suitable for the proper development of life (*Peace
on Earth,* no. 11).

The Supreme Court, in its recent decision striking down the laws of Texas
and Georgia regulating abortion, has stated that the unborn child is not a
person in the terms of the Fourteenth Amendment. Moreover, the Court held
that the right of privacy encompasses a woman's decision to terminate a
pregnancy, although the right of privacy is not an absolute right, and is not
explicitly mentioned in the Constitution. In effect, the Court is saying that
the right of privacy takes precedence over the right to life. This opinion of the
Court fails to protect the most basic human right—the right to life.
Therefore, we reject this decision of the Court because, as John XXIII says,
"If any government does not acknowledge the rights of man or violates them,
... its orders completely lack juridical force." (*Peace on Earth,* no. 61)

The Court has apparently failed to understand the scientific evidence
clearly showing that the fetus is an individual human being whose pre-natal
development is but the first phase of the long and continuous process of
human development that begins at conception and terminates at death.
Thus, the seven judge majority went on to declare that the life of the unborn
child is not to be considered of any compelling value prior to viability, i.e.,
during the first six or seven months of pregnancy, and of only questionable
value during the remaining months. Ultimately this means that the fetus,
that is, the unborn child, belongs to an inferior class of human beings whose
God-given rights will no longer be protected under the Constitution of the
United States.

We find that this majority opinion of the Court is wrong and is entirely
contrary to the fundamental principles of morality. Catholic teaching holds
that, regardless of the circumstances of its origin, human life is valuable
from conception to death because God is the Creator of each human being,
and because mankind has been redeemed by Jesus Christ (cf. *Peace on
Earth,* nos. 9 and 10). No court, no legislative body, no leader of government, can legitimately assign less value to some human life. Thus, the laws
that conform to the opinion of the Court are immoral laws, in opposition to
God's plan of creation and to the Divine Law which prohibits the destruction
of human life at any point of its existence. Whenever a conflict arises between
the law of God and any human law, we are held to follow God's law.

Furthermore, we believe, with millions of our fellow Americans, that our
American law and way of life comprise an obvious and certain recognition of
the law of God, and that our legal system is both based in it, and must conform to it. The Declaration of Independence holds that all men are endowed
by "their Creator with certain unalienable rights," among which are "life,
liberty and the pursuit of happiness." The Preamble to the Constitution
establishes as one goal of the people of the United States "to secure the bless-

ing of liberty to ourselves and to our posterity." Without the right to life, no true liberty is possible.

The basic human rights guaranteed by our American laws are, therefore, unalienable because their source is not man-made legislation but the Creator of all mankind, Almighty God. No right is more fundamental than the right to life itself and no innocent human life already begun can be deliberately terminated without offense to the Author of all life. Thus, there can be no moral acceptance of the recent United States Supreme Court decision which professes to legalize abortion.

In light of these reasons, we reject the opinion of the U.S. Supreme Court as erroneous, unjust, and immoral. Because of our responsibilities as authentic religious leaders and teachers, we make the following pastoral applications:

(1) Catholics must oppose abortion as an immoral act. No one is obliged to obey any civil law that may require abortion.

(2) Abortion is and has always been considered a serious violation of God's law. Those who obtain an abortion, those who persuade others to have an abortion, and those who perform the abortion procedures are guilty of breaking God's law. Moreover, in order to emphasize the special evil of abortion, under Church law, those who undergo or perform an abortion place themselves in a state of excommunication.

(3) As tragic and sweeping as the Supreme Court decision is, it is still possible to create a pro-life atmosphere in which all, and notably physicians and health care personnel, will influence their peers to see a value in all human life, including that of the unborn child during the entire course of pregnancy. We hope that doctors will retain an ethical concern for the welfare of both the mother and the unborn child, and will not succumb to social pressure in performing abortions.

(4) We urge the legal profession to articulate and safeguard the rights of fathers of unborn children, rights that have not been upset by this Supreme Court opinion.

(5) We praise the efforts of pro-life groups and many other concerned Americans and encourage them to:

(a) Offer positive alternatives to abortion for distressed pregnant women;

(b) Pursue protection for institutions and individuals to refuse on the basis of conscience to engage in abortion procedure;

(c) Combat the general permissiveness legislation can engender;

(d) Assure the most restrictive interpretation of the Court's opinion at the state legislative level;

(e) Set in motion the machinery needed to assure legal and constitutional conformity to the basic truth that the unborn child is a "person" in every sense of the term from the time of conception.

Bringing about a reversal of the Supreme Court's decision and achieving respect for unborn human life in our society will require unified and persistent efforts. But we must begin now—in our churches, schools and homes, as well as in the larger civic community—to instill reverence for life at all stages. We take as our mandate the words of the Book of Deuteronomy: *I set before you life or death ... Choose life, then, that you and your descendants may live ...*

Statement of the Administrative Committee on the Anti-abortion Amendment

NCCB, September 18, 1973

The Administrative Committee of the National Conference of Catholic Bishops reaffirms its commitment to a constitutional amendment in defense of unborn human life. While abortion transcends legal and constitutional issues and involves fundamental questions of individual and social morality, a constitutional amendment is now the only viable means to correct the disastrous legal situation created by the Supreme Court's rulings on abortion.

We therefore urge early hearings in the Senate and House on pending constitutional amendments to protect the unborn. We also urge pro-life supporters to call on their senators and representatives to support congressional hearings at an early date.

We are strongly encouraged by the fact that numerous pro-life amendments have been introduced in both houses of Congress. We commend the many members of Congress who have sponsored such amendments. In view of the evidence of widespread popular and congressional support for an amendment, we feel that prompt and positive congressional consideration is in order.

Furthermore, independent of the hearings, we recognize the need for grassroots pro-life organization on behalf of such an amendment. Local action can render an essential service by example, by public information programs on the subject of abortion, by contacts with congressmen, and by encouragement to state legislatures to petition Congress—as several have done—on behalf of a constitutional amendment. Men and women of good will, regardless of creed, who support the cause of human life must prepare now to make an effective, united, long-term effort.

The complex legal issues relating to an amendment are now under intensive and continuing study by the bishops' conference and by the legal staff and advisors of the United States Catholic Conference. At present we do not single out any specific pending amendment. Our detailed views regarding the wording of an amendent will be stated at an early date, in the context of congressional hearings or some other appropriate forum. Our immediate concern, however, is that Congress take action to insure prompt and favorable consideration of this urgent matter and that pro-life individuals and groups prepare now for the supportive action which will be necessary to win congressional approval and ultimate ratification of an amendment.

Resolution on the Pro-Life Constitutional Amendment

NCCB, November 13, 1973

On repeated occasions since January 22, 1973, offices of the National Conference of Catholic Bishops have expressed opposition to the Supreme Court's ruling on abortion. Abortion, the destruction of a living human being in the womb of its mother, is morally wrong. No law or judicial opinion can change the moral judgment. We are convinced that the decision of the

Supreme Court is wrong, and must be reversed. The only certain way to repair effectively the damage perpetrated by the Court's opinions is to amend the Constitution to provide clearly and definitively a constitutional base for legal protection of unborn human beings. A number of constitutional amendments have been introduced in Congress, but to date, no definite action has been taken.

We wish to state once again, as emphatically as possible, our endorsement of and support for a constitutional amendment that will protect the life of the unborn. We urge Congress to conduct hearings and move with all deliberate speed to pass a pro-life amendment. We reaffirm the statement of the NCCB Administrative Committee of September 18, 1973.

At the same time, we remind our people that the passage of the amendment will require concerted and continued efforts on their part to convice the Congress and the American people of its absolute necessity. Specifically, we urge public information programs and petitions to state legislatures to memorialize Congress in behalf of a pro-life amendment. In all of this, well-planned and coordinated political organization by citizens at the national, state and local levels is of highest importance. Our system of government requires citizen participation, and in this case, there is a *moral imperative* for political activity.

Thus, we commend and encourage pro-life groups that have already initiated programs of political action to bring about congressional action on a constitutional amendment. We urge continued and unified efforts directed toward convincing the Congress to hold hearings at the earliest possible date. We especially invite the collaboration of other religious leaders in pursuing a pro-life constitutional amendment.

Finally, we wish to make it clear beyond doubt to our fellow citizens that we consider the passage of a pro-life constitutional amendment a priority of the highest order, one to which we are committed by our determination to uphold the dignity of the human being and by our conviction that this nation must provide protection for the life, liberty and pursuit of happiness for all human beings, before as well as after birth.

Pastoral Plan for Pro-Life Activities

NCCB, November 20, 1975

> All should be persuaded that human life and the task of transmitting it are not realities bound up with this world alone. Hence they cannot be measured or perceived only in terms of it, but always have a bearing on the eternal destiny of men. . . . For God, the Lord of life, has conferred on men the surpassing ministry of safeguarding life in a manner which is worthy of man. Therefore from the moment of its conception life must be guarded with the greatest care, while abortion and infanticide are unspeakable crimes.
>
> *Constitution on the Church*
> *in the Modern World*

Respect for human life has been gradually declining in our society during the past decade. To some degree this reflects a secularizing trend and a rejection of moral imperatives based on belief in God and His plan for creation. It also reflects a tendency for individuals to give primary attention to what is personally rewarding and satisfying to them, to the exclusion of responsible concern for the well-being of other persons and society. These trends, along with others, have resulted in laws and judicial decisions which deny or ignore basic human rights and moral responsibilities for the protection and promotion of the common good. In this category are efforts to establish permissive abortion laws, the abortion decisions of the United States Supreme Court in 1973 denying any effective legal protection to the unborn child, and the growing attempts to legitimatize positive euthanasia through so-called "death with dignity" laws.

In the Declaration of Independence, our Founding Fathers point to the right to life as the first of the inalienable rights given by the Creator.

In fulfillment of our pastoral responsibilities, the members of the National Conference of Catholic Bishops have repeatedly affirmed that human life is a precious gift from God; that each person who receives this gift has responsibilities toward God, toward self and toward others; and that society, through its laws and social institutions, must protect and sustain human life at every stage of its existence. Recognition of the dignity of the human person, made in the image of God, lies at the very heart of our individual and social duty to respect human life.

In this Pastoral Plan we hope to focus attention on the pervasive threat to human life arising from the present situation of permissive abortion. Basic human rights are violated in many ways: by abortion and euthanasia, by injustice and the denial of equality to certain groups of persons, by some forms of human experimentation, by neglect of the underprivileged and disadvantaged who deserve the concern and support of the entire society. Indeed, the denial of the God-given right to life is one aspect of a larger problem. But it is unlikely that efforts to protect other rights will be ultimately successful if life itself is continually diminished in value.

In focusing attention on the sanctity of human life, therefore, we hope to generate a greater respect for the life of each person in our society. We are confident that greater respect for human life will result from continuing the public discussion of abortion and from efforts to shape our laws so as to protect the life of all persons, including the unborn.

Thus this Pastoral Plan seeks to activate the pastoral resources of the Church in three major efforts:

1. an educational/public information effort to inform, clarify and deepen understanding of the basic issues;
2. a pastoral effort addressed to the specific needs of women with problems related to pregnancy and to those who have had or have taken part in an abortion;
3. a public policy effort directed toward the legislative, judicial and administrative areas so as to insure effective legal protection for the right to life.

This Pastoral Plan is addressed to and calls upon all Church-sponsored or identifiably Catholic national, regional, diocesan and parochial organizations and agencies to pursue the three-fold effort. This includes ongoing dialogue and cooperation between the NCCB/USCC on the one hand, and priests, religious and lay persons, individually and collectively, on the other hand. In a special way we invite the continued cooperation of national Catholic organizations.

At the same time, we urge Catholics in various professional fields to discuss these issues with their colleagues and to carry the dialogue into their own professional organizations. In similar fashion, we urge those in research and academic life to present the Church's position on a wide range of topics that visibly express her commitment to respect for life at every stage and in every condition. Society's responsibility to insure and protect human rights demands that the right to life be recognized and protected as antecedent to and the condition of all other rights.

Dialogue is most important—and has already proven highly fruitful—among churches and religious groups. Efforts should continue at ecumenical consultation and dialogue with Judaism and other Christian bodies, and also with those who have no specific ecclesial allegiance. Dialogue among scholars in the field of ethics is a most important part of this interfaith effort.

The most effective structures for pastoral action are in the diocese and the parish. While recognizing the roles of national, regional and statewide groupings, this Plan places its primary emphasis on the roles of diocesan organizations and the parish community. Thus, the resources of the diocese and parish become most important in its implementation.

I. Public Information/Education Program

In order to deepen respect for human life and heighten public opposition to permissive abortion, a two-fold educational effort presenting the case for the sanctity of life from conception onwards is required.

The first aspect, a public information effort, is directed to the general public. It creates awareness of the threats to human dignity inherent in a permissive abortion policy, and the need to correct the present situation by establishing legal safeguards for the right to life. It gives the abortion issue continued visibility, and sensitizes the many people who have only general perceptions of the issue but very little by way of firm conviction or commitment. The public information effort is important to inform the public discussion, and it proves that the Church is serious about and committed to its announced long-range pro-life effort. It is accomplished in a variety of ways, such as accurate reporting of newsworthy events, the issuance of public statements, testimony on legislative issues, letters to editors.

The second aspect, an intensive long-range education effort, leads people to a clearer understanding of the issues, to firm conviction, and to commitment. It is part of the Church's essential responsibility that it carry forward such an effort, directed primarily to the Catholic community. Recognizing the value of legal, medical and sociological arguments, the primary and ultimately most compelling arguments must be theological and moral. Respect for life must be seen in the context of God's love for mankind reflected in creation and redemption and man's relationship to God and to other members of the human family. The Church's opposition to abortion is based on Christian teaching on the dignity of the human person, and the responsibility to proclaim and defend basic human rights, especially the right to life.

This intensive education effort should present the scientific information on the humanity of the unborn child and the continuity of human growth and development throughout the months of fetal existence; the responsibility and necessity for society to safeguard the life of the child at every stage of its existence; the problems that may exist for a women during pregnancy; and more humane and morally acceptable solutions to these problems.

The more intensive educational effort should be carried on by all who participate in the Church's educational ministry, notably:

—Priests and religious, exercising their teaching responsibility in the pulpit, in other teaching assignments, and through parish programs.

—All Church-sponsored or identifiably Catholic organizations, national, regional, diocesan and parochial, carrying on continuing education efforts that emphasize the moral prohibition of abortion and the reasons for carrying this teaching into the public policy area.

—Schools, CCD and other Church-sponsored educational agencies providing moral teaching, bolstered by medical, legal and sociological data, in the schools, etc. The USCC Department of Education might serve as a catalyst and resource for the dioceses.

—Church-related social service and health agencies carrying on continuing education efforts through seminars and other appropriate programs, and by publicizing programs and services offering alternatives to abortion.

Although the primary purpose of the intensive educational program is the development of pro-life attitudes and the determined avoidance of abortion by each person, the program must extend to other issues that involve support of human life: there must be internal consistency in the pro-life commitment.

The annual Respect Life Program sets the abortion problem in the context of other issues where human life is endangered or neglected, such as the problems facing the family, youth, the aging, the mentally retarded, as well as specific issues such as proverty, war, population control, and euthanasia. This program is helpful to parishes in calling attention to specific problems and providing program formats and resources.

II. Pastoral Care

The Church's pastoral effort is rooted in and manifests her faith commitment. Underlying every part of our program is the need for prayer and sacrifice. In building the house of respect for life, we labor in vain without God's merciful help.

Three facets of the Church's program of pastoral care deserve particular attention.

1) Moral Guidance and Motivation

Accurate information regarding the nature of an act and freedom from coercion are necessary in order to make responsible moral decisions. Choosing what is morally good also requires motivation. The Church has a unique responsibility to transmit the teaching of Christ and to provide moral principles consistent with that teaching. In regard to abortion, the Church should provide accurate information regarding the nature of the act, its effects and far-reaching consequences, and should show that abortion is a violation of

God's laws of charity and justice. In many instances, the decision to do what is in conformity with God's law will be the ultimate determinant of the moral choice.

2) *Service and Care for Women and Unborn Children*

Respect for human life motivates individuals and groups to reach out to those with special needs. Programs of service and care should be available to provide women with alternate options to abortion. Specifically, these programs should include:

—adequate education and material sustenance for women so that they may chose motherhood responsibly and freely in accord with a basic commitment to the sanctity of life;

—nutritional, pre-natal, childbirth and post-natal care for the mother, and nutritional and pediatric care for the child throughout the first year of life;

—intensified scientific investigation into the causes and cures of maternal disease and/or fetal abnormality;

—continued development of genetic counseling and gene therapy centers and neo-natal intensive care facilities;

—extension of adoption and foster care facilities to those who need them;

—pregnancy counseling centers that provide advice, encouragement and support for every women who faces difficulties related to pregnancy;

—counseling services and opportunities for continuation of education for unwed mothers;

—special understanding, encouragement and support for victims of rape;

—continued efforts to remove the social stigma that is visited on the women who is pregnant out of wedlock and on her child.

Many of these services have been and will continue to be provided by Church-sponsored health care and social service agencies, involving the dedicated efforts of professionals and volunteers. Cooperation with other private agencies and increased support in the quest for government assistance in many of these areas are further extensions of the long-range effort.

3) *Reconciliation*

The Church is both a means and an agent of reconciliation. As a spiritual entity, the Church reconciles men and women to God. As a human community, the Church pursues the task of reconciling men and women with one another and with the entire community. Thus all of the faithful have the duty of promoting reconciliation.

Sacramentally, the Church reconciles the sinner through the Sacrament of Penance, thereby restoring the individual to full sacramental participation. The work of reconciliation is also continually accomplished in celebrating and participating in the Eucharist. Finally, the effects of the Church's reconciling efforts are found in the full support of the Christian community and the renewal of Christian life that results from prayer, the pursuit of virtue and continued sacramental participation.

Granting that the grave sin of abortion is symptomatic of many human problems, which often remain unsolved for the individual woman, it is important that we realize that God's mercy is always available and without limit, that the Christian life can be restored and renewed through the sacraments, and that union with God can be accomplished despite the problems of human existence.

III. Legislative/Public Policy Effort

In recent years there has been a growing realization throughout the world that protecting and promoting the inviolable rights of persons are essential duties of civil authority, and that the maintenance and protection of human rights are primary purposes of law. As Americans, and as religious leaders, we have been committed to governance by a system of law that protects the rights of individuals and maintains the common good. As our founding fathers believed, we hold that all law is ultimately based on Divine Law, and that a just system of law cannot be in conflict with the law of God.

Abortion is a specific issue that highlights the relationship between morality and law. As a human mechanism, law may not be able fully to articulate the moral imperative, but neither can legal philosophy ignore the moral order. The abortion decisions of the United States Supreme Court (January 22, 1973) violate the moral order, and have disrupted the legal process which previously attempted to safeguard the rights of unborn children. A comprehensive pro-life legislative program must therefore include the following elements:

a) Passage of a constitutional amendment providing protection for the unborn child to the maximum degree possible.

b) Passage of federal and state laws and adoption of administrative policies that will restrict the practice of abortion as much as possible.

c) Continual research into and refinement and precise interpretation of *Roe* and *Doe* and subsequent court decisions.

d) Support for legislation that provides alternatives to abortion.

Accomplishment of this aspect of this Pastoral Plan will undoubtedly require well-planned and coordinated political action by citizens at the national, state and local levels. This activity is not simply the responsibility of Catholics, nor should it be limited to Catholic groups or agencies. It calls for widespread cooperation and collaboration. As citizens of this democracy, we encourage the appropriate political action to achieve these legislative goals. As leaders of a religious institution in this society, we see a moral imperative for such political activity.

MEANS OF IMPLEMENTATION OF PROGRAM

The challenge to restore respect for human life in our society is a task of the Church that reaches out through all institutions, agencies and organizations. Diverse tasks and various goals are to be achieved. The following represents a systematic organization and allocation of the Church's resources of people, institutions and finances which can be activated at various levels to restore respect for human life, and insure protection of the right to life of the unborn.

1. State Coordinating Committee

A. It is assumed that overall coordination in each state will be the responsibility of the State Catholic Conference or its equivalent. Where a State Catholic Conference is in process of formation or does not exist, bishops' representatives from each diocese might be appointed as the core members of the State Coordinating Committee.

B. The State Coordinating Committee will be comprised of the Director of the State Catholic Conference and the diocesan Pro-Life coordinators. At this level it would be valuable to have one or more persons who are knowledgeable about public traditions, mores and attitudes and are experienced in legislative activity. This might be the Public Affairs Specialist referred to under the Diocesan Pro-Life Committee, or, e.g., an individual with prior professional experience in legislative or governmental service. In any case, it should be someone with a practical understanding of contemporary political techniques.

C. The primary purposes of the State Coordinating Committee are:

—to monitor the political trends in the state and their implications for the abortion effort;

—to coordinate the efforts of the various dioceses; and to evaluate progress in the dioceses and congressional districts;

—to provide counsel regarding the specific political relationships within the various parties at the state level.

2. The Diocesan Pro-Life Committee

a) *General Purpose*—The purpose of the Committee is to coordinate groups and activities within the diocese (to restore respect for human life), particularly efforts to effect passage of a constitutional amendment to protect the unborn child. In its coordinating role, the Committee will rely on information and direction from the Bishops' Pro-Life Office and the National Committee for a Human Life Amendment. The Committee will act through the Diocesan Pro-Life Director, who is appointed by the Bishop to direct pro-life efforts in the diocese.

b) *Membership*

—Diocesan Pro-Life Director (Bishop's Representative)

—Respect Life Coordinator

—Liaison with State Catholic Conference

—Public Affairs Advisor

—Representatives of Diocesan Agencies
 (Priests, Religious, Lay Organizations)

—Legal Advisor—Representative of Pro-Life Groups

—Representatives of Parish Pro-Life Committees

—Congressional District Representative(s)

c) *Objectives:*

1. Provide direction and coordination of diocesan and parish education/ information efforts and maintain working relationship with all groups involved in congressional district activity.

2. Promote and assist in the development of those groups, particularly voluntary groups involved in pregnancy counseling, which provide al-

ternatives and assistance to women who have problems related to pregnancy.

3. Encourage the development of "grassroots" political action organizations.

4. Maintain communications with National Committee for a Human Life Amendment in regard to federal activity, so as to provide instantaneous information concerning local Senators and Representatives.

5. Maintain a local public information effort directed to press and media. Include vigilance in regard to public media, seek "equal time," etc.

6. Develop close relationships with each Senator or Representative.

3. The Parish Pro-Life Committee

The Parish Pro-Life Committee should include a delegate from the Parish Council, representatives of various adult and youth parish organizations, members of local Knights of Columbus Councils, Catholic Daughters of America Chapters and other similar organizations.

Objectives:

a) Sponsor and conduct intensive education programs touching all groups within the parish, including schools and religious education efforts.

b) Promote and sponsor pregnancy counseling units and other alternatives to abortion.

c) Through ongoing public information programs generate public awareness of the continuing effort to obtain a constitutional amendment. The NCCB, the National Committee for a Human Life Amendment and the State and Diocesan Coordinating Committees should have access to every congressional district for information, consultation and coordination of action. A chairperson should be designated in each district who will coordinate the efforts of parish pro-life groups, K of C groups, etc., and seek ways of cooperating with non-sectarian pro-life groups, including right-to-life organizations. In each district, the parishes will provide one basic resource, and the clergy will have an active role in the overall effort.

d) Prudently convince others—Catholics and non-Catholics—of the reasons for the necessity of a constitutional amendment to provide a base for legal protection for the unborn.

4. The Pro-Life Effort in the Congressional District

Passage of a constitutional amendment depends ultimately on persuading members of Congress to vote in favor of such a proposal. This effort at persuasion is part of the democratic process, and is carried on most effectively in the congressional district or state from which the representative is elected. Essentially, this effort demands ongoing public information activity and careful and detailed organization. Thus it is absolutely necessary to encourage the development in each congressional district of an identifiable, tightly-knit and well-organized pro-life unit. This unit can be described as a public interest group or a citizens' lobby. No matter what it is called:

a) its task is essentially political, that is, to *organize people* to help persuade the elected representatives; and

b) its range of action is limited, that is, it is focused on passing a constitutional amendment.

As such, the congressional district pro-life group differs from the diocesan, regional or parish pro-life coordinator or committee, whose task is pedagogic and motivational, not simply political, and whose range of action includes a variety of efforts calculated to reverse the present atmosphere of permissiveness with respect to abortion. Moreover, it is an agency of the citizens, operated, controlled and financed by these same citizens. *It is not an agency of the Church, nor is it operated, controlled, or financed by the Church.*

The congressional district pro-life action group should be bipartisan, nonsectarian, inclined toward political action. It is complementary to denominational efforts, to professional groups, to pregnancy counseling and assistance groups.

Each congressional district should have a chairperson who may serve as liaison with the Diocesan Coordinating Committee. In dioceses with many congressional districts, this may be arranged through a regional representation structure.

Objectives of the Congressional District Pro-Life Group

1. To conduct a continuing public information effort to persuade all elected officials and potential candidates that abortion must be legally restricted.

2. To counterbalance propaganda efforts opposed to a constitutional amendment.

3. To persuade all residents in the congressional district that permissive abortion is harmful to society and that some restriction is necessary.

4. To persuade all residents that a constitutional amendment is necessary as a first step toward legally restricting abortion.

5. To convince all elected officials and potential candidates that "the abortion issue" will not go away and that their position on it will be subject to continuing public scrutiny.

6. To enlist sympathetic supporters who will collaborate in persuading others.

7. To enlist those who are generally supportive so that they may be called upon when needed to communicate to the elected officials.

8. To elect members of their own group or active sympathizers to specific posts in all local party organizations.

9. To set up a telephone network that will enable the committee to take immediate action when necessary.

10. To maintain an informational file on the pro-life position of every elected official and potential candidate.

11. To work for qualified candidates who will vote for a constitutional amendment, and other pro-life issues.

12. To maintain liaison with all denominational leaders (pastors) and all other pro-life groups in the district.

This type of activity can be generated and coordinated by a small, dedicated and politically alert group. It will need some financial support, but its greatest need is the commitment of other groups who realize the importance of its purposes, its potential for achieving those purposes, and the absolute necessity of working with the group to attain the desired goals.

Conclusion

The challenges facing American society as a result of the legislative and judicial endorsement of permissive abortion are enormous. But the Church and the individual Catholics must not avoid the challenge. Although the process of restoring respect for human life at every stage of existence may be demanding and prolonged, it is an effort which both requires and merits courage, patience, and determination. In every age the Church has faced unique challenges calling forth faith and courage. In our time and society, restoring respect for human life and establishing a system of justice which protects the most basic human rights are both a challenge and an opportunity whereby the Church proclaims her commitment to Christ's teaching on human dignity and the sanctity of the human person.

Birth Control

In a 1966 statement, The Government and Birth Control, *the American bishops vigorously protested the tendency of governments to persuade, and even to coerce, the underprivileged to practice birth control. They further called upon all Catholics to oppose local and national campaigns by tax-supported agencies to adopt birth prevention as a public policy, especially in connection with welfare benefit programs.*

The 1969 and 1970 statements likewise protest government promotion of birth control programs.

The Government and Birth Control

NCCB, November 14, 1966

1. The good of the individual person and that of human society are intimately bound up with the stability of the family.[1] Basic to the well-being of the family is freedom from external coercion in order that it may determine its own destiny.

2. This freedom involves inherent personal and family rights, including the freedom and responsibility of spouses to make conscientious decisions in terms of nuptial love, determination of family size and the rearing of children. The Church and the State must play supportive roles, fostering conditions in modern society which will help the family achieve the fullness of its life and mission as the means ordained by God for bringing the person into being and maturity.

3. We address ourselves here to certain questions of concern to the family,

---

[1] Because the documents of Vatican II were issued in 1965, the American bishops decided not to issue their own pastoral that year. At the November 14-18, 1966 meeting the National Welfare Conference, which had served as the general secretariat of the American Bishops since 1919 was reorganized as the United States Catholic Conference and the bishops' organization was restructured as the National Conference of Catholic Bishops.

with special reference to public policies related to social conditions and the problems of our times.

4. In so doing, we speak in the light of the Pastoral Constitution on the Church in the Modern World adopted by Vatican Council II. Faced with our Government's stepped-up intervention in family planning, including the subsidizing of contraceptive programs at home and abroad, we feel bound in conscience to recall particularly the solemn warning expressed in these words:

5. "... [There] are many today who maintain that the increase in world population, or at least the population increase in some countries, must be radically curbed by every means possible and by any kind of intervention on the part of public authority. In view of this contention, the Council urges everyone to guard against solutions, whether publicly or privately supported, or at times even imposed, which are contrary to the moral law. For in keeping with man's inalienable right to marry and generate children, the decision concerning the number of children they will have depends on the correct judgment of the parents and it can in no way be left to the judgment of public authority." (Church in the Modern World, Section 2, Number 87.)

6. Therefore, a major preoccupation in our present statement must be with the freedom of spouses to determine the size of their families. It is necessary to underscore this freedom because in some current efforts of government—federal and state—to reduce poverty, we see welfare programs increasingly proposed which include threats to the free choice of spouses. Just as freedom is undermined when poverty and disease are present, so too is freedom endangered when persons or agencies outside the family unit, particularly persons who control welfare benefits or represent public authority, presume to influence the decision as to the number of children or the frequency of births in a family.

7. Free decision is curtailed when spouses feel constrained to choose birth limitation because of poverty, inadequate and inhuman housing, or lack of proper medical services. Here we insist that it is the positive duty of government to help bring about those conditions of family freedom which will relieve spouses from such material and physical pressures to limit family size.

8. Government promotion of family planning programs as part of tax-supported relief projects may easily result in the temptation and finally the tragic decision to reduce efforts to foster the economic, social and indeed moral reforms needed to build the free, enlightened society.

9. In connection with present and proposed governmental family limitation programs, there is frequently the implication that freedom is assured so long as spouses are left at liberty to choose among different methods of birth control. This we reject as a narrow concept of freedom. Birth control is not a universal obligation, as is often implied; moreover, true freedom of choice must provide even for those who wish to raise a larger family without being subject to criticism and without forfeiting for themselves the benefits or for

their children the educational opportunities which have become part of the value system of a truly free society. We reject, most emphatically, the suggestion that any family should be adjudged too poor to have the children it conscientiously desires.

10. The freedom of spouses to determine the size of their families must not be inhibited by any conditions upon which relief or welfare assistance is provided. Health and welfare assistance should not be linked, even indirectly, to conformity with a public agency's views on family limitation or birth control; nor may the right to found a large family be brought properly into question because it contradicts current standards arbitrarily deduced from general population statistics. No government social worker or other representative of public power should in any way be permitted to impose his judgment, in a matter so close to personal values and to the very sources of life, upon the family seeking assistance; neither should he be permitted to initiate suggestions placing, even by implication, public authority behind the recommendation that new life in a family should be prevented.

11. For these reasons, we have consistently urged and we continue to urge, as a matter of sound public policy, a clear and unqualified separation of welfare assistance from birth control considerations—whatever the legality or morality of contraception in general or in specific forms—in order to safeguard the freedom of the person and the autonomy of the family.

12. On previous occasions we have warned of dangers to the right of privacy posed by governmental birth control programs; we have urged upon government a role of neutrality whereby it neither penalizes nor promotes birth control. Recent developments, however, show government rapidly abandoning any such role. Far from merely seeking to provide information in response to requests from the needy, Government activities increasingly seek aggressively to persuade and even coerce the underprivileged to practice birth control. In this, government far exceeds its proper role. The citizen's right to decide without pressure is now threatened. Intimate details of personal, marital and family life are suddenly becoming the province of government officials in programs of assistance to the poor. We decry this overreaching by government and assert again the inviolability of the right of human privacy.

13. We support all needed research toward medically and morally acceptable methods which can assist spouses to make responsible and generous decisions in seeking to cooperate with the will of God in what pertains to family size and well-being. A responsible decision will always be one which is open to life rather than intent upon the prevention of life; among religious people, it includes a strong sense of dependence upon God's Providence.

14. It should be obvious that a full understanding of human worth, personal and social, will not permit the nation to put the public power behind the pressures for a contraceptive way of life. We urge government, at all levels, to resist pressures toward any merely mathematical and negative effort to solve health or population problems. We call upon all—and especially

Catholics—to oppose, vigorously and by every democratic means, those campaigns already underway in some states and at the national level toward the active promotion, by tax-supported agencies, of birth prevention as a public policy, above all in connection with welfare benefit programs. History has shown that as a people lose respect for any life and a positive and generous attitude toward new life, they move fatally to inhuman infanticide, abortion, sterilization and euthanasia; we fear that history is, in fact, repeating itself on this point within our own land at the moment.

15. Our government has a laudable history of dedication to the cause of freedom. In the service of this cause it is currently embarked upon a massive, unprecedented program of aid to underdeveloped nations. Through imaginative and constructive efforts, it shows itself willing to do battle with the enemies of freedom, notably poverty and ignorance. We gladly encourage our government to press this struggle with all the resources at its disposal and pledge our cooperation in all the ways in which we or those responsive to our leadership can be of assistance. Our nation's duty to assist underdeveloped countries flows from the Divine Law that the goods of the earth are destined for the well-being of all the human race.

16. In the international field, as in the domestic field, financial assistance must not be linked to policies which pressure for birth limitation. We applaud food supply programs of foreign aid which condition our cooperation on evidence that the nations benefited pledge themselves to develop their own resources; we deplore any linking of aid by food or money to conditions, overt or oblique, involving prevention of new life. Our country is not at liberty to impose its judgment upon another, either as to the growth of the latter or as to the size of its families.

17. Insofar as it does so, our country is being cast in the role of a foreign power using its instrumentalities to transgress intimate *mores* and alter the moral cultures of other nations rather than in the historic American role of offering constructive, unselfish assistance to peoples in need. Indeed, we are aware of existing apprehension in the minds of many of the peoples of the world that the United States, in its own great affluence, is attempting, by seeking to limit their populations, to avoid its moral responsibility to help other peoples help themselves precisely that they may grow in healthy life, generous love and in all the goods which presuppose and enrich both life and love.

18. Programs inhibiting new life, above all when linked to offers of desperately needed aid, are bound to create eventual resentment in any upon whom we even seem to impose them and will ultimately be gravely detrimental to the image, the moral prestige and the basic interests of the United States.

19. Obviously, therefore, international programs of aid should not be conditioned upon acceptance of birth control programs by beneficiary nations. Equally obvious, however, should be the fact that, in the practical ad-

ministration of overseas assistance, neither direct nor indirect pressures should be exerted by our personnel to affect the choice of spouses as to the number of children in their family. In the international field, as in the domestic field, both our government in its policy and our American representatives in their work, should strive above all to bring those economic and social advances which will make possible for spouses conscientious family planning without resort to contraceptive procedures fostered among them by controversial policies backed by American political power and financial aid.

20. Sobering lessons of history clearly teach that only those nations remain stable and vigorous whose citizens have and are encouraged to keep high regard for the sanctity and autonomy of family life among themselves and among the peoples who depend in any way upon them. Let our political leaders be on guard that the common good suffer no evil from public policies which tamper with the instincts of love and the sources of life.

Programs Against the Right to Life

NCCB, November 14, 1969

A statement of the National Conference of Catholic Bishops "in protest of U.S. Government programs against the right to life."

1. Every human person is made in the image of God and is called to share the eternal life with God. No price can be set on human life.

2. In 1959, the Bishops of the United States warned against the involvement by the U.S. Government in programs of population control by immoral means. In 1966, we reiterated our serious concern. We now speak out again because of the ever increasing and ever-expanding programs against the right to life in many areas. We cautioned in 1966 that programs of birth control related to public welfare could hardly fail to be coercive. Today that element of coercion is being openly advocated by some of the leading exponents of population control.

3. Government sponsored programs of birth control have already made use of methods, such as the intrauterine devices, which informed scientists tell us may produce harmful effects after conception. Projected research programs, sponsored by the National Institute of Child Health and Human

Development, include the quest for effective methods of inducing abortion early in an established pregnancy. In effect, the government is supporting birth control by early abortion.[1] Besides some private organizations[2] that receive government funding are considering seriously means of population limitation that go beyond family planning; these will involve coercion and abortion as well as other objectionable elements.

4. In the present situation, we reaffirm our stand in defense of the right to life and we affirm that there is a role for government sponsored scientific research for the preservation of life. Commendable work had been done, for example, in the development of a vaccine which would prevent German measles, and thus eliminate this source of harm to unborn children, a source of harm often mentioned by advocates of relaxed criminal laws against abortion.

5. We continue to believe that the proper answer to population problems is development—development of natural resources and of technological means, and development also of human beings themselves. Given educational opportunity and the economic means that go with it, we believe couples will make judgments about family size that will be in harmony with the common good. We affirm that parents themselves, and no government official, should make that judgment.

6. We also continue to believe that the common welfare requires government not only to avoid but also to forbid and prevent methods of population limitation that attack human life from conception onward. The equal protection of the laws, guaranteed by the Fourteenth Amendment of the U.S. Constitution to all persons, should not be withheld from the unborn. Anglo-American law has recognized the rights of the unborn.

7. Certainly no one should be deprived of life merely because it is more convenient for some that he should die.

8. In the name of the priceless dignity of the right to life, we the Catholic Bishops of the United States, protest the continuing and ever-expanding role both at home and abroad of the government in the matter of population control through the limitation of births. We hope that our fellow Americans will appreciate the soundness of our stand.

---

[1] A new Contract Research Program for the Development of new contraceptives (Research and Development Resources sought).

[2] e.g., Federation of Planned Parenthood; Population Council "Studies in Family Planning" (February, 1969).

Birth Control Laws

NCCB, November 20, 1970

1. We are strongly opposed to involvement of the federal or state governments in the area of population control or family planning.
2. These are always inherent risks to human freedom, danger of invading human rights and too great a danger of assuming that family planning will solve all the problems of poverty, racism and social injustice by this over-simplified expediency.

Call to Action

In October 1976, an NCCB Committee organized a conference at Detroit entitled A Call to Action. This conference, attended by 1,350 delegates from all parts of the country and 1,000 observers, considered the results of hearings and discussions on the local and national level held during the preceding two years under the auspices of the same NCCB committee. The intent of the program and its theological setting is outlined in the conference's opening address by John Cardinal Dearden, Chairman of the committee. In the spring of 1977, the American bishops made a preliminary and partial response to the more than 180 recommendations produced by A Call to Action Conference.

The bishops noted that most recommendations on domestic and international issues were consistent with their own public positions. They accepted conference recommendations for a formal statement on racism and for the establishment of a "family year" (cf. Family Life). The NCCB expressed disagreement, however, with the conference's suggestions for a change in Church discipline regarding priestly celibacy, ordination of married men as priests, and ordination of women to the priesthood.

The bishops concluded their statement by noting with approval the keen interest of conference participants that the Church participate in the formation of public policy and the political ethos. Finally, the bishops directed the

NCCB president to set up an ad hoc *committee to develop a five-year "Plan of Action" for the social apostolate of the Church.*

On May 4, 1978, the NCCB outlined a five-year plan for the Catholic community in the U.S. in a document entitled To Do the Work of Justice. *The NCCB selected for itself and the USCC six major areas of emphasis. These are: Education for Justice, Family Life, Church Parishes and Communities, Economic Justice, Human Rights, and World Hunger.*

More than twenty individual programs or steps are outlined in the plan. The NCCB ad hoc *committee is to monitor the progress of carrying out these measures and report in 1983 on the overall impact of the plan for the Church and society.*

The Call to Action Conference:

Opening Address, John Cardinal Dearden, Archbishop of Detroit, Chairman, NCCB Ad Hoc Committee for the Bicentennial October 1976

The journey to this day and this place has been long. You have come to Detroit in October of the bicentennial year, 10 years after Pope Paul VI issued his "Call to Action" urging us to take up the cause of justice in the world, and two years after our own bishops summoned us to consider our responsibilities for the preservation and extension of the national promise of "liberty and justice for all." We are here to participate in an extraordinary assembly of the American Catholic community. This assembly has been convened to respond to the needs of our people as these have been revealed through two years of discussions, hearings and reflection. All of us are here to assist the American Catholic community to translate its sincere commitment to liberty and justice into concrete programs of action designed to make those ideals a living reality in Church and society. We will do all this in a setting of prayerful reflection on the call of the Holy Spirit. Our central preoccupation here should be how we can more authentically as a Christian community live our faith in God and His Son, bearing witness to our confidence in Him and our awareness of His image in every person, and, together as a Church and individually as workers, citizens and Church members, serve the cause of justice and human development.

Never before has there been an attempt to bring together in this way representatives of the whole ecclesial community of the United States: bishops, priests, religious and laity. Yet, this extraordinary assembly is not a radical departure from our traditions. Our first bishop, John Carroll, initiated a policy of practical collegiality among the American hierarchy which resulted in seven provincial and three plenary councils of Baltimore between 1829 and 1884. In these meetings, the bishops and archbishops of the country, working closely with the Roman authorities, legislated for the Church in America. The hierarchy cooperated to insure that, despite the rapid expansion of the nation across the continent and the even more rapid growth of the Catholic people from the polyglot nationalities of Europe, the American Church would remain one in spirit, practice and discipline. In the latter part of the century, in 1889 and 1893, national assemblies of the laity met to discuss what role the lay people of the Church could play in spreading the Gospel and providing a fuller and freer life for all Americans. The enthusiasm spurred by these meetings did not last. Later efforts to bring about unity through federation of hundreds of lay organizations met with only modest success. Yet, there was a tradition of fostering regional, sectional and ethnic diversity, and out of it to form a unified Church which could communicate among the groups and regions, and lead to mutual enrichment and provide a basis for united action.

Our efforts at renewal require both an affirmation of our rich pluralism and a strong national organization, and both must take account of the pressing needs of our own people and the people of our country and our world. To forward these objectives, the American Catholic bishops decided to dedicate the Church's bicentennial celebration to the theme of justice. With the help of many people, we formulated a unique plan: we would hold a series of regional hearings, where teams of bishops would sit and listen to the concerns of our people on issues of justice in the Church and in the world. These hearings were a marvelous experience. At each of the hearings—held in six different cities: Washington, San Antonio, Minneapolis, Atlanta, Sacramento and Newark—we heard clearly the cries of people for a chance to raise their families in peace and dignity, pass on their distinctive cultural traditions to their children, find a responsible government and a responsive Church. Later, in a special hearing at Maryknoll, New York, we heard a number of invited guests from around the world tell us of the issues of human rights, economic justice and human survival in nations struggling for development and liberation. The hearings were an exhilarating and challenging experience for all who took part. People today, rich and poor, are often studied by scholars and pollsters; their needs, hopes and concerns are defined by questionnaires or by computers. Only rarely are they asked directly to speak up and be heard; so rarely, in fact, that many greet the invitation with understandable skepticism. Yet, that is what we have tried to do, in our perhaps inefficient way. We are left with an enormous sense of responsibility and an equally strong feeling that there is great power in the spirit and faith of the people who appeared before us. The human resources of our Church and our nation are vast; our task is to carry forward, today, together, the work that has been begun—to unlock the structures of Church and world so that the spirit and energy of our people can flourish and contribute to renewing our communities. No one who sat through those 21 days of hearings could doubt that it can be done and that it must be done.

The regional hearings presented a model of a listening, learning and caring Church. We hoped that the model would be reproduced in parishes and dioceses around the country. And we were right. More than half the nation's dioceses sponsored parish discussions. These and other dioceses held their own regional and diocesanwide meetings to hear the voice of the people and, in some cases, to begin formulating new goals and objectives for the local churches. From parishes around the country came over three-quarters of a million responses, listing the people's own perception of the major issues before us and their recommendations to deal with those issues. Of course, it was not a scientific sample; many sections of the country held no program; even where there was a program, the level of participation depended upon many factors. Together with the testimony of the regional hearings, this massive body of material represents the hopes and fears, the anxieties and the aspirations of many of our people.

Today it rests in the cold form of "feedback sheets" and computer print-outs; yet, it is far more than that, for each document represents the personal investment of the people who took part. They deserve our full attention, and our measured, responsible, serious and sincere consideration.

Since the end of the consultation, teams of bishops, scholars and people active in the ministry of the Church have been examining the results, trying to piece together from the complex fabric of testimony and parish reports some sense of the major concerns that emerge, some summary of the issues of most pressing importance to the Catholic people. On the basis of their reading of this mass of material they have framed some proposals for our consideration. Though a very full agenda for action, these recommendations do not cover all the hundreds of issues raised or the thousands of actions proposed. Instead they suggest some priorities, and begin the process of moving all of us towards a compassionate, realistic and effective response to the voices of our people. It is our task to consider these proposals, to accept them, reject them, revise them, frame our response to the problems on the basis of our experience, our considered judgment and, most of all, in the light of the Gospel.

I will not try to evaluate any or all of these proposals here. Yet a few comments are in order. For one thing, there appears to be an overwhelming acceptance of this process. Throughout America, wherever Catholics were asked, they expressed their desire to share responsibility for the Church and the nation. They like parish and diocesan pastoral councils; they criticize their shortcomings, but they want these new structures. They want to work closely with their priests and bishops, and they want their leaders to trust them and be accountable to them for the use of Church resources. Everywhere this program took place the participants were respectful, even deferential, towards Church leaders, modest in their demands, wary of quick judgment on questions they perceive as theological or doctrinal. They spoke of the existence of injustice in the Church, but they did not fix blame. They urged all Catholics to work together to make the Church a more fitting witness to the truths that it proclaims. Anyone who attended these programs at any level knows that they were conducted not in a spirit of complaining or faultfinding, but with a strong affirmation by our people of their Church, of Vatican II and of one another. The agenda that emerges is the agenda of a hopeful, energetic, self-confident people, determined to keep trying.

But there are problems. We have as a people made less progress than we all had hoped in learning and making our own the teaching of our Church during and since Vatican II. There are many who do not yet know what the Council taught, even more, perhaps, who have little understanding of the social message of the Church as it has developed in recent years. Perhaps because of the pressures arising from life in our advanced industrial society, many of our people are not certain that their Church should even be discussing issues of justice and liberty. We Catholics are always prepared to respond with warmth, generosity and compassion to people in need. We are not always so quick to seek out those responsible for suffering or those abuses of society which cause those needs to arise. While the bishops have often spoken clearly on matters of social justice, the hearings and parish discussions indicate that not only have we not often been heard, but that we have not always convinced our people that we take our words with complete seriousness ourselves. As pastors, we bishops must be alarmed at the failures of our community to share more fully the works of justice; as Catholics, all of us must be dismayed at our common failure to make our tradition of social action a living reality at all levels of our community. To remain a vital resource for the Church, our tradition must be studied and applied to ever-changing situations, which themselves must be analyzed with the help of the social sciences and with respect for personal experience. And study and reflection must lead to action; that is the hardest part.

In addition, many Catholics have become skeptical of the ability of Church leaders to take them seriously. Again and again the listener heard people say that while they would speak up, they were doubtful anyone would really listen and would really try to respond. Many have had the experience of failure, and they are becoming more and more convinced that their leaders in the Church, like their leaders in the community, really don't care what they think. Perhaps it is the ambiguities that have surrounded the development of parish councils; perhaps expectations of laity and religious have outstripped the ability of priests and bishops to deliver; perhaps the Church simply cannot carry all the hopes which people place in it. In any event the same deepening fatalism which grips American culture generally affects the Church; if we fail to respond to the needs expressed, fail even to demonstrate convincingly that, while we cannot solve all the problems, we do care, then we will reinforce the conviction that it simply can't be done, that we can't really become a community of faith and friendship as Vatican II said we should.

The needs, anxieties and hopes expressed throughout the last two years are addressed to the bishops, but through the bishops they are addressed to all the Catholic people, to the nation and the world. They challenge all of us to respond by becoming a more caring, a more faithful, and more responsible community of men and women. Our response must come in our hearts, and then back home in our local communities. The National Conference of Catholic Bishops is going to consider the results of this meeting. I would hope that their response will be full and candid, continuing the process of dialogue, joining their voice with those who have already spoken, seeking to incorporate what has happened during the last two years into the ongoing life of the Church. All of us will try, as best we can, to join in the tasks that will be outlined at this conference; all of us will try, where we disagree, to express clearly the reasons for our disagreement and provide mechanisms for ongoing communication. If we do this job assigned to us by our Church, I am certain that not only will the bishops respond, but we still have made significant progress toward the renewal of our Church and the restoration of confidence in the American promise of liberty and justice for all.

Some may be surprised that a program designed to focus our attention on the concrete responsibilities of American Catholics in response to the "call to action" for justice of Pope Paul and the Synod of Bishops should end up giving a great deal of attention to such matters as pastoral renewal, accountability and responsibility within the Church, and personal growth and development. Yet, this surely could not have been unanticipated. In opening the initial hearing in Washington in February of last year, I stated that the "integrity of our work will depend upon our willingness to make our ecclesial life a witness to liberty and justice and to the possibilities of love, friendship and service which liberty and justice create." To renew the Church and to participate in the transformation of the world are not separate and distinct tasks; every major document of the renewal makes that clear. Rather, they are two sides of the same coin of clarifying our faith and the demands which it makes upon us.

Even more practically, we must see that these tasks go together. We cannot preach a justice to the world that we do not practice ourselves; we cannot demand recognition of the dignity and worth of every human person by governments in combating war and torture and hunger while even one person in our own community is homeless or hungry or mistreated. Of course, none of us can expect to attain an individual perfection before doing our best to live the Christian life in the community; but, neither can we expect others to respond to our prescriptions and challenges if we are not trying with all that is in us to practice what we preach. Nor is it out of place to suggest that only as we build in our urban neighborhoods, in our rural communities, in our homes and places of work a way of life which is a source of joy and happiness for ourselves will we be able to be something more in the nation than moralistic prophets of doom. One guesses that the ancient world knew that Christians loved one another by the fact that they seemed at least relatively happy and content with their lives and with one another. In our own country the friendship and support our immigrant forebears found in their parishes and religious associations certainly had something to do with their success in building new lives for themselves, sharing in the building of this great nation. We are, in a very real sense, the heirs of their common endeavors. The record of our hearings and discussions demonstrates that our people possess a degree of fairness, compassion and commitment which would stand well against any comparative test. Much pain and anguish was expressed, to be sure, but the people who attended and testified and talked with one another were not hopeless or joyless or lacking in energy, talent or friendly faces. They were, on the contrary, welcoming and sharing and caring people. And they, and we, are that way because we have learned in our families and Church that no matter what the world may say of us, we are, in fact, of infinite worth and value because our Creator cares for us and we have through our Church the gift of His Spirit.

The trap, of course, is to conclude that our experience of faith and God and sacrament and friendship is sufficient, that our task is accomplished. Let us remember that we do all this, engage in the often discouraging tasks of building parish and diocesan pastoral councils, revising the forms of sacrament and worship, spending endless hours in meetings on parish finances and educational policy, and organizing to bring about justice, not simply because we want to create a community of peace and energy and care, but so that we may all be better prepared to do the Lord's will in our times. It is in order to be more fit instruments of His will that we do these things; we must carry what we receive in and from the Church into the marketplace, there to redeem all of human life by participating and sharing in the struggles of humankind for dignity, justice, peace and liberation. And what we learn there, in the midst of struggle and work, we carry back to the community, to share the experience, to reflect upon it, to make our Christian life in the world a source of enrichment for the *ecclesia,* the community called out from the world, while the experience of the *ecclesia* is the center from which we must always return to renew the face of the earth.

For myself, I can say only one thing with full assurance, and that is that there are no clear, ready-made answers to the problems of Church and society. If by chance some day we should reverse the process we have been through, and send teams of lay people, priests and religious around the country to listen to the testimony of bishops, I suspect that what would be heard would differ only in specific details from what we have heard during the last two years. We, too, remain excited and challenged by the renewal of the Church initiated by the Second Vatican Council and chastened by the experience of having tried, as best we could, to implement that spirit in our own local churches. We have been frustrated and angry with ourselves, with our priests and people; we have made some mistakes, had some moments of heroism and some moments of weakness. We have tried to learn from the experience, have tried to keep moving forward in spite of the setbacks. Like most people of our generation, we bishops have had to try to grasp and make our own the new visions and hopes excited by renewal while remaining faithful to the beliefs and customs of our childhood and our families. Like them, too, we have probably sometimes wished things would just slow down a bit, that something—the family, the parish, the liturgy—would just regain some of the strength we think it had not too long ago. Most of all, I think we have all wished there were some way we could relate more directly and intimately with our people, share their burdens and have them share ours, know their anguish and let them know our own. If nothing else has happened to those of us who took part in this process, we at least learned this: that when we take the risk of listening and being open to our people, they demonstrate almost without exception a sensitivity to our feelings and a willingness to share our problems with us, if we will only let them.

So, in the next few days, we are going to deliberate about the response we should make to the issues before us. We will discuss and debate; we will have considerable controversy within this hall and will probably generate some controversy outside it. We are a fairly representative gathering of the American Catholic community; as such, we contain within ourselves many, if not most, of the ethnic, racial, cultural, economic, sociological and theological differences which characterize our diverse people and country. If we could meet and easily agree on policy for the Church and nation, we probably would not have wrestled with any problem of serious consequence. All of us in this hall are against racism and war and hypocrisy and violence; all of us are committed to the Gospel of Jesus, a Gospel of peace and justice and love and brotherhood and sisterhood; the tough part is translating all that into action. Translating it into a community of faith which conducts worship and prayer and education and works of charity and social service. Translating it into a moral position on questions of public significance, impacting on the processes by which legislation and public policy are made, because it is there that the basic work of justice is done in modern society. Both the pastoral task of building the Church, and the political task of building the world, involve choices, concrete and specific choices of how to spend our money, make our decisions, allocate our resources, direct our personal and collective allocation of time, treasure and talent. None of us knows for sure how best to do these things, none of us can be certain that our program of reform is exactly what the Lord intends for us today. So we have no choice, if we are to be a community of both faith and freedom, except to meet, debate and make some decisions. That is what we are trying to do here. We are trying to begin a new way of doing the work of the Church in America. We may fail, but let us try and let people in the nation say of us that they cared enough to try.

In conclusion, one more thought should be expressed. We meet here as *Church*. Penetrated by the Spirit of Christ, we seek His will, not our own. We are conscious of our identity as the Church in the United States. At the same time, we are well aware of our bond in Christ with the Church throughout the world. We are one in our common concerns, in our traditions and in our faith. No one of us could fail to see and appreciate the profound significance of our Holy Father addressing us as we open this conference. What we do is meaningful for the entire Church. Let us begin our work, prayerfully, reflectively, conscientiously. With due accommodation, I voice the hope stated by Paul in his letter to the Church in Philippi: "It is my wish that you may be found rich in the harvest of justice which Jesus Christ has ripened in you to the glory and praise of God." (Phil. 1:11).

The Bicentennial Consultation: A Response*

NCCB, May 5, 1977

I.

For two years, as part of the Catholic contribution to the bicentennial, a committee of our conference sought to involve people across the nation in a reflection on justice. At the national level it conducted 7 three-day hearings at which bishops and other Church leaders listened to invited experts and

---

*Collective statement of the American bishops reflecting an initial response to the NCCB bicentennial program and the recommendations of the Call to Action conference.

concerned local persons. At the local level dioceses were encouraged to join a parish program and invite Catholics to reflect on their experience and practice of justice.

Many bishops, scholars and persons active in social ministry reviewed and summarized the results of this consultation. Finally, 1,350 delegates and 1,000 observers gathered last October at a conference entitled A Call to Action to consider the results of the hearings and discussions as reflected in working papers on humankind, personhood, nationhood, ethnicity and race, the Church, neighborhood, family and work. The convocation met for three days and produced more than 180 recommendations.

We invited this process of structured public discussion in the Church so that we might listen to the needs of our own people and through their voices come to know more specifically and to share more intimately "the joys and the hopes, the griefs and the anxieties" of the people of our age. Admittedly, the process of consultation was imperfect and there are some conclusions which are problematical and in some cases untenable. This has been a source of concern. Yet, this two-year process was marked by trust and respect among nearly all who took part. It gave many people a good opportunity to speak directly to Church leaders. It identified issues and a number of constructive suggestions for action. It helped dramatize how the Church and its leadership are perceived by some. We are grateful to all who shared their insights with us. We reaffirm our commitment to the principle of shared responsibility in the contemporary Church, and we assert our intention to improve consultation with our people.

The bicentennial program must be understood in light of what Vatican Council II has said about the Church. Throughout the universal Church, pastors and people have been engaged in the work of designing methods, structures and processes for bringing the conciliar vision of the Church to fruition at the level of the parish, the diocese, the nation and, indeed, the world. The conciliar vision is contained in a unique way in the two documents on the Church: *Lumen Gentium* (The Dogmatic Constitution on the Church) and *Gaudium et Spes* (The Pastoral Constitution on the Church in the Modern World). It is in the light of the ecclesiological principles of these documents that the process, results and future implications of the bicentennial program must be evaluated.

Fundamental to the theological vision of *Lumen Gentium* is its description of the Church as the people of God.[1] The focus given to this concept by the Council has opened the way for many movements of renewal in the last decade. The image of the Church as the people of God affirms that all of us derive our dignity from the same source: the free, unmerited love of God who has called us out of darkness into His own wonderful light to share in the life of the risen Lord Jesus Christ, thus giving us a new identity as a people

---

[1] *Lumen Gentium*, 9, 10, 11, 12.

uniquely His own. At this most fundamental level of the life of the Church, there are no distinctions among us. Holiness and openness to grace are the most important aspects of the life of the Church, to which everything is ordained. The hierarchical ministry in the Church is ordained entirely to the service of this plan of God, making it possible for those He has called to hear His word, become His people and enjoy the life of the community of Jesus, the Messiah.[2] Thus the Second Vatican Council teaches that bishops, as successors of the apostles, have received from the Lord the mission of teaching authoritatively all peoples so that all may attain salvation through faith, baptism and the observance of the commandments.[3] As pastors who are teachers, we are called both to listen and to learn from our people and also to respond to what we hear by announcing the Good News in all its implications, unfolding its riches and applying it to contemporary circumstances.

In any process of dialogue in the Church, we listen, as all Christians do, for the voice of the Spirit in the Church[4] and the world; we also exercise the charism of judgments and discernment in the Church in a special way. For bishops are "authentic teachers, that is, teachers endowed with the authority of Christ, who preach the faith to the people assigned to them, the faith which is destined to inform their thinking and direct their conduct."[5] In responding to the consultative process we have begun, therefore, we are seeking to judge and discern, to guide and direct a process which we believe can bear much fruit in the Church today. We have to be both pastors who can listen and teachers who can speak. We seek to do this sensitively, intelligently and compassionately. We are addressing our response especially to those Christians whose faith in Christ is nurtured within the Roman Catholic Church. In this community, with its specific understanding of authority, we are called to live in truth and by love and to be free with the liberty Christ has gained for us. One of the greatest tests of the Catholic Christian's interior freedom is to respond to God's word in the Church even when a decision may be contrary to one's own views and to abide by that decision with a profound inner peace and joy.

The particular process of consultation which culminated in the proposals of the Call to Action conference was helpful and important. However, it cannot be the sole factor in determining the pastoral agenda for the Church. It is our task to assess those proposals in the context of God's plan as revealed in and through Christ.

One of the demands of the divine plan is action to support a way of life in conformity with the justice which God has revealed and communicated to us in Christ Jesus. Both *Gaudium et Spes* and the synodal document, *Justice in the World,* affirm direct and intimate connection between the mission of the

---

[2] *Lumen Gentium,* 18.
[3] *Lumen Gentium,* 24.
[4] *Lumen Gentium,* 4.
[5] *Lumen Gentium,* 25.

Church and the ministry of justice.[6] This connection is so strong that the plan of salvation, which the Church is meant to proclaim and serve, is understood by the Bible as one of "justification," that is, as the transformation of human life by the righteousness or justice of God. This has powerful implications for the entire Church. In communion with our people, we have an obligation to address many issues of individual and social life in the light of this divine justice.[7] The bicentennial program was initiated by us to clarify and specify the implications for the Church in the United States of a social ministry at the service of the justice of God.[8]

Because this is the justice we preach, we also recognize that we may not simply equate earthly progress with the spread of the kingdom of God or confuse the Church's role and competence with respect to each. The principles of revelation do not provide specific solutions to many social problems, nor do they constitute a blueprint for organizing society. In proposing concrete policies in the social order, the Church is aware that often, the more specific a proposal or program, the more room there may be for persons of sincere faith to disagree.

The Church is called to engage in continuing self-examination in order to make its own structures and procedures more effective instruments of and witness to this divine justice. In doing this, we must keep in mind that the Church is a unique reality into which we are graciously incorporated and a society which is essentially designed by Christ. In reflecting upon its structures, therefore, we can learn much from human organizations but we may not draw too heavily upon them. The Christian life is given to us as an undeserved gift, a grace; it does not originate in our efforts and aspirations although it requires our full cooperation. Reflection upon the roles and rights of members of the Church must take place in light of this fact.

In this preliminary and partial response we can speak to only some of the many recommendations, general and specific, presented to us. All are being referred for study to committees of the National Conference of Catholic Bishops and the United States Catholic Conference. How they will be addressed is described in the final section of this document. Our purpose at this time is to provide an overall assessment of what has been placed before us.

---

[6] *Gaudium et Spes,* 40, 43; *Justice in the World:* Introduction; Parts I and II.

[7] *Lumen Gentium,* 25; cf. also *Christus Dominus,* 12: "Let (bishops) explain also how high a value, according to the doctrine of the Church, should be placed on the human person, on his liberty and bodily life; how highly we should value the family, its unity and stability, the procreation and education of children, human society with its laws and professions, its labor and leisure, its arts and technical inventions, its poverty and abundance. They should expound likewise the principles governing the solution of those very grave problems concerning the possession, increase and just distribution of material goods, concerning peace and war, and the fraternal coexistence of peoples."

[8] *Octagesima Adveniens,* 4.

II.

The bicentennial consultation reflected the participants' willingness to take personal responsibility for building the Christian community and sharing in its mission. Forthright in requesting episcopal action, they were equally direct in challenging one another and the community at large. The most lasting response will be in dioceses, parishes and the lives of individuals.

The consultation, itself an exercise in shared responsibility, appropriately recommended "the further development of both structures and practices of consultation and shared responsibility at every level of the Church."[9] We shall seek to develop such ways of helping to discern the needs and gifts of the faithful in the light of the Gospel. We have already encouraged the formation of parish councils and diocesan pastoral councils. We wish to encourage these councils again as good forums for this dialogue to take place.

We support the thrust of recommendations for continued efforts to eradicate racial and ethnic discrimination, even when unconscious and unintended, in both the Church and society; to protect and foster the rights of Church employees; to carry forward the practice of financial accountability; and to observe due process procedures in Church life. Catholic institutions and officials should regularly engage in formal review of their personnel policies and other practices in this light.

Hispanic, black and Indian Catholics deserve continued support in their efforts to articulate their needs, as do the many other ethnic groups which demonstrate the values of cultural diversity and pluralism within the Church and society. We readily express our "desire to respond to proposals for action which come from ethnic, racial and cultural organizations," and we further strive to "facilitate and encourage efforts of such groups to formulate pastoral and social action programs to meet their needs."[10] There is much to commend in recommendations calling attention to minority needs of a cultural, liturgical and social nature. We see the value of new forms of training for ministry, responsive to cultural diversity,[11] and of efforts to foster appropriate multicultural expressions within the Church, especially in relation to worship, pastoral planning and education. Clearly, though, all such efforts must be consistent with the essential unity of the community of faith.

Since racism is "among the most persistent and destructive evils in our nation,"[12] we shall continue to address this abuse in words and actions. In view of the recommendation for a collective pastoral "on the sin of racism in both its personal and social dimensions,"[13] we shall seek to develop such a document, either as a pastoral letter or in some other appropriate form.

---

[9] Call to Action, *Church,* I, 3.

[10] CTA, *Ethnicity and Race,* II, 2.

[11] Cf. *Ethnicity and Race,* II, 3.

[12] NCCB, *To Live in Christ Jesus.*

[13] *Ethnicity and Race,* IV, 8.

Inner-city neighborhoods clearly require "priority attention by the Church,"[14] yet there is also a great need for its efforts "to improve the quality of life in rural areas."[15] The dilemma with which such recommendations can confront the Church in allocating its limited resources does not permit us to abandon one area of need in favor of another; it underlines the urgent need for all the people of the Church, not only its bishops, to be sensitive and generous in responding.

The consultation spoke often of family concerns and the need for family ministry. Participants found much evidence of discrimination against families in society today, and some expressed the belief that even the Church gives too little attention to family life. "The whole Church, through the example of the lives of its members and through action undertaken in cooperation with other religious and civic groups, [should] combat those contemporary social, economic and cultural forces which threaten families."[16] Comprehensive pastoral planning for family ministry is required, involving Church leadership and family representatives.[17] On the national level this effort has begun and will continue through our Commission on Marriage and Family Life. Families, diocesan offices and national Church bodies, together with other religious and civic groups, should give particular attention to the media's impact on family life and undertake programs to encourage their wholesome use by families "as part of a pastoral social justice program related to media."[18] We encourage our national communication structures to move forward vigorously in this area. Also, noting the recommendation for a "family year,"[19] we ask the appropriate NCCB/USCC structures, in collaboration with other interested bodies, to give immediate attention to this suggestion as a possible vehicle for new initiatives in this critically important field.

Recommendations supportive of vocations to the priesthood, the diaconate and the religious life reflect a commendable appreciation of these forms of service to God and humanity. Beyond question, God's people who have "the right to competent pastoral care," also have "the responsibility to further vocations . . . by prayer, by participation in religious vocation programs and by active encouragement of those in seminaries and those training for the religious life."[20] Moreover, the Catholic community should offer understanding and support to bishops, priests, deacons and religious in their work. While continuing to seek ways to improve the quality of pastoral care available to our people, we urge them also to assume their own responsibilities in this regard.

---

[14] *Neighborhood,* II, 7.
[15] *Neighborhood,* IV.
[16] CTA, *Family,* I, 3.
[17] *Family,* I, 3.
[18] Cf. *Family,* II, 4.
[19] *Family,* I, 3.
[20] *Church,* I, 5.

Some recommendations suggested the possibility of change in the Church's discipline concerning priestly celibacy and the ordination of married men as priests. We concur instead with the longstanding view of the Church, as expressed overwhelmingly by the 1971 Synod of Bishops. Priestly celibacy has great value as an eschatological sign and an instrument for pastoral service, and "the law of priestly celibacy existing in the Latin Church is to be kept in its entirety." Also, "excepting always the right of the Supreme Pontiff, the priestly ordination of married men is not permitted, even in particular cases."[21]

Much attention has been given the several recommendations concerning the ordination of women to the priesthood. We affirm the conclusion of the Holy See's recent *Declaration on the Question of the Admission of Women to the Ministerial Priesthood*—that the Church "does not consider herself authorized to admit women to priestly ordination."[22] We invite theologians to join us in a serious study of the issues to which the document addresses itself. Further study and clarification of these issues may allay some of the anguish felt by many whose love for the Church is unquestioned. There is a pressing need to "identify, formally authenticate and expand ministries" performed by women in the Church.[23] Efforts to open up new and greater opportunities for leadership by women are imperative. We shall vigorously pursue this matter, as well as questions of justice for women in society, within our conference and other Church structures.

Other specific recommendations pertaining to pastoral ministry concern the aged, youth and young adults. The needs of the elderly in our parishes and communities are urgent. In our pastoral approach to the elderly we must all recognize "the principle of dynamic growth in every age span and give consideration to the spirituality of the aging as a resource to the Church."[24] As we indicated a year ago in our statement, *Society and the Aged: Toward Reconciliation*, we intend to increase our efforts to insure that their pastoral needs are met, that they are included in all phases of the Church's life, and that Church agencies and institutions for social service and social action give them high priority. Youth and young adults need similar attention, including opportunities for greater direct participation in the Church's life and work.[25] We welcome creative, practical proposals by agencies and individuals familiar with youth and young adult ministry. Similarly, recognizing "the unique gifts handicapped persons have to offer the Church," we shall seek ways more effectively to achieve "their integration into full participation in the Christian community."[26]

---

[21] *The Ministerial Priesthood.*
[22] Sacred Congregation for the Doctrine of the Faith, October 15, 1976.
[23] *Church,* II, 5.
[24] CTA, *Personhood,* II, 5.
[25] Cf. *Personhood,* II, 5.
[26] *Personhood,* II, 6.

Other issues addressed during the consultation concern contraception, ministry to homosexuals and the pastoral care of separated and divorced Catholics.

We have frequently expressed our fidelity to the Church's teaching on birth control. As pastors and teachers we, too, are concerned over "conflict and anguish" with respect to this issue.[27] In rejecting contraception as a morally legitimate means of limiting births, the Church is proclaiming and defending the value of procreation itself, "a value attacked, though in different ways, by both the ideology of contraception and by contraceptive acts."[28] For this reason, we have urged, and urge again, prayerful reflection concerning the necessity to live according to this teaching, so that the grace of God will give to all couples the power to be faithful to their mission of expressing in their lives the lifegiving love of Christ for His people. In continuing to seek effective means of "safeguarding the holiness of marriage"[29] in our times, we are determined to observe the dual reminder given us by Pope Paul: "To diminish in no way the saving teachings of Christ constitutes an eminent form of charity for souls. But this must ever be accompanied by patience and goodness, such as the Lord Himself gave example of."[30]

While we acknowledge the need for sensitive and compassionate ministry to homosexuals and support their basic human rights[31] we also emphasize that "homosexual activity . . . as distinguished from homosexual orientation, is morally wrong."[32] The moral obligations for such persons which arise from this fact carry a corollary obligation for all of us to respond to their need for pastoral care.

Recommendations concerning separated and divorced Catholics call for a clear but sensitive response in deeds as well as words.[33] In fidelity to Christ, the Church teaches firmly that sacramental marriages are indissoluble. The staggering rate and number of divorces in our country at the present time, many of them involving Catholics, reflect the tragedy of marital failure in a society which shows little appreciation for the sanctity of marriage. In light of this, the Church has a two-fold responsibility. It must proclaim more strongly, not less, the indissolubility of Christian marriage. It must also extend special pastoral care to separated and divorced Catholics, so that, even as they experience the heartache of marital failure, they may also experience Christ's loving concern and understanding mediated through their Church.

---

27 *Personhood*, III, 2.

28 *To Live in Christ Jesus.*

29 *Humanae Vitae*, 30. The encyclical adds that this "implies concerted pastoral action in all the fields of human activity, economic, cultural and social; for, in fact, only a simultaneous improvement in these various sectors will make it possible to render the life of parents and of children within their families not only tolerable, but easier and more joyous."

30 *Humanae Vitae*, 29.

31 Cf. *Personhood*, III, 4.

32 *To Live in Christ Jesus.*

33 Cf. *Family*, III.

This pastoral care must include a strong effort to strengthen, where needed, the personnel and expertise of those exercising ministry in our marriage tribunals. These must be properly equipped to render justice expeditiously to those who request adjudication of their marriage status by a plea of nullity.

Participants in the consultation spoke forcefully of their concern for many issues of justice and peace in our country and world. Recognizing that only with sacrifice will this nation be able to provide meaningful jobs, decent housing, quality education and equal opportunity for all its people, while furthering the cause of peace, development and human rights internationally, the recommendations express a clear commitment, which we share, to continue to work for these goals. In particular, we encourage our national offices to seek to develop "new models of justice education at all levels" and to encourage research and evaluation projects in this area.[34]

The concern for human life expressed in the consultation and the recognition of the need to restore legal protection to the unborn are praiseworthy. Comprehensive and consistent commitment to the sanctity of life in all contexts and at all stages of its development, before birth as well as after, is demanded of us as followers of Christ. Such commitment requires many practical forms of action, including restoration to the unborn of their legal right to life through an amendment to the Constitution.[35]

The consultation proposed a large agenda for national policy on many other issues also concerned with the sanctity of life. There were recommendations on such matters as public action to achieve full employment, income security, decent housing and health care, equal access to quality education, public and private, responsive agricultural and resouce policy, sensitive immigration laws, reform of the criminal justice system, respect for human rights in foreign policy, arms control and disarmament and many other issues. We wish in particular to state our recognition of "the dangers and evils of the arms race and an aggressive military posture" and to acknowledge our responsibility, in collaboration with others, to encourage "peace education programs" which will illuminate the moral dimensions of this urgent issue and foster responsible efforts on behalf of arms control and disarmament.[36]

In most cases, the recommendations on domestic and international issues are consistent with our publicly stated positions and provide a welcome impetus for continued efforts. A few, however, involve matters with which we have not dealt up to now; in some cases, the issues appear more complex than the recommendations would suggest. We strongly encourage our committees and offices to continue to study these questions and develop policy recommendations for our consideration. These efforts should go forward in

---

[34] CTA, *Humankind*, I, 5.
[35] Cf. *Personhood*, II, 2.
[36] *Humankind*, III, 3.

recognition of the responsibility of the Church "to promote a critical reordering of national priorities and policies to give primary consideration to human rights and human needs"[37] in this country and abroad.

III.

As these remarks suggest, the different recommendations of the bicentennial consultation must be approached in several different ways. Some pertain to the teaching or discipline of the universal Church; in regard to them we recall our duty, as members of the college of bishops united with the Holy Father, to respect the principles of collegiality and universality and, in particular, our fundamental obligation of fidelity to the teaching of Christ entrusted to the Church. The conflict, between a few of the recommendations and what the Church teaches, underlines our responsibility to express this teaching more clearly and effectively. As bishops we cannot compromise Catholic teaching. Yet we have the responsibility to do whatever we can, with God's grace, to clarify the evangelical principles which lie behind these teachings, as we strive to improve our efforts to catechize on these matters. Other recommendations pertain specifically to dioceses, parishes, other structures and individuals, and the final response must come at these levels. Some matters involve existing programs of NCCB/USCC or questions now being studied by it; in such cases the recommendations will be fully considered in planning future initiatives at the national level. Still others raise new, complex questions; these too, will be examined very carefully. As part of the evaluation process, the availability of material resources to accomplish what has been suggested must necessarily be given serious and realistic consideration.

Among matters which are beyond the competence of our conference, as such, to influence directly, we note several themes, concerning the parish, which emerged from the consultation. It is worth doing this in order to indicate our support in principle.

In speaking of their parishes, some Catholics tend to measure the health of the Church by the presence of the sense of commitment. They express a desire to experience community in ways they find more meaningful. Requests for home Masses, parish welcoming and outreach committees, greater liturgical variety, more opportunities for cultural expression and reinforcement and improved communication between priests and people all point to the importance of developing the community of faith in families, parishes and informal gatherings of Christians.[38]

Clearly, the parish community must become closely involved with the neighborhood and its problems, to witness Christian concern for a better life for all and its work for justice at the local level. Parish life should provide

---

[37] *Nationhood,* II.
[38] *Neighborhood,* I, 3.

challenges and opportunities for the believing community to confront sin, suffering and injustice within and beyond the local community. This theme was articulated in repeated requests for adult education programs, especially those involving formation in Christian responsibility in the political and social realm.[39] Effective utilization of the new sacramental rites and of catechetical instruction for the young was also urged. Other recommendations, made in relation to social justice, noted the need to involve the parish in the surrounding neighborhood or rural community through prayer, service and education. This underlines the need for supportive structures and programs at the diocesan level relating to pastoral planning for social justice, increased support for community organization, education for justice, the achievement of equal opportunity and family life.

The Church in the United States is both a community of believers, pledged to fidelity to the Gospel, and a body of concerned citizens. Reflecting this dual role and the obligations arising from it, participants in the consultation expressed a keen interest in the Church's involvement in the formation of public policy and the political ethos. We, too, are intensely interested in the quality of Catholic citizenship, and, we agree that "parishes, dioceses and other groups within the Church . . . [should] continue or initiate programs of education aimed at greater understanding of: a) the way public policy is made; b) the relationship between the public policy and the Gospel of Jesus Christ and the traditions and experiences of the Catholic people themselves, and c) the duties of citizenship."[40]

We cite these two areas as representative of those where response must essentially come at the local level and where early positive action is to be encouraged. In doing so, we also note the desirability of continued consultation at various levels in the Church concerning the implementation of such recommendations.

As we have already said, every recommendation from the bicentennial consultation will also be studied by one or more of the committees of NCCB/USCC. Conscious of the fact that the hearings and the Detroit conference aimed at providing us the material for a five-year "Plan of Action," we direct the president of the NCCB to appoint, as soon as possible, an ad hoc committee to be chaired by a bishop, and to be composed of members of the NCCB and of members drawn from the Advisory Council. This committee will have as its charge to develop the five-year "Plan of Action," in consultation with our NCCB and USCC committees. It will establish appropriate deadlines for its work, and once the "Plan of Action" has been accepted by the NCCB, it will have responsibility for oversight of its implementation. Finally, this committee will submit a written report on the implementation process at each of our general meetings in November for the next five years.

---

[39] Cf., for example, *Church*, III, 2.
[40] *Nationhood*, I, 1.

We believe these steps will insure effective implementation and responsible accountability, to us and to all others, on the part of our national structures.

The present preliminary and partial response is not intended as a total response to the bicentennial consultation. Such a response must come in carefully planned actions carried out over a period of time. But we do not forget the fact that hundreds of people came to us to describe how their lives are troubled by social injustice. Others came to describe situations of injustice which they had seen or worked in. All came with hope that the Church can be a sign and source of social justice and peace in the world today. We have been moved by these voices. Perhaps the major result of this extensive consultation is the hope it has given us that together we can bear witness to the unity of the Church of Christ by the justice and peace in which we all live.

To Do the Work of Justice:
A Plan of Action for the
Catholic Community in the U.S.*

NCCB, May 4, 1978

Christian faith continually calls the Church and each of its members to decisive action to bring faith alive in the concrete circumstances of human history. Throughout the world today churches are bearing witness to Christ's saving presence by courageous efforts to speak God's word boldly; to renew themselves; and to confront with hope and courage the critical issues of human rights, social justice and world peace. Sharing and having shared in this renewal, we seek here to identify some of the work which remains to be done in the years ahead. This plan of action springs from our vision of our Church's ministry to the pressing needs of all the world's people. A challenge to us and our people, it is also an invitation to every bishop, priest, religious and lay person in the Catholic Church in the United States to join in a deliberate, systematic effort to be of service to all people in their struggle for dignity, justice and peace.

A year ago we issued a preliminary response to the consultation on social justice entitled "Liberty and Justice For All," which we conducted on the occasion of our national bicentennial. This consultation, in which the bishops

---

*Call to Action plan approved by the Catholic bishops May 4, 1978.

listened to the voices of many groups and individuals, was intended to help us formulate a plan to establish goals and programs in the area of social justice over the next five years. As bishops we were called both to listen and to exercise judgment in teaching an extremely vital part of the Gospel of Jesus pertaining to the mission on behalf of social justice. Through this process of structured public dialogue, we learned much about the needs of our own people and about the problems of justice and peace which they face in their own lives and communities. Convinced that this program could bear much fruit in the Church today, we undertook a detailed evaluation of all of the recommendations through the committees of the National Conference of Catholic Bishops and the United States Catholic Conference. In addition, we directed the President of the NCCB to appoint an ad hoc committee to coordinate the evaluation process and develop a five-year pastoral plan of action based on its results. We are now prepared to set forth this plan and we invite the cooperation of the entire Catholic community in its implementation. We do so in the firm conviction that our growth as the community of God's people and our ministry of service to the world are inseparable dimensions of our common Christian commitment. We must, and we will, continue to grow in love and care for one another even as we enter more actively into the pursuit of justice and peace. Our participation in that pursuit, indeed, will be authentic and productive only if it truly reflects the quality of our life of fellowship with one another.

The programs and activities proposed here are not our only response to the needs expressed during the bicentennial consultation. Our continuing, collective commitment to the social mission of the Church and the achievement of a more just social order has long been evident in the work of our episcopal conference, its secretariats and committees. Resolutions adopted by the Call to Action conference on such issues as full employment, human rights, disarmament, housing, political responsibility, the aged, criminal justice and world hunger echo similar positions adopted and advocated by the USCC and the NCCB in recent years. The Campaign for Human Development, the Catholic Relief Services, the USCC Migration and Refugee Services and other social services, education and advocacy programs carried out under the auspices of the bishops reflect our determination to meet human needs and to serve the cause of social justice.

Since our meeting a year ago, we have responded to many of the concerns reflected in the Call to Action program. We have created a new Secretariat for the Laity and we have launched new initiatives pertaining to parish life and the family. We have engaged in consultation and articulated principles on teacher unionization in parochial schools, adopted standards for fund raising within the Church and issued statements of concern on the American Indian, human rights in Eastern Europe, the Panama Canal treaties, the U.S. defense policy and crime. Our sponsorship of the Segundo Encuentro Pastoral, a national conference designed to identify and promote the pastoral and human needs of our Hispanic people, and our continuing consultation on increasing leadership opportunities for women in the Church are illustrative of the wide range of activities in our episcopal conference designed to renew the life of the Catholic community in this nation.

Many dioceses, parishes, schools and Catholic organizations have already undertaken programs of response to the Call to Action conference. Some dioceses, for example, have sponsored consultations focusing upon its recommendations, while others have instituted significant pastoral and social programs which respond to the needs articulated. Still other dioceses and organizations have incorporated the program's results into their planning processes. These various responses are in keeping with our statement last spring inviting action at every level of Church life.

During the bicentennial consultation, we found that the vision of the universal Church as an effective agent of social justice and as an advocate for human rights lives in the people of our dioceses and parishes. In expressing, from their living experience, their aspirations for the Church in our day, they reaffirmed their hopes for justice and peace. We began our bicentennial consultation as part of an attempt to implement the directive of Pope Paul VI that each Christian community, through a process of reflection and action, should apply the norms of the Gospel and the teachings of the Church to the conditions in its nation and local communities. The issues which people specified for us reflected the abiding interests of the Church today: the dignity of the person, the welfare of the family, the quality of life in cities and rural areas, the horror of modern war and the need to abolish hunger and poverty from our land and our world.

We cannot address all these issues—or indeed any of them—as a conference of bishops. The call to a ministry of justice and peace is a call to the whole Church. It is a call for the Church to do the work of justice in society and, equally important, a call for the Church to be just in its own life. In shaping a response by NCCB/USCC we have selected six major areas of emphasis. They do not exhaust the total agenda in the ministry of justice and peace, but they do reflect some of its major components. These issues are both local and national; they touch our own land and our relations with other nations. They are chosen because of their intrinsic significance and because they symbolize the larger range of issues which we challenge others in the Church and in the nation to address, even as we try, with others, to address them.

I. Education for Justice

We believe that to realize the goals we have set we must expand and improve our programs of education for justice. This education must cut across generational lines, institutional structures and various educational agencies. It requires teaching and learning the tradition of Catholic social thought, the creation of an environment for learning that reflects a commitment to justice and an openness on the part of all Catholics to change personal attitudes and behavior. In Catholic thought, social justice is not merely a secular or humanitarian matter. Social justice is a reflection of God's respect and concern for each person and an effort to protect the essential human freedom necessary for each person to achieve his or her destiny as a child of God. Because education for justice is such a vast and all-encompassing process, we choose, within the framework of the principle of subsidiarity, to suggest here only a few of the actions we can take at the national level to encourage and complement local programs in families, schools, parishes and dioceses.

We shall establish within the USCC Office of Social Development and World Peace a center for the coordination of ongoing activities in justice education. A staff person, working closely with other national agencies concerned with education for justice, will identify areas in which further initiatives are needed, make available consultative services, facilitate the exchange of information among diocesan and regional offices of social justice and provide materials and resources for schools, workshops, symposia, and other programs requested by diocesan offices and other appropriate agencies. Recognizing the indispensable role of catechesis in forming individuals and communities in the Church, we request that social justice be given appropriate attention and treatment in catechetical programs, using the *National Catechetical Directory* as a base, particularly Chapter VII, "Catechesis for Social Ministry."

The NCCB/USCC will invite scholars and universities to undertake serious research into issues of justice and peace. In doing so we will seek funding from potential sources of research grants, besides cooperating, as circumstances may dictate, in the establishment of a structure for the selection of grantees and a method of collaboration with associations involved in Catholic higher education. We shall co-sponsor with appropriate groups seminars on topics, such as shared responsibility, which are central to the full development of this plan of action.

To those responsible for directing seminaries, we encourage in-service courses, workshops and seminars for faculties and administrators to help them develop programs of justice education and we request that these programs be strengthened. Seminarians and others preparing for ministry should continue to be instructed in the social thought of the Church and have a variety of experiences with social problems and cultural conditions in order to deepen their awareness of injustice and develop the knowledge and skills which will enable them to provide leadership in the Church's ministry of justice and peace.

We request that preparation for ministry for justice continue to be included as an integral part of pastoral preparation in seminaries. Commitment to the promotion of justice should continue to be among the criteria used in evaluating candidates for ordination. We ask the NCCB Committee on Priestly Formation to assess carefully the commitment to justice ministry on the part of a seminary within the committee's regular program of seminary visitation.

We also request that preparation for ministry for justice be continued, and where intensified, as an integral part of diaconate training programs and that positions in ministry for justice be identified and supported as works for permanent deacons. Commitment to the promotion of justice should be among the criteria used in evaluating candidates for ordination.

We urge Catholic colleges and universities to develop degree programs in justice and peace education and to provide resource centers for local justice education projects. We ask all Catholic educational institutions, including elementary and secondary schools, to insure that their students are exposed to fundamental Catholic social teaching as reflected in papal encyclicals and pronouncements, conciliary and synodal documents and episcopal teaching. At the same time, we strongly urge dioceses to seek actively to extend career opportunities in the areas of social ministry and justice education.

We request each diocese to initiate an in-service justice education program for teachers, school administrators and school boards, as well as health care personnel. We request that diocesan offices of religious education develop programs of preparation for the sacraments which will highlight their social as well as individual dimension. Finally, in dioceses where such instrumentalities do not exist, we recommend that consideration be given to the establishment of agencies to promote and coordinate justice education and social action; or, where this is not possible, that the sharing of resources and programs on a regional basis be investigated instead. In this connection, we pledge the assistance and support of the USCC Department of Social Development and World Peace.

II. Family Life

The Church's mission to create and sustain community runs as a theme throughout the Call to Action resolutions. The resolutions place special emphasis on the basic community of the family. Participants in the bicentennial consultation called upon their Church to support family life, foster reconciliation within and among families, enhance the family's teaching, sacramental and social ministries. The family is a vital agent in both Church and society; it preserves tradition and develops the values of the past; it supports persons in their present responsibilities and actively prepares them to meet the challenges of the future. Effective family ministry supports these indispensable functions while embracing all the diverse living situations in which people find themselves.

At this time our episcopal conference is preparing to undertake a special plan of pastoral action for family ministry designed as a response to the report of the USCC Commission on Marriage and Family Life. This plan takes into account the results of the bicentennial consultation and involves a comprehensive approach to family ministry—one that sees the development and strengthening of family life as integral to the total mission of the Church in society. It seeks as well to extend the impact made by Christian families on the formation of public policy and social legislation.

A diocesan family life committee or advisory board, under the direction of the family life officer, will be asked to assess family needs and to evaluate present diocesan ministry and social involvement programs. Programs to be taken into account include marriage preparation, family planning, human sexuality education, marriage and family enrichment practices, family social policy, education and leadership training for couples and families.

The 1980 Family Year will highlight parish programs of family ministry and encourage assessment of them. This assessment and subsequent planning should give consideration to ministry to six groups: the premarried, including young adults and engaged couples; married couples, including newlyweds, middle-aged, and retired couples; parents, including the widowed, parents of the very young, expectant parents, parents of adolescents in crisis, with particular attention to the unique pastoral and social needs of single-parent families; "developing" families, including those facing the needs of beginning their families, issues pertaining to family spirituality and technological pressures upon and within families; "hurting" families, including those confronting the problems of poverty, alcoholism, drug abuse, issues of sexuality, separation and divorce; and "leadership" families, including parish coordinating couples and couples engaged in family social action and the family apostolate, together with their children.

While this plan of action for total family ministry is designed to involve the Church at all levels, it places special emphasis on the parish. The year 1979 has been designated as a year of special diocesan preparation and planning, leading to a Family Year in 1980 and to a decade of family research and renewed ministry thereafter. The USCC, through its departmental agencies, will design educational programs for family social missions and family involvement in social policy formation. It will also continue preparation for the 1980 White House Conference on Families through a special coordinating committee involving other Catholic agencies, organizations and movements.

This parish-level action plan will reach out to involve families in parish ministry, small support groups and social action programs. The aim of the plan is to renew the family, the neighborhood and the parish community, a goal vital to the Church and society.

III. The Church: People, Parishes and Communities

The Church is the community of God's people sharing a common faith while engaged in responding to the needs of all. A pastoral plan of action for justice must involve efforts to deepen our life as a community and improve our ways of living and working together. This present plan recognizes certain basic pastoral principles designed to strengthen our community as we go forth to serve. These include the creative interaction of bishops, theologians and Church leaders and the people and their authentic representatives; specification of pastoral needs based on listening to one another in parishes and dioceses and in the nation; and careful efforts to develop consensus through open and informed discussion, prayerful deliberation and equitable procedures for making decisions. In this section we recommend programs to bring our people into closer touch with one another and to strengthen our ability to establish pastoral objectives based upon people's real needs. Community at the local level, especially in the parish, will have our closest attention during the next five years; it is there that all of us participate most directly in the life and mission of the Church.

The NCCB has already established an Ad Hoc Committee on the Parish to carry out a parish renewal project. Enlisting the cooperation of every diocese, this program will be a major priority of our episcopal conference. It will consider pastoral care, liturgical life, ethnic, cultural and doctrinal pluralism, parish councils and their roles in the mission of the Church. Its work will involve not only studies of parish life, but the preparation of aids, identification and communication of successful renewal programs and the gathering of parish personnel to share experiences.

In reporting to the episcopal conference on its work, we suggest that the Ad Hoc Committee on the Parish highlight progress in the following areas: (a) steps by which parishes can become more creatively involved in the life of their communities; (b) effective models for parish programs of social service and social action; (c) steps by which the rich multicultural heritage of the Church can be strengthened at the local level; and (d) proposals for policies which will insure to every Catholic, whatever his or her income, sex, age, race or social status, the right to share fully in the life of a vital Christian community, and through that community, to participate fully in the mission of the Church.

While continuing our support for the work of the NCCB/USCC Secretariat for Hispanic Affairs, we shall also seek means to encourage development of a National Hispanic Research Center. We request that our Committee for Liaison with the National Office for Black Catholics report by 1980 on further steps which may be taken, beyond those recommended elsewhere in this plan, to improve and encourage community life among black Catholics. Committees of our conference have indicated that they will be striving to improve ministry to diverse ethnic communities so as to incorporate multicultural awareness in Christian education and to insure adequate formation of candidates for ministry in the social teachings of the Church. We will request that these committees provide annual public reports on their progress.

Each diocese is asked to undertake an evaluation of its rural ministry, profiling the social and pastoral needs of its rural people and assessing current resources and programs. Each diocese is encouraged to designate a person to coordinate this program and to make recommendations to diocesan agencies concerning needed reform.

Interested in the quality of Catholic citizenship, we shall ask our Catholic conference directors to undertake a consultation on political responsibility with the goal of devising programs and methods to promote a greater understanding of the way public policy is made and the duties of citizenship.

IV. Economic Justice

Catholic social teaching has consistently maintained that economic life must serve people's needs and be governed by justice. Over the past century, papal encyclicals, conciliar documents and the statements of bishops have often called attention to the social and moral dimensions of economic life. In its teaching, the Church has noted a number of basic human rights in economic life, including the right to productive employment, the right to just wages, the right to an adequate income, the rights of workers to organize and bargain collectively, the right to own property for the many as a protection of freedom and the right to participation in economic decisions.

Each of these rights carries with it responsibilities, such as the duty to work, the duty of property owners to exercise ownership for the common good and the obligation to provide a just wage. These rights and responsibilities are still not fully guaranteed in our society. While poverty and joblessness still plague millions, workers are subject to harassment for their attempts at collective bargaining, and full employment and economic security are not yet operative goals of public policy. The Christian community must intensify its efforts on behalf of these human rights. We propose the following program to make our rich heritage of Catholic teaching come alive in the ministry of the Church and the life of every believer.

Our episcopal conference will continue to speak out for full employment, adequate income, the rights of workers to organize and defense of the poor and the victims of economic injustice. In particular, we shall seek to make our voice heard more effectively in our own Catholic community and where public policy is made. Economic injustice will be a major concern in our teaching ministry and in our relations with the government. In addition, economic justice as well as economic development will continue to be a major emphasis of concern of our Campaign for Human Development. We shall continue to call for a more responsible rate of economic consumption on the part of the people of our nation in order to effect economic justice for the poor in our country and throughout the world.

In 1981, the USCC will convene a major consultation on economic justice. We will bring together leaders of government, business, labor and consumers, economists and theologians to dialogue on how the Christian community can best apply its teaching of economic justice to contemporary conditions. The consultation will focus on ways by which the Church, business, labor and government, as well as individual citizens, can contribute to greater respect for human rights and basic justice in our national economy and in the international economic order. In all such discussions, the poor and those suffering from economic injustice will share. From these discussions may come the feasibility of forming a National Commission on Economic Justice. Such a commission might contribute to broadening and deepening our involvement in the moral and social dimensions of economic issues, make our efforts more effective, visible and productive and provide an ongoing forum for dialogue over Catholic principles and economic life. The scope and purpose of such an undertaking will be dependent upon the above planned consultation.

V. Human Rights

The Church has seen increasingly the defense and promotion of human rights as inseparable from its Gospel mandate. The tradition of Catholic social teaching is clear and emphatic in calling the community to justice. It is also consistent in linking justice to the protection of human rights and the satisfaction of human needs on the local, national and international levels. The recent USCC publication, *Human Rights/Human Needs—An Unfinished Agenda,* provides a tool for educating the community to the wide range of human rights addressed by and rooted in Catholic tradition. We call for a coordinated educational effort in the Catholic community regarding this significant topic during 1978, the 30th anniversary of the *U.N. Universal Declaration of Human Rights.*

The right to life, as a most fundamental human right, is and will remain the object of priority efforts on the part of the Church. We are committed to this work by our vision of human life and destiny, by the teaching of the Church and, in a special way, by our own *Pastoral Plan for Pro-Life Activities.* Therefore, in speaking of our determination to work for human rights, we deem it fitting to speak first of our intention to strive to win greater recognition and respect for this right, which had a prominent place among the Call to Action recommendations. Further consideration of human rights in this section, however, will be limited to only a few of the issues emphasized in the Call to Action recommendations.

Racism remains a major concern. This blight on American society is of special concern for the Church because of its deep moral implications. We hope to issue a pastoral letter dealing with this issue in 1979 and anticipate that it will treat such themes, noted in the Call to Action recommendations, as discrimination in both Church and society, pluralism, as well as the distinction between race and ethnicity and the need to enhance and strengthen cultural pluralism. We shall attempt to address individual, cultural and institutional racism and to initiate a process aimed at overcoming all forms of racism in the Church and in society.

Discrimination based on sex, because it radically undermines the personal identity of both women and men, constitutes a grave injustice in our society. At this point in history, marked, as Pope John indicated in *Pacem In Terris,* by the growing struggle of women to achieve full development, it is urgent that the Church give tangible evidence of its commitment to the rights of women, affirming their dignity as persons and promoting their expanded participation in ecclesial and civic life. We will further purposefully study and dialogue regarding issues of concern to women and the eradication of sexist discrimination in current practices and policies.

Cutting across race, ethnicity, sex and age, discrimination in American society urgently demands our attention. In addition to the pastoral letter we shall undertake the following actions: (1) A USCC statement will be issued by the fall of 1979 which will analyze the pluralism of the American experience, affirm it as a positive value in our culture with profound moral implications for social justice and peace and include appropriate pastoral directives. (2) A set of guidelines for affirmative action will be published by mid-1979 for diocesan evaluation and implementation. Our own conference offices, in their hiring practices, are prepared to take leadership in the implementation of such guidelines. (3) An organized program of action based on the USCC statement, *Society and the Aged: Toward Reconciliation,* will begin in mid-1980. Action will emphasize parish programs of ministry to the elderly and advocacy programs by Church agencies to assist the elderly and to protect their human rights, especially as they are affected by legislative and governmental action.

In order to ensure an increasingly effective response to the pressing needs of the handicapped, we will continue our work with them through the National Advisory Committee on Ministry to the Handicapped and other appropriate groups. The advisory committee, it is to be noted, came into being as a result of our direct invitation, and the conference continues to serve the committee in the role of both convenor and participant. Our pressing efforts in this regard are focusing on a mutual determination of the most effective approach to ensuring across-the-board involvement of our national conferences as well as that of other Church organizations at the regional and local levels.

This involves, as a necessary precondition, an in-depth needs analysis to identify more specifically the priority concerns of this important segment of the Church and of society in general. Although more specific action awaits completion of this present stage of dialogue, one important item already of our forward agenda is a pastoral letter on ministry to the handicapped.

Better understanding of the international dimensions of human rights is urgently needed. A consultation of diocesan representatives on this topic, sponsored by the USCC, by the spring of 1979, will assist the Church at the local level to engage its constituents in this vital work. From such a consultation, specific programs for promoting human rights internationally should emerge; e.g., the celebration of a World Day of Peace and the formation of groups for disarmament, for opposition to the arms race, for promotion of international economic structural changes and for providing support to the suffering Church in the Third World and in Eastern Europe.

VI. World Hunger

The basic human right to eat continues to be denied to hundreds of millions of people in the United States and overseas.

In an effort to combat world hunger, our offices at the United States Catholic Conference will continue to monitor U.S. food policy, including constant appraisal of national policies affecting food exports, domestic food programs (e.g., food stamps, school lunch programs) and agricultural policies. We shall also continue to prepare educational materials on these matters and to present testimony before appropriate congressional committees.

Dioceses are urged to continue to support local efforts to provide remedial programs such as food banks and food kitchens for the needy, advocacy support for persons eligible for government assistance and support for programs such as the Catholic Relief Services, Operation Rice Bowl, Bread for the World and World Food Day.

On the domestic level, the USCC will provide dioceses and parishes with a Lenten program in 1980 designed to provide American Catholics with a prayer period for examining their personal lifestyles in relation to eating habits and patterns of energy consumption.

Conclusion

In setting forth this six-part program, we pledge ourselves for the next five years to an ongoing effort to monitor and evaluate its implementation. At the end of that five-year period there will be an evaluation and review of the plan of action which we have set forth in terms of its impact on the Church and society. Further, we call upon the Department of Social Development and World Peace, the Department of Education and the Department of Communication of the United States Catholic Conference to assist in the implementation of this plan by calling together national, regional and diocesan social ministry, catechetical and communications personnel to enlist their aid in publicizing and implementing this plan of action.

We are all learning how to live the Gospel anew today. We have truly heard a "call to action" both from our Holy Father and from our Catholic people across the land. The programs we have outlined offer a sufficient challenge to all our leadership groups to engage in generous service to the word.

Ultimately, the call is directed to each Catholic in America. It is an invitation to each to make a personal commitment to seek justice and to live justly. There is no "program" for bringing this about. The action needed does not lie essentially in plans, projects or statements. Rather, we know as Christians that the most effective response to the ills of the world is ours to make, the duty to seek justice and equality resides with each of us. Here, in the painfully slow changing of our own lives and in the agony of living out our vocations, lies the essential key to a more decent and more human world.

We pray and we trust that God's love, alive in the hearts of our people, will fire their imaginations and enkindle in them a desire for a more simple way of life, free from dependency on luxuries mistaken for necessities; that it will liberate them from prejudgments about others which are an obstacle to sharing the faith with them; and will enable them to view with an objective eye the deleterious effects on human beings of unjust social structures and to strive with courageous hearts to change these for the better; that it will intensify their commitment to service out of love for the One Who has first loved us. So also we pray and trust the same for ourselves.

Crime and Punishment

In November 1973, the USCC issued a formal statement entitled "The Reform of Correctional Institutions in the 1970s." The basic thrust of the statement is that rehabilitation, not punishment, should be the primary concern of correctional institutions. The bishops argue further that a system should be worked out to compensate victims of crime or their survivors. They also recommend higher wages and realistic safety provisions for prison staff and urge society to accept released offenders with compassion so that they will not become recidivists.

Having discussed the problems besetting correctional institutions, the USCC offers twenty-two recommendations for their reform. These recommendations are so extensive and detailed they do not permit short summary. It suffices here to reiterate the USCC's rationale for speaking out in such detail on this issue: ". . . to insure protection for all the civil rights of confined offenders in an atmosphere of human compassion conducive to reconciliation and rehabilitation."

In 1974, the USCC issued a one-line statement declaring its opposition to the reinstitution of capital punishment.

The USCC Committee on Social Development and World Peace entered the debate on handgun violence in September 1975. The bishops' statement contains several policy proposals meant to reduce the number of deaths caused by handguns. The bishops acknowledge that their proposals are only stop-gap measures that will not solve the problem of handgun violence. What really must be done, they argue, is to prohibit the importation, manufacture, sale, possession, and use of handguns with the obvious exceptions of the police, military, security guards, and pistol clubs.

Early in 1978, the USCC's Committee on Social Development and World Peace issued a comprehensive statement on the subject of crime and punishment. In it, the bishops of the committee point out four major causes of crime: (1) society's tendency toward materialism, excessive individualism, and acceptance of violence; (2) social and economic deprivation; (3) family and neighborhood breakdown; and (4) lack of moral leadership from government, the business community, labor, medicine, education, social service professions, the media, and religious leaders.

The bishops believe the Church has a two-fold role to play in response to the problem of crime. First, they suggest twenty-two initiatives for parishes, dioceses, and religious orders to undertake, such as establishing a system of "block patrols" and citizen watches in high crime areas, providing a forum for the discussion of crime issues, and aiding parolees to find suitable work. Second, the committee encourages the USCC and dioceses around the country to support certain public policy initiatives. For instance, the committee suggests support for handgun control, opposition to the reinstitution of the death penalty, greater efforts to combat white collar crime, and opposition to electronic surveillance.

The Reform of Correctional Institutions in the 1970s

USCC, November 1973

I was ill and you comforted me, in prison and you came to visit me. Then the just will ask him: "Lord ... when did we visit you when you were ill or in prison?" The King will answer them: "I assure you, as often as you did it for one of my least brothers, you did it for me."

(Matt. 25:36ff)

Introduction

In the preparation of this statement, more than a score of persons were consulted, both in their individual professional capacities and, in some instances, as representatives of particular groups. Included in this consultation were prison chaplains, minority group representatives, administrative and custodial personnel of correctional institutions and representatives of an ex-offender organization. Comments of the Federal Bureau of Prisons were helpful, particularly in verifying certain factual points and the feasibility of specific recommendations, without implying endorsement of this statement by the bureau.[1] To all who assisted us we are indebted for their contribution.

Concern

In recent years Americans have experienced deepening concern over the presence and nature of crime in our nation.[2] We share this concern. Fully adequate law enforcement and protection of law-abiding citizens are clear but unmet needs. We oppose violence, whether in defiance of law and order or under the cover of preserving law and order. We oppose both "crime in the streets" and "white collar crime." Dedicated people throughout the country are earnestly striving to identify and deal with the roots of crime.[3] Some, very properly, are questioning society's reaction to victimless crimes. Others are

---

[1] Larry F. Taylor, Executive Assistant, Federal Bureau of Prisons, to John E. Cosgrove, 5 November 1973, Personal Files of John E. Cosgrove, Division of Urban Affairs, U.S. Catholic Conference, Washington, D.C.

[2] Harry Fleischmann, "Crime" (to be published in the *Encyclopedia Yearbook 1973*) pp. 8- 9.

[3] Milton Rector, President, National Council on Crime and Delinquency, to John E. Cosgrove, 26 December 1972, Personal Files of John E. Cosgrove.

addressing themselves to the issues of law enforcement and the procedures of our criminal courts. Still others are concentrating their attention upon the manner in which suspects and convicted criminals are dealt with and provided for while incarcerated.

The numerous reports issued by representatives of this last group, coupled with incidents of violence in correctional institutions across the nation, have aroused many consciences. In a few instances, federal district court orders have dealt positively with abuses in local institutions of incarceration, because some of the constitutional rights of the resident offenders were being violated. We believe it is timely and urgent that we express ourselves on the moral problems involved in sentencing and incarcerating violators of the law.

We wish it clearly understood that most administrators, guards and other staff members of our correctional institutions are decent, dedicated public servants and that those confined—aside from those awaiting trail—are there because they have been found guilty of crimes or contempt of court.

Crime and punishment are pre-eminently moral issues.[4] Much of the amorality in society today arises from contemporary man's neglect or refusal to place his affairs ultimately in God's hands. In attempting to take control away from God one begins the process of losing control over himself. The immorality of crime results from disregard for the love and worship owed to God; from lack of consideration and esteem for one's neighbor; and from failures in self-knowledge and in self-discipline.

It behooves us to be aware that, despite well-publicized exceptions, prisons are largely filled with the poor, the disadvantaged minorities and the "losers" of our society. We need to examine whether we may not have a "poor man's" system of criminal justice. Often the petty thief—the shoplifter or the pickpocket—goes to jail while the clever embezzler, the glib swindler, the powerful racketeer, the polished profiteer may only undergo the litigation of the civil courts. In the case of the open "vices" prohibited by law, the "town drunk" is sentenced by a judge while the "country club alcoholic" is treated by a physician. We insist that punishment, in order to fulfill its proper purpose, must fit the nature of the crime; it must be considerate of the offender's human dignity; and, it must be tempered by mercy and constantly aimed at reconciliation.

In our response to the urging of Jesus, recorded in St. Matthew's Gospel, to "visit" those in prisons, it is necessary that we not only visit individuals confined in prison but "visit" the correctional system itself. Our concern for correctional institutions does not exist in isolation from other related issues. The injustices and inequities that plague our society affect both the incidence of crime and the administration of correctional institutions. The problems in these institutions are also intimately bound up with the inadequacies of our judicial system. These include unreasonably delayed trials, particularly ag-

---

[4] Archbishop Philip M. Hannan to John E. Cosgrove, 24 January 1973, Personal Files of John E. Cosgrove.

gravating when the accused is jailed; the lack both of quality and adequate quantity of legal counsel for the needy; difficulties with bail bonds; and widespread abuses of such useful expedients as plea bargaining.

What happens in the correctional institutions of this nation should not be considered apart from what is happening in the courts, in the executive offices of powerful corporations where major economic decisions affecting millions of people are often made, in the legislatures, in police stations, in employment offices, in schools, in homes and on the streets. Society's most serious failings—in the ugly and despicable forms of racism, disrespect for life, physical violence, political repression and corruption, erosion of individual and civil liberties, setting profit for the few over the necessities of the many, sexual perversion and materialistic inducements—all add explosive fuel to the smoldering problems in the field of correction.

Several broad issues of criminal justice are distinct from, but related to, conditions in correctional institutions. One is the general slowness and inadequacy of federal and state criminal judicial procedures. Delays and overloads by themselves raise serious questions of equity, most often adversely affecting the poor. The rights of the accused should be protected before and during trial. Before formal changes are made, adequate evidence should be an absolute requirement. Additional analyses and funding to reorganize the criminal justice system to accord with the best aspirations of all our people should be given urgent priority.

Recompense for the innocent victims of crime is a sensitive and painful problem. Society must share at least some of the responsibility for compensating innocent victims of crime. When a way is found to pay offenders a fair rate for the work they do in confinement, provisions should be made for regular court-determined payments as at least partial recompense to the victims, or the survivors of the victims of their crimes. This also could become a more personalized aspect of programs such as now exist in several states to compensate innocent victims of violent crimes.

Purpose of Correctional Institutions

Whether the penal system of the United States should not seek to deal with all except dangerous offenders outside of penal institutions is a question which merits much attention. This is a challenging concept clamoring for a fair chance to prove itself—a chance which society should give it forthwith. There is increasing and strongly convincing evidence that a large center of incarceration should *not* be the major instrument for dealing with convicted offenders. Bigger, better, more modern buildings are not the answer.

Smaller, community-based facilities are beginning to prove that they are more appropriate and effective. Half-way houses, work contracts and other alternatives need to be more fully explored. A sympathetic consideration of such approaches should precede any extensive remodeling of existing buildings or construction of contemplated new structures.

In the meantime, however, we must deal with the correctional system as it is. When one examines the situation of confined, convicted criminals, one finds an urgent need to clarify precisely what society is seeking to achieve through their incarceration. Is a correctional institution an instrument of punishment whereby a criminal "does time" in expiation for his misdeeds? Is it a place of custody where a dangerous citizen is detained in order to protect and restore order in society? Is it a means of retribution designed to deter the criminal himself and/or the populace at large from engaging in unlawful behavior? Is a correctional institution ultimately a place for rehabilitation in which a criminal is re-educated or reconciled to a lawful way of life? We feel it is, or ought to be, a composite of all of these, but that pre-eminently it is a place for rehabilitation.

Correctional institutions in fact do harm if they do not offer opportunity for rehabilitation. We are unequivocally committed to the view that rehabilitation should be their primary concern and will do all in our power to make this a reality. There are, however, limitations in this concept. The ideal of rehabilitation cannot, for example, justify investing members of the criminal justice system with excessive discretion to extend a prisoner's term of incarceration. Because of the very common practice of indeterminate sentencing and the frequently arbitrary decisions of overburdened parole boards, a criminal's confinement time can be unjustly and inhumanly extended beyond any reasonable criterion of retribution for his offense. There is need for a mechanism by which parole board decisions can be reviewed, with provision for judicial intervention if necessary.

Those engaged in motivating confined individuals should bear in mind that they are dealing with human beings, created in the image and likeness of God and endowed with free will. Rehabilitation cannot be imposed. The offender has to be convinced of its value and led freely to desire it. Moreover, methods of rehabilitation whose appropriateness can be called into question by reasonable persons should not be forced upon any and all indiscriminately. Certain kinds of group therapy or chemico-psychological treatments or experimentation should not be required of those unwilling or unable to make an intelligent and free decision to submit to them. Furthermore, when such unwillingness results in prolonging the term of incarceration or other discretionary penalties, basic freedoms of the incarcerated are affronted. "Hiring out" the sentenced, as is occasionally done with illegal immigrants in particular, is a wholly unacceptable practice. As the intention to rehabilitate does not exempt from the obligations of retributive justice, so retribution does not legitimatize assaults upon human dignity. Although we speak in the defense of rights of prisoners, we are not unaware of their responsibilities and obligations. They should obey reasonable regulations, serve the just sentences imposed, respect the staff and other residents of the institution and cooperate in the process of rehabilitation.

There is general agreement among qualified commentators that the correctional institutions of our land have, in most cases, failed in the matter of rehabilitation. The numbers of those who are re-incarcerated tend to prove this. Chief Justice Warren E. Burger recently argued the need to reform penal institutions and to develop processes to determine whether particular convicted persons should or should not be confined.[5] The widespread failure to rehabilitate, the Chief Justice observed, is demonstrated by the degree of recidivism. It is true, of course, that rehabilitation is not the only purpose of prisons and that their historic purpose has been to incarcerate. However, even the effectiveness of prisons in incarcerating is related to their effectiveness in rehabilitation. Certainly with regard to rehabilitation, they are, in general, not performing acceptably. All blame, however, for recidivism cannot be attributed to the institutions. Society's unwillingness to accept released offenders with compassion and understanding is a large factor in recidivism.

Operation of Correctional Institutions

Whatever the professed intentions of society may be, our correctional institutions are fundamentally places of custody, strongholds for the secure removal of certain citizens from our midst. Accordingly, the rehabilitative staff (psychologists, sociologists, chaplains, teachers, instructors, etc.) is regularly subordinated to the custodial staff (wardens, guards, etc.), not only on the organization chart of the institution's administration but also in regard to budget. In addition, correctional institutions are commonly located far from urban centers from which the majority of convicted criminals come and to which they are likely to return. Consequently, inmates have little opportunity gradually to learn or re-learn conventional societal living through controlled educational and social contacts or even through regular visits from relatives, friends or sympathetic volunteers. Distance from urban centers also greatly reduces the likelihood of recruiting a staff whose racial, ethnic and social backgrounds are similar to those of the inmates. Thus, alienation and lack of understanding between staff and residents are almost inevitable; and rehabilitation remains largely an abstract ideal rather than a concrete achievement.

Add to all of this in some cases such positive injustices as minimal opportunities for academic or vocational training, unsatisfying work experience with pay that is frequently demeaning, sexual assaults, inadequate diet, meager bathing and recreational facilities, insufficient psychological and medical care, fear, loneliness and shame, plus the all-too-common outrage of associating youthful first offenders with hardened criminals, and the result can be the very reverse of an institution of rehabilitation. It is instead an instrument of punishment or perhaps just a means of deterring the criminally

---

[5] Warren E. Burger, Chief Justice of the United States, address to the National Conference of Christians and Jews Annual Dinner, Philadelphia, Pennsylvania, 16 November 1972, p. 3.

inclined from engaging in unlawful behavior; it may also be a setting which generates further crimes in a spirit of vindictiveness.

Rights of Prisoners

The conditions which prevail in many of our correctional institutions cannot be defended on the grounds of either punishment or deterrence. Christian belief in the potential goodness of man and recognition of every human being's dignity as a child of God redeemed by Jesus Christ causes us to recoil from any form of punishment which is degrading or otherwise corrodes the human personality. Society has a right to protect itself against lawbreakers and even to exact just and measured retribution, but the limits of what is reasonable and just are far exceeded in too many penal institutions. Abuses cannot be justified on the basis of their effectiveness as deterrents to crime. The disturbing statistics of recidivism demonstrate that our correctional institutions have little deterrent effect. It is necessary in any case to raise serious moral objection to tormenting one man unjustly in order to instruct or caution another.

All these considerations bring us back to the primary purpose of houses of correction in the United States as commonly articulated in law and accepted by society. Correctional institutions should be institutions of rehabilitation. They should help men and women rebuild their lives so that, with few exceptions, they can return to society as considerate, free and law-abiding citizens. They are places of custody, but they are never to be only that. They are also instruments of retribution and in a measure strategies for deterrence. These purposes, nevertheless, are to be kept in balance with the need to safeguard the moral order in society while at the same time assisting in the rehabilitation of offending human beings who urgently need society's understanding and care.

Such an analysis clearly derives from a religious conception of man and commitment to the virtues of justice and charity. However, even apart from religious and humanitarian motivation, society's self-interest will best be served by adopting such a view of correctional institutions and working to make it a reality. Nothing whatever is gained by permitting correctional institutions to function as mere fortresses within which self-hatred and embitterment thrive. Confined offenders are not our "enemies." They are fellow human beings, most of whom will one day move freely in our midst, either better or worse for their prison experience. If worse, either they have failed themselves or we have failed both them and ourselves. If better, we have acted in righteousness before God and man; and we have also made an important, essentially positive, contribution to safety and tranquillity in society. In addition, we are ever mindful that each resident offender has individual needs. We emphasize this even as we urge that the correctional institutions develop a relationship—far closer than heretofore—to society in general.

Recommendations

With all this in mind, we offer the following suggestions for reform in the correctional institutions of the United States. Some of these proposals are already being implemented in various places. We add our own endorsement not as experts in penology but as concerned citizens and men of faith. There is no intent to coddle criminals or to harass administrators of correctional institutions. We speak with a view to motivating all those with responsibilities in the field of correction so that their efforts may render correctional facilities more efficacious instruments for the rehabilitation of offenders and for deterrence of further crime. In the prayerful hope of sustaining the best efforts of the often heroic men and women who staff correctional institutions and whose skill, patience, prudence, kindness and dedication are vital to the rehabilitative process, we strongly recommend a higher scale of remuneration with realistic provisions for safety and security in the performance of their duties. Our fundamental purpose remains throughout—to insure protection for all the civil rights of confined offenders in an atmosphere of human compassion conducive to reconciliation and rehabilitation.

1. Correctional institutions whose residents come mainly from urban centers should usually be located near these centers. This will facilitate such desirable things as visitation by relatives, friends and volunteers, recruitment of prison staffs from among members of racial, ethnic and social groups similar to those to which the residents belong, and even the gradual reintegration of the residents into free society.

2. Staffs should be recruited on the bases of ability, training and experience without reference to partisan politics.[6] The most modern sociological and psychological means should be used to screen and select the staff. Salaries should be competitive with those paid persons engaged in education and training activities in the private sector. The custodial and rehabilitative staffs should be integrated so that rehabilitation is furthered rather than subordinated to other purposes. Staff members should be encouraged to seek further training through courses in universities and colleges and through regular participation in "in-service" training programs. Advancement and salary increases should be determined at least in part by the extent of such continuing education.

3. In developing programs and facilities careful consideration to the varying needs of men and women is important. Male residents should

---

[6] Joseph R. Rowan, Executive Director of the John Howard Association, to John E. Cosgrove, 20 December 1972, Personal Files of John E. Cosgrove.

be separated from female residents in different facilities; juveniles from adults; first offenders from repeaters; sexual offenders in specialized treatment centers. The emotionally disturbed should be treated in institutions designed for this purpose. The availability of educational training and any other appropriate programs for men and women together should be investigated. Extraordinary efforts should be made to rehabilitate juvenile offenders. Few, if any, offenders should be deprived of access to families and friends.

4. Discrimination because of race, religion or national or ethnic background is never tolerable. Inspectors should be especially alert to expressions of such discrimination in work assignments, the granting of privileges and the manner in which residents are addressed, responded to, given orders and corrected by members of the staff.

5. Free exercise of religion should be guaranteed in every institution. Religious services of various faiths and denominations should be regularly available; chaplains should be welcomed on a continuing or an occasion-by-occasion basis, as needed; and dietary laws should be respected. Residents should be free to consult their chaplains in private and at length. The chaplains should never be constrained to testify before parole boards or to share privileged information with members of the staff. Chaplains should not be required to serve on administrative boards which make decisions about discipline, parole or probation.

6. All residents should be given the regulations of the institution in writing. They should be advised of their rights and privileges, their responsibilities and obligations, punishments to which they are subject for infractions of regulations and established grievance procedures. When necessary, the regulations should be read to residents, in a language they understand. The regulations should be available not only to inspectors but also to the general public.

7. Residents should never be authorized to punish one another. Members of the staff should not inflict any punishments other than those stipulated in the regulations for a particular infraction. Whipping, shackling as a punishment and other penalties which are of their nature cruel or degrading are to be excluded. If solitary confinement is necessary as a last resort, the cell should be standard size, well lighted and ventilated, and the resident should be properly clothed. Adequate diet and facilities for bodily hygiene are to be provided together with regular visitation by a medical officer.

8. All residents should be afforded protection against all assaults, sexual or otherwise, even if this requires a transfer.

9. At least elementary and secondary education and vocational training that is truly useful in free society should be provided all residents who wish to take advantage of these opportunities. In vocational and apprentice training the wholehearted cooperation of industry and labor is indispensable and could very well become a key factor in personal readjustment for the residents.

10. The work to which a resident is assigned should be—and appear to be—worthwhile and compatible with the dignity of a human being. Nothing is so devastating to human aspirations as a work assignment which both parties know is really useless. National standards* should be adopted and promulgated regarding compensation for work. Enabling the residents to work at a fair wage may, among other things, help keep their families off the welfare rolls, either totally or partially. Much greater emphasis is needed on practical job training and post-release employment opportunity. Government agencies should make it their policy to purchase products produced in correctional institutions whenever possible.

11. National standards should be adopted and promulgated regarding residents' diets, the lighting and ventilation of their living and working environments, their access to toilet and bathing facilities, the extremes of temperature in which they are required to live and work, the quality and cleanliness of their clothing and the medical and psychiatric care available to them. Undue regimentation in clothing and grooming should be eliminated.

12. A resident should be free to refuse treatments, aimed at social rehabilitation, whose appropriateness can be called into question by reasonable persons in and outside the institution. No penalties of any kind should result from such refusal.

13. National standards should be adopted and promulgated regarding the residents' right to send and receive mail, censorship of mail (allowing for necessary inspection), access to printed literature within the institution and from without, and opportunities to listen to the radio and watch television. In developing these standards, it should be borne in mind that most resident offenders are preparing to return to

---

*Reference here and elsewhere to "national standards" implies the hope that states would voluntarily adhere to them. However, consideration should be given to making adherence a precondition of any federal grants to the state's criminal justice system.

free society, where their survival will depend largely upon the persons with whom they maintained contact during their confinement and their knowledge and understanding of current events and thinking.

14. Authorities should encourage visiting by residents' relatives, friends and acquaintances. The design and appointments of visiting rooms should create an atmosphere of dignity, warmth and as much privacy as possible. Where feasible, opportunity and facilities for conjugal visits should be provided for married residents and their spouses. Where possible, family celebrations, picnics and such events as "father-son" and "mother-daughter" days should be arranged. Furloughs should be more liberal, when this is prudent in order to strengthen family life. Furloughs can help offenders apply for jobs, visit sick relatives, attend funerals and maintain social ties useful toward rehabilitation. The experience can also be a helpful forerunner to parole. In some states this has proven to be a success.[7] Several states have developed the work-release system for felony offenders; happily, even more have done so with regard to residents of local county jails. Work-release programs should be extended as far as feasible. Obviously the above opportunities could be made available only to offenders who exhibit an interest in rehabilitation.

15. A national committee of lawyers, state and federal legislators, members of correctional staffs, offenders and ex-offenders and other knowledgeable citizens should be assigned the task of establishing a national code of civil rights for the incarcerated and the development of standardized grievance and due-process procedures as well as a bill of rights clearly defining the extent of duties and limits of obligations of the incarcerated. A similar committee should be assigned to develop a plan of self-governance in such areas as recreation, entertainment, and voluntary educational and vocational training.

16. National standards should be adopted and promulgated regarding the inspection of correctional institutions. Educational requirements for inspectors should be specified. All inspectors' reports should be required to follow a standardized form in order to facilitate comparison from year to year and between various areas of the nation and various institutions. These reports should be available to the general public.

17. No resident should be detained simply because employment is not available. If employment is a condition for release and no private employment is available, federal, state or local government should make every effort to assist the resident. Career counseling, testing,

---

[7] *Ibid.*

guidance and bonding—where applicable—should be offered all who are preparing to be released.

18. A resident should be informed of the date beyond which further detention demands another intervention of the court.

19. Parole is a vital function, both for the offender and for society. Consideration should be given to shifting the "burden of proof" by making a parole automatic after a defintely determined period of confinement unless there is sound reason against it.

20. Congress should investigate the feasibility of extending the Social Security Act (OASDI) coverage to residents of correctional institutions.

21. After release, ex-offenders, upon their resumption of life in society, should have their civil rights completely restored. Limiting the activities of an ex-offender in public life could undo what took years to build-up. Individual and community acceptance of ex-offenders with love and understanding is absolutely necessary for their complete integration into normal community living. Community-based correctional efforts, therefore, should be high on the list of priorities.

22. The use and dissemination of arrest records should be strictly controlled. The revelation of arrest records, where there was no conviction, should be forbidden, as should the denial of employment for reason of an arrest without conviction. (There may, however, be some exceptions to these principles in the case of persons who have been committed for actions resulting from emotional disturbances, or where an inquiry can be demonstrated to be justified in terms of personal or community security. But care should be taken that the exceptions do not degenerate into abuses.)

Parole and Pre-Trial

Closely allied with concerns about correctional reform are two other issues: parole and conditions in jails for those awaiting trial. Both matters urgently need study and attention.

On every side, one hears of institutional case workers obliged to prepare recommendations for parole boards on the basis of meager records and little or no contact with the custodial or training staffs. Parole officers are commonly overburdened with lengthy reports and unreasonable numbers of persons to serve. Parole boards themselves often include members who have only token preparation for their responsibility and who frequently do not have the time even to grant a hearing to those upon whose freedom they are to rule. The effect of all of this on morale is devastating.

In our nation a man is presumed innocent until proved guilty. Yet after arrest he may spend many months awaiting trial in jail under conditions that can only be described as penal. Usually it is the poor who suffer most under these circumstances. Deprived of freedom, forced to idleness, associating with persons who in many instances are dangerous, the accused may well wonder just how much value the legal presumption of innocence really has. The result all too often is that he grows angry, bitter and is started—or confirmed—in a life of crime. If the prisons of our nation need reform, so also do the jails—a great many of which are houses of terror.

Responsibility

We wish to bring all these matters to the attention of chief executives, legislators and judges and of the staffs of correctional institutions, for we believe that they have an obligation in law and in conscience to undertake or continue a thoroughgoing reform of the American criminal justice system. At the same time, we recognize our own duty to alert all the Catholic faithful and to call these considerations to the attention of all our fellow Christians and citizens of his nation to the need for such reform and to the part they can take in urging, supporting and participating in it. Significant achievement in the reform of our correctional system will benefit society more than it will benefit the reformed criminal. The replacement of just a small tile in a grand mosaic makes a noticeable difference in its composite beauty.

Suggested Action Steps

Among other appropriate actions, and with whatever modifications are appropriate and prudent, the following steps are indicated.

The United States Catholic Conference will undertake widespread distribution of this statement. In addition, under coordination of the Conference's Division for Urban Affairs, each staff office, department and division of the USCC and the committee secretariats of the National Conference of Catholic Bishops will be asked—as will the National Catholic Community Service, the National Conference of Catholic Charities, and the National Council of Catholic Laity—to develop programs furthering the purposes of this statement. The USCC will also consider joint ventures with other organizations in the field of correctional institution reform.

The state Catholic conferences should consider the many aspects of this problem which will require state legislation, interventions with the executive branches of the state governments and—as appropriate—the filing of briefs *amicus curiae* in cases of special significance. State Catholic conferences may also wish to develop more specific documents on reform, relating to conditions in their own states.

Dioceses will, we trust, continue or undertake a major role in fostering the concern of the clergy, religious and laity for the human rights of offenders. Diocesan newspapers and other programs of communication can highlight the moral considerations involved in correctional reform and urge action. As bishops we will make every effort to provide qualified chaplains to serve the offenders.

Parishes have a singular opportunity to serve by helping to improve local institutions within their boundaries. This will include support of the chaplains or providing such periodic services where there are no chaplains. In addition, parishes can maintain continuing contact with correctional institutions by committees or groups of concerned parishioners and can work to overcome neighborhood resistance to community-based institutions.

Religious orders, because of their dedication and knowledge in various disciplines, can bring special assistance to administrative and custodial officials, as well as to the residents in our correctional system. They can offer the People of God a greater understanding of the problems of our correctional system and of all of the people concerned with it. In addition, religious communities can literally "visit" those "in prison." Perhaps some will make service to confined offenders their special apostolate as counselors and educators.

College and university groups, including those engaged in campus ministry, can bring companionship and comfort to prisoners by visiting and otherwise assisting them. Visits to prisons by local groups of the National Council of Catholic Women have proven valuable. Various groups can offer special services to the families of prisoners such as providing transportation for visits to the prisoners.

Recognizing that accountability at every level is a major ingredient for making our nation's criminal justice system truly a system of justice, we urge specific methods for evaluation and reasonable community accountability of the work of criminal justice professionals. This applies at every level of the system to both custodial and treatment personnel, pre-sentence investigators, parole and probation officials and all other workers involved.

Finally, each of us should responsively recall that Christ our Lord was a prisoner and according to His living gospel is still present in the person of those who are prisoners today. His apostles knew the agonies of dark dungeons. Many of His original disciples experienced the inhuman cruelty of primitive jails. To this day—in many lands—many of His most dedicated followers find themselves in penal cells or isolated under house arrest.

May our contemplation of these facts inspire us to provide a humble human presence—touched with the sacred—for those accused and those convicted. Let our standing by them or walking with them reunite us as good neighbors and true friends worthy of sharing in the lasting joys of the only absolute unity, God our heavenly Father.

Conclusion

We ask for the prayers and support of all God-fearing people and all those of good will in a renewed effort to improve our criminal justice system; to bring law, order and justice to society; and to strengthen correctional institutions as places where human dignity will be protected and advanced by serious, innovative programs directed to rehabilitation. We ask God's blessing on such efforts and on all who take part in them.

Statement on Capital Punishment

USCC, November 1974

"The United States Catholic Conference goes on record in opposition to capital punishment."

Handgun Violence: A Threat to Life

*USCC, Committee on Social
Development and World Peace
September 11, 1975*

The Problem

There are currently 40 million handguns in the United States.[1] More than 2½ million new handguns will be manufactured and sold this year. In most of our cities and rural areas, purchasing a weapon is as easy as buying a camera.

In 1973, the last year for which complete figures were available, there were 28,000 firearms deaths.[2] In 1975, it is estimated that nearly 30,000 will die from gunshot wounds. Added to this are over 100,000 people wounded by guns each year, the victims of 160,000 armed robberies and 100,000 assaults with guns.[3]

Gun accidents are now the fifth most common accidental cause of death according to the National Safety Council. In 1973, 2,700 people died in gun-related accidents.

Some have suggested that homeowners and citizens should arm themselves to protect their families from murder, assault or robbery. The sad fact is that a handgun purchased for protection is often used in a moment of rage or fear against a relative or acquaintance. A recent study in the Cleveland area indicates guns purchased for protection resulted in the deaths of six times as many family members, friends and neighbors as intruders or assailants.[4] The *1973 FBI Uniform Crime Report* indicates that of all murders almost 25% involved one family member killing another and an additional 40% occur among people who are acquainted. Most homicides are not the result of criminal design but rather they are the outcome of quarrels and arguments

---

[1] Estimate of the Division of Alcohol, Firearms and Tobacco, U.S. Department of the Treasury. Handgun refers to a firearm held and fired by the hand, usually a pistol or revolver. It does not include rifles, shotguns, long guns or other shoulder arms.

[2] There were 13,070 murders involving firearms according to *Crime In The United States 1973*, the FBI Uniform Crime Report (September, 1974). In addition, there were 2,700 deaths involving firearms accidents according to *Accident Facts*, National Safety Council. And, approximately 13,317 people committed suicides with firearms according to the National Center for Health Statistics.

[3] *Crime In The United States 1973*, FBI Uniform Crime Report. September, 1974.

[4] A 1968–1972 study of the Medical School of Case Western University. Of the 131 persons killed, 114 were family members or acquaintances killed because a gun was present in the home and 17 were robbers or other persons engaged in criminal activity.

among spouses, friends and acquaintances. In these situations, it is the ready availability of handguns that often leads to tragic and deadly results.

Handguns play a disproportionate role in gun violence. They account for 53% of all murders, yet make up only 20% of all firearms. The problem is growing. The annual sales of handguns have quadrupled in the last ten years.

A National Firearms Policy

The growing reality and extent of violent crime is of great concern to the Committee on Social Development and World Peace and to all Americans. It threatens more and more of our citizens and communities. The cost of this violence in terms of human life and suffering is enormous. We speak out of pastoral concern as persons called to proclaim the Gospel of Jesus, who "came that they may have life and have it to the full." (John 10:10). We are deeply committed to upholding the value of human life and opposing those forces which threaten it.

One of these factors is the easy availability of handguns in our society. Because it is so easily concealed, the handgun is often the weapon of crime. Because it is so readily available, it is often the weapon of passion and suicide.

This is clearly a national problem. No state or locality is immune from the rising tide of violence. Individual state and local action can only provide a partial solution. We must have a coherent *national* firearms policy responsive to the overall public interest and respectful of the rights and privileges of all Americans. The unlimited freedom to possess and use handguns must give way to the rights of all people to safety and protection against those who misuse these weapons.

We believe that effective action must be taken to reverse this rising tide of violence. For this reason, we call for effective and courageous action to control handguns, leading to their eventual elimination from our society. Of course, reasonable exceptions ought to be made for the police, military, security guards, and pistol clubs where guns would be kept on the premises under secure conditions.

We recognize that this may be a long process before truly comprehensive control is realized. We therefore endorse the following steps to regulate the use and sale of handguns:

1. A several day cooling-off period. This delay between the time of the sale and possession of the handgun by the purchaser should result in fewer crimes of passion.

2. A ban on "Saturday Night Specials." These weapons are cheap, poorly made pistols often used in street crime.

3. Registration of handguns. This measure could provide an improved

system of tracing weapons by law enforcement officials. Registration will tell us how many guns there are and who owns them.

4. Licensing of handgun owners. Handguns should not be available to juveniles, convicted felons, the mentally ill and persons with a history of drug or alcohol abuse.

5. More effective controls and better enforcement of existing laws regulating the manufacture, importation and sale of handguns.

These individual steps will not completely eliminate the abuse of handguns. We believe that only prohibiting the importation, manufacture, sale, possession and use of handguns, with the exceptions we have already cited, will provide a comprehensive response to handgun violence.

Conclusion

We realize this is a controversial issue and that some people of good faith will find themselves opposed to these measures. We acknowledge that controlling possession of handguns will not eliminate gun violence, but we believe it is an indispensable element for any serious or rational approach to the problem.

We support the legitimate and proper use of rifles and shotguns for hunting and recreational purposes. We do not wish to unduly burden hunters and sportsmen. On the contrary, we wish to involve them in a joint effort to eliminate the criminal and deadly misuse of handguns.

We are, of course, concerned about the rights of the individual, as these rights are grounded in the Constitution and in the universal design of our Creator. We are convinced that our position is entirely in accord with the rights guaranteed by our Constitution, and particularly with the Second Amendment to the Constitution as these rights have been clarified by the United States Supreme Court. We affirm the traditional principle that individual rights to private property are limited by the universal demands of social order and human safety as well as the common good.

Statement on Capital Punishment

Joseph L. Bernardin, President
NCCB, January 26, 1977

Capital punishment involves profound legal and political questions; it also touches upon important moral and religious concerns. In 1974, the United States Catholic Conference declared its opposition to the reinstitution of capital punishment. Since that time a number of individual bishops, State Catholic Conferences and other Catholic organizations have actively opposed the death penalty. Many have expressed the view that in this day of increasing violence and disregard for human life, a return to the use of capital punishment can only lead to further erosion of respect for life and to the increased brutalization of our society.

At the same time, crime in our society cannot be ignored; criminals must be brought to justice. Concern for human life also requires reaffirmation of the belief that violent crime is a most serious matter. It calls for seeking effective ways to prevent crime, insuring swift and certain punishment for its perpetrators, the reform of the criminal justice system, and steps to eliminate the complex causes of crime in our society.

I do not challenge society's right to punish the capital offender, but I would ask all to examine the question of whether there are other and better approaches to protecting our people from violent crimes than resorting to executions. In particular I ask those who advocate the use of capital punishment to reflect prayerfully upon all the moral dimensions of the issue. It is not so much a matter of whether an argument can be advanced in favor of the death penalty; such arguments have already been forcefully made by many people of evident good will, although others find them less than convincing. But the more pertinent question at this time in our history is what course of action best fosters that respect for life, all human life, in a society such as ours in which such respect is sadly lacking. In my view, more destruction of human life is not what America needs in 1977.

The Catholic bishops of the United States have manifested deep commitment to the intrinsic value and sacredness of human life. This has led to our strong efforts on behalf of the unborn, the old, the sick and victims of injustice, as well as efforts to enhance respect for human rights. While there are significant differences in these issues, all of them touch directly upon the value of human life which our faith teaches us is never beyond redemption. It is for this reason that I hope our leaders will seek methods of dealing with crime that are more consistent with the vision of respect for life and the Gospel message of God's healing love.

Community and Crime

USCC, Committee on Social
Development and World Peace
February 15, 1978

I. Introduction

1. The people of the United States are clearly and legitimately concerned about crime. This concern is reflected in public opinion polls, in widespread fear that exists in many communities, and in the vast sums of money spent on crime prevention and detection devices.

2. The level of crime is alarmingly high in the United States. In 1976, for example, more than 18,000 people were murdered in cities, suburbs and rural areas; 56,000 women were reported to have been the victims of forcible or attempted rape; there were 400,000 robberies and 3 million burglaries; shoplifting, purse snatching and bicycle thefts cost American $1.2 billion.[1] There has also been a resurgence of gang violence in some of our major cities. Furthermore, in the recent past, some high-ranking persons in government have resigned from office in the face of evidence of their apparent misconduct as officials; numerous industries and corporations have been charged with violating health standards and neglecting the safety of their workers; and over a thousand Americans were convicted of federal tax offenses.[2] Crime statistics, however, indicate only the recorded and nationally reported crimes and therefore only part of the problem. More important than the numbers is the fact that these figures represent human beings inflicting harm on other human beings.

3. There are various forms of criminal behavior. While murder, rape and armed robbery are the most obvious, any exclusive focus on violent crime neglects a significant proportion of criminal behavior. "White collar crime," abuse of power by public officials, discrimination and consumer fraud, among others, seriously harm our society by contributing to the destruction of trust among people and the breakdown of community. These crimes, although less violent, also undermine the common good and victimize people.

4. Fear of crime has been the focus of a great deal of political rhetoric.

---

[1] Statistics were taken from: *Crime in the United States 1976: Uniform Crime Reports*, Federal Bureau of Investigation, U.S. Department of Justice (Washington, D.C.: Government Printing Office, 1976).

[2] *Annual Report of the Attorney General of the United States*, U.S. Department of Justice (Washington, D.C.: Government Printing Office, 1975), p. 146.

Partisan political rivalry has not provided the most suitable context for analysis and positive action. It has at times led to proposals inconsistent with our religious and legal traditions. Our national response to the problem of crime ought to reflect certain basic values and principles—commitment to justice, respect for life and human dignity, concern for safety and community, recognition of personal moral responsibility and the rule of law.

5. The cost of crime is overwhelming. It includes the loss of life, personal injury and billions of dollars in property and financial losses from fraud, theft and embezzlement. Crime creates fear and distrust of individuals and institutions. Many people believe our institutions of law can no longer protect them from injury, theft or the abuses of power. Others believe they will not be treated fairly and justly by these institutions. This fear and distrust tears deeply into the social fabric of our nation.

6. We are shocked by the level of crime in our nation and the human suffering it leaves in its wake. Our concern is intensified by the fact that the impact of crime and the criminal justice system falls disproportionately on the weakest in our society—the poor, the minorities and the elderly. How can we remain silent about a problem which affects so many?

7. Crime is obviously a moral issue in itself, but it also has long range effects on society. In this document, our basic concern is with what crime is doing to American families, neighborhoods and communities. The human cost of crime undermines the trust and mutual respect that are the foundation of any successful society. The factors that contribute to crime are intensified where family and community life are weakened and personal responsibility lessened. These factors include: economic and social deprivation, toleration of injustice and discrimination, false values of materialism and greed, lack of respect for one another, loss of personal responsibility for one's actions and moral choices, failure to love one's neighbor, and toleration and condoning of organized and white collar crime by some officials and citizens. Until these basic concerns are addressed, the nation will not make significant progress against crime, despite future improvements in technology and increased financial expenditures. Any effective response to crime ought to focus on improving our community life, on strengthening our families and neighborhoods, on rooting out economic deprivation and social injustice and on teaching basic values of personal responsibility, human dignity and decency.

8. This means that the criminal justice system and its correctional institutions cannot be expected to shoulder alone the burden of crime. The efforts of law enforcement agencies, courts and correctional facilities are doomed to failure if they do not engage the interest and participation of the entire community in overcoming crime. Real progress in the struggle against crime can only be brought about by concerted community action that unites the efforts of citizens, ecumenical and Church groups, civic organizations, business, labor and professionals in a comprehensive effort to improve our common quality of life.

II. Principles

9. The complexity of crime and criminal justice issues requires a keen sensitivity to the many competing interests and values which influence public policy and individual action on crime. The differing concerns of crime victims, offenders, criminal justice officials and taxpayers need to be balanced in a search for a just response. Too often, basic principles seem to conflict with each other. For example, concern for community safety sometimes conflicts with the legal tradition of respect for the civil liberties of offenders. In light of these tensions, it is necessary to state briefly the principles and values which underlie our analysis of the problem of crime and our proposals for action.

10. As Americans, we are blessed with rich resources which can be brought to bear on this problem—the tradition of freedom of religion, our American constitutional framework and strong legal traditions. As believers, we find strength in the Judeo-Christian heritage and in the teachings and example of Jesus Christ.

A. Christian Tradition

11. Jesus, who was crucified and died between two thieves, preached a gospel of forgiveness and brought compassion and mercy to those whom society rejected.[3] He manifested the love that the Father offers to all and taught us to regard with charity even those who injure us.[4] His Church has constantly affirmed the basic rights of the human person: the right to life; the right to human dignity; and the right to those things necessary for life, including personal safety and freedom from fear. These rights are regarded as necessary for a free and responsible fidelity to God's commands and to our obligations as members of society. While affirming these rights, the Church has also recognized the corresponding duties, especially the responsibility to assure that the rights of all our fellow human beings are protected. Christian teaching recognizes human sinfulness and affirms the realities of moral choice, personal responsibility and obedience to rightful authority, at the same time that it proclaims the message of God's infinite love and saving grace.[5]

B. American Tradition

12. The equality of all persons before the law, due process, trial by jury and the right to protection against unlawful search and seizure are basic principles of the American constitutional tradition. Their purpose is to assure that no person will be deprived of life, property or freedom without just legal proceedings.

---

[3] Mk. 15:27; Lk. 23:34a; Lk. 4:18f.
[4] Mt. 5:11–12, 38–48
[5] Col. 3:2, 5–10; Rom. 14:7–8; Rom. 13:1–7; Rom. 14:9.

13. The American legal system seeks to insure equal justice and the protection of the rights of offenders, victims and society as a whole. Too often, we have fallen short of the promise of our legal tradition. In many instances, a double standard has afforded the affluent and influential better and more lenient treatment than the poor and the powerless. Such failures, however, by no means invalidate these principles.

14. Criminal law is the responsibility of civil society and is aimed at securing justice, harmony and correction. Criminal laws are moral expressions of the community, but they are not morality itself nor the source of morality. Behavior that is legal is not necessarily moral. For example, the practice of abortion is clearly immoral, but according to recent Supreme Court decisions, it is legal in the United States. Yet, there are instances of behavior which are presently regulated by criminal law, which could be dealt with more effectively by other means. For example, rather than relying solely upon criminal law and law enforcement officials, the active participation of community leaders, Church groups and the schools is needed to develop policies and programs for the research and treatment of drug and alcohol abuse. Greater community involvement can lead to the more humane and effective treatment of these problems. In the case of drugs, such a community approach can promote the development of measures to impede and eventually to eliminate organized crime's increasing corruption of law enforcement, the recruitment of youthful pushers, as well as to reduce the incidence of defiance of and confrontation with the criminal justice system by numerous persons.

15. The relationship between morality and criminal law is complex. The scope of moral responsibility often exceeds that of the law. As believers, we should not simply be satisfied with obeying the letter of the law. We are called to follow the Gospel message, which demands more than the civil law, but which offers us Christ's promise of help and saving grace.[6]

III. Causes of Crime

16. No one can determine with precision and certainty the causes of criminal behavior. Several factors do, however, significantly contribute to an environment which fosters crime. Efforts to address these problems should be part of any attempt to reduce crime, although we recognize that even their eradication would not totally eliminate the problem of crime in our nation.

A. *False Values*

17. Our society is increasingly marked by false values which are inconsistent with Christian life and which contribute to crime. We refer here to materialism, excessive individualism, acceptance of violence and loss of respect for human life. We fear that an ethic of consumption and greed is a

---

[6] Mt. 6:33.

dominant force in our society. The desire for unlimited consumption of material goods, for excessive profit and for pleasure above all else, contributes to many forms of illegal and immoral behavior. Intense personal and corporate competition also contributes to crime by fostering an uncontrolled quest for power and personal achievement which often leads to abuse of power and neglect of more important values, such as those pertaining to family life and ethical conduct. The absence of respect for life and acceptance of excessive violence have led to a devaluation of human life and to apathy in the face of the suffering of others. False values foster the violation of the spirit of the law by many citizens which, in turn, may contribute to the violation of the letter of the law—crime—by others.

B. Social Injustice

18. Another major factor contributing to crime is the serious lack of social justice in our society. In the past few years, unemployment and social and economic deprivation in our nation have risen sharply and remained at very high levels. Decent housing, health care and education are unavailable to millions of Americans. Hunger continues to affect families in slums and rural shacks. The distribution of economic opportunities and rewards is still grossly inequitable. Our society, despite great dreams and some progress, is still characterized by serious injustice.

19. Most often it is the weak and unfortunate, the poor, the aged, the young, minorities and women who are forced to bear injustice. They are frequently the victims of crime and of the failures of the criminal justice system. Families mired in poverty, without adequate income, housing, education or health care, too often witness their children convicted and incarcerated as juvenile offenders. In many of our inner cities where unemployment approaches 50 percent, crime has become the major industry, filling the vacuum left by departing businesses and jobs. The studies of the Federal Bureau of Prisons indicate a high positive correlation between the rate of prison commitments and unemployment.[7] Although not solely problems of the poor, drug addiction and alcoholism fester in deprived areas and contribute to an unending cycle of crime and fear. Without major efforts to combat injustice, our struggle against crime will lack effectiveness and credibility.

C. Family and Neighborhood Breakdown

20. Another factor which often contributes to increased crime is the decline of basic social institutions, particularly the family and neighborhood. This is critical, because they are the environments in which we learn how to

---

[7] "Interview With Norman A. Carlson," *Corrections Digest 5* (June 12, 1974):464.

relate to others. Furthermore, studies indicate that numerous crimes occur within families and among friends.

21. The indicators of increasing family stress are well known: rising divorce rates, increased irresponsible parenting, high incidence of domestic violence—child and spouse abuse. These problems are found in families of all racial, economic, cultural and social groups. In addition, family life is threatened by social and economic forces—deprivation, unemployment, lack of housing or health care, the influence of false values—as well as the debilitating effects of alcoholism and drug abuse. Inadequate family life, whether in the lower, middle or upper class, clearly contributes to crime. The breakdown of family relationships is probably the most commonly stated explanation for criminal behavior. We have to work more diligently to strengthen the stability of the American family and restore it to a role of importance in our society, for it is in the family that we learn to respect one another and to harmonize our personal needs with those of others.[8]

22. Where the quality of neighborhood life declines, some of the most effective defenses against crime disappear. The sense of mutual concern and the community support, which are often effective curbs to the isolation and alienation that contribute to crime and fear, disintegrate. Positive relationships between community and police are broken down. Changes in the quantity and quality of city services and private investment, as well as the decline of community involvement, also help to erode community defenses against crime. It is important to reestablish neighborhood values and institutions since they, along with strong family life, are the most promising bulwarks against crime. Cooperation between neighborhoods should also be encouraged in order to respond to problems which reach beyond neighborhood boundaries.

D. Lack of Moral Leadership

23. Still another factor contributing to crime is the lack of moral leadership within our society's major institutions. Too often those in authority have not demonstrated an attitude of respect for law. Although most people seek decency and morality in their relationships and lives, individuals may become caught in institutional pressures that diminish their ability to provide moral leadership. This breakdown in moral leadership pervades the community.

24. Within government, in the recent past, we have seen too much evidence of corruption and abuse of power. Unfortunately, some public servants have put their own thirst for power and money above their responsibility to the people and the common good. In some cases, political leaders have

---

[8] "The Pastoral Constitution on the Church in the Modern World," *The Documents of Vatican II,* ed. Walter M. Abbott, S.J. (New York: Guild Press, 1966; U.S.A.: America Press and Association Press, 1966), p. 257.

sought to manipulate legitimate concerns about crime for political advantage by feeding the fears of citizens in order to urge proposals inconsistent with our constitutional and legal traditions.

25. We have seen within the business community unfortunate examples of the pursuit of profit overwhelming concerns about the safety of workers, service to customers and the environmental impact of corporate actions. At times, some business leaders have become involved in illegal activity in their search for greater economic return. Monopolistic practices, price manipulation, failure to observe labor-management and environmental regulations, illegal campaign contributions and a variety of other abuses have left the impression in some quarters that many in business are not willing to abide by the law or provide examples of corporate responsibility.

26. Lack of moral leadership is not limited to business and government officials. Abuses are evident in labor, medicine, education and the social service professions, among others. Labor leaders have been found guilty of corrupt practices. Recent reports indicate that the Medicaid and Medicare programs, which were developed to assist the needy and the aged, have been misused by some members of the medical profession. Some educational institutions have failed to meet their leadership responsibilities by failing to address discriminatory policies and practices; by favoring institutional needs above educational concerns; and by not providing the ethical training and example which are needed to preserve a just and moral society.

27. In addition, the entertainment and news media have contributed to this lack of moral leadership. By emphasizing and appearing to condone materialism, violence, greed and indecency and by glorifying the activities of the law-breaker, the media may have contributed to criminal behavior. Many programs and movies being produced today exalt the "supercop" and public officials who break laws which have been designed to protect individual rights. This glorification of illegal behavior by law enforcement and political officials undermines the values of honesty and respect for law, which are essential underpinnings of the good society. Others in the entertainment media have supported and condoned indecency, pornography and the exploitation of sex. These activities exploit the children and adults who participate in the production of these materials, as well as the problems of those who purchase or view them. The news media often sensationalize crimes, especially crimes of violence. This may lead to community demoralization as well as to the creation of an adverse image of a minority group or young people in general.

28. Finally, religious leaders also have to share the burden stemming from the lack of effective moral leadership. We have not spoken out as strongly and effectively as we should. We have not acted effectively enough to overcome the causes of crime and the circumstances which contribute to criminal behavior. In our own teaching and educational institutions, perhaps we have not stressed sufficiently personal responsibility, moral formation and social

concern. Activities have been permitted which not only violated the spirit of the law, but which were illegal. If we are to provide effective moral leadership, it will be necessary to ensure that all Church activities demonstrate strict conformity to the law.

29. Many of those in government, business, labor, education, the media, religious life and other institutions have sought to provide moral leadership. The failure of others to do so and the acceptance of this failure by many in our society may have undermined the efforts of those who have tried. If we are to address crime effectively, it will be necessary to challenge those in positions of moral leadership to act. The leadership, participation and support of those in public life, business, education, labor, the media, the religious community, among others, need to be coordinated in programs of education and action to prevent and reduce crime and in efforts to eliminate the root causes of crime.

IV. Approaches for Action

30. There are two basic approaches to overcoming crime: one focuses on the individual while the other aims at society and the community.

31. First, we wish to affirm the personal moral responsibility of each individual. Without discounting the many powerful forces at work in our society, we believe that the individual makes basic choices about personal action and sometimes the result of these choices is the violation of criminal as well as moral law. Thus, crimes are frequently sins as well as illegal acts. We therefore urge that extensive research, education and other efforts be undertaken to understand and to foster the proper moral formation of each person, the development of Christian values and the acceptance of personal responsibility by every individual. Families and religious institutions have a primary responsibility in this area. The strengthening of family and religious life, in light of their influence on personal moral development, is a critical element of a religious, communal and effective response to crime.

32. Second, we recognize that these choices are also influenced by community and social factors. Individuals' perceptions of themselves, their future and the fairness of society obviously affect the likelihood of their becoming involved in crime. Religious organizations cannot restrict themselves solely to concern for the individual and his or her individual conscience. Actions for a more just and equitable society are clearly elements of the Church's ministry and are a part of any Christian response to the problem of crime.

33. An excessive emphasis on either personal responsibility or the social causes of crime is fundamentally inadequate. An integrated and comprehensive response to crime is necessary, if we are to deal with it in an effective way, which is consistent with our own ministry and teaching.

V. Criminal Justice Issues

34. Criminal justice issues are complicated and difficult to resolve, because they involve many legitimate but divergent and competing interests. Since most crimes involve a threat to person and property, interactions among these interests are often highly charged. In the midst of this diversity, it is imperative that our analysis of the issues reflect Christian values, the American constitutional and legal traditions, and a concern for social justice and human rights.

A. Prisons/Jails vs. Community Alternatives

35. Identifying the just and charitable response to the criminal offender is a troubling challenge for any morally sensitive person. The community defines what behavior is legally criminal. It determines what response best communicates to the offender and to the community the condemnation of criminal behavior, and also sets forth the conditions for reintegration of those who have broken the law. Christians, as members of the civil society, participate in the determination of the community's response to criminal behavior. As Christians, however, we have a particular responsibility to see that the message communicated to the offender and to the community reflects Christian principles, including: the right to life and human dignity; responsibility to protect the rights of all persons; mercy and compassion for those less fortunate; forgiveness of those who offend or harm us; and the openness of a loving and healing community.[9]

36. Our present prison system clearly does not reflect Christian values. Numerous studies document the fact that prisons are dehumanizing and depersonalizing. Prison life denies individual decision-making and responsibility; it provides the opportunity for an education in crime rather than for rehabilitation.[10] Rather than developing the skills of offenders for future employment, the purpose of prison job assignments is to provide for institutional needs. These job experiences are acknowledged by those in the correctional system as being useless. Research has also shown that crime is caused not only by personal inadequacies, but also by the complex interaction of social and economic forces. Yet prison life cannot address these problems. A prison system does not and cannot provide long-term employment opportunities, increase family stability, encourage responsibility or improve the ties between the offender and the community, because it is separated from the community in which the offender ultimately has to learn to function.

---

[9] Mt. 5:11–12; Lk. 15.

[10] For example: Gresham Sykes, *Society of Captives* (New Jersey: Princeton University Press, 1958); *Theoretical Studies in Social Organization of the Prisons,* ed. Richard Cloward (New York: Social Research Council, 1960); Tom Wicker, *A Time To Die* (New York: Quadrangle, 1975).

Prisons communicate a message of hopelessness and of community anger devoid of concern.

37. As a Christian community, we should seek to express to the offender disapproval of his or her criminal behavior together with a strong willingness to accept that individual's reintegration into society as a contributing member. To do this, we should seek alternatives to our present approach to incarceration. It should be remembered that prisons, as we know them, are a relatively recent historical creation. Prior to the beginning of the 19th century, responses to crime other than confinement were utilized. Some were more brutal than incarceration, others less. Many alternatives[11] have now been developed and tried both here and abroad. These include having an offender perform a community service or provide restitution to the victim of his or her crime; conciliation of citizens' disputes through a community mediation program rather than the courts; drug and alcohol abuse programs to which defendants are diverted before trial; employment programs run through corporations; and many others. It should be borne in mind, however, that these programs are alternatives to incarceration and not post-release efforts or new ways to bring more people into the criminal justice system. To address the problem of the criminal offender effectively and thereby secure the safety of every citizen, it will be necessary to use the creativity and talents of all our people.

38. Admittedly, a small proportion of those now in our prisons have committed acts of violence or other serious crimes and either cannot or should not be placed in unstructured settings. We need not, however, confine even these people in our present prisons. Small community-based facilities appear to provide the potentiality for a more humane and suitable environment. Our creativity is needed to develop positive and truly rehabilitative programs for these offenders. Caution, however, must be exercised to ensure that these facilities do not become small prisons.

39. Incarceration of accused individuals in jails prior to trial is another serious problem.[12] Too often, the difference between those who await their trial in jail rather than out on bail is the ability to pay, rather than the probability of court appearance or seriousness of the offense. A number of community groups have developed programs through which an accused person is released into the custody of a program participant. Other groups have established programs through which the information on the employment, residence and level of income of the accused is confirmed and provided to the

---

[11] National Advisory Commission on Criminal Justice Standards and Goals, *Corrections* (Washington, D.C.: Government Printing Office, 1973), pp. 232–236; Ira Schwartz, "Prisons Run for Humans—Not Animals," *Chicago Tribune,* August 23, 1976; Robert B. Coates, Alden D. Miller and Lloyd E. Ohlin, *Exploratory Analyses of Recidivism and Cohort Data on the Massachusetts Youth Correctional System* (Cambridge, Massachusetts: Harvard Law School Center for Criminal Justice, 1975).

[12] National Advisory Commission on Criminal Justice Standards and Goals, *Corrections,* p. 274.

court by a project volunteer. A reasonable bail should be set according to the following considerations: probability of court appearance, seriousness of charge and income of the accused. There are some individuals accused of crimes who appear to present a serious threat to the community and should not be released on bail. If, however, greater court resources were provided, the length of their pre-trial detention could be shortened by speeding up the adjudication process.

40. The effective rehabilitation and reintegration of criminal offenders requires active community participation. Having communicated our disapproval of criminal behavior, it behooves us to be willing to greet the ex-offender in the spirit of reconciliation and forgiveness of our Lord.[13]

B. Sentencing

41. In addition to its prison system, America's failure to reduce crime has often been attributed to the disparity in sentences as a consequence of the policy of indeterminate sentencing. Under this system, the judge imposes a sentence as a minimum and maximum time to be served. (For example: one to 10 years.) An individual, once incarcerated, must serve a proportion of the minimum sentence before being eligible for release. Up to the maximum sentence, the release of the offender on parole or to other programs is usually at the discretion of correctional authorities. The disparity and inequity created by these sentencing procedures often create feelings of anger, frustration and a sense of mistreatment in the offender.

42. Several studies have been made which document these problems and which propose alternatives for change.[14] In our statement, *The Reform of Correctional Institutions in the 1970s* [reprinted in this compendium], we recognized the rehabilitative inadequacies of the penal system and the problems associated with indeterminate sentencing. We also articulated our belief that the correctional system should perform several functions, including the rehabilitation of the offender, restitution for the victim and the protection of society.[15] The present system of prisons and sentencing practices clearly does not achieve these goals nor does it, in practice, reflect Christian values.

43. We therefore believe that the sentencing procedures should be restructured to enhance the possibility of achieving these goals and to reflect more

---

[13] Mt. 18:21-22.

[14] Among them were: Andrew on Hirsch, *Doing Justice* (New York: Hill and Wang, 1976); *Fair and Certain Punishment,* Report of the Twentieth Century Fund Task Force on Criminal Sentencing (New York: McGraw-Hill Book Company, 1976); David Fogel, *We Are the Living Proof* (Cincinnati: W. H. Anderson, 1976).

[15] *The Reform of Correctional Institutions in the 1970s* (Washington, D.C.: United States Catholic Conference, November 1973).

closely the values and teachings of the Christian tradition. The type and length of sentence should be based upon the following principles:

- Use of imprisonment as a measure of last resort;

- Utilization of community alternatives for most criminal offenses;

- Consideration of the seriousness of the offense;

- Reduction of arbitrary disparity in sentences by placing primary consideration on the seriousness of the offense and previous convictions for similar offenses;

- Consideration of aggravating or mitigating circumstances in individual cases;

- Promotion of respect for and understanding of the law;

- Concern for adequate specific deterrence with safeguards against general deterrence being abused and utilized as a justification for punishment; and

- Reconciliation of the victim and the offender.

These changes should contribute to the development of fairer and more effective sentencing practices.

C. Capital Punishment

44. The use of the death penalty involves deep moral and religious questions as well as political and legal issues. In 1974, out of a commitment to the value and dignity of human life, the Catholic bishops of the United States declared their opposition to capital punishment.[16] We continue to support this position, in the belief that a return to the use of the death penalty can only lead to the further erosion of respect for life in our society.

45. Violent crime in our society is a serious matter which should not be ignored. We do not challenge society's right to punish the serious and violent offender, nor do we wish to debate the merits of the arguments concerning this right. Past history, however, shows that the death penalty in its application has been discriminatory with respect to the disadvantaged, the indigent and the socially impoverished. Furthermore, recent data from corrections

---

[16] *Motion on Capital Punishment* (Washington, D.C.: United States Catholic Conference, November 1974).

resources[17] definitely question the effectiveness of the death penalty as a deterrent to crime.

46. We are deeply troubled by the legislative efforts being undertaken under the guise of humanitarian concern to permit execution by lethal injection. Such a practice merely seeks to conceal the reality of cruel and unusual punishment. We find this practice unacceptable.

47. The critical question for the Christian is how we can best foster respect for life, preserve the dignity of the human person and manifest the redemptive message of Christ. We do not believe that more deaths is the response to the questions. We therefore have to seek methods of dealing with violent crime which are more consistent with the Gospel's vision of respect for life and Christ's message of God's healing love. In the sight of God, correction of the offender has to take preference over punishment, for the Lord came to save and not to condemn.

D. Youth Crime

48. Perhaps one of the most disturbing aspects of the crime problem is the youthful age of many serious offenders. In 1976, 76 percent of all persons arrested for robbery, 84 percent of those arrested for burglary, and 57 percent of those arrested for forcible rape were under 25 years of age. Twenty-four percent of those arrested for murder were between the ages of 20 and 22.[18]

49. Most juveniles designated as offenders have not committed violent crimes. In almost all states, children who run away from home, who are truant or who are declared incorrigible by their parents can be sent to juvenile institutions. Such offenses are generally referred to as status offenses. They are crimes solely because of a child's status as a child; they are not crimes if committed by an adult. In 1975, 75 percent of the females and 25 percent of the males in facilities for juvenile offenders were there because of status offenses.[19] The status offender is often incarcerated longer than a child who has committed a crime, because in many cases there is no home to which the runaway or incorrigible child can be returned.

50. Most youthful offenders are the victims of broken families, unresponsive school systems, turbulent neighborhoods or limited job opportunities. Many have become insensitive and cynical after having been neglected,

---

[17] For example: T. Sellin, *The Death Penalty* (Report for the Model Penal Code of the American Law Institute, 1959); *Idem.,* "Capital Punishment," *Federal Probation* 25 (September 1961); David C. Baldus and James W. L. Cole, "A Comparison of the Work of Thorsten Sellin and Isaac Ehrlich on the Deterrent Effect of Capital Punishment," *Yale Law Review* 85 (December 1975): 170–186; William J. Bowers and Glenn J. Pierce, "The Illusion of Deterrence in Isaac Ehrlich's Work on Capital Punishment," *Yale Law Review* 85 (December 1975): 187–208; Peter Passell, "The Deterrent Effect of the Death Penalty," *Stanford Law Review* 28 (November 1975): 61–80.

[18] *Crime in the United States, 1976: Uniform Crime Reports.*

[19] Rosemary Sarri, *Under Lock and Key: Juvenile Jails and Detention* (Ann Arbor, Michigan: National Assessment of Juvenile Corrections, University of Michigan, December 1974), p. 18.

abused, battered and even raped by members of their families.[20] Some with average or above average intelligence have learning disabilities, such as dyslexia, which, untreated, have resulted in academic failure, in frustration and ultimately in truancy and/or delinquency.

51. We stated in our document on correctional reform that extraordinary efforts should be made to rehabilitate the juvenile offender.[21] These efforts should begin before the juvenile is sent to the youth facility. The Christian community has to address itself to the needs of all youth. Children have to be taught self-respect and respect for others; however, only by our actions can we hope to demonstrate to them effectively the meaning of these values. Juvenile offenders should be kept and treated within the community. We support efforts to decriminalize status offenses in all states. Community programs and alternatives, such as foster care, special education, family counseling, recreation programs and other noninstitutional supportive services, should be available to youth and their families without resorting to the juvenile justice system and without stigmatizing those who participate in these programs.

52. Our primary goal for youth care should be to keep our children out of the juvenile justice system by providing them with the needed attention and services. While we do not condone acts of violence by young people, we recognize that institutionalizing them in the juvenile system is usually a brutalizing rather than a rehabilitative experience and serves to further embitter them as well as oftentimes to teach them how to be more clever criminals rather than better citizens.

E. Nonviolent Crimes

53. Since nonviolent crimes are so often viewed with laxity, we feel compelled to stress their seriousness and costliness to society. One category of nonviolent crime is referred to as "white collar crime." This term generally means crimes committed by persons in the course of their employment. It may be an act of an individual, for example, forgery or embezzlement; or it may be a crime committed in a corporation's name, for example, commercial bribery, antitrust crimes such as price-fixing, product safety and health crimes, and financial crimes. It may be committed by or perpetrated against corporations, firms, non-profit organizations, clients, customers, govermental units, et al. It has been estimated that "white collar crimes" such as embezzlement; bank, stock and consumer fraud; pilferage; computer crimes; check and credit card fraud (but excluding antitrust violations) cost $40 billion each year. This is 200 times the amount stolen by the country's

---

[20] For example: Gisela Konopka, *The Adoleslcent Girl in Conflict* (Englewood Cliffs, New Jersey: Prentice-Hall, 1966); Kenneth Wooden, *Weeping in the Playtime of Others* (New York: McGraw-Hill Book Company, 1976).

[21] *The Reform of Correctional Institutions in the 1970s.*

bank robbers in 1974.[22] In 1973, $135.6 million was lost in bank frauds and embezzlement, while $22 million was lost in robberies.[23] Although the economic costs are staggering, we are most concerned about the human costs; therefore, we reiterate our opposition to "white collar crime," as stated in our 1973 document on correctional reform.

54. Failure to comply with attainable and practical air or water pollution standards, mine safety regulations or safety standards for nuclear reactors can cause death and destruction. Violations of these regulations can create conditions that shorten the lives of workers, people living near the industry and consumers.

55. At times, the regulations themselves are developed under questionable circumstances. The human costs of not implementing stringent standards are weighed against the anticipated profit losses from observing them. The resulting regulations often reflect a greater concern for industrial profit than for human life. For example, government agencies may issue licensing criteria which have been opposed by their own experts, but are supported by the manufacturers or the producers of the particular product.[24]

56. Our national political institutions—political parties, state, local and federal governments—are sometimes instruments for criminal activity. Our recent national scandals are particularly shocking because they took place at the highest levels of government. They were not, however, unique. Scandals also pervaded our state and local governments.[25] Crimes by public officials violate the public trust and encourage the belief that some people are above the law. In many instances, political corruption has been related to the need of politicians to raise large sums of money for election campaigns. Reform of campaign finance laws is a necessary element of any attempt to address the problem of political crimes effectively.

57. The response of the criminal justice system to the white collar offender also undermines respect for law in our society. A study of the New York Southern District Court during the period from July 1, 1971, to June 30, 1972, indicated that the likelihood of imprisonment for those convicted of embezzlement was 23.2 percent; for bribery, 25 percent; and for bank robbery, 82.3 percent. The average length of the sentences was 18 months for embezzlement, 11 months for bribery, and 69.6 months for bank robbery.[26]

58. Many citizens who are usually law-abiding commit acts for which they could be prosecuted, if they were caught. Today, many regard the taking of questionable income tax deductions or driving while intoxicated as normal.

---

[22] "White Collar Justice," *Law Week,* April 13, 1976.

[23] Hearings before the Senate Subcommittee on Criminal Laws and Procedures of the Committee on the Judiciary on S. 1 and S. 1400, 94th Cong., 1st sess., (July 19, 1975).

[24] Daniel F. Ford and Henry W. Kendall, "Nuclear Safety," *Environment,* September 1972, pp. 1–6.

[25] Hearings on S. 1 and S. 1400, p. 7893.

[26] "White Collar Justice," p. 11.

This type of activity and the individualistic philosophy which it reflects were condemned by the Second Vatican Council.[27]

59. "White collar crime" imperils our lives and the social fabric of our society. Yet, our law enforcement agencies devote only a small portion of their resources to these crimes. In fiscal year 1974, less than 15 percent of the Department of Justice's legal activities, manpower and budget were allocated for tax, antitrust and consumer fraud activities.[28] Only a few officials maintain useful data on these crimes.[29] More important, however, is the fact that many of these crimes are viewed with indifference by the community.

60. An effective response to "white collar crime" ought to begin with the community. No longer should we tolerate "white collar crime" as normal. We should also examine our own lives to determine how we contribute to this problem by our actions, attitudes or indifference. While the "white collar" offender should be treated with compassion and we should seek the individual's reconciliation with the community, we ought to respond vigorously to these crimes and seek their elimination from our society.

F. Handgun Control

61. In 1976, crime statistics indicated that 64 percent of all murders were committed with a firearm and 49 percent were committed with handguns. Twenty-four percent of all aggravated assaults and 43 percent of all robberies were committed with firearms. Eighty-five percent of the police officers killed were killed with firearms.[30] Other studies have shown that most homicides are committed against friends and relatives, not strangers. Since such a significant number of violent offenses are committed with handguns and within families, we believe that handguns need to be effectively controlled and eventually eliminated from our society. We acknowledge that controlling the possession of handguns will not eliminate gun violence, but we believe it is an indispensable element of any serious or rational approach to the problem.[31]

G. Law Enforcement and Legal Professionals

62. The swift apprehension, judgment and correction of offenders are necessary to uphold the law and to secure justice. This requires a law enforcement and criminal justice system which has strong community support and is provided with the resources and personnel necessary to perform its functions justly and effectively. We recognize that most law enforcement and court per-

---

[27] "The Pastoral Constitution on the Church in the Modern World," p. 228.

[28] Hearings on S. 1 and S. 1400, p. 7893.

[29] Ibid.

[30] Crime in the United States, 1976: Uniform Crime Reports.

[31] Handgun Violence: A Threat to Life (Washington, D.C.: Committee on Social Development and World Peace, United States Catholic Conference, September 1975).

sonnel work hard to enforce and uphold the law. This task is often difficult and dangerous. Cooperation between those professionally involved in the criminal justice system and citizens and community groups is quintessential to any effort to control crime effectively.

63. The preservation of law and justice does, however, place a particular burden on those who enforce the law. As they are often perceived as symbols of the law and the criminal justice system, they have a special responsibility to demonstrate respect for law, the community and the rights of others. Too often in recent years, there have been incidents of police brutality, of illegal wiretaps on American citizens, of illegal searches and even of burglaries being committed by law enforcement officials. At times, widely-publicized trials have presented a circus-like image of the judicial process. Many citizens have become aware of the fact that most offenders do not receive a jury trial, but rather that their case is decided through an informal process called plea bargaining. In its most prevalent form, plea bargaining involves an arrangement between the prosecutor and the defendant or the defense lawyer whereby the accused pleads guilty to a less serious charge than could be proven at trial. "Less serious" usually means a charge carrying a lower maximum sentence; thus, this confines the judge's sentencing power.[32] This approach to arriving at a criminal conviction demeans the criminal justice process.[33]

64. A sufficient quantity of quality legal services for indigent clients is critical to a just criminal justice system. Studies indicate that in spite of the constitutional guarantee of counsel, many poor defendants are not properly represented.[34] Quality legal counsel is a right and not a privilege dependent upon one's financial resources. It is the responsibility of the legal profession, the appropriate levels of government and lay citizens to ensure that this right is protected for all citizens.

65. We recognize that most law enforcement and court officers do not engage in illegal activities. Too often, they suffer loss of essential support from the community because of the misdeeds of others. Those who do engage in illegal acts should be disciplined if respect for law and law enforcement is to be maintained and if those who seek to justly enforce the law are to receive the respect due to them. Many of the problems of administering criminal justice, however, often lie deeper than individual errors. For example, plea

---

[32] President's Commission on Law Enforcement and Administration of Justice, *Task Force Report: Courts* (Washington, D.C.: U.S. Government Printing Office, 1967), pp. 10–11.

[33] National Advisory Commission on Criminal Justice Standards and Goals, *Corrections,* pp. 168–169.

[34] For example: David L. Bazelon, "The Realities of Gideon and Argersinger," *Georgetown Law Journal* 64 (March 1976): 811–838; National Advisory Commission on Criminal Justice Standards and Goals, *Courts* (Washington, D.C.: Government Printing Office, 1973), pp. 250–252; *Idem., A National Strategy to Reduce Crime* (Washington, D.C.: Government Printing Office, 1973), pp. 105–106; *Guidelines for Legal Defense Systems in the United States: The Report of the National Study Commission on Defense Services* (Washington, D.C.: National Legal Aid and Defender Association, 1976).

bargaining, some instances of corruption within police departments and the illegal use of wiretaps have come to be viewed as acceptable procedures by many criminal justice professionals. Some of these activities have become common practice as a consequence of the limited resources of the criminal justice system. Others have endured because of poor management or political pressures. Better administrative management and greater community support are needed to reorganize the criminal justice system in order that it may achieve the best aspirations of all our people.

H. Grand Jury

66. The grand jury system has come under attack for its use as a mechanism to abuse the rights of many Americans.[35] A grand jury is generally selected at random from a voter registration list and sits either for a period of time or for a specific case. Its purpose is to examine in private session evidence against those accused of serious crimes and, on the basis of just cause, to decide whether or not to indict the individual for the crime. During a grand jury hearing, practices are permitted which can lead to abuse, including: the government's ability to call any witness without explanation and without advance notice; the barring of the witness' attorney from the court room; the practice that, once a witness begins to answer questions, the Fifth Amendment right to silence has been waived; the ability to place a witness in jail for contempt for the length of the grand jury because of refusal to testify; and the government's ability to forcibly impose immunity upon a witness and thereby require the person to choose between jail or testifying. These powers have in many instances been used by government prosecutors against government critics, political opponents and even leaders of churches.

67. Out of a concern for the life and liberty of our people and for social justice in our society, we believe the time has come to reform the grand jury system. Reforms should reflect a concern for the human dignity of each person; the constitutional rights which would be afforded during a regular trial; and the recognition that the purpose of the grand jury process is to ensure justice and to protect against capricious accusation, but not to secure a conviction.

I. Community Crime Prevention

68. Recent discussions about crime have often focused on community action to prevent crime,[36] as well as on sophisticated weapons and the training of criminal justice professionals. In spite of the "community" rhetoric, however, most of the responsibility for efforts to reduce and prevent crime has continued to be relinquished to professionals using modern techniques.

---

[35] *Grand Jury,* No. 1-4 (1976).

[36] President's Commission on Law Enforcement and Administration of Justice, *The Challenge of Crime in a Free Society* (Washington, D.C.: Government Printing Office, 1967), p. 39.

69. While we recognize that criminal justice professionals should be trained and that new technologies facilitate the detection of crime, they alone cannot effectively respond to the causes which contribute to crime in our society. Any effective response to crime has to be sought in the community. This approach requires the participation and talents of all members of the community—professionals, nonprofessionals, young, old and middle-aged. Without this mobilization of all citizens, we shall remain at the mercy of crime.

J. Research

70. It is evident that the cause of crime and the development of an effective response to this problem are complex. Further study is needed of both the root causes of crime and of various alternative approaches to crime. In recent years, federal and state agencies have funded research, but too many of these efforts have been directed toward the development of hardware and equipment. Furthermore, the limitations of self-evaluative research—in this case, agencies studying their own programs—are well-documented.

71. What is needed is research, which may be governmentally funded, but which focuses on the objective study of the causes of crime and appropriate responses. Catholic educational institutions have a particular capability to promote such research as they possess the expertise and background in both the relevant academic disciplines and in the moral and social teachings of the Church. As a consequence of this unique position, they have a responsibility to both the Church and to the society to apply their resources to the study of crime and criminal justice.

K. Special Concerns: the Crime Victim/the Elderly/the Media

72. The victims of crime are often forgotten by the community and by the criminal justice system. This experience can engender hatred, which often harms the individual more than the crime did. As Christians, we should demonstrate a deep compassion for the victims of crime and be practically concerned that they receive the compensation and restitution due to them.

73. The elderly are often the victims of violent and nonviolent offenses. Many of these crimes can be prevented by providing community efforts as simple as better lighting at a bus stop or informing people about techniques used to defraud the elderly of their savings. The elderly can assist in crime prevention efforts by working as volunteers in law enforcement agencies, with ex-offenders in transition or by becoming involved in programs for juveniles. Recently, we have also found examples of programs through which young people, even gang members, have worked to assist and protect senior citizens from crime. These efforts provide meaningful employment for the young, needed help to the elderly and create a means to develop love and

understanding between the two generations. By seeking to utilize the skills of both the young and the old, the community not only receives assistance in its anticrime efforts, but also reaffirms the human dignity of those who are all too often cast aside.

74. While strongly supporting the constitutional rights of free speech and press, we believe that those in the media should exercise, as many are doing already, greater moral responsibility in the development of entertainment and news programs and materials. We also believe that efforts should be made within the family and through schools and parishes to help children develop a critical sense with which to approach media presentations and to provide alternatives to the quick thrills and simplistic problem-solving approaches depicted by the media.

VI. The Role of the Church

75. As a Christian community, we have a responsibility to utilize our resources to respond to the problem of crime in America. Our actions should reflect our Christian values, as well as our constitutional and legal traditions. We should seek to revitalize our basic social institutions, which are our strongest weapons against the destruction caused by crime. Action should be taken at the local level through parishes and dioceses and at the national, public policy-making level.

A. The Responsibility of the Local Church

76. The most important setting for Church activities to reduce and prevent crime is the local church. It can join with other local groups to assess and respond to the problem of crime in a community. Many parishes and dioceses are already involved in a variety of anti-crime activities. We extend our support to this work and encourage other parishes and dioceses as well as religious orders to undertake or cooperate with others in efforts such as:

(1) More actively seeking to foster Christian values through education, liturgy and the media, in order to prevent as well as to respond to crime. The Church, as a community of Christians, needs to reflect a positive image of uncompromising respect for the law and the human rights of all persons, as well as a strong desire for the rehabilitation and reintegration of the individual offender into the community.

(2) Providing forums for the discussion of the nature and types of crime and criminal justice issues.

(3) Sponsoring discussions and developing materials on Christian approaches to reduce and prevent all types of crime.

(4) Organizing exchanges between criminal justice professionals and citizens and ex-offenders about the problems, services and needs of the community.

(5) Organizing discussions among business professionals and between professionals and citizens to discuss and seek effective ways of responding to all types of "white collar crime."

(6) Encouraging Catholic lawyers, psychologists, psychiatrists and other professionals to offer their expertise to the indigent and the disadvantaged.

(7) Providing educational, employment and recreational opportunities for youth to assure that they are presented with a clear alternative to the false values of violence and materialism often idealized in our society.

(8) Initiating or supporting community efforts to improve housing conditions, city services, safety and the general quality of life in the area.

(9) Sponsoring crisis intervention and family counseling projects, especially to respond to the problems of battered wives, abused spouses and battered children.

(10) Establishing a system of "block patrols" and citizens watches in high crime areas. Developing strong, supportive neighborhood groups.

(11) Providing assistance and protection to the elderly, particularly in high crime areas, and encouraging their participation in crime prevention efforts.

(12) Supporting or sponsoring efforts to assist the accused, such as pre-trial release projects and legal services programs.

(13) Sponsoring programs to monitor court proceedings in order to assure that the rights of all citizens who come before the court are protected.

(14) Establishing, supporting, as well as educating people about the importance of: community correctional alternatives, such as, half-way houses, group homes and drug and alcohol abuse centers; community service sentencing alternatives; community mediation centers; and other models.

(15) Supporting foster care, group home and nonresidential community

programs for youthful offenders and encouraging their participation in community crime prevention efforts.

(16) Supporting efforts to assist and work in cooperation with offenders and their families, for example, in third party custody release programs, projects to facilitate visiting by the offenders' families, furlough programs and educational and job training programs.

(17) Aiding parolees to find suitable work and encouraging employers to hire these individuals.

(18) Creating programs to respond to the physical and emotional needs of the victims of crime.

(19) Sponsoring special Dismas Sunday liturgies.

(20) Providing subsidies to correctional chaplains through the diocese or religious order, where needed, in order to permit those in prison ministry to exercise more fully and freely their mission as ministers of Christ.

(21) Implementing adequate guidance programs for those choosing to minister to residents of correctional facilities. Whenever possible, these should be ecumenical in spirit.

(22) Supporting and encouraging the development of research on the causes of crime and alternative responses, particularly through Catholic universities, colleges and research organizations.

77. Many of these efforts can and should be undertaken in cooperation with other religious and community groups, as well as governmental agencies. They should be developed in conjunction with efforts to secure greater social justice in other areas, such as health, housing, welfare, economics and discrimination. Although the needs and therefore the response of each community will differ, it is evident that the Church has a responsibility to act to reduce crime and that this involvement ought to reflect values and principles which are consistent with the Gospel and the American constitutional traditions.

B. Public Policy

78. Crime and criminal justice have traditionally been the concern of state and local authorities in the United States. Only a few specific offenses, such as bank robbery and crimes involving interstate activities, have fallen under

the jurisdiction of federal authorities. Since the 1960s, the federal government has expanded its role in the criminal justice field. It now exerts a much greater influence over state and local criminal justice policies as a consequence of several U.S. Supreme Court decisions and the policies and programs of the Law Enforcement Assistance Administration of the U.S. Department of Justice. In light of the complex network of government controls in criminal justice, a comprehensive response to crime will require governmental action at the national and state levels, as well as the local level.

79. In accordance with the principles expressed earlier in this document, we encourage the United States Catholic Conference and the dioceses of this country to support governmental action and public policy initiatives in several areas:

(1) *An effective response to the socioeconomic causes of crime.* Action has to be taken to end socioeconomic deprivation through full employment and a guarantee of a decent income for all Americans. We also urge that measures be adopted to secure the right to a decent home, quality education and adequate medical care.[37] We need to mobilize our national and community resources to respond to the inadequate social conditions which contribute to certain types of crime.

(2) *Response to "white collar crime."* "White collar crime" is a complex problem which will have to be addressed on a variety of levels. In order to approach this problem effectively, we believe that it will be necessary to develop measures to respond both to the different types of white collar offenses and to provide for relief for the victims of these crimes. Much of the public policy effort will involve technical issues on which we cannot comment. We do believe, however, that public policy initiatives to address white collar crimes are needed and that they should reflect the seriousness of these offenses with respect to individuals and society. Strict codes of ethics and conduct should be adopted and enforced by institutions, organizations, professions and associations. Educational initiatives are needed to assist the potential victims of these crimes—members of the business community, professionals and citizens—to recognize these crimes and thereby help to prevent them.

(3) *Handgun control.* We support the development of a coherent national handgun control policy that includes: a several day cooling-off period between the sale and possession; a ban on "Saturday Night Specials"; the registration of handguns; the licensing of handgun

---

[37] *The Right to a Decent Home* (Washington, D.C.: United States Catholic Conference, November 1975); *The Economy: Human Dimensions* (Washington, D.C.: U.S. Catholic Conference, November 1975).

owners; and more effective controls regulating the manufacture, sale and importation of handguns. We recognize, however, that these individual steps will not completely eliminate the abuse of handguns. We believe that only prohibition of the importation, manufacture, sale, possession and use of handguns (with reasonable exceptions made for the police, military, security guards and pistol clubs where guns would be kept on the premises under secure conditions) will provide a comprehensive response to handgun violence.[38]

(4) *Juvenile justice.* Our primary goal should be to keep our youth out of the juvenile justice system and to provide the resources to meet their needs within the community. Status offenses should be decriminalized in all states and, at the same time, the needed services and community assistance to these youths should be provided outside the confines of the juvenile justice system. We support the development of job training programs, meaningful employment opportunities, recreational facilities and other community alternatives to assist our youth to develop self-respect and respect for others.

(5) *Federal criminal justice assistance.* Federal criminal justice monies should be primarily utilized for state and local community development and for crime prevention efforts rather than for sophisticated equipment.

(6) *Community-based alternatives.* For most offenders, we support the utilization of federal, state and local correctional funds for community-based alternatives, including requiring the offender to perform a service for the community, providing restitution to the victim, utilizing other forms of nonresidential alternatives and placement in community-based facilities in limited cases. Primary concern should be placed on developing creative alternatives to incarceration. We recognize, however, that there are a few individuals who cannot function in the community. They should be cared for in small and secure facilities which respect their dignity and protect the community. While prisons are operative, efforts should be made to assure humane conditions for the incarcerated. Funds should be directed toward community-based alternatives and rehabilitative programs. At the pre-trial stage, community alternatives, such as third party release programs and projects to identify and verify the residence and employment of the accused, should be developed to permit the more frequent release of offenders on bail while protecting the security of the community. These practices should not be used to discriminate against the poor, the weak and minorities.

---

[38] *Handgun Violence: A Threat to Life.*

(7) *Local, state and federal sentencing policies.* Our primary goal in reforming sentencing policies should be to assure the following: the limited use of imprisonment, the utilization of community alternatives for most criminal offenders and the elimination of arbitrary disparity in sentences in order that those committing essentially the same crime receive equivalent sentences. Committees comprised of citizens and experts should be created to review sentencing procedures and policies periodically, as well as to establish the types of mitigating and aggravating circumstances that may be considered in individual cases.

(8) *Capital punishment.* We continue to oppose efforts to reinstitute the death penalty.

(9) *Electronic surveillance.* In general, we oppose the use of wiretaps and other electronic surveillance mechanisms for the purpose of gathering economic and political information from conversations customarily considered private. We believe that there is a need for further study of the ethical dimensions of surveillance for the purpose of national security. We support the creation of legislative regulations which would limit the use of these devices to cases of extreme national danger and permit the Congress to review the use of wiretaps by the executive branch.

(10) *Victim compensation.* We support the creation of systems of victim compensation at the federal, state and local levels. We believe that the community has to share in the responsibility of providing restitution to the victims of crime. Such a program should provide compensation for personal injuries which were the result of a crime; compensation for surviving dependents of an individual whose death was a consequence of a crime; compensation for a percentage of the property lost as a consequence of a crime. Where possible, the offender should be a participant in the process of restitution.[39]

(11) *Grand jury reform.* We support the reform of the grand jury system so as to assure the constitutional rights of grand jury witnesses.

80. The need for action in these areas exists at the state and local levels as well. We encourage individuals, parishes, dioceses, those in religious orders and other organizations to support such efforts in their communities.

---

[39] *The Reform of Correctional Institutions in the 1970s,* p. 6.

VII. Conclusion

81. The magnitude and complexity of the American crime problem are so formidable that they create a feeling of hopelessness and a temptation to accept crime as a fact of life because solutions are difficult. Rather than allowing ourselves to succumb to these feelings, what is needed is a united and widespread effort to address this problem.

82. At this time, our concern is not to console those who are discouraged by the dimensions of the crime problem but to challenge our people, and all Americans, to confront crime and the attitudes, conditions and false values that foster it, in spite of the immensity of the task. We seek the talents, initiatives, responses and support of all God's people.

83. As believers, we have strong traditions from which to develop a response to crime. As Americans, we can find real support in our constitutional heritage and our fundamental social institutions—the family, the community and the neighborhood.

84. In efforts to reduce and prevent crime, believers have to strive to exemplify the attitude of Christ our Lord, who loved His enemies, who forgave those who persecuted and executed Him, and who taught that love and forgiveness are the only forces that can overcome evil and hatred.[40] Despite the difficulty of this task, we should endeavor to create communities which incarnate this saving love. We also need to balance the competing interests of those involved with the criminal justice system, in accordance with the protections which are guaranteed in the American Constitution.

85. It is recognized that many of the solutions to the problem of crime, such as the elimination of deprivation and unemployment and changes in attitudes and values, will take time, patience, financial resources and considerable self-sacrifice. Yet, we are hopeful that as a community in the land of the free and home of the brave, we can respond effectively to the problem of crime in our society.

86. This very difficult task of responding to the problem of the curtailment and the elimination of crime in America needs a commitment full of faith, hope and charity—one that embodies the teaching of Jesus who is both Lord and Messiah.[41]

---

[40] Lk. 23:34; Rom. 12:17, 20-21.
[41] Acts, 2:36.

Economic Issues and Other Human Needs

The American bishops issued eight statements on economic issues between 1967 and 1977. The most comprehensive and significant is entitled The Economy: Human Dimensions *(November 20, 1975).*

The bishops contend that they will address the moral, human, and social aspects of the economic crisis and the impact of the economy on individuals and families, but not "technical, fiscal matters, particular economic theories or political programs." Their general perspective is that "economic life must reflect broad values of social justice and human rights."

As a moral guide for citizens and policymakers, the bishops enunciate seven principles to guide economic activity. Then they briefly examine the three economic problems they consider most serious: unemployment, inflation, and unequal distribution of wealth and income. They argue that the reality of high unemployment in the U.S. indicates that the nation no longer appears to be fully committed to genuine full employment. To stress the urgency of achieving full employment, the bishops cite the devasting effects of unemployment: high crime rates, drug addiction, alcoholism, mental illness and social tension, erosion of family relationships, dulling of the spirit, and the destruction of human dreams and hopes. Joblessness causes people to "lose a key measure of their place in society and a source of individual fulfillment." Furthermore, people out of work means billions of dollars in lost productivity and great expense to all.

In discussing inflation, the bishops stress that it is unjust to "tolerate high levels of unemployment for some in order to avoid ruinous inflation for all." They reject the economic view that low unemployment and high inflation are necessarily related. They claim, instead, that the best protection for many citizens against inflation is a decent job at decent wages.

In the view of the USCC, the major economic problem is unequal distribution of income and wealth. The bishops cite statistics to demonstrate this inequality and then assert that Catholic social teaching condemns "gross inequality in the distribution of material goods."

The last part of the bishops' statement contains specific policy suggestions, including effective national commitment to full employment, improvement of the unemployment compensation system, adequate assistance for victims of recession, income policy for the sick, old and disabled, better use of land to insure more employment, and preservation of small family farms. They call upon the public and private sectors to promote fairness in taxation, to halt the harmful effects of inflation, and to distribute more evenly the burdens and opportunities of society.

252

Poverty Legislation

NCCB, November 14, 1967

1. The Catholic bishops of the United States, convened in formal session in Washington, D.C., November 14, 1967, planning the fulfillment of their own responsibilities in fields of education and welfare as these are related to the services of the Church to the nation, respectfully recommend the immediate passage of strong and adequate legislation supporting the War on Poverty. We urge the House of Representatives to defeat amendments which would destroy the ability of our nation and its citizenry to keep faith with the commitments already made to the socially and economically handicapped segment of our population. To formalize this conviction of the Catholic bishops of this country, the following resolution was passed unanimously.

2. *Resolved,* that the National Conference of Catholic Bishops strongly urge the House of Representatives to maintain the momentum of our national attack on poverty and its causes, thus reinforcing the confidence of our impoverished brothers that the United States and all its citizenry will keep faith with them in the increasing pursuit of justice, fairness and equal opportunity for all citizens by enacting legislation continuing the War on Poverty as administered by the Office of Economic Opportunity with an adequate budget which will enable it to preserve the basic program now in force.

This statement was issued by the National Conference of Catholic Bishops and was immediately forwarded to leaders of the U.S. House of Representatives.

Crusade Against Poverty

NCCB, November 14, 1969

1. The problems of poverty, racism and minority tensions require of us a constant re-evaluation of our investments of human energy and financial resources. Such a re-appraisal highlights the professional services of our Catholic Charities agencies, the generous financial support—running into many millions of dollars—that is supplied by our Catholic people, often at the cost of considerable personal sacrifice.

2. Notwithstanding this record of genuine service, these are the human conditions we face at the present moment. In 1968 there were 22 million people certified as poor—that is, living below the level of manageable poverty as defined by the U.S. Social Security System. Sixty-six percent of these poor people are white; fifty percent of these poor families lived in the South in rural-oriented communities, with little hope of developing economic and social independence under existing conditions.

3. The magnitude and complexity of these problems in a time of rapid social change challenges us to a constant re-dedication of our efforts and at the same time, calls for the creation of a new source of financial capital that can be allocated for specific projects aimed at eliminating the very causes of poverty.

4. Besides the services in finances and personnel that can be grouped under present programs of Catholic Charities, inner-city parochial schools, and other Church-sponsored agencies, there is an evident need for funds designated to be used for organized groups of white and minority poor to develop economic strength and political power in their own communities. This requires private sources of funding not now available through government and foundation sources.

5. These self-help funds can be distributed according to definite criteria for such projects as voter registration, community organizations, seed money to develop non-profit housing corporations, community-run schools, minority owned cooperatives and credit unions, capital for industrial development and job training programs and setting up of rural cooperatives.

6. These funds can be made available on a two- or three-year basis with the understanding that the enterprises will become self-sufficient or will find other sources of funding within this trial period.

7. The goal of such support is self-sufficiency and the development of people caught within the cycle of poverty and dependence.

8. We are encouraged by the willingness of our Catholic people to volunteer their time and energy and to assure a financial base to the present

Church-sponsored efforts. But we are also convinced that our ability to find new pathways should not further stretch our present resources, but should be based on a new funding effort. We also believe that this new effort can lead the People of God to a new knowledge of today's problems, a deeper understanding of the intricate forces that lead to group conflict, and a perception of some new and promising approaches that we might take in promoting a greater spirit of solidarity among those who are successful, those who have acquired some share of the nation's goods, and those still trapped in poverty.

Resolution:

9. Therefore, be it resolved that the National Conference of Catholic Bishops establish a National Catholic Crusade Against Poverty.

10. The crusade will commit the Church to raise a fund of $50 million dollars over the next several years.

11. To effect this, the conference directs that the president of the NCCB appoint a committee to formulate a specific proposal for the approval of the administrative board at its next meeting.

Welfare Reform Legislation

USCC, April 23, 1970

1. *Whereas:* Poverty in the midst of affluence is indefensible, particularly the privation of children, the old and the handicapped, who are poor through no fault of their own, and who make up the great bulk of those receiving assistance; and

2. *Whereas:* The welfare system, including the Aid for Families with Dependent Children (AFDC) Program, has proven wholly inadequate to provide either a decent standard of living or incentive to the "beneficiary" families but, instead, is in many cases counter-productive and destructive of family life; and

3. *Whereas:* The Family Assistance Act of 1970, passed by the House of Representatives and pending before the Senate Finance Committee, would constitute a substantial social advance in providing a federal minimum pay-

ment to poor families and in helping the "working poor" as well as the poor who are unemployed;

4. Now Therefore be it resolved: That the Catholic Bishops of the United States assembled as the United States Catholic Conference urge prompt enactment of the Family Assistance Act or some similar family assistance program, at the same time urging that the minimum dollar amount of $1,600 for a family of four, be substantially raised. Strong and clear federal guidelines, to assure equitable administration, must be provided. If training for, or acceptance of, employment by the family head is a condition precedent to the obtaining of benefits, it is important that such employment be truly suitable.

5. We consider this legislation one of the most important and urgent issues to come before the Congress in recent years. We express the hope that the Governmental responsibility will be met. We ask all people of good will to address their attention to this problem and the pending landmark legislation.

Statement on National Health Insurance

USCC, Committee on Health Affairs
February 2, 1971

Whereas society, which is concerned for the total well-being of its members, has the responsibility to provide health care in the broadest sense which includes health education as well as preventive and environmental medicine together with curative and restorative measures;

Whereas health, as broadly defined, includes physical and mental aspects, contributes to the total well-being of and is consistent with man's personal dignity and respect for himself as well as his human condition;

Whereas physical and mental health care should be equally available to every citizen in our society as a right;

Whereas access to and availability of services which promote physical and mental well-being are essential to health maintenance; and

Whereas health services in our society are being provided and funded through the collaboration of both voluntary and governmental components of our society; therefore

We endorse and offer our support to the development of a national program for health which has as its foundation the above principles and which is designed to define and remedy deficiencies which mitigate against these principles.

Statement on Feeding the Hungry: Toward a U.S. Domestic Food Policy

USCC, Department of Social Development and World Peace April 16, 1975

The Department of Social Development and World Peace of the United States Catholic Conference takes the occasion of "Food Day," April 17, 1975, to urge Catholics to deepen their understanding of the food crisis and commit themselves to continued reflection and action to feed the hungry both here and abroad. The Church has a particular responsibility with regard to the food crisis since Jesus identified himself with the poor and hungry. We recognize with the 1974 Synod of Bishops the "right to eat" as a fundamental right which flows from the basic and inalienable right to life itself. It is for this reason that we look upon feeding the hungry as a requirement of justice.

Last November the Catholic Bishops of the United States adopted a pastoral plan of action on the world food crisis. The response to the Bishops' program has been widespread and significant. Many dioceses, parishes, and other organizations instituted educational programs and raised funds for international humanitarian relief efforts.

The USCC has engaged in a sustained effort to influence public policy on food issues. Working with the National Catholic Rural Life Conference, Catholic Relief Services and the National Conference of Catholic Charities, the USCC has testified before Congress on food and agricultural policy, and the Food for Peace Program. The USCC has also opposed efforts to increase the price of food stamps, and has supported increased funding for food and nutrition development in our foreign assistance programs.

The grave international consequences of food shortages must be a continuing concern of the American people. However, we must not neglect the very serious food and nutrition needs in our country. The United States has a responsibility in both domestic and international areas. These responsibilities should not be seen in conflict with each other, but viewed as different aspects of the same problem.

The development of a comprehensive food policy is an urgent priority for the nation. Our government is currently considering various food issues. It will be necessary to weigh the competing interests of consumers, producers, and middlemen in the food distribution system. Farmers seek reasonable prices for their products; food processors, retailers and distributors are concerned about adequate return on their investment; consumers worry about rising food costs. Lower income consumers have a particular concern about the future of food stamps and other federal nutrition programs. In addition, policymakers need to evaluate the interests and unique responsibilities of the United States vis-a-vis world markets and international needs.

In the midst of these competing interests, our food policy should work toward full production, equitable distribution and price stability. At a time when world food shortages mean starvation for millions, a U.S. agricultural policy of full production is absolutely essential. At the same time, U.S. food policy should not force low and middle income consumers and independent farmers to bear an unfair burden.

In view of these considerations, we shall address three areas of immediate concern: U.S. food needs and nutrition programs, ownership and control of resources, and full production and target prices.

I. U.S. Food Needs and Nutrition Programs

Many people in the United States continue to suffer from hunger and serious malnutrition. Rapid inflation in food prices, high levels of unemployment and a deep recession have meant a significant increase in hunger in America. While the problem is less severe in the United States than in other countries, it is no less harsh for those who endure it.

Hunger and malnutrition in this country are essentially the result of economic factors. Nutritional studies indicate that malnutrition rises as income declines and that the worst hunger is among the very poor. The consequences of malnutrition are very serious, especially for young children. It reduces productivity, motivation and educational performance, lowers resistance to disease, inhibits growth and development, and can even result in a shorter life-span.

There are over 37 million poor people in the United States. Many people lack adequate nutrition because they lack employment and income that would enable them to buy sufficient food. Their situation has worsened as the economy has declined. Public assistance and social programs have not kept pace with inflation. Jobs have become almost impossible to find as unemployment approaches nine percent. In addition, many elderly persons living on fixed incomes are also victims of serious malnutrition. Middle and working class families are victims of similar economic pressures. Caught in the web of inflation, recession, and high taxes, many of them have lost ground in their battle to provide their families an adequate diet.

In the last decade, the federal government has expanded programs aimed at providing an adequate diet for all Americans. Expenditures on domestic food programs have risen to an estimated $5.8 billion in the present fiscal year.

Recently it has been proposed that existing child nutrition programs be eliminated and a block grant approach be substituted which would cut $600-700 million from nutrition assistance. The USCC opposes reductions in domestic food aid. We urge Congress to resist attempts to eliminate these nutrition programs or reduce funding for food assistance. Instead, these programs should be reformed to eliminate inequities and administrative problems that may prevent eligible persons from participating. They must be expanded to meet increasingly serious needs during this time of economic decline.

A. Families

The food stamp program is the basic form of federal nutrition assistance for American families. This program now serves more than 18 million people, although studies indicate that it reaches less than half of those who may be eligible.

The food stamp program must be maintained and improved. We strongly oppose any increase in the price of food stamps. We support the recent action of Congress to prevent the proposed food stamp price increases and commend the President for his decision to accept that action. Appropriate steps should be taken to guarantee that the benefits of the program go to those who are actually in need. In addition, modifications are required to speed up the certification process and improve the outreach effort to involve other qualified families while guaranteeing that eligibility requirements are enforced.

B. School Children

The federal government now provides nutritional assistance to nearly 25 million children through the National School Lunch Program. The program has both nutritional and educational value and should be extended and improved. Specifically, we support efforts to include the children of unemployed parents in the free lunch program and include orphanages and daycare centers in the subsidy program. We also support proposals to provide additional subsidies to cover increased costs in school lunch programs resulting from inflation.

The School Breakfast Program serves an adequate breakfast to almost two million children every school day. A nutritional breakfast has obvious educational and health benefits for low-income children who would otherwise go to school hungry. The level of the present program does not begin to meet the overall need. Additional funding and permanent status for the breakfast program are required.

Another undertaking that merits continued support is the special milk program. Many schools, especially those without hot lunch programs, benefit from this successful effort to provide milk to school children at reduced prices.

Many Catholic school students participate in these three programs. The Congress should be commended for recognizing the nutritional needs of non-public school children. We urge all qualified Catholic schools to provide these services for their students.

C. Mothers and Young Children

Infants, young children and expectant or nursing mothers have special nutritional needs. Food assistance at these stages can have major impact on the elimination of birth defects, mental retardation, and malnutrition in newborn children. The Women, Infants, and Children Program (WIC) is designed to provide high protein diet supplements to low-income women, infants, and young children. We strongly support the continued existence and expansion of this unique and important program.

D. Older Americans

The nutritional problems of the elderly living alone and on fixed income are especially tragic. They often lack the financial resources or physical health necessary to provide an adequate diet. The Older Americans Act provides funds for community feeding programs for the elderly through communal dining rooms and meals-on-wheels programs along with a range of supportive services. Unfortunately, many of our senior citizens with nutritional problems are not reached by this program. In addition to its food benefits, a fully implemented program would diminish our society's reliance on institutional care for the elderly. We endorse the program and efforts to expand its availability. It is an important effort to meet the needs of our senior citizens.

E. Nutrition Education

An essential element of a national policy against hunger and malnourishment is nutrition education. Consumers need opportunities to improve their knowledge regarding foods and eating habits and to better understand the relationship between health and nutrition. Schools and other institutions should be encouraged to provide broader programs in practical nutrition education.

II. Ownership and Control of Resources

Recent food shortages have made us acutely aware that U.S. food and agricultural policies have a massive impact on the availability, quality and prices of food not only in this country but throughout the world. Because food is a unique resource, necessary to life itself, our great capacity to produce it carries with it awesome responsibilities. Our food policy must not be governed by profit considerations alone, but by the needs of hungry people.

A disturbing phenomenon in the United States is the increasing concentration occurring in the food production system. We have experienced a rapid decline in the number of farms in the U.S. over the last two decades and a substantial migration of families from rural areas to already overcrowded urban centers. The high costs of land, technology and credit make it virtually impossible for young people to go into agricultural production on their own. Governmental policies have often fostered the promotion of capital incentive, corporate controlled agriculture. Our federal and local tax structures create incentives for wealthy non-farm investors in agriculture, but do little for the competent full-time farmer. We support an agricultural system based upon widespread ownership of resources and the means of production. Legislation is needed now to inhibit further encroachment upon agriculture by non-farm corporations and to insure that our land is kept in the hands of those who work it.

We are also concerned about the diminishing level of competition in the food processing and distribution system. In some sectors of the food industry fewer companies are controlling more and more of the market. This trend toward increasing concentration of control can lead to excessive profit and even higher prices for consumers. We urge a comprehensive study of non-competitive forces in the food industry and appropriate anti-trust action to eliminate monopolistic practices.

Decisions about the use of land and resources are often made without rational planning or sufficient concern for the environmental and human costs of those decisions. Suburban sprawl, surface mining, industrial development and other demands on the land are diverting over one million acres from agricultural use each year with potentially serious consequences for future food production. A more integrated and rational process for land use planning is necessary. With regard to agricultural land, the primary objective of land use legislation should be the conservation of such land for its unique food producing value and protection of a dispersed pattern of ownership.

III. Full Production and Target Prices

In light of present food needs, farmers must be encouraged to produce to full capacity. To cut back on production in the face of unmet world needs would be morally and ethically untenable. Neither is it acceptable, however, to ask farmers to assume total financial responsibility for the risks involved in full production without some protection. Widely fluctuating prices for farm products mean at least uncertainty, and perhaps disaster, for small farmers. A system of equitable target prices should be established and reviewed at regular intervals to assure farmers a fair return on their investment and labor. Price supports can be set at levels that will not result in excessively high food prices for consumers, yet provide adequate protection for producers.

At the same time, we support the establishment of reserves of essential commodities to maintain price stability and to safeguard against future world food shortages. These reserves must be federally regulated in a manner that does not jeopardize a just return for farmers.

Conclusions

The debate over American food policy must be seen in a larger context. Hunger and malnutrition flow from basic failures in our society's social and economic structures. Hunger is often the result of persistent poverty, and food programs only supplement inadequate income. They cannot substitute for economic resources, jobs, decent wages, equal opportunity or the power to change economic and political institutions. These programs are not a solution to poverty, racial discrimination, inequitable taxation, or the isolation of the elderly. Fundamentally, our nation must provide jobs for those who are able to work and a minimal income to those who cannot. The U.S. Catholic Conference has consistently supported programs that would guarantee an adequate income for all Americans. We renew that call today.

At this point, however, Church institutions, parishes, and individual church members must seek out and help those in our midst who lack food. For as Pope Paul has said, it is not enough to point to injustice and human need. "Such words will lack real weight unless they are accompanied for each individual by a livelier awareness of personal responsibility and effective action."

At the same time, the Church must also participate in a rigorous and competent analysis of structures and systems that result in poverty and hunger. We must become advocates of change so that structures are adapted to meet the serious needs of those who now go hungry. In his Apostolic Letter, *A Call to Action,* Pope Paul says Christian organizations "have to express in their own way and rising above their particular nature, the concrete demands of

Christian faith for a just, and consequently, necessary, transformation of society."

The hungry of the world have voiced their cries of anguish. We must respond to them not only with words of hope, but with actions that will mobilize the energies, talents, and resources of the Catholic community to assist people not only around the world but in this nation as well.

The Economy: Human Dimensions

USCC, November 20, 1975

> "This unemployment returning again to plague us after so many repetitions during the century past is a sign of deep failure in our country. Unemployment is the great peacetime physical tragedy of the nineteenth and twentieth centuries, and both in its cause and in the imprint it leaves upon those who inflict it, those who permit it, and those who are its victims, it is one of the great moral tragedies of our time."

> The Bishops of the United States,
> *Unemployment*, 1930.

1. This was the judgment of our predecessors as they responded to the economic crisis of 1930. As pastors, teachers and leaders, we recall and emphasize their words as our country faces important economic, social and moral decisions in the midst of the highest unemployment since the 1930s.

I. The Church's Concern

2. Despite recent hopeful signs, the economy is only slowly and painfully recovering from the recent recession, the worst since World War II. We are deeply concerned that this recovery may lack the strength or duration to alleviate the suffering of many of the victims of the recession, especially the unemployed. It is the moral, human and social consequences of our troubled economy which concern us and their impact on families, the elderly and children. We hope in these limited reflections to give voice to some of the concerns of the poor and working people of our land.

3. We are keenly aware of the world-wide dimensions of the problem and

the complexity of these issues of economic policy. Our concern, however, is not with technical fiscal matters, particular economic theories or political programs, but rather the moral aspects of economic policy and the impact of these policies on people. Our economic life must reflect broad values of social justice and human rights.

II. The Church's Teaching

4. Our own rich heritage of Catholic teaching offers important direction and insight. Most importantly, we are guided by the concern for the poor and afflicted shown by Jesus, who came to "bring good news to the poor, to proclaim liberty to captives, new sight to the blind, and to set the downtrodden free" (Luke 4:18). In addition, the social encyclicals of the Popes and documents of the Second Vatican Council and the Synod of Bishops defend the basic human right to useful employment, just wages and decent working conditions as well as the right of workers to organize and bargain collectively. They condemn unemployment, maldistribution of resources and other forms of economic injustice and call for the creation of useful work experiences and new forms of industrial organization enabling workers to share in decision-making, increased production, and even ownership. Again and again they point out the interrelation of economics and ethics, urging that economic activity be guided by social morality.

5. Catholic teaching on economic issues flows from the Church's commitment to human rights and human dignity. This living tradition articulates a number of principles which are useful in evaluating our current economic situation. Without attempting to set down an all-inclusive list, we draw the following principles from the social teachings of the Church and ask that policymakers and citizens ponder their implications.

a. Economic activity should be governed by justice and be carried out within the limits of morality. It must serve people's needs.[1]

b. The right to have a share of earthly goods sufficient for oneself and one's family belongs to everyone.[2]

c. Economic prosperity is to be assessed not so much from the sum total of goods and wealth possessed as from the distribution of goods according to norms of justice.[3]

d. Opportunities to work must be provided for those who are able and

---

[1] Vatican II, *The Church In The Modern World*, 64; John XXIII, *Mater et Magistra*, 38–39.
[2] Vatican II, *The Church In The Modern World*, 69.
[3] John XXIII, *Mater et Magistra*, 73.

willing to work. Every person has the right to useful employment, to just wages, and to adequate assistance in case of real need.[4]

e. Economic development must not be left to the sole judgment of a few persons or groups possessing excessive economic power, or to the political community alone. On the contrary, at every level the largest possible number of people should have an active share in directing that development.[5]

f. A just and equitable system of taxation requires assessment according to ability to pay.[6]

g. Government must play a role in the economic activity of its citizens. Indeed, it should promote in a suitable manner the production of a sufficient supply of material goods. Moreover, it should safeguard the rights of all citizens, and help them find opportunities for employment.[7]

6. These are not new principles. They are drawn directly from the teachings of the Church, but they have critical relevance at this time of economic distress. Under current conditions, many of these principles are being consistently violated.

III. Dimensions of the Economic Situation

7. In these reflections we wish to examine briefly the dimensions of our economic problems in three areas: unemployment, inflation and distribution of wealth and income.

A. Unemployment

8. In October, government figures show eight million persons were unemployed, representing 8.6% of the work force.[8] Millions of other persons have given up seeking work out of discouragement or are in part-time jobs although they desire full-time work. Taking this into account, the actual level of unemployment in our country is over 12%. It is estimated that 20 million people will be jobless at some time this year, and that one-third of all Americans will suffer the traumatic experience of unemployment within their families.

---

[4] Pius XI, *On The Reconstruction of The Social Order,* 74; John XXIII, *Pacem in Terris,* 11, 18; Vatican II, *The Church In The Modern World,* 67; Paul VI, *A Call To Action,* 6.

[5] Vatican II, *The Church In The Modern World,* 65.

[6] John XXIII, *Mater et Magistra,* 132.

[7] John XXIII, *Mater et Magistra,* 20; Vatican II, *The Church In The Modern World,* 67, 70.

[8] The Employment Situation: October 1975; U.S. Department of Labor, Bureau of Labor Statistics; November 7, 1975.

9. The official unemployment rate does more than underestimate the true extent of joblessness. It also masks the inequitable distribution of unemployment. The figures for October indicate that minorities, blue collar workers, young people and women bear a disproportionate share of the burdens of joblessness.[9]

10. These realities clearly indicate that the nation's commitment to genuine full employment has been seriously eroded, if not abandoned. Since World War II, unemployment has been substantial, persistent and drifting upward. In fact, when joblessness rose dramatically during the latest recession, it took the form of an acute and visible crisis, superimposed on a long-term unemployment problem which has persisted for decades.

11. The costs of this tragic under-utilization of our country's human resources are enormous. In economic terms, these high levels of unemployment cost literally hundreds of billions of dollars in lost productivity and tens of billions of dollars in lost revenue and increased expenses for all levels of government.

12. As lamentable as these financial costs are, the social and human impact is far more deplorable. In our society, persons without a job lose a key measure of their place in society and a source of individual fulfillment; they often feel that there is no productive role for them. Many minority youth may grow up without meaningful job experiences and come to accept a life of dependency. Unemployment frequently leads to higher rates of crime, drug addiction, and alcoholism. It is reflected in higher rates of mental illness as well as rising social tensions. The idleness, fear and financial insecurity resulting from unemployment can undermine confidence, erode family relationships, dull the spirit and destroy dreams and hopes. One can hardly bear to contemplate the disappointment of a family which has made the slow and painful climb up the economic ladder and has been pushed down once again into poverty and dependence by the loss of a job.

13. The current levels of unemployment are unacceptable and their tremendous human costs are intolerable. Unemployment represents a vast and tragic waste of our human and material resources. We are disturbed not only by the present levels of joblessness, but also by official government projections of massive unemployment for the rest of this decade. We sincerely hope that these figures do not represent resignation to the human and economic waste implied in these rates of unemployment. As a society, we cannot accept the notion that some will have jobs and income while others will be told to wait a few years and to subsist on welfare in the interim. For

---

[9] Department of Labor figures for October 1975 indicate:
- One out of five teenagers were jobless.
- Over 11% of all blue collar workers were out of work.
- 14.2% of all minority persons were unemployed.
- Nearly 40% of all minority teenagers were jobless.
- 134 of our 150 major urban areas were officially listed as areas of substantial subemployment.

work is more than a way to earn a living. It represents a deep human need, desired not only for income but also for the sense of worth which it provides the individual.

B. Inflation

14. There are those who insist that we must tolerate high levels of unemployment for some, in order to avoid ruinous inflation for all. Although we are deeply concerned about inflation, we reject such a policy as not grounded in justice. In recent years, our country has experienced very high levels of inflation. During this past year, there has been some reduction in inflation, but there are already signs of its renewal, spurred by large increases in food and fuel prices.

15. Inflation weakens the economic stability of our society and erodes the economic security of our citizens. Its impact is most severe on those who live on fixed incomes and the very poor. The double distress of inflation and recession has led to a painful decline in real income for large numbers of people in recent years. Clearly, steps must be taken to limit inflation and its impact.

16. However, low unemployment and high inflation are not inevitable partners, as history and the experience of other industrialized countries bear out. Policymakers should seek and use measures to combat inflation which do not rely upon high rates of joblessness. For many of our fellow citizens, the major protection against inflation is a decent job at decent wages.

C. Distribution of Income and Wealth

17. Within our country, vast disparities of income and wealth remain. The richest 20% of our people receive more income than the bottom 60% combined. In the area of ownership, the disparities are even more apparent. The top one-fifth of all families own more than three-fourths of all the privately held wealth in the United States while over one-half of our families control less than 7% of the wealth.

18. The distribution of income and wealth are important since they influence and even determine our society's distribution of economic power. Catholic social teaching has condemned gross inequality in the distribution of material goods. Our country cannot continue to ignore this important measure of economic justice.

IV. Policy Directions

19. Fundamentally, our nation must provide jobs for those who can and should work and a decent income for those who cannot. An effective national commitment to full employment is needed to protect the basic human right to useful employment for all Americans. It ought to guarantee, through ap-

propriate mechanisms, that no one seeking work would be denied an opportunity to earn a livelihood. Full employment is the foundation of a just economic policy; it should not be sacrificed for other political and economic goals. We would support sound and creative programs of public service employment to relieve joblessness and to meet the vital social needs of our people (housing, transportation, education, health care, recreation, etc.).

20. The burden and hardship of these difficult times must not fall most heavily on the most vulnerable: the poor, the elderly, the unemployed, young people and workers of modest income. We support efforts to improve our unemployment compensation system and to provide adequate assistance to the victims of the recession. Efforts to eliminate or curtail needed services and help must be strongly opposed.

21. We continue to support a decent income policy for those who are unable to work because of sickness, age, disability or other good reason. Our present welfare system should be reformed to serve our country and those in need more effectively.

22. Renewed efforts are required to reform our economic life. We ask the private and public sectors to join together to plan and provide better for our future, to promote fairness in taxation, to halt the destructive impact of inflation and to distribute more evenly the burdens and opportunities of our society. We also ask that consideration be given to a more efficacious use of the land, the nation's primary resource in order to provide gainful employment for more people. We should also explore the impact of technology and endeavor to preserve the small family farm and other approaches to economic life which provide substantial and productive employment for people. It is not enough to point up the issues in our economy and to propose solutions to our national problems while accepting uncritically the presupposition of an economic system based in large part upon unlimited and unrestrained profit.

23. We pledge our best efforts in support of these goals. We call on local parishes, dioceses, Catholic institutions and organizations to undertake education and action programs on issues of economic justice. We renew our commitment to assist the needy and victims of economic turmoil through programs of financial assistance and active participation in the dialogue over the formulation and implementation of just economic policies. We call on our people to pray for our country in this time of need and to participate in the difficult decisions which can still fulfill the promise of our land.

24. Working together with renewed vision and commitment, our country has the productive capacity and human and material resources to provide adequately for the needs of our people. We take this opportunity to renew the challenge of our fellow Bishops of 45 years ago:

"Our country needs, now and permanently, such a change of heart as will, intelligently and with determination, so organize and distribute our work and wealth that no one need lack for any long time the security of being able to earn an adequate living for himself and for those dependent upon him."

The Bishops of the United States,
Unemployment, 1930

Appendix

In adopting this resolution, the Bishops sought to link this effort to a major statement issued in 1919 on similar matters. Entitled, "The Bishops' Program For Social Reconstruction," the statement called for: minimum wage legislation; unemployment insurance and protection against sickness and old age; minimum age limit for working children; legal enforcement of the right of labor to organize; a national employment service; public housing; and a long term program of increasing wages.

It also urged: prevention of excessive profits and incomes through regulation of public utilities and progressive taxes on inheritance, income, and excess profits; participation of labor in management; a wider distribution of ownership through cooperative enterprises and worker ownership in the stock of corporations; and effective control of monopolies even by the method of government competition if that should prove necessary.

Most of these proposals have been enacted. Partial progress has been made toward others. The 1919 statement provides a historical framework for the current resolution and evidences a longstanding concern for economic justice on the part of the Catholic community in this country.

Resolution on New York City

USCC, Administrative Board
November 15, 1976

"The current crisis facing the 8 million people of New York City is more than a fiscal crisis. It is a human crisis as well, it involves people and their health and welfare. Moreover, it is not just a problem of one city or one state. It is part of a larger urban crisis confronting many American cities and threatening the common good and dignity of many millions of our fellow citizens.

"We are convinced that default and bankruptcy are not adequate answers.

Default will mean that human life in New York City will be paralyzed. Assistance in human services for the poor and the sick, the young and the aged, will all but cease to exist. Hospitals may well have to suspend their services, furlough their staffs, and discharge their patients. Nursing homes and senior citizen centers are also in jeopardy. Schools, day care centers, and child care facilities may not be able to survive.

"We are not unaware of the many factors which have contributed to New York City's problems. The dire effects of recession and inflation—the loss of thousands of jobs, the erosion of tax base and the costs of municipal and human services to sustain the less fortunate have all contributed to the problem. We are also aware of the serious charges that poor judgments, over spending, political opportunism and at times inefficient management have all played their part and must be corrected. Specific steps in this direction have already been taken.

"We call upon our national leaders and the people of New York City; as just and equitable solutions are sought, there is no room for sectionalism and partisanship.

"Therefore we earnestly urge that the Congress enact and the President sign appropriate loan guarantee legislation for the City of New York. This legislation should be designed to avert default by the City and the adverse economic and social consequences that would result for the people of New York. We support these guarantees in order to provide sufficient time for the City to make the necessary program and financial adjustments to restore the City to financial stability."

Welfare Reform in the 1970s

USCC, Department of Social Development and World Peace February 25, 1977

The Department of Social Development and World Peace issued a letter on reform of the welfare system in this country on February 25, 1977. The letter was in response to a request by the Department of Health, Education and Welfare soliciting the views of the United States Catholic Conference on present problems in the welfare system and methods of resolving them. The

Federal Government has undertaken a major study of welfare problems and alternative approaches to public assistance programs, and has invited insights and recommendations from religious, civic and governmental organizations.

Since the 1930s the Bishops of the United States have participated in discussions on public welfare assistance. In 1969 the USCC presented testimony before Congress on a proposal entitled: the Family Assistance Plan. This measure signaled the first attempt of the Federal Government to substantially revise public assistance programs. The proposal, however, never reached enactment.

With the recent initiatives of the Department of HEW, the subject of welfare reform is again in the forestage of national debate.

In submitting its position on this timely question, the USCC has called for national policies which reflect the values of human rights and social justice while placing primary attention on assuring family values. Welfare reform, the USCC asserts, must also include commitments to the provision of jobs for those who can work and adequate income assistance for those who cannot. The text follows:

The Department of Social Development and World Peace, United States Catholic Conference, welcomes the opportunity to contribute to discussions on the reform of the welfare system in this country. As religious leaders and pastors, the primary concern of Catholic Church leadership is with the human and moral dimensions of welfare policies, rather than with specific technical or administrative provisions of public assistance programs.

We are not new participants in the national debate on public welfare assistance. The Catholic Bishops of the United States, through the U.S. Catholic Conference and its predecessor, the National Catholic Welfare Conference, have been involved in this issue since the 1930s. More recently, the USCC presented testimony in the United States Senate and the House of Representatives on the Family Assistance Plan of 1969 and on full employment and national economic policy in 1976.

We bring to these discussions two important resources: a rich heritage of Catholic social teaching and over two centuries of experience in providing for the needs of the poor of this country. Through their pastoral statements and anti-poverty efforts, the American Bishops have continually called attention to the needs of the poor. Moreover, the Catholic Charities agencies throughout the country constitute one of the largest and most effective networks of voluntary providers of social services in this nation. Through this involvement and experience we have come to appreciate the extent of poverty in America and the hardships that many of our citizens face in meeting their daily needs.

America must seek to protect her greatest resource—her people. To accomplish this, there must be jobs for all those who can work and adequate income assistance for those who cannot. In providing for those who cannot work, we firmly believe that our nation's policies should reflect the values of human rights and social justice while placing primary attention on assuring family stability. These principles must guide our consideration of welfare reform proposals.

Unfortunately, we are presently far from achieving the goal of providing all citizens with an adequate income. Too many American families suffer from the devastating effects of unemployment and of poverty. The human costs of our failure to provide an adequate income for all Americans are tremendous. Suffering, alienation, the breakdown of family life, alcoholism, and drug abuse are only some of the ramifications of acute poverty. Unemployment and poverty statistics are not simply numbers, but represent our nation's underdeveloped and lost potential.

We must all—government officials, religious leaders, professionals and citizens—work to assure that every American receives a just share of our earthly goods. It is for this reason that we are eager to contribute to this most recent national effort to address the needs of the poor. In our response we will draw upon our tradition and experience in order to examine several elements of welfare reform including a discussion of those welfare reform issues which we find most troublesome; an outline of nine basic principles against which we believe any welfare reform proposal should be examined; and a statement of several policy considerations.

Issues and Concerns

As most of us well know, there are numerous problems inherent in establishing a fair income assistance program. This fact is evident from the present welfare system as well as the debate surrounding alternative approaches. We do not intend to address all of these problems, but only those which we believe most directly bear upon the moral and human dimensions of welfare reform.

Inadequacy and Inequity of Assistance

We are greatly disturbed by the inadequate benefit levels and inequities of benefit distribution across the country. Presently among the states there exists a wide disparity in the amount of payments received by those eligible for assistance through the Aid to Families with Dependent Children (AFDC) program. In some states, families are forced to live on substandard incomes. The variations in benefit distribution is such that a family of four in one state can receive $60 monthly, while in another state a family of the same size is eligible to receive $476. This disparity of benefit distribution is most evident in the case of families with unemployed fathers. In only half of the states are these families eligible for AFDC benefits. Perhaps the greatest injustice of the existing system is that there is no permanent or adequate program to provide support for the head of household working full-time whose wages are insufficient to support a family. Reform of the welfare system must mean the elimination of inequity and arbitrary disparity in benefits among the states.

Employment

The employment of the poor has a critical bearing on any efforts to reform our public welfare system. We share the belief of most Americans, including many of the poor themselves, that the poor should work for a living if they are able to do so. The vast majority of the underemployed and unemployed seek the dignity, security, financial gain, and the measures of success which useful work provides. Our nation must guarantee that no one seeking work will be denied an opportunity to earn a livelihood. Yet, the problem of providing adequate employment is not one that can be solved simply by short-term job creation and occasional economic stimulus. As the Catholic Bishops declared in their statement, *The Economy: Human Dimensions* (1976), "An effective national commitment to full employment is needed to protect the basic human right to useful employment for all Americans." Through comprehensive economic planning, sound job creation in both the private and public sectors and coordinated fiscal and monetary policies, our nation should move swiftly and directly toward an economic policy which harnesses the talents and energies of all of our people to meet basic human needs.

The Family

In their recent statement on moral values entitled, *To Live in Christ Jesus,* the United States Bishops asserted that "every human being has a need and right to be loved, to have a home where he or she can put down roots and grow." The family, the Bishops continued, "is the first and indispensable community in which this need is met." As such a community, it is the primary moral, social and educational institution of our society; and, therefore, its health and stability are of critical importance to our nation. Our present welfare system often contributes to the destruction rather than the strengthening of family life by not assuring an adequate income; by creating incentives for a father to leave his family; by not sufficiently providing for the basic needs of some families, particularly those of low income working men and women. Any proposed welfare reform should include measures to rectify the provisions of our present system that are detrimental to family life. It should reflect a recognition of the importance of parents being in the home and of parental responsibility for the care and welfare of their children. The well-being of the family should be a primary focus embodied in any welfare reform program.

Administration

Administrative complexities and inefficiencies impact the human dimensions of welfare. Complex forms, multi-agency processing, variations in regulations and requirements between programs not only create confusion and frustration for recipients, but also impede efficient administrative practices. Such complexities make program oversight difficult; promote overzealous, abusive and demeaning surveillance of recipients; and increase the possibility of fraud and administrative abuse. Simplified procedures and the greater coordination of programs should reduce the difficulty of applying for assistance and the need for an intensive monitoring program to assure the proper distribution of funds. Moreover, these changes would help to keep administrative costs under control, as well as facilitating accountability of public assistance administrators to the public.

Special Needs

It must be recognized that among the poor there are populations with special needs—migrant workers, American Indians, those not protected under unemployment or disability compensation programs, minimum wage laws, or old age social security benefits. Some of these needs can best be met by expanding existing programs and protections, such as by the extension of the social security program. The response to the needs of certain others, however, should be integrated into any welfare reform or employment programs.

Principles

In view of the problems of the present welfare system, we believe that there is an immediate need for change. Our heritage of Catholic social teachings and long experience in providing services to the poor, provide us with a sound basis from which to address the problem of poverty in our society. Based on these traditions, we believe that there are certain principles which should be reflected in any approach to welfare reform. We will evaluate proposed reforms in light of the following norms:

> I.—Every human person has the right to an income, sufficient to insure a decent and dignified life for one's self and one's family.

The earth and all its goods ought to be shared by every human being, not just a select few. As a nation, we must recognize our responsibility to assure that all citizens share this wealth. Every individual and family should have an income or income assistance, as well as additional program support, in order to assure them adequate food, clothing, medical care, shelter, care of children, personal well-being and the resources to exercise community responsibilities.

> II.—Welfare reform should be developed in conjunction with broader economic policies directed toward the development of a genuine full employment economy that serves all our people.

The problem of welfare reform is related to the overall inequitable distribution of jobs, income, wealth, economic and political power in our society. The richest twenty percent of our people receive more income than the bottom sixty percent of our people combined. Unemployment and underemployment fall disproportionately on the young, minorities and women. Inflation erodes the economic security of all of our citizens, but particularly those on fixed incomes. To alleviate these problems and to provide for effective welfare reform, what is needed is sustained governmental action to achieve a genuine full employment economy.

III.—Our nation must provide jobs at a decent wage for those who can work and a decent income for those who cannot work.

Work is valued both because of the income it provides and for the sense of self-worth and dignity it affords the individual. Accordingly, we believe that those who can work should be provided with meaningful jobs through the private or public sector. Where there is no employable household member or where requiring the employment of a household member would damage the family structure our nation must assure these individuals an adequate income.

IV.—The maintenance and revitalization of family life should be a primary concern.

We are deeply concerned about the impact of poverty and our present welfare system upon the family. Since family life is the primary source of our moral and social education, it is essential to the proper functioning of society that the family be sustained. Public authorities should regard the maintenance and protection of the integrity of the family as a vital responsibility. Programs should be structured so as to support the presence of both parents in the home rather than encouraging desertion by a parent in order to obtain assistance for the family.

V.—Income assistance should be available to those who are employed but who do not receive an adequate income.

One of the greatest tragedies in our society is the fact that there are many Americans who work hard, but for a variety of reasons do not receive an adequate income. Public assistance should be given to these individuals and to their families, solely on the basis of need. Job training and suitable employment opportunities should also be available to the low income working men and women. This supplemental income program should be designed so as to avoid creating work disincentives.

VI.—Income assistance should be determined solely on the basis of need.

Assistance should be available to all those in need. There should be no discrimination against families or persons because of race, creed, sex, ethnicity, age, marital status or family size.

> VII.—Any income assistance program should permit the poor to manage their own income and personal needs.

About half of those who receive assistance under the present system are adults. Yet, through certain eligibility requirements and programs that specify how benefits are to be spent, e.g., food stamps, the government directs the purchasing patterns of the poor. This system can be demeaning to the recipients. The poor should have the right to manage their income just as any other citizen does.

> VIII.—The processes through which welfare policies and regulations and standards are formulated should involve the poor as participants.

The determination of state and national welfare policies affect the quality of life of millions of poor people. We believe that they should be able to participate in the policy-making that so directly affects their lives. Involvement of the poor should be required in the development and operation of any welfare program.

> IX.—The administration of welfare assistance should be improved and simplified.

Uniform minimum standards for welfare benefits should be established on a simple formula and benefits distributed through understandable and nondemeaning procedures. An evaluation mechanism should be set up to check administrative abuse and inefficiency and to reduce the possibility of recipient fraud. National minimum standards should be created to assure that all Americans receive a basic income.

Policy

While we recognize that these principles are not exhaustive, we do feel that they should be reflected in any reformed welfare system. Based on these principles we also believe that the following policy provisions should be part of a comprehensive reform of the welfare system.

A Full Employment Economy

In order to protect the basic human right to employment of Americans, what is needed is a comprehensive full employment program which includes: comprehensive economic planning; mechanisms to create jobs in the private and public sector; job training and placement programs as well as just economic, monetary and fiscal policies. These strategies ought to be implemented in order to reach a level of genuine full employment.

Full employment will not eliminate the need for an income assistance program as there are individuals who cannot work. Employment should not be used as an excuse to harass the unemployable. We also believe that there are cases, such as the single head of household with a preschool or school age child, or the single head of household with a disabled dependent where competing responsibilities may make it desirable that the individual be allowed to choose whether to work full-time, part-time, or not at all.

While full employment will not solve the entire welfare problem, it will assure that for those who are employable there are jobs at a sufficient income to provide for their families; it will reduce the human and financial costs of unused talent; and it will generate economic growth.

National Income Assistance Program

To provide for those who cannot work, there is a need for a national income assistance program substantially funded by the federal government to assure a universal guaranteed income at a level less than but not substantially disproportionate to the median family income. The program should be primarily supported by the federal government to assure benefit levels, greater uniformity of assistance levels across the country and sufficient resources. States should be encouraged to supplement the program by providing for special needs and for the cost of additional regional variations above the nationally established assistance level. The basic federal assistance level and actual recipient benefits should reflect changes in the cost of living.

Distribution of Benefits

Benefits under the national income assistance program should be distributed solely on the basis of need. Families with unemployed fathers and low income working men and women should be eligible for assistance. For those who can work, but whose income is insufficient; those who can only work part-time; or those seeking job training for future employment, the benefit reduction system should be structured on a sliding scale that provides a positive work incentive. Benefit reductions should not be so great as to make dependency on income assistance more profitable than working.

We recognize that there are some who abuse the present welfare system. Although elimination of such abuse should be one of the purposes of welfare reform, reform should not lead to diminished assistance to those in need or signify a decreased commitment to the poor in our society.

Participation of the Poor

Where possible provision should be made for the participation of the poor on task forces, policy making committees, and supervisory boards which treat state and federal benefit assistance policies, standards, and regulations. We were disappointed by the initial failure to include low income individuals and welfare recipients on the Administration's welfare reform task force. We hope that the role of the poor will be expanded and that henceforth they will be considered by the Administration as necessary participants in any welfare reform or programmatic efforts.

State and federal governments should continue to support self-help and community development efforts by the poor. These provide the opportunity for community groups to determine and respond to local needs of a broader scope and magnitude than individual income assistance.

Special Benefit Programs

All benefit programs, such as low income housing, food stamps, medicaid should be integrated with a reformed welfare system. While responding to specific needs of the poor some of these programs limit the ability of the poor to choose how to spend their money and in some cases those programs do not meet actual family needs. (For example, by providing a family of four with $153 worth of food stamps and $47 for the rest of their expenses.) Many present non-cash benefit programs can be replaced by providing a family with an adequate income. Where those programs are replaced or phased out an equivalent level of cash benefits should be made available. We continue to support the need for low income public housing and rehabilitation and housing maintenance programs, the purpose of which is to increase the supply of available housing to the poor, while recognizing that there are other housing subsidies which might be replaced by direct cash payments to the poor. These changes, however, should not be designed to eliminate large numbers of recipients from the benefit rolls or to reduce benefit levels. In the case of the food stamps and other similar programs, the substitution of cash payments for in-kind services should not be made until equivalent cash payments can be provided. We believe that the poor should have the same right as every other American—to determine family needs and expenditures.

Administration and Accountability

The primary concern of those providing services through the income assistance program should be to respond to the needs of their clients. To facilitate the distribution of benefits, forms, application and appeals procedures should be easily understood; should not discriminate on the basis of race, sex, ethnicity; and should not be applied in a punitive manner. A system of administrative evaluation and accountability should be established to assure the prompt processing of applications and appeals, the delivery of benefits to those in need, and review and control of administrative costs.

Proper administrative procedures and safeguards are necessary to assure that those in need receive their benefits; that abuse of the system be held to a minimum; and that administrative waste and inefficiency are curtailed. We do not believe that these problems require the intensive surveillance of welfare recipients or elaborate application forms and procedures as are now used. Rather, a simpler system would permit easier and less offensive checks for fraud and inefficient administration.

In Conclusion

In this memorandum our focus with respect to principles, issues and policy has been on the human dimensions of welfare reform. This perspective is reflected in our earlier Congressional testimony and in numerous documents that have been issued by the USCC during the past few years, including: *Human Life In Our Day* (1968); *The Economy: Human Dimensions* (1975); and the resolution passed by the USCC in 1970 supporting the overall direction of the Family Assistance Plan legislation.

Too many Americans today suffer the devastating effects of poverty and unemployment. This country has been blessed with many God-given gifts and abilities. Our present challenge is to utilize our talents and resources to provide for a true reformation of our economic and welfare policies. Such a change will require that we direct our energies toward providing jobs for the employable and adequate assistance to those in need.

As religious leaders, we feel an obligation to speak out on this matter in the hope that our insights will contribute to the public discussion of this subject. We shall continue to pray that our nation succeeds in this most important endeavor.

Family Life

In preparation for 1980, designated as Family Year by the American bishops, the NCCB published a statement entitled The Plan of Pastoral Action for Family Ministry: A Vision and Strategy. *The bishops explain the four principles on which the plan of action is based. For example, one principle is to make people more aware of the sacramental nature of Christian marriage and of the problems married couples and families face. They speak of*

*the planning process for Family Year and discuss six areas of the pastoral
ministry to which parishes should pay particular attention: ministry for pre-
marrieds and singles, ministry for married couples, ministry for parents,
ministry for developing families, and ministry for families in situations of
social need.*

The Plan of Pastoral Action
For Family Ministry: A Vision
and Strategy

USCC, May 1978

Changing circumstances in today's world call for a new approach within the
Church to pastoral service to families. The Catholic community is becoming
increasingly aware of the crucial issues facing contemporary marriage and
family life. In view of this, a plan of pastoral action is needed so that a genuine renewal might take place in the family ministry of the Church.

At the outset we affirm that the faithful proclamation of the Gospel in
word and sacrament is fundamental to all such planning in the Church. Also,
integral to this plan of action is the deep conviction that the Church's leadership considers it essential to listen perceptively, trustingly and compassionately to what people are saying about their Christian understanding of
marriage, sexuality and family life. The potential for development as well as
the problems confronting people in their daily lives will be perceived correctly
only if this openness is central to our pastoral outlook and ministry.

Preparatory Steps

The actual process of listening and discernment began over two years ago.
At that time a special Ad Hoc Commission was established within the United
States Catholic Conference to address the issues of marriage and family life.
In addition, family concerns surfaced as a central theme in the hearings that
formed part of the Bishops' Bicentennial Consultation. This led in turn to
certain recommendations on families in the 1976 Call To Action Conference.

The concerns voiced by married couples, single people and others aware of the needs of young people and families were brought to bear on the work of the USCC Commission on Marriage and Family Life. This Commission composed of bishops, diocesan family life personnel, married couples and scholars, was instructed to devise a "comprehensive strategy"[1] to be carried out at all levels of the Church in the United States in support of marriage and family life.

As a prior step to convening this Commission, diocesan family life personnel in twelve regional meetings were asked to assess the present condition of the family, survey existing programs and articulate issues in family ministry.[2] The Marriage and Family Life Commission then met in late 1976 and early 1977 to analyze the results. It studied various research reports and pastoral surveys. Proposals were developed to deal with the wide range of issues and concerns expressed. To cover the whole span of family pastoral and social needs, the Commission's work culminated in a report with forty-five recommendations.

Certain basic themes run through these recommendations and point to the crucial areas where the Church's mission to young people, married couples and families must be developed.

The need for research is frequently mentioned. A number of recommendations call for deeper theological study of sexuality and the foundations of family ministry along with a spirituality of marriage and family life. Others recommend research into successful forms of family living as well as problematic areas. The formation of better curricula relating to marriage and family life is indicated as an urgent need. Clearly, interdisciplinary dialogue and scholarly exchange with social scientists are strongly recommended.

The development of programs for all persons engaged in family ministry—priests, deacons, religious and lay people—receives considerable attention. Note is also made of programs for professionals—physicians, lawyers and educators. Affirmative, developmental and preventive programs are proposed that should be adapted to the needs of particular groups and family styles. In such programs the concept of family should include the engaged, newly marrieds, those in the middle and later years of married life, extended families and young singles searching together for a Christian understanding of sexuality and marital commitment. Special attention should be given to military families and minority families with particular racial, cultural and ethnic heritages. Not to be overlooked are the widowed, separated and divorced Catholics and one-parent families.

Certain major issues are identified within the area of family ministry. Particular attention is asked to be given to sexist discrimination and the Christian clarification of men's and women's roles. The pastoral issues arising in the areas of contraception and natural family planning are also pointed to.

---

[1] See *Final Report on the United States Catholic Conference Ad Hoc Commission on Marriage and Family Life*, Washington, D.C., Nov. 14, 1977, p. 2.
[2] *Ibid.*, pp. 6-7.

The importance of assisting families to deal with problems related to technological change and mass media, especially television viewing, is indicated.

Great emphasis is placed on the need to develop family social consciousness. Proposals call for education in family social mission to enable the family members to understand their social role as part of total family ministry, which also includes family-centered prayer and catechesis. The development of ministries for ethnic and racial minority families receives special attention and recommendations that call for a thorough assessment of present approaches, especially those to Hispanic, Black and Native American families. In conjunction with the development of governmental policy for families, the potential of the 1981 White House Conference on Families is cited.

Certain key recommendations call for adequate staffing, funding and structuring of family ministries and programs. Planning and needs assessment at *all* levels of the Church with continuing consultation of families themselves are urged. Finally, the Commission assigns the highest priority to a comprehensive vision and planning process, a plan of action that would embody a "practical and pastoral"[3] response to family issues. Its intent is to be sensitive, discerning and adaptable to local conditions as well as to draw on grassroots opinion and scholarly research.

Planning Process

This plan of action focuses primarily on a *process* designed to involve the Church at all levels. Guided by the teaching of the Church, it is founded on four specific principles, which will help the Church itself to touch the real needs of families. Moreover, since the family is called to be an expression of God's creative and redemptive love, this process unites the spiritual with the material and psychological dimensions of human existence.

First, this pastoral plan seeks to raise the awareness of the Church to the sacramental nature of Christian marriage and to the realities now facing married couples and families. In addition, it aims to help families themselves become aware of their special charisms, talents and potential for self-help and ministry to others.

Such awareness can be encouraged in a variety of ways. First of all, it should come through participation in the liturgical and sacramental life of the Church and prayerful reflection on lived experience. At other times, dialogue, assessment of needs and shared mutual insights into family life are necessary to bring it about. Such consciousness-raising can be assisted by experts and the instruments of professional research properly and sensitively employed.

---

[3] *Ibid.*, p. 44.

Secondly, the Church is seeking through this plan of action ways to enable couples and families to be caring. It is concerned with helping family members develop their potential for nurturing and healing each other, for reaching out in active concern to others. This caring involves a participation in God's creative action and the redemptive mission of Jesus.

As it responds to those in need, active caring takes the step beyond mere awareness and reaches out to touch individuals and groups by showing God's loving, renewing presence. The need for such a presence is obvious today. For it to happen, a positive climate is encouraged by this process, an atmosphere of warmth that will enable people to reflect on their experience more deeply, judge it in the light of Gospel values and then make the decision to act.

Thirdly, when we speak of a true and authentic Christian service of families, we speak of a ministry that flows from a sense of Christian mission. This call to real ministry involving the lay person in the family, not only the priest, deacon, or religious, is the genuine realization of Christian vocation and the basis of the apostolate.

The call from the Holy Spirit and recognition from the Church community will lead a couple or even a whole family to a deeper sense of vocation as family life ministers. Such a calling must be adequately supported and formed. In this way the Church will come to have deeply motivated, well-trained and competent leadership in this and other areas of pastoral ministry.

Attention should be given to another factor that will help to form family ministers who can truly serve. Notably we point to the importance of like-to-like ministry, whereby people with similar experience and inclination help others. Examples of this are married couples ministering to engaged or young people interested in marriage; parents with longer experience helping newer parents; older married couples assisting newlyweds; the widowed or persons with a particular difficulty ministering to others in similar life circumstances.

Fourthly, this plan of action stresses the need to establish structures that will facilitate marriage and family ministry. This is not a call to a multiplicity of new structures for their own sake; it may even require phasing out irrelevant or cumbersome structures. Yet structures that truly facilitate are important for helping the Church as a community care for and effectively serve those in need.

It will first of all be necessary to make sound and wise decisions about the various structures of the Church's operation on the national and regional levels. But more concretely and directly, family ministry committees or advisory commissions on the diocesan and parish levels should themselves sensitively discern the types of structures and programs needed. They should especially have a voice in forming the structures that will make family ministry effective within the everyday lives of people in the thousands of parishes and millions of families in our country.

In summary, this plan of action calls for a process directed to awareness that understands, caring that enables, ministry that serves and structures that truly facilitate.

National Effort for Family Ministry

To begin such a plan we will concentrate on developing the resources and program aids during 1978 and 1979 to enable dioceses and parishes to do their vital part. These resources will include a more detailed outline of the approaches to the planning process as applied concretely to diocesan and parish communities. They will also include specific programmatic models which allow for local application and variations.

We designate 1979 as a year of special diocesan preparation and planning, leading to a Family Year in 1980. We hope that this Family Year, dedicated to the celebration of family values and ministry, will usher in a decade of research into Christian marriage and family life and a time for the development of outstanding programs in family ministry.

To oversee this plan and related family life issues, we have established a new Commission on Marriage and Family Life. Through its membership, consisting of bishops, priests, and married lay people, which will include adequate representation from ethnic and racial minorities, we hope to communicate our concern for the value and vitality of sacramental marriage and Christian family life.

Already in 1978 the Department of Education of the United States Catholic Conference has been directed to serve diocesan offices in this area of ministry. It has been instructed to publish the results of its survey on marriage and family enrichment programs in order to encourage further diocesan efforts. Likewise, the emphases placed by the *National Catechetical Directory* on family-centered religious formation are to be encouraged.

The Department has been authorized to develop curriculum guidelines for family living and sexuality education from early childhood through young adulthood. These are to include design principles for teacher and parent preparation with suggestions for diocesan implementation. This Department will involve bilingual-bicultural personnel to assist in curriculum development and the process of implementation.

Several other projects also call for the attention of the Education Department. In consultation with educators and other specialists, educational guidelines are to be developed to help fathers and mothers improve their parenting skills. Resource materials and program information for families with handicapped members are to be provided. Help is to be given to diocesan offices in designing educational programs relating to family social mission and policy. New programs are to be initiated for ethnic groups to meet their special needs.

Because the family always exists in relationship to the wider society, careful attention must be given toward the constructive influence of public policy as it relates to family life. Implicit government policy and explicit government planning and programs can contribute to an erosion of the health and vitality of the family. Examples of this process are urban and neighborhood revitalization developments which favor the wealthy rather than the displaced poor, the creation of suburban sprawl which is determined primarily by the priorities of big business and real estate developers, and the spread of giant agribusiness at the expense of the small family farm.

Comprehensive decisions of a national or regional scope must take into account their impact on family life. Families, especially those whose influence is lessened by poverty or social status, must be allowed their rightful input in those decisions which affect their daily lives. This delicate, yet decisive, relationship between the society and the family demands careful study, and, where destructive influences on family are apparent, society ought to be challenged in support of the rights of families.

In order to influence the development of family governmental policy based on principles of Christian social justice, an effort will be made to encourage Catholic participation in the White House Conference on Families. This is especially to be effected through the Catholic Coordinating Committee for the White House Conference on Families.

Diocesan Planning for Family Ministry

During 1979 diocesan planning should begin. It is to be coordinated by the diocesan family life committee or advisory board working in cooperation with other diocesan agencies, such as education and Catholic Charities offices. The diocesan family life office is to take the initiative in this process through its director, who should oversee the planning process as well as other family-related programs, organizations and movements. Research and consultation with representative families of diverse backgrounds should help the diocese make the necessary allocation of funds and staff.

We pledge to give particularly close attention to leadership formation in family ministry. This training will include both ordained and non-ordained leaders. Unless this takes place, the total implementation of this plan will not be realized in the diocese.

We pledge to foster communication and coordination among various movements and organizations in this field such as Engaged Encounter, Marriage Encounter, Christian Family Movement, Families for Prayer, Teams of Our Lady, Marriage Retorno, Movimiento Familiar Cristiano and Cursillo. These and other groups are reminded to pay particular attention to the unity of the family apostolate within the diocese and the needs of the parish community.

To promote sound laws and better public policies pertaining to marriage and family life, we will, where possible, work with our state Catholic conferences. State, county and city laws should be evaluated for their impact upon the quality of family life. Full use of the communication media will be encouraged in order to promote support for favorable public policy as well as to publicize this plan of pastoral action.

Parish Implementation

Looking beyond this initial period of diocesan planning, we designate 1980 "Family Year" during which parishes are asked to join the total diocesan effort to renew family life. It is to be a particular time for the celebration of family values and for initiating the decade of total family renewal.

During this year every parish should begin to undertake its own planning process with appropriate support from the diocesan family life office or bureau. Resource materials, which will help them assess their families' needs, develop a plan for family ministry, select suitable programs and activities, train parish-level leadership and begin to implement their own action plan, will be made available. The Family Year effort at the parish level will lay the foundation for parish family ministry renewal for the decade.

Emphasis is placed within this entire plan on flexibility so that dioceses, parishes and interrelated institutions, such as Catholic schools, social justice offices, retreat centers, Catholic Charities and health care facilities can proceed in ways that work best for them.

In assessing the pastoral needs of its people, the parish in particular should give attention to six areas of pastoral ministry. These areas are not rigidly divided from one another, but together form a comprehensive approach for building up Christian family life through total family ministry.

1. Ministry for Pre-Marrieds and Singles

To undertake the renewal of marriage and family life the Church must address the question of its ministry to young people and those who are not married. This begins in the remote preparation of young people for their vocation through quality programs in family living and sexuality education from their earliest years. The proximate preparation for marriage calls for ministry for engaged couples who should be encouraged through their engagement period to deepen their commitment to creative fidelity and sacramental marriage. A number of programmatic efforts already exist, but do not always touch the majority of the engaged, especially at the parish level. These programs should treat all significant topics related to contemporary married life. The need for the development of a sensitive ministry for single persons of all ages is likewise encouraged. This includes ministry programs and activities for middle-aged and elderly people who live alone.

2. Ministry for Married Couples

The need for spiritual growth and continuing development in the marriage relationship is more pronounced today than ever before. Particular attention should be given to helping couples understand communications and practical

Christian approaches to questions of economics and sexuality. A special aspect of this ministry is directed to newlyweds, since many marriages end in divorce in the early years. The recent emergence of a number of programs and movements for enriching the relationship of married couples of all ages, including the middle and older years, offers parishes a variety of ways to minister. This ministry needs to touch the lives of many more couples from all economic and cultural backgrounds within the parish.

3. Ministry for Parents

More and better ways are needed for helping Christian parents—including widowed and other "single" parents—to carry out their responsibilities. Parenting programs are growing in numbers and depth. The need for this ministry extends from expectant parents and parents of very young children to parents of adolescents. The last mentioned often express the need for help in intergenerational communication skills and in understanding cultural change. Special help is needed for parents of children with learning disabilities. All need assistance in their role as the primary catechists of their children.

4. Ministry for "Developing" Families

Families with children of varying ages need different approaches designed to foster Christian family development and enrichment. Special needs are voiced by families just beginning and families with adolescent members. Supportive association, in the context of a community of faith with other families of like ideals, is a crucial element in family stability and enrichment. Family spirituality needs to be promoted through various approaches involving family sacramental preparation, home prayer formation, family nights, parish family liturgies, and other religious cultural events. Family social ministry programs require particular support in order to encourage the development of a sense of the social mission of the family toward the total human community.

5. Ministry for "Hurting" Families

The anguish and fragmentation of so many married couples and family members call for both a preventive and a remedial ministry for families. This includes specialized counseling, and a ministry of reconciliation that touches the psychological, economic and spiritual realities of family life. Clergy and couples engaged in family ministry should be encouraged and helped to acquire specialized skills for dealing with such complex issues as poverty, aging, alcoholism, drug abuse and homosexuality. There is a great need for ministry to separated and divorced persons as well as to children of divorced parents. The needs of families with handicapped members and those with members living in institutions should not be overlooked in this area of pastoral ministry.

6. *Ministry for Leadership Couples and Families*

The need for ministry to families and couples actively involved in family ministry can easily be overlooked. This area of ministry should include parish coordinating couples, family social action couples and leadership people in family movements. These generous, dedicated people deserve help in their efforts to grow spiritually and emotionally through their own experience of marriage and family life, and their involvement in family ministry. They need assistance in learning leadership skills as well as knowledge of how to deepen their understanding of the Christian principles influencing marriage and family life.

In order to plan its own family ministry program, every parish should have a family ministry committee chaired by a volunteer couple or a full or part-time coordinator of family ministry. Responsibility for particular areas of ministry or programs (e.g., marriage preparation, natural family planning, education in human sexuality, parenthood education, marriage and family enrichment, family social education) can then be assigned to designated lay leaders with appropriate training and formation. Parishioners involved in lay apostolic movements should be encouraged to place their talents at the service of the parish.

Existing parish structures and institutions (e.g., parish councils, parish catechetical programs, parochial schools, etc.) are reminded of their potential for marriage and family ministry within their special areas of competence. Parish schools and parent-teacher associations can develop effective home programs and lines of communication with families. Likewise, parish religious education structures can attend to family needs through different types of family-centered approaches. These and other opportunities exist at the parish level and can be acted upon through alert pastors, parish ministry teams, principals, teachers, coordinators and parish councils.

Future Action Areas

That the apostolic concern expressed in this initial effort move ahead, we see a number of other areas that require a response during the coming years.

Candidates for the priesthood and permanent diaconate should receive better preparation for family ministry; this ministry should also be a major element in the continuing education of the clergy.

There is a need for theological reflection on the family's role as an agent of evangelization, as well as for practical steps to involve more family members in the full apostolate of the laity and the renewal of parish life as a whole. There must be careful coordination of evangelization, parish renewal and family life ministry.

Family participation in the liturgical life of the Church should be encouraged, especially through the development of forms of family prayer and sacramental celebration.

Research is needed concerning the factors which influence religiously "mixed" marriages. This analysis should study the impact of such marriages on the Catholic identity of spouses and children and on ecumenical cooperation.

The high priority need for the Church to investigate appropriate ways of ministering to minority and ethnic families should be recognized and acted upon. Specific attention should be given to the familial needs of Blacks, Hispanics, Asians and American Indians. The unique sense of the extended family among Catholic racial and ethnic groups in our national experience should be examined.

Solid research about the impact of sociocultural and technological change on the family should be undertaken and related to the ways in which one generation passes on its beliefs and values to the next.

The role of women in society and the Church requires further investigation. Particular attention should be paid to the phenomenon of a family situation in which both parents work outside the home.

Additional efforts should be made to offer couples education and counseling in the natural methods of family planning and to inform them of the scientific advances in this field.

There is likewise a serious need for deeper study of theological and interdisciplinary issues related to human sexuality so as to overcome the present malaise or credibility problem among many Catholic couples and individuals.

While pledging to move forward in these areas, we affirm the need for cooperation with other agencies in society for continued research into and necessary action for the renewal of marriage and family life.

Vital Participation of Families

If this plan of pastoral action does not touch or change the lives of family members and their relationship to the total Church community, then it will have failed in its purpose. The plan's success, however, presupposes efforts on the part of families themselves, supported by others in pastoral ministry. It is crucial that this pastoral vision focus on the need for spiritual renewal and conversion within the lives of families as is indicated in the teachings of conciliar, papal and other documents of the Second Vatican Council and of the Church's magisterium in the times following the Ecumenical Council. [4]

---

[4] Cf. *Lumen Gentium, Gaudium et Spes, Apostolicam Actuositatem, Humanae Vitae* (1968), *Address to Teams of Our Lady* by Pope Paul VI (1970), *Evangelii Nuntiandi* (1975) as well as *Human Life in Our Day* (1969), *To Teach As Jesus Did* (1973) and *To Live in Christ Jesus* (1975) of the United States Bishops.

Wherever possible, husband and wife should set aside time to reflect on their vocation as a couple to make their marriage an effective sign of Christ's self-giving, faithful love. They should examine their ministry to each other, the opportunities they share for spiritual growth, the responsibility as Christian parents to lead their children to Christ, their call as individuals and as a couple to a wider mission within the Church, especially to their parish, and to society with particular concern for their own neighbors. They should explore the possibility of forming a network of friends and neighbors who will mutually reinforce marriage and family ideals.

Likewise, families with children should try to dialogue about their role in witness, worship and service. They should look for opportunities beyond the immediate family to minister to the needs of others, especially needy neighbors, relatives and parishioners. Christian charity and justice call them to go out to serve the physical and spiritual needs of others in the local community, the country and the world. Support groups of other families can reinforce their Christian idealism and way of life.

Ideally, this family-centered ministry should be based on a perception of the Gospel foundations of the family's own mission. These have been initially elaborated upon in the teachings of the Second Vatican Council[5] and in the apostolic exhortation on "Evangelization in the Modern World."[6] In these documents the importance of the family's Christian ministry as a witnessing community, a worshipping community and a serving community is communicated.

A Word of Hope

This plan of action provides the framework for far-reaching pastoral renewal. Since it involves commitment to a type of ministering not only to but *with* people through a particular participation of the family members themselves, it also presents a challenge.

The Fathers of Vatican II in pointing out the importance of family ministry spoke to the family as the "foundation of society."[7] They declared that: "The well-being of the individual person and of human Christian society is intimately linked with the healthy condition of that community produced by marriage and the family."[8] More recently Pope Paul VI pointed out: "Today, concern for marriage and family is one of the most pressing duties of any pastoral work . . . the family is the chief cell, not only of human society, but also of the Church."[9]

---

[5] Cf. *Lumen Gentium #11*, 30-37; *Apostolicam Actuositatem #11*; *Gaudium et Spes #48-50*, 52.

[6] *Evangelii Nuntiandi #71*.

[7] *Gaudium et Spes #52*.

[8] *Ibid., #47*.

[9] Pope Paul VI, Address to the Bishops of Austria, *L'Osservatore Romano*, Eng. ed., Sept. 29, 1977, p. 10.

The pressures of social change and the ensuing moral crisis are indeed to be acknowledged. However, we see this primarily as a time to be hopeful. What could be viewed as a breakdown of marriage and family life, we hope will be a breakthrough for families and society itself. Our Christian optimism, based as it is on Christ's own victory in the face of apparent defeat, gives us reason to see a time coming when, through the renewal of the Church's ministry, a better world will come about for the entire human family.

Free Exercise of Religion

In November 1971, the USCC issued a statement on parental rights and the free exercise of religion. The bishops argue that the Supreme Court's interpretation of the Constitution gives parents a constitutional right to send children to non-public schools. Inflation, taxation, and rising governmental costs, however, often prevent the exercise of this constitutional right. Consequently, government has an obligation to provide parents with economic assistance so that they will, indeed, have the freedom to choose private education for their children.

In September 1973, the Administrative Board of the USCC called for a constitutional amendment that would permit religious instruction and prayer in public schools. The Board justifies the proposal of this amendment in two ways. First, ratification of the amendment would protect the religious liberty of parents and children. The freedom to learn the truths of the parents' faith within the setting of formal education would help the child understand the importance of religion in his life. Second, if religion is not taught in schools, the religious heritage of the nation is in danger of being supplanted by a pervasive secularism.

Statement on Parental Rights and The Free Exercise of Religion

USCC, November 15, 1971

The Constitution of the United States guarantees religious and political liberty to every citizen. Precisely for this reason, we, the Catholic Bishops of the United States, feel compelled to speak to our fellow citizens about certain implications of the recent United States Supreme Court decision relating to government assistance for teachers' salaries in parochial schools. Our purpose is not to discuss the particular programs upon which the Court ruled, nor indeed the related tax and educational crisis affecting the citizens of many states. Rather we address ourselves to features of the decision which, left unchecked, would affect basic freedoms of all. These freedoms relate to parental rights, the free exercise of religion, and the liberty of every citizen to speak, assemble, petition and vote on matters affecting the public role of religion in American life.

The fundamental right of parents to educate their children in non-public schools is guaranteed by our Constitution and was recognized a half century ago in the *Pierce* case, wherein the Supreme Court said:

"The child is not the mere creature of the State."

But today the highest court of the land—dealing with a case intimately related to parents—makes no explicit mention of that right. Instead, by its decision this well recognized right could become an illusion if it results in a state educational monopoly in which parental rights—if acknowledged at all—will be enjoyed only by the wealthy, by those who can bear both the burden of school taxes and of the separate added cost of non-public schooling.

Today the effects of taxation, inflation and rising governmental cost make it increasingly impossible for parents to exercise their constitutional freedoms in education without enabling assistance. Government plainly has an obligation in justice to make those accommodations necessary to secure parental rights in education. In order to exercise this right today, parents need and are entitled to a measure of economic help—a share of the tax dollars they pay. Government should not tip the economic scales so heavily in favor of the public schools that parents can exercise their right to choose non-public schools only with severe personal sacrifice.

We are hopeful and confident that the Congress and the states will promptly enact legislation, in conformity with the Constitution, which will aid parents in the exercise of their rights in education. In no way, however, should such legislation be construed as contributing to the creation or support of racially segregated schooling.

Furthermore, we trust that the Supreme Court will use its vast powers, in appropriate cases, to emphasize parental rights in education and to repudiate every effort to make the child a "mere creature of the State."

The Supreme Court has said that the public discussion and political activity required to achieve enactment of certain types of state aid to church-related education must be kept out of the public forum because they present "hazards of religion intruding into the political arena." This kind of reasoning is unacceptable.

The Supreme Court has also stated that "religion must be a private matter for the individual, the family and the institutions of private choice." Religion is indeed a private matter, but it is far more than that. Since the founding of the Republic it has been deemed, in an important sense, a very public matter. The separation of church and state is a wise policy. The separation of religion from public life is dangerous folly. We Americans have always known that religious liberty demands, by its very nature, that it be exercised publicly.

There can be no political liberty in a society in which religious groups and individual believers, as such, may not speak out on public issues. There can be no religious liberty in a society in which public issues may not be discussed in their religious dimension.

We trust that citizens concerned for the protection of parental rights, religious liberty, diversity and excellence in education, and the avoidance of the increased taxation resulting from a state monopoly of education, will now work, peaceably and with renewed vigor, for viable programs of aid to the education of all children.

We trust that religious-minded citizens of all faiths will continue to bear public witness to the truths they hold, so that—as always before in American history—religion will continue to have its proper role in the life of our nation.

Statement on Prayer and Religious Instruction in Public Schools

USCC, Administrative Board
September 19, 1973

"Section 1. Nothing in this Constitution shall be construed to (i) forbid prayer in public places or in institutions of the several States or of the United States, including schools; (ii) forbid religious instruction in public places or in institutions of the several States or of the United States, including schools, if such instruction is provided under private auspices whether or not religious.

"Section 2. The right of the people to participate or not to participate in prayer or religious instruction shall never be infringed by several States or the United States."

The Constitution of the United States

"An amendment permitting religious instruction and prayer in public schools and other public institutions is vitally important to protect the religious liberty of parents and children.

"Such a liberty has an obvious two-fold aspect: an opportunity to learn the truths of one's faith, and freedom from imposition, through the power of the state, of values hostile to one's faith or its moral precepts.

"Many parents today are deeply concerned over the fact that their children who attend public schools are being denied such religious liberty.

"They are acutely concerned for the faith and morality of their children. They are also rightly concerned lest the religious heritage of the nation be supplanted by a pervasive secularism. They do not find the Supreme Court's suggestions for 'teaching about' religion, or for teaching 'religion as culture' acceptable.

"Nor do these parents believe that the religious training which a child may receive at home or through extra-school instruction is ordinarily sufficient for his religious formation. They feel that religious instruction should be part of the child's formal educational experience, and that to deprive him of such instruction may diminish the importance of religion in his eyes and deprive him of the knowledge of moral values. There is evidence of this in statistics which document an alarming increase in recent years in the number of crimes committed in our country by teen-aged and younger children.

"Since the Supreme Court has interpreted the Constitution to forbid genuine religious freedom in public education, the people of the United States have no recourse but to amend the Constitution. The question then is how the Constitution shall be amended.

"The U.S. Catholic Conference believes an amendment limited to allowing prayer would be inadequate to meet the national need. The amendment which is needed must cover prayer and religious instruction.

"Such an amendment will be a powerful factor in restoring to all Americans a basic liberty of which they are now deprived. It can be an effective instrument in thwarting the trend toward universal secularizing of the education of the young.

"The amendment does no violence to the views and rights of non-believers. Rather, it protects their rights while restoring equal rights to believers."

Housing

Early in 1973, the USCC Committee on Social Development and World Peace protested a government decision to place a freeze on federal funds and loan guarantees for low and moderate income housing. The Committee called for the lifting of the moratorium and called upon the government and the nation "for renewed dedication to a truly adequate housing program."

Late in 1975, the entire body of bishops addressed the housing crisis in a major statement entitled The Right to a Decent Home: A Pastoral Response to the Crisis in Housing. *The USCC presents five approaches the Catholic community can take to promote better housing. First, Catholics should do all they can to promote understanding of housing problems. The bishops themselves promise "to educate people regarding the demands of justice in the area of housing. . . . " The second approach the bishops recommend is for the Church to analyze housing needs in the light of the Gospel and then to advocate various policies before the appropriate government body. To revitalize neighborhoods, for example, the USCC suggests the abolition of "redlining," a practice by which banks and lending institutions restrict or deny mortgage and home improvement loans in certain areas, and the disclosure of lending patterns by banks and loan associations.*

A third way the Catholic community can help is by providing services for low-income people and for the elderly, such as housing, financial and personal counseling, and education in their rights. A fourth contribution would be to exercise more responsible stewardship over Church property. And finally, the bishops call upon local Catholic parishes to develop a ministry of "community building." Parishes are in a good position to participate in the life of the community and to encourage members to get involved in community affairs and housing issues.

Statement on Housing Subsidies Moratorium

USCC, Committee on Social Development and World Peace
February 1973

"We protest the Federal government's action, announced January 8, placing a freeze on Federal funds and loan guarantees for housing for families of low and moderate income. An annual rate of construction of only 250,000 units for the next 18 months will not alleviate the suffering of untold thousands of Americans forced to reside in substandard housing—housing in which vermin, the danger of lead poisoning, and the threat of respiratory diseases associated with inadequate plumbing, heat and ventilation are grim realities.

"While we agree that many of our housing subsidy programs have not worked very well and that there is need to 're-evaluate and seek better ways' of achieving their objectives, we cannot agree that the 'pause' required for re-evaluation must be as drastic as the one proposed by the Federal government. Many of our nation's most complex programs—the effort to place a man on the moon is a dramatic example—have encountered frustration and failure in their early stages, but have undergone re-evaluation simultaneous with continued development culminating ultimately in brilliant success. Is one to conclude from the policy announced on January 8 that our national commitment to decent housing for all Americans is less than our commitment to sending men to the moon, or that the scientists and social planners working in the housing field are less capable than those involved in space technology? We hope not.

"We are also deeply concerned about the potential effect of this announcement on the economy in general and the construction sector in particular. It is our understanding that many smaller contractors are under-capitalized and that the availability of capital to these entrepreneurs depends to a large degree on projected construction in their areas and their ability to bid successfully on these contracts. We are anxious for the future of these businessmen and alarmed at the loss of employment opportunities resulting from a cutback. We are also concerned at the prospect that this new policy will undermine efforts to increase opportunities for minority employment in the construction field.

"Finally, we note that the efforts of many persons of good will have led to the emergence of healthy partnership between the public and voluntary sectors in the housing field. While all involved in this partnership recognize the need for improvement, a useful mechanism has been set in motion to begin to meet the challenge of adequate housing. We fear that the moratorium policy, as announced by the Department of Housing and Urban Development, will reverse the momentum of this partnership and that in the future it will be extremely difficult to generate such momentum anew.

"We support any efforts to devise more effective housing programs and promise our cooperation for this purpose. But for the sake of the thousands of Americans who have yet to realize their aspiration and right to decent housing, any 're-evaluation' should be carried out in a manner that does not involve a drastic pause in current housing programs, such as that now envisaged. We therefore urge that the moratorium be lifted, and we call upon the government and the nation for renewed dedication to a truly adequate housing program."

The Right to a Decent Home: A Pastoral Response to The Crisis in Housing

USCC, November 20, 1975

I. Introduction

1. The United States is in the midst of a severe housing crisis. This is a broader, more pervasive and more complicated phenomenon than the customary photographs of urban slums and rural shacks indicate. It involves more people, more neighborhoods and communities than was thought to be the case even a few years ago. It touches millions of poor families who live in inhuman conditions, but it also involves many middle-income families whose ability to provide themselves with decent housing is being painfully tested. Rising costs of shelter, maintenance and utilities—as well as high interest rates and regressive property taxes—are forcing many families to live in inadequate housing or to do without other basic essentials. Other low- and middle-income families have been confined to neighborhoods without adequate services, minimal safety or necessary community life.

2. The dimensions of our housing crisis are apparent in the following statistics:

—One of every five families in the United States suffers from serious housing deprivation. They either live in physically inadequate buildings, suffer from severe overcrowding, or spend an excessive proportion of their income for shelter.[1]

—Housing costs have increased to the point that millions of families cannot obtain decent housing unless they deprive themselves of other essentials of life. Only 15% of American families can afford to purchase a median-priced new home.[2]

—4.7 million housing units lack adequate plumbing facilities and 5 million families live in overcrowded housing.[3]

---

[1] "America's Housing Needs: 1970 to 1980," Joint Center for Urban Studies of the Massachusetts Institute of Technology and Harvard University. (Cambridge, 1973) pp. 4–7.

[2] "Availability of Homes for Middle-Income Families," Congressional Research Service, Library of Congress. (Washington, 1975), p. 19.

[3] "General Housing Characteristics for the United States: 1970." Bureau of the Census, U.S. Department of Commerce. March 1972, p. 1–53.

—80% of those with incomes under $5,000 experience some form of housing inadequacy.[4]

—Two-thirds of officially substandard housing is in rural areas and small towns.[5]

—It is estimated that over 23.3 million new homes will be needed between 1970 and 1980, yet housing production for the first quarter of 1975 was at the lowest level since World War II.[6]

—40% of our available housing stock is more than 30 years old and the accompanying deterioration and abandonment are threatening many neighborhoods.[7]

—It is authoritatively estimated that 13.1 million American families suffer serious housing deprivation.[8]

3. Over 25 years ago, the United States Congress declared the housing policy of this country to be "a decent home in suitable living environment for every American family."[9] This goal has not been achieved. The harsh and frustrating reality is that it certainly will not be achieved in the near future and may never be achieved at all. This means that millions of American families are condemned to live in poor housing or in unsuitable environments unless dramatic action is taken.

II. Housing: a Pastoral Imperative for the Church

4. In the face of this cruel and discouraging condition, we, the Bishops of the United States, cannot remain silent. The reality of this housing crisis provides a challenge to our country as we approach the bicentennial. In the past 200 years our nation, with the abundant blessing of God, has overcome many other complex problems and has provided a standard of living previously unknown to the world.

5. We are not so naive as to believe that there are easy solutions to the crisis. The housing crisis is overwhelming. It touches facets of our economic,

---

[4] "America's Housing Needs: 1970 to 1980." *Op. cit.*, pp. 4–12.

[5] "General Housing Characteristics for The United States: 1970." *Op. cit.* Officially substandard refers to units lacking adequate plumbing and overcrowded conditons.

[6] "America's Housing Needs: 1970 to 1980." *Op. cit.*, pp. 3–13. Also, Bureau of the Census, U.S. Department of Commerce: (1) *Housing Construction Statistics, 1889 to 1964*, p. 18, table A-1; (2) *Construction Reports, Housing Starts 1959 to 1971*, C 20 supplement; and (3) *Construction Reports, Housing Starts*, series C 20.

[7] "Detailed Housing Characteristics of The United States: 1970." Bureau of the Census, U.S. Department of Commerce, June, 1972, pp. 1–287.

[8] "America's Housing Needs: 1970 to 1980." *Op. cit.*, pp. 4–7.

[9] *The Housing Act of 1949.* Section 2.

political and social life that are extremely complicated. Any attempt to solve these intricate problems can give rise to petty self-interest and alarming divisions. Addressing ourselves to our own people and to the whole country, we plead with all, in both the private and the public sector, to confront our housing crisis with the courage, conviction and talent that have brought about our greatest achievements in the past.

6. As preachers of the gospel, we proclaim the message of Jesus Christ who identifies Himself with the needs of the least of the brethren. The second great commandment is to love our neighbor. We cannot deny the crying needs for decent housing experienced by the least of the brethren in our society. Effective love of neighbor involves concern for his or her living conditions.

7. We begin with the recognition that decent housing is a right. Our Catholic tradition, eloquently expressed by Pope John XXIII[10] and Pope Paul VI,[11] insists that shelter is one of the basic rights of the human person. The Second Vatican Council has said with great directness: "There must be made available to all men everything necessary for leading a life truly human, such as food, clothing and shelter. ..."[12]

8. As teachers, pastors and leaders, we have the responsibility to articulate the principles and values that govern the Church's concern for housing. We believe that each individual possesses an inherent dignity and priceless worth because he or she is created in the image and likeness of God. We also believe each person should have the opportunity to grow and develop his or her potential to the fullest extent possible. Human dignity and development are threatened whenever social and economic forces imprison or degrade people. We call on Catholics and all citizens to join us in working against these debilitating forces.

9. In particular, we take this opportunity to reflect on the consequences of poor housing. The physical and social environment play an important role in forming and influencing the lives of people. We cannot ignore the terrible impact of degrading and indecent living conditions on people's perception of themselves and their future. The protection of the human dignity of every person and the right to a decent home require both individual action and structural policies and practices.

10. Our faith teaches us that "the earth is the Lord's" (Psalm 24) and that wealth and private property are held in trust for others. We are trustees of God's creation, and as good stewards we are required to exercise that trust for the common good and benefit of our brothers and sisters.

11. The role of those who own land or other wealth is one of stewardship. While the Church has traditionally recognized the right to private property,

---

[10] *Peace on Earth,* 11. Pope John XXIII. April 1963.
[11] *A Call to Action,* 11–12. Pope Paul VI. May 1971.
[12] *Pastoral Constitution on the Church in the Modern World,* 26. December 1965.

that right is always subject to certain limitations. As the Second Vatican Council pointed out:

> God intended the earth and all that it contains for the use of every human being and people. ... Whatever the forms of ownership may be, as adapted to the legitimate institutions of people according to diverse and changeable circumstances, attention must always be paid to the universal purpose for which created goods are meant. In using them, therefore, a man should regard his lawful possessions not merely as his own but also as common property in the sense that they should accrue to the benefit of not only himself but of others.[13]

12. This teaching is central to a discussion of the ethical and moral dimensions of the housing crisis. It imposes major responsibilities on those whose land and shelter resources or skills might help society guarantee the right to a decent home.

13. This concept of stewardship must be reflected in our concern and action on housing. It must be practiced not only by individuals, but also by institutions. The Church must give witness to this trusteeship in the use of its own property and resources. Just as individual property holders are bound by this principle, so it must be reflected in public policy at each level of government.

14. Our concern is not simply for houses or programs but for the people who inhabit these dwellings or are affected by these programs. These include families whose attempts to create a stable and wholesome family life are inhibited by inadequate living conditions; people and parish communities in neighborhoods without the housing services or community life which foster love and Christian service; the many elderly whose meager incomes are consumed by housing maintenance costs, utility bills and property taxes; and countless young families who lack the resources to acquire decent housing. The statistics we cite are not simply numbers or points on a graph; they are individual human tragedies. We are shocked by the pervasiveness and depth of our housing crisis and what this means for our country and our people.

III. National Housing Goal

15. We affirm the national housing goal first articulated in 1949: "a decent home and a suitable living environment for every American family." We believe this inclusive goal is in line with the values and principles we have already articulated, and is a suitable basis for national policy. We take this opportunity, however, to suggest two needed qualifications of this goal. First, decent housing must be within the *means* of each family. The cost of such a home or apartment should not deprive the family of other essentials. Secondly, our housing goal must allow families *freedom of choice* as to where they will live and whether they will rent or own their homes. Equal housing

---

[13] *Ibid.*, 69.

opportunity and the possibility of home ownership for those who desire it should be integral components of our national housing policy.

16. As we have already stated, this national goal is far from being realized. Even now, social and economic forces—and current housing policy—make its realization more and more difficult. We are faced with the cruel paradox of urgent and growing housing needs and the inability of our present system of housing production, delivery and financing to meet this challenge.

17. The achievement of this housing goal will require a reordering of priorities and a substantial increase in expenditures for housing and community development. A realistic appraisal of our housing needs indicates that the resolution of our present crisis will be expensive and difficult.

18. In many ways the housing crisis is an institutional one, reflecting the limitations of our political, economic and social institutions. Effective action for better housing will depend on a competent analysis and significant changes in the structures and policies that have helped create and maintain our current housing delivery system. Our present way of financing and building housing seems not to lend itself to the resolution of our problems. The traditional law of supply and demand has not proved adequate to the task of providing decent housing for all our people. The demand, as we have seen, is present and growing, yet the response is clearly inadequate, especially for low- and middle-income people.

19. The housing crisis is, of course, part of a larger pattern of neglect. It is intricately linked to other social and economic problems. In fact, poor housing is often cited as an index or symptom of general social deprivation. We do not undertake here an in-depth examination of the relationship between housing and employment, income, education, health, crime, discrimination, environment or transportation. However, we recognize that a lasting solution to our housing problems will require a comprehensive attack on a variety of social injustices. An essential dimension of comprehensive housing strategy is action on unemployment and inadequate income, which severly limit the ability of families to acquire decent housing. A comprehensive response to our shelter needs will include more than increased housing production and elimination of blight. This broader response requires a serious analysis of economic and tax policies, the treatment accorded neighborhoods and rural areas, the use of land and resources, as well as issues of environmental preservation and civil rights.

IV. Housing Issues

20. Questions of housing and community development are extremely complex and often technical. They involve a variety of interests: private enterprise and government participation; maximum production and environmental and consumer protection needs; increased housing needs and tight

budgetary restraints; public interest and private gain; as well as questions of equity and efficiency.

A. Housing and the Economy

21. The housing crisis and proposed solutions to it are often stated in economic terms. The present housing crisis itself is often attributed to the critical state of the economy in a period of inflation and recession. However, there has been a serious housing problem for at least the last 25 years, during which we have experienced unparalleled prosperity. Since the problem has persisted in both good and bad economic times, it is apparent that we cannot rely on economic recovery alone to meet our housing needs.

22. Nonetheless, it is obvious that current economic difficulties have greatly intensified housing problems. For example, during the recent recession, housing production has been approximately one-half of the annual need of over 2.3 million units.[14] At this level of production, almost no housing for the poor is being constructed. Recession, inflation and monetary policies have combined to leave the housing industry in a lamentable condition. The recent steep decline in housing production was the fifth and sharpest in the last 20 years. This situation is particularly ominous for low-income families and apartment dwellers since the production of multi-family developments is even lower. Recent economic projections show some signs of hope, but even the most optimistic forecasters predict a level of housing starts well below our requirement.

23. Another serious factor in our current difficulties is the devastating impact of inflation. Rising construction costs, high interest rates and increasing utility bills have combined to make decent housing an unrealizable goal for many families. Studies indicate that 85% of American families cannot afford to purchase the median-priced new home.[15] The price of that median home rose from $23,400 in 1970 to $39,900 in May of 1975.[16] An income of $21,170 is needed to support the median-priced *existing* home.[17] Declining production, shrinking real income and the tendency of builders to produce higher-priced homes have severely limited the number of new homes available to middle- and moderate-income families. Low-income people face even bleaker prospects. Their rents and utility costs are climbing, yet they have virtually no place to go.

24. Another important economic factor is the availability and cost of housing credit. High interest rates substantially increase the cost of housing

---

[14] The National Association of House Builders estimates that housing starts for 1975 will not exceed 1.2 million starts. The Harvard-MIT Study previously cited estimates a ten year need of 23 million new units.

[15] "Availability of Homes for Middle-Income Families." *Op. cit.*, Page 19.

[16] "New One-Family Houses Sold and For Sale," Bureau of the Census, U.S. Department of Commerce. Series C-25.

[17] "Availability of Homes for Middle-Income Families." *Op. cit.*

and often lead to a downturn in housing production. For example, the increase in the cost of buying a $25,000 home at 10% interest rather than 6% is $19,800 over the life of a 25-year mortgage.[18] National monetary policy must insure an adequate supply of affordable credit for socially desirable purposes such as housing.

25. The number, intensity and durability of these economic downturns in housing point out the necessity for fresh approaches. More efficient use of land and materials must be sought through the use of attached dwellings, planned unit developments and other innovations.

26. The focus of the housing crisis is shifting from problems associated with the *condition* of the structure to problems associated with the *cost* of housing. It is not that the problem of substandard housing has been solved, although progress has been made. Rather, the impact of economic factors has become so great that they must now become the central focus of efforts to remedy our housing problems.

B. Neighborhoods

27. Housing conditions cannot be separated from the surrounding environment. City services, education, community cohesiveness, safety, government responsiveness, and taxation policies are critical factors in the creation and maintenance of decent housing.

28. In our view, the key element in the deteriorating urban environment is the decline of neighborhoods. In the past, the neighborhood has played a critical role in the lives of its residents. More recently, neighborhoods have lost some of their influence and importance. Centralized decision-making, suburban migration, deteriorating city services and the loss of ethnic identity have contributed to this decline and resulted in less responsibility for local concerns. A psychological and physical process of abandonment has set in, and fewer resources and people have been available to assist neighborhoods in combating blight and indifference.

29. Our cities are composites of smaller communities. Strong neighborhoods are the cornerstone of strong cities, and decent housing is a critical factor in the survival and viability of neighborhoods.

30. We applaud the renewed interest in neighborhoods by those who live in them and govern them. The neighborhood is the most logical basis for a positive housing policy. We hope that recognition of this fact will be translated into policies and provide neighborhoods with the tools and resources necessary to survive. The local parish has a critical role to play in the revitalization of neighborhoods. Effective use of revenue-sharing and community development funds can be a step in promoting neighborhood recovery.

---

[18] Interest on a $25,000 mortgage, payable in 25 years, at 6% is $23,300; at 10%, $43,100.

C. Disinvestment

31. We are particularly concerned about the abundant evidence of "red-lining" or disinvestment. This is the practice by which financial institutions deny or restrict mortgage and home improvement loans in particular areas. This practice often becomes a self-fulfilling prophecy leading to the rapid decline of a neighborhood or community. Where it exists it must be condemned; discrimination based on geography is as destructive as other forms of discrimination. We must insure fair and equal access to available credit.

32. We urge banks and savings and loan associations to meet their responsibilities in central city areas. We commend financial institutions which have chosen to intensify programs of investment in these neighborhoods. We support the principle of disclosure of lending patterns. Savers and consumers are entitled to information about the lending practices and patterns of the institutions seeking their business. We also urge individual depositors and those responsible for Church funds to encourage a responsible and sensitive lending policy on the part of the financial institutions which they patronize.

D. Racial and Economic Segregation

33. There are disturbing signs of increased racial and economic segregation in urban areas. We deplore discrimination, still present in our society, against persons because of their race, economic status, sex, or religion. Such attitudes contradict the Christian belief in the equality and inherent dignity of all people and they must be opposed.

34. Central cities are increasingly becoming islands of economic hardship populated by the elderly, racial and ethnic minorities and the working poor. The eroding tax base of cities follows the trend of suburban migration. Exclusionary zoning continues as a major factor which limits housing opportunities for low and middle income families and minority persons in suburban areas. In addition to these economic hurdles, many persons still find their housing choice limited by discriminatory practices in the sale or rental of housing. Suburban communities must recognize and act on their responsibilities without utilizing improper zoning, overly rigid building codes, onerous referendum requirements, or other barriers to avoid contact with the less affluent.

35. Continued vigilance is necessary in the struggle to expand equal housing opportunity. We take this occasion to renew our support, expressed in 1966, for:

> Sound programs to assure equal housing opportunities for all, without discrimination of race, creed or color. Here is a unique chance for respon-

sible dialogue, for learning from successes and failures and thus constructing harmonious communities in every part of the nation.[19]

36. The uniqueness of neighborhoods and diversity of communities are
healthy signs. We have a pastoral responsibility to respond creatively to questions of ethnicity and race. Positive ethnic identity, whether it be Black-
American, Hispanic-American, Irish-American, Italian-American, or any
other, recognizes the worth of the individual and respects his or her particular cultural heritage and lifestyle.

37. However, heightened awareness of ethnic background cannot be
allowed to lead to exclusionary practices or intergroup competition. Rather,
a healthy sense of cultural pluralism should lead to a greater ability to in-
teract with neighbors of different backgrounds in a positive way.

38. The housing needs of racial minorities remain critical and the un-
fulfilled dream of open housing cannot be abandoned. An absence of racial
discrimination is no longer enough. We must insist upon effective programs
to remedy past injustice.

E. Rural Housing

39. The housing crisis is often thought of as a predominantly urban problem. This misconception has resulted in unfortunate consequences for rural
people. According to 1970 Census figures, 30% of Americans live outside
metropolitan areas; at the same time, over 60% of all overcrowded housing
or units without plumbing are in rural areas and small towns.[20] The housing
crisis is at least as severe in rural areas as in urban centers.

40. The housing delivery system is inadequate in many small towns and
rural areas. Almost half of all rural counties have no public housing agency.
In addition, many rural areas do not have sufficient construction or financial
institutions which make private development feasible. While some progress
has been made, disparities remain.

41. Economic factors also account for widespread housing deprivation in
rural areas. The gap between housing costs and income is even wider in rural
communities than in cities. Only one rural family in twenty can afford the
median-priced newly constructed home. In recent years, one-third of all new
housing units in rural areas have been mobile homes.

42. The simple fact is that neither rural people nor rural communities
have the resources to solve their housing problems without outside assistance. It is clear that too often national housing policy has neglected rural
areas.

---

[19] "On Poverty and Race Relations." United States Catholic Conference. November 1966.
[20] "General Housing Characteristics for the United States: 1970." *Op. cit.*, pp. 1–53.

F. Special Needs

43. Several groups in our society have particularly severe housing problems. The poor suffer disproportionately in this regard. They lack the income and economic resources to acquire and maintain adequate housing. Rising rents and utility costs, as well as a decline in the availability of low-cost housing, have intensified their problems. Four out of five families with incomes below $5,000 suffer some form of housing deprivation.[21]

44. Many elderly people have special housing problems resulting in part from their small fixed incomes, growing isolation, rising property taxes and housing maintenance costs. New approaches to housing maintenance and health care are needed to enable the elderly to remain in their own homes and communities. Present government housing programs for the elderly do not begin to meet the need. A recent survey of federal housing for the elderly revealed that, for every senior citizen in an apartment for the elderly, there is another on a waiting list for such an apartment. The average waiting time is over twenty months.[22]

45. Migrant farmworkers also suffer serious housing deficiencies. Their high mobility, low income and regular periods of unemployment seriously hamper their efforts to obtain decent shelter. The housing available in migrant farm labor camps is often deplorable, yet effective enforcement of housing standards is rare.

46. The high levels of poverty and unemployment among Native Americans in both rural and urban areas have seriously affected their ability to acquire good housing. On Indian reservations the problems are particularly severe. Two-thirds of the housing on reservations either lacks adequate plumbing or is overcrowded. Most lending institutions are reluctant to make loans to Native Americans whose reservation land is held in Federal trust. In addition, housing assistance is often caught in the bureaucratic maze surrounding the provision of services on Indian reservations.

47. People with physical handicaps often experience difficulty in obtaining suitable housing at a cost they can afford. The planning and construction of housing often restrict it to able-bodied people. Architectural barriers are often put in the way of handicapped people in conventional housing as well as public buildings and accommodations.

48. Housing policy must be more sensitive to the needs of these particular groups, whose problems have too often been neglected or intensified by past housing practices.

G. Housing Stock

49. The existing housing stock of nearly 70 million units is perhaps the largest single component of our national wealth. According to the 1970 Cen-

---

[21] "America's Housing Needs: 1970 to 1980." *Op. cit.*, pp. 4–12.

[22] Senate Subcommittee on Housing for the Elderly, July 1975.

sus, 27.4 million of these units are more than 30 years old. We must act now to preserve and maintain this valuable resource or it will be abandoned and lost to us.

50. Too often older housing has been allowed to simply deteriorate. Conservation of existing housing must be encouraged by modifying tax and fiscal policies which penalize those who seek to maintain and rehabilitate existing housing. These approaches can help preserve part of our housing supply and prevent the destruction and large-scale displacement of people which marked earlier urban renewal efforts.

51. Rehabilitation and housing maintenance programs which are innovative, imaginative and economically feasible should be encouraged and implemented. The preservation of existing housing is an essential and economical approach to meeting our housing goal.

H. The Resource of Land

52. There is increasing awareness of the limitations of land and resources and the implications of these limitations on efforts to house our citizens. Since only a fixed amount of land is available and housing needs are growing, legitimate questions may be raised regarding the amount of land a person owns, the manner in which that land is used and regulation of land ownership by society.

53. The principle of stewardship discussed earlier has specific application to this question. As Pope Paul said in *Populorum Progressio:*

> ... Private property does not constitute for anyone an absolute and unconditional right. No one is justified in keeping for his exclusive use what he does not need, when others lack necessities. In a word, according to the traditional doctrine, as found in the Fathers of the Church, and the great theologians, "the right to property must never be exercised to the detriment of the common good."[23]

54. Land speculation is a particularly vexing problem. Where basic human rights are concerned, one person simply must not take an unreasonable gain at the expense of another. Huge increases in the cost of land, resulting in part from such speculation, seriously impair efforts to provide affordable housing to people of low- and moderate-income.

55. The demand for land to meet a variety of competing growth needs, such as urban expansion, highway and mineral development, parks and recreation, is forcing upon us difficult decisions with respect to the use and control of our land resources. These decisions can no longer be left to the private market alone to resolve. Since land use decisions are characteristically irreversible and hold consequences for the nation as a whole, they should be

---

[23] *Populorum Progressio,* 23. Paul VI. March 1967.

opened to some degree of public participation. Legislation is urgently needed to facilitate such participation.

V. Governmental Housing Activity

56. The federal government has for decades exerted a major influence upon the production and consumption of housing. Its involvement in the housing field is intricate and tangled, including economic and taxation policies, regulation of mortgage financing, as well as provision of housing subsidies.

57. Since decent housing is a human right, its provision involves a public responsibility. The magnitude of our housing crisis requires a massive commitment of resources and energy. Government must supplement and regulate the activities of private individuals and institutions in order to achieve our housing goals. A creative partnership of private enterprise and government is necessary. Public agencies have a particular responsibility to aid those in need as well as to oversee the development of a comprehensive housing and community development policy.

58. Fiscal and monetary policy has a dominant influence on housing. The rise and fall of inflation, employment and productivity are felt to a pronounced degree in the housing market. Monetary policy, the availability and rate of credit are likewise critical factors in the system of housing production and consumption.

59. Beyond these broad economic policies the federal government utilizes two basic approaches in housing: indirect subsidies to homeowners through the tax system and direct subsidies to producers and consumers of housing.

A. Indirect Action

60. Indirect housing subsidies through the tax system make up the largest share of federal housing activity. In 1972, federal housing expenditures and tax subsidies rose to a level of $15 billion of which only $2.5 billion went for direct housing subsidy programs. This indirect tax subsidy consists primarily of the deduction of mortgage interest and property taxes by home-owners. It is estimated that this deduction alone will cost $11.3 billion in 1976.

61. The higher a person's income, the more likely it is that he will be entitled to this kind of subsidy, and the higher the subsidy is likely to be.[24] In 1972, less than 5% of the taxpayers with incomes below $5,000 were entitled

---

[24] In 1973, 112,000 people with incomes below $3,000 claimed these subsidies, and the average subsidy was $23. At the other end of the income scale, 118,000 people with incomes of $100,000 or more claimed these subsidies and the average subsidy was more than 100 times the subsidy for the low income person: $2,449.

to this kind of subsidy, as against more than 80% of all taxpayers with incomes above $20,000.[25] This means:

—Four out of five households with incomes over $20,000 received housing subsidies though the tax systems.

—Only one out of 20 households with incomes below $5,000 received this form of housing subsidy.

In addition, it is estimated that in 1976:[26]

—The 1% of the population with incomes over $50,000 will receive more than 10% of both direct and indirect housing subsidies (an estimated $1.4 billion in 1976).

—The 14% of the population with incomes below $3,000 will receive less than 7% of either direct or indirect housing subsidies ($0.9 billion).

62. We do not quarrel with the objectives of these policies. The use of tax incentives to achieve desirable social goals (i.e., home ownership) can be appropriate, but it inevitably raises questions of equity which must be addressed through public policy.

B. Direct Housing Programs

63. Since the 1930s the federal government has used seven basic approaches to provide more direct forms of assistance to builders and consumers of housing.

1) Mortgage insurance, begun during the Great Depression, enabled millions of middle-income families to buy homes with long-term, low down payment mortgages.

2) Insurance of bank deposits and purchase of mortgages from private institutions—sometimes with a subsidy—have provided a flow of credit into housing and sustained construction during periods of tight money.

3) Low interest rates for rental and sales housing have been direct subsidy programs since 1968. Under these programs, the federal government can reduce interest costs, thus substantially lowering the monthly cost to the consumer.

---

[25] *Housing in the Seventies.* Report of the Department of Housing and Urban Development (HUD). (Washington, 1973). Pp. 2–8.
[26] By the National Rural Housing Coalition. Washington, D.C., 1975.

4) Public housing is the oldest direct housing subsidy program. Begun in 1937, it provides for building, buying, or renting housing by local housing authorities. Over one million public housing units are occupied primarily by families with incomes below $4,000.

5) Block grants recently have been made available to assist local communities in their efforts to provide adequate community development.

6) Housing assistance payments to families and individuals are currently being tested as a new approach to the housing problems of low-income people.

7) Large-scale leasing of housing units is a relatively new and untested approach to assist low-income people in gaining decent housing.

64. The Department of Housing and Urban Development (HUD) is responsible for administering a variety of programs in metropolitan areas across the country. The Farmer's Home Administration serves rural areas with direct lending and other programs. In the past, many of these federal programs were designed to encourage the participation of non-profit housing development corporations. A large number of these have been established by religious organizations or community groups.

65. Currently, the federal government relies almost exclusively on its leased housing program to meet national housing needs. This is not enough. The housing crisis requires a variety of tools responsive to the many dimensions of housing need. No single program will be the answer. Programs which might be improved and used as effective vehicles for the production of housing should not be abandoned. The country needs a firm commitment by the federal government to meet our housing goal. The agencies charged with this duty must move forcefully and creatively to meet their responsibilities. Adequate funds and administrative staff must be made available to them. The free market, acting alone, cannot supply a sufficient quantity of low- and moderate-income housing to meet our needs. A new commitment of will and resources is needed if we are to make progress in providing "a decent home and suitable living environment" for all Americans.

C. Local and State Activity

66. Local governments control housing development through zoning and building codes and the provision of such community facilities as streets or roads, water, sewers, schools and health and recreation centers. Many communities with older housing also have housing codes which set basic standards for all existing housing.

67. Unfortunately, on some occasions these local controls have been used to exclude minorities and the less affluent from communities and to evade

common responsibilities for housing and community development. On a more positive note, however, many communities have initiated housing rehabilitation and construction programs aimed at providing adequate housing at costs which low- and middle-income people can afford.

68. Recently, many state governments have set up housing finance agencies or departments of community affiars. They assist local communities with advice and resources, sometimes providing financial assistance and often using federal subsidy programs to help local groups.

69. These local and state efforts to provide greater housing opportunities for all our people are encouraging and should be expanded. We urge state and local governments to develop sensitive and responsible policies regarding land use and zoning disputes. We also hope local governments will use their new community development funds to assist the victims of housing deprivation.

VI. The Role of the Catholic Community

70. The Catholic community has a responsibility to act effectively to help meet the needs of those who lack adequate housing. We must confess that we have not done all we could. It is not enough for us to point to the reality of poor housing and recommend that government and other institutions take appropriate action. We must also reflect on our own responsibilities and opportunities for action. We call on individual Catholics, dioceses and parishes, as well as other Catholic organizations, to join us in a new commitment to those who suffer from poor housing.

71. The Church alone cannot provide a significant quantitative answer to the cries for better housing. This is not its specific role, nor does it have the financial and technical resources to build all the required homes. However, it is our responsibility to proclaim the Gospel of Jesus Christ and its implications for our society. We must analyze in a competent and critical manner the aspects of housing which pertain to social justice. We must point constantly to human rights—and human suffering—involved in this issue. We must apply Christian social teaching to the resolution of the problem. We must seek to have a qualitative impact on the problem of housing deprivation in our society by attempting to change the systems and the policies that result in housing deprivation. There seem to be five possible approaches for Church involvement in housing: awareness, advocacy, providing services, stewardship and community-building.

A. Awareness

72. The first element of the Church's response is building awareness of the extent of the housing crisis and our participation in it. Christ's concern for those in need is an essential dimension of our Faith. The Catholic community

must remind itself and all others that indecent housing is a moral and ethical issue demanding a response.

73. We cannot be at peace with ourselves while so many of our brothers and sisters suffer from inadequate housing. We are often unconscious participants in the systems that result in poor housing. All of us, through our involvement in the community, can assist in the development of humane and just policies pertaining to shelter. We encourage individual Catholics to join and support organizations which have demonstrated a sincere and effective concern for better housing for all people.

74. Particular persons have particular responsibilities. Those who own rental property must maintain and manage it in a way that provides decent, sanitary and safe housing. Landlords must respect the human dignity and rights of tenants and observe the principles of justice in setting their rents. Tenants must cultivate a respect for property and their neighbors and meet their financial obligations. Those employed in the housing field should seek to encourage a sensitive response on the part of private industry, labor unions and government agencies.

75. We urge parishes and organizations within the Catholic community to undertake programs to promote understanding of housing problems and the role each of us might play in meeting those needs.

B. Advocacy

76. As an advocate, the Church should analyze housing needs in the light of the Gospel, make judgements and offer suggestions. On the national level, we should attempt to educate people regarding the demands of justice in the area of housing and suggest principles upon which proposals for change might be based. We should also involve ourselves in the ongoing dialogue over housing policy and underline the moral dimensions of the problem.

77. The United States Catholic Conference will continue to monitor and participate in the development of housing and community development policy. In line with the following principles we shall encourage governmental action that:

1) Affirms and advances the realization of the national housing policy of "a decent home and suitable living environment for all American families."

2) Provides a variety of programmatic tools and sufficient resources to meet the housing needs of low- and moderate-income families, including the continued participation of non-profit, community-based housing corporations.

3) Focuses programs and resources on the special needs of the following:

low-income people, rural Americans, the elderly, farmworkers, Native Americans and the handicapped.

4) Adapts our housing delivery system to meet the economic realities of inflation, recession and unemployment.

5) Recognizes the central role of the neighborhood in the survival of viable urban areas by encouraging rehabilitation and reinvestment in central cities.

6) Encourages land use policies that provide for adequate planning and effective controls on unreasonable and wasteful development and speculation.

7) Encourages a monetary policy and credit allocation system that provides a sustained supply of affordable credit for housing production.

8) Encourages the integral participation of housing consumers and tenants in decisions regarding housing at local, regional and national levels.

9) Encourages equal housing opportunity, within a framework of cultural pluralisms, through voluntary compliance and, where necessary, legal remedies.

78. We applaud the involvement of the National Conference of Catholic Charities, the National Catholic Rural Life Conference and the Interreligious Coalition for Housing in this area. We hope to work in collaboration with them and other groups in advancing these principles.

79. The same responsibility for action exists on the local and regional levels. We encourage local and regional organizations to work with their people and political leaders to achieve these same ends.

80. The parish is the setting for perhaps the most important Catholic response to poor housing. With its roots deep in the community, the parish can play a critical advocacy role regarding the housing problems of its people. Working with individuals, community organizations and members of the private sector, it can harness its own resources and energies to combat decay, blight and indifference. Parish programs of rehabilitation and housing maintenance could be initiated. In addition, parishes can join with others to utilize government programs and monitor public and private efforts to alleviate poor housing.

81. Through education and involvement, the local church can help its people gain a wider measure of justice in the area of housing.

C. Providing Services

82. The Catholic Church in this country has a long tradition of providing services to those in need. Our concern must also extend to the shelter needs of people.

83. Many dioceses, Catholic Charities and parishes have already sponsored the development of housing for low-income people and the elderly or have initiated rehabilitation programs. Using federal programs, Catholic institutions and organizations have provided a substantial amount of housing for low- and middle-income people and for the elderly. A 1974 survey of 60 dioceses conducted by the National Housing and Human Development Alliance indicated that more than 25,000 units have been built under Catholic sponsorship in the past ten years. Over 20 congregations of religious men and women are involved in housing, with 2,600 units already constructed.

84. We strongly support these efforts and are deeply impressed by what has been achieved thus far. Given the compelling need for new housing, we believe there is an important role for non-profit developers willing to sponsor viable and creative housing where the private market is unable or unwilling to build.

85. This special "housing ministry" requires sensitivity and adequate technical expertise. Housing sponsorship inspired by Christian values should bring a qualitative difference to housing. The housing development motivated by Christian concern must reflect a lively awareness of human need and the dignity of the person in its treatment of tenants, in its relationship to the local community, in its planning, location and employment practices.

86. There are a variety of other social and human services relating to shelter. Housing management, education in tenant rights and responsibilities, financial and personal counseling, housing and appropriate services provided by Catholic organizations and individuals.

87. Providers of housing services should endeavor to involve tenants and the local community in an integral way in housing management and the provision of services. Housing sponsorship and management under Church auspices should provide models for others. This housing ministry must be encouraged, for it offers us an opportunity to act on our principles and give witness of our concern for the poorly housed.

D. Stewardship

88. In proclaiming the principle of stewardship, we must take note of the fact that the Church is also an institution possessing land, economic and personnel resources. While speaking to other organizations about the promotion of human rights and social justice, the Church must examine its own con-

science and actions to determine if its efforts and use of resources are just. In the 1971 Synod document, *Justice in the World*, the Bishops state:

> While the Church is bound to give witness to justice, she recognizes that anyone who ventures to speak to people about justice must first be just in their eyes. Hence we must undertake an examination of the modes of acting and of the possessions and lifestyle found within the Church itself.[27]

89. In the particular area of housing, we might take an inventory of our property and real estate, reflect upon its utilization and examine how it might better be put at the service of those who lack adequate shelter. We might also consider how we could make better use of our economic and personnel resources to assist those who need housing. In addition, a review of our investment policies may indicate how we might better harness our economic resources to assist in resolving the housing crisis.

E. Community Building

90. The alienation and isolation in our communities are important components of the housing problem. This more subtle concern is central to the resolution of the housing crisis. The Church is called to reconcile people with God and with one another, to bring them into a community of mutual support and love. We have noted that the Church must identify with the needs and aspirations of the community it serves. The Church should encourage the development of community organizations, neighborhood institutions and programs concerned with housing. As Pope Paul VI pointed out in *A Call To Action:*

> There is an urgent need to remake at the level of the street, of the neighborhood, the social fabric whereby man may be able to develop the needs of his personality. Centers of special interest and of culture must be created or developed at the community and parish levels with different forms of associations, recreational centers, and spiritual and community gatherings where the individual can escape from isolation and form anew fraternal relationships.[28]

91. It is important to recognize that historically neighborhoods often developed side by side with the growth of the local parish. If the neighborhood is the foundation stone of the city, it is obvious that the local parish plays a critical role in many neighborhoods. Often in rural areas and small towns a similar relationship exists between the local church and the community.

92. This fact imposes great responsibilities and provides important opportunities for the local church. With the encouragement of the local diocese,

---

[27] *Justice in The World.* November 1971.
[28] *A Call To Action,* 11. Pope Paul VI. May 1971.

Catholic parishes in urban areas should seek out a creative pastoral role in the development of sound and healthy neighborhoods. In metropolitan and rural areas alike, parishes must develop a ministry of "community-building," helping to identify and resolve serious problems through education and participation in the life of the community. It should encourage its members to become informed and involved in community affairs and housing issues.

93. The parish itself should join with other community groups and churches to gain greater housing opportunities for all people. Traditionally, the Catholic parish has rendered a major service in meeting the educational needs of communities; it should now also attempt to meet other critical human needs, including the need of a decent home and a suitable living environment.

VII. Conclusion

94. The dimensions of the crisis in housing seem overwhelming in the number of people and communities affected, the complexity of the problem, and the magnitude of the effort required to meet our housing needs. There is a temptation to feel discouraged in the face of this situation.

95. However, we do not address this crisis to emphasize the difficulty, but to issue a challenge. The greatest obstacle is apathy and indifference. We ask all those in our society—individuals, private enterprise, government, social and religious organizations—to reexamine what role they might play in eliminating poor housing in our nation. Responsibility for this problem has been passed from one segment of the community to another for too long. We pray that this statement will not further divide, but rather unite us in a common effort to meet our housing needs. For our part, we pledge to work with others in a renewed effort to promote awareness and action on the housing crisis. Shared responsibility, ecumenical coordination and cooperation with any group sharing our concern will mark our housing activities.

96. We are hopeful. We have faith in the basic values of people. We believe that once they understand the nature and extent of housing problems and their moral responsibility, they will respond with individual and collective action to meet housing needs. They believe, as we do, that every person has a right to a decent home in a decent environment.

97. Our hope flows from the core of the Gospel: new life springs from suffering and death. We believe our cities and rural areas can be resurrected and bloom again with renewed vitality and community life. As the prophet said:

> They shall rebuild the ancient ruins,
>   the former wastes they shall raise up
> And restore the ruined cities, desolate
>   now for generations. (Isaiah 61,4).

98. Our Faith tells us that men and women are called by God to continue the work of creation, to fashion a better, more just society as we wait for the coming of the Kingdom of God. Effective action for decent housing is an essential dimension of this continuing creation.

99. This is a time for renewed dedication and action. Decent housing for all our people is a moral imperative. We pledge our support to those who carry out the demand of the traditional corporal work of mercy, "to shelter the homeless."

100. We are not suggesting a project or a program for this year or the next, nor are we calling for a reassertion of a public policy already declared, but never realized. What we are proposing is a long and determined effort, with all its frustrations, toward a better life for millions of Americans. This task is more than an element of a better society or an aspect of the common good; it is indispensable to the future health of America and its people.

101. In this undertaking, we summon our fellow Catholics and all who recognize this pressing concern to a task that calls for intelligence, resiliency and unremitting vigor. We will find allies in this work, and we must welcome them; we will find foes who think our dream utopian and unrealizeable, and we must persuade them. The one thing we cannot do is to acknowledge the immoral situation of indecent, inadequate housing and do nothing about it. We seek in this statement to initiate a fresh response to the unanswered pleas for help that come from the oppressed, neglected and forgotten. We pledge our continuing efforts as we set out on the long road that offers a lasting hope for decent shelter to this nation and its people.

Immigrants

Late in 1976, the NCCB went on record in favor of amnesty for illegal aliens. In addition, the Conference made four other recommendations including measures that would allow increased emigration of persons from Canada and Mexico, as well as less restrictive immigration policies toward refugees.

The Pastoral Concern of the Church for People on the Move

NCCB, November 11, 1976

"I was a stranger and you made me welcome." (Mt. 25:35)

The movement of people seeking their daily bread and the protection of their human rights is a growing phenomenon of our times. Large scale international migration is due chiefly to demands for plentiful and cheap labor created by technological progress and patterns of investment or to political unrest. People cross international borders for seasonal work, for temporary work, and for permanent resettlement. In all too many cases human considerations, such as family life and family values, are sacrificed to economic ones.

Massive migration from underdeveloped countries and regions is a special phenomenon of our age. The United States alone receives about 400,000 new immigrants each year. Our country continues to attract immigrants as workers and refugees.

Many of today's immigrants are doubly marginal: they are forced to migrate because of inadequate resources and unequal distribution of goods; then, in their countries of adoption, they are sometimes ignored or subjected to new injustices. Perhaps it is because of such compounded injustice that Jesus specifically promises His Kingdom to those who recognize Him in the immigrant.

In his Motu Proprio *On the Pastoral Care of Migrants* Pope Paul called for a careful balance of the immigrant's rights and duties: to the right of emigration corresponds the duty to serve the common good, especially in developing countries (e.g., the problem of 'brain drain'); the right to be accepted as an immigrant is limited by the common good of the country receiving the immigrant; to the right of immigration corresponds the duty of adapting to the new environment; to the duty of serving the common good in the country of origin corresponds the duty of the state to create jobs in the country of origin.

As a leaven in the world, the Church is called to participate in human affairs and to recognize in the poor, the afflicted, and the oppressed the presence of the Lord summoning the Christian community to action.

Seen in this evangelical perspective, immigrants, refugees, migrant workers, seamen and other people uprooted and on the move for survival and human dignity are a theological sign to the Christian community. They are among those signs of the times to which the Second Vatican Council called our attention in order to discern the working of God's will.

While the pastoral care of the Church is directed to all, it is especially imperative that it be extended to newcomers "driven by political or economic forces to move abroad." (*On the Pastoral Care of Migrants*, I, 1). Their human and spiritual needs are great. Furthermore, the Church has a natural concern in this area, for at least three reasons.

First, a high percentage of the new immigrants to our nation come from traditionally Catholic countries such as Mexico, Cuba, the Philippines, the Dominican Republic, Colombia, Portugal, Haiti, etc. Second, the changed character of the new immigrant population, now predominantly Latin American, Caribbean, and Asian, finds in the transnational character of the Church an appropriate catalyst for a healthy adaptation to a new life. Third, the background of many of these immigrants has accustomed them to look to the Church not only as a source of spiritual guidance, but also as a natural point of cultural and social reference.

Among the concrete issues facing newcomers to our country are questions pertaining to legislation and the administration of immigration laws, employment opportunities, and health and education benefits. Many special problems affect children, women, seamen and undocumented immigrants.

We are particularly concerned with the passage in October of 1976 of Public Law 94-571. While it does equalize visa issuance for both the eastern and western hemispheres, it causes a most serious hardship in the matter of family reunification, especially for natives of Mexico and Canada.

This is exemplified, first, by the fact that, whereas over the past few years immigration from Mexico, chargeable to the numerical ceiling, has averaged in excess of 40,000 visas per year, this present law now restricts it to 20,000. Secondly, restrictive conditions have been placed in this law which affect alien parents who have children born in the U.S. Both of these restrictions will hinder family reunification.

Therefore, we recommend:

1. That quota-ceilings for natives of Mexico and Canada be increased to 35,000 persons per year.

2. That the American citizen child, regardless of age, be in a position to facilitate his or her parents' immigration.

3. That in the light of humanitarian concerns and the preservation of family unity, a generous amnesty procedure be enacted for the undocumented aliens presently residing in the U.S.

4. That the administration and implementation of the immigration laws be reviewed and revised in order to eliminate arbitrary selective enforcement and to reflect humanitarian concerns.

5. That a new and broader definition of the category of "refugee" be given in order that we may provide a haven for oppressed people from any part of the world, regardless of their race, religion, color, or creed.

All of these concerns are treated in the pastoral response which has been prepared by the Conference's Committee on Migration and Tourism.

The Church, the People of God, is required by the Gospel and by its long tradition to promote and defend the human rights and dignity of people on the move, to advocate social remedies to their problems, and to foster opportunities for their spiritual and religious growth. We pledge ourselves and urge our brothers and sisters in the Lord, to resist injustices against immigrants, to assist them in their need, and to welcome them into our nation and our community of faith as fellow pilgrims on the journey to the Father. It is our duty and our privilege to respond in this way to the biblical injunction: "The stranger who sojourns with you shall be as the native among you and you shall love him as yourself." (Lv. 19:34)

Labor Issues

November 1968 brought the first formal statement on farm labor from the NCCB. The Conference expressed great sympathy for the farm workers, who were receiving low wages and no assistance from social legislation. The bishops were especially desirous that farm workers receive "legislative protection for their natural rights to organize for purposes of collective bargaining." Hence, they urged Congress to include farm workers under the National Labor Relations Act as well as under a national employment insurance program and a national minimum wage.

In 1972, the Committee on Social Development and World Peace at the USCC endorsed and urged support of the lettuce boycott begun by the United Farm Workers (UFW), who resorted to a boycott when the growers in the Salinas Valley and in the Santa Maria area of California refused to bargain with them even though they represented a majority of the farm workers in those areas.

One year later, the same USCC Committee issued another statement on behalf of the UFW because of "union busting" by the International Brotherhood of Teamsters. The teamsters signed contracts with growers in the table grape industry, who already had been under contract with the UFW for three years. To remedy this injustice, the USCC Committee called on the teamsters union and the growers to accept UFW's request for a secret ballot election, in which the farm workers themselves could choose which union they preferred. Until the growers agreed to enter into collective bargaining with the union preferred by the farm workers, the USCC Committee urged continued support of the table grapes and iceberg lettuce boycotts.

In 1974, the bishops' Committee on Farm Labor of the NCCB issued a short resolution calling for legislation, on either the national or state level, which would assure farm workers the right to choose their union by secret ballot. Finally, in 1975, the entire body of bishops issued a resolution on farm labor in response to the passage of the California Agricultural Labor Relations Act, which guaranteed the right of farm workers to determine by secret ballot which union, if any, they wanted as their representative at the bargaining table. The bishops called the legislation an historic step toward the resolution of the farm labor problem, congratulated all those who participated in the process of passing the California law, and expressed their own willingness to work with all parties for an era of peace and justice in the agricultural industry.

In November 1973, the USCC's Committee on Social Development and World Peace concluded, after appropriate investigation, that the Farah company was treating its workers unfairly. To help remedy the injustice, the committee endorsed a strike by Farah workers and supported a boycott of Farah products.

Farm Labor

NCCB, November 15, 1968

1. The problems of farm workers have been receiving increased attention in this country in recent years. Greater awareness on the part of the general public has resulted in some progress such as is mirrored in the Migrant Health Act. However the workers' dramatic struggle to improve their lot has sometimes produced divisions and protracted conflict in the relations between the two parties.

2. We, the Catholic bishops of the United States, address ourselves to this problem with the high hope of assisting in a reconciliation between grower and worker.

3. For 30 years the disadvantaged field workers of this nation have stood by helplessly and listened to other Americans debating the farm labor prob-

lem. Burdened by low wage scales, mounting health problems, inadequate educational opportunities, substandard housing and a lack of year-round employment, they have often been forced to live devoid of security, dignity and reasonable comfort. For the past three years, however, many of them have been attempting to take their destiny into their own hands. This is a very healthy development.

4. Farm workers are now very painfully aware that not only do they have to struggle against economic, educational and social inequities, but they have also been excluded from every piece of social legislation as well.

5. The conflict that began in California is now spreading throughout the nation and is clearly a national issue. Farm workers are demanding legislative protection for their natural rights to organize for purposes of collective bargaining. They are demanding inclusion under a law which has protected the bargaining rights of other American workers for 33 years, namely the National Labor Relations Act.

6. Tragic as is the plight of farm workers, American growers and farmers also find themselves in a sea of difficulties. Mounting costs, foreign competition, water shortages and many other problems are closing in upon them.

7. We are aware that the small grower is often the victim of circumstances beyond his control, and that his sincere willingness to pay higher wages meets with obstacles which he cannot overcome without a realistic co-ordination of all his strengths. We urge him to examine his situation carefully in order to see that his so-called independence is unreal and could result in his vanishing from the American economy. We believe that this would be tragic for our country. To protect himself, his interests and the interests of farm workers, we plead with him to unite with his fellow farmers and growers in associations proper to themselves. This is their natural right and even their duty at this moment of our history.

8. At the same time we wish to note that throughout this century, our State and Federal governments have done much to assist growers and farmers with their difficulties. The same, unfortunately, cannot be said for the men working in the fields.

9. Catholic bishops in several of the States most deeply affected by the current crisis in the field of farm labor have already addressed themselves to the need for Federal legislation to provide machinery for the peaceful settlement of disputes between growers and farm workers. In this statement, speaking in the name of the National Conference of Catholic Bishops, we wish to add our support to the position taken by these individual bishops, since the problem and its solution are national in scope.

10. We urge the 91st Congress to provide the legislation necessary both to protect the rights of farm workers and to provide the peace and stability so essential to the well being and prosperity of the agricultural industry. Specifically we urge that Congress enact legislation:

a.) To include farm workers under the National Labor Relations Act.

b.) To include farm workers more effectively under a national minimum wage which will ensure them a decent standard of living.

c.) To include farm workers under the national employment insurance program.

11. As a servant of justice, the Church must speak out on controversial issues such as these even with knowledge that she might be misunderstood. Sensitive to the problems of both sides, the Church must encourage dialogue by helping to create an atmosphere of charity and justice. It was in this spirit and for this purpose that the Second Vatican Council reaffirmed the traditional teaching of the Church with regard to the right of workers to organize and bargain collectively and, under certain conditions, to resort to the strike. These matters were treated by the Council in its *Pastoral Constitution on the Church in the Modern World,* which reads, in part, as follows:

12. "Among the basic rights of the human person must be counted the right of freely founding labor unions. These unions should be truly able to represent the workers and to contribute to the proper arrangement of economic life. Another such right is that of taking part freely in the activities of these unions without risk of reprisal. Through this sort of orderly participation, joined with an ongoing formation in economic and social matters, all will grow day by day in the awareness of their own function and responsibility, thus they will be brought to feel that according to their own proper capacities and aptitudes they are associates in the whole task of economic and social development and in the attainment of the universal common good.

13. "When, however, socio-economic disputes arise, efforts must be made to come to a peaceful settlement. Recourse must always be had above all to sincere discussion between the parties. Even in present-day circumstances, however, the strike can still be necessary, though ultimate, means for the defense of the workers' own rights, and the fulfillment of their just demands. As soon as possible, however, ways should be sought to resume negotiations and the discussion of reconciliation." (68).

14. In calling for the legal protection of the rights of farm workers, we, the bishops of the United States, do so in this same spirit and with sympathetic awareness of the problems faced by the growers and, more specifically, by family farmers. It is our prayerful hope that ways can be found at the earliest possible date "to resume negotiations" and to bring a "reconciliation" between the parties to the current farm labor dispute. We pledge our united efforts to achieve this objective.

The Farm Workers' Lettuce Boycott

*USCC, Committee on Social
Development and World Peace
July 10, 1972*

Following the successful completion of the Delano table grape dispute, the United Farm Workers advised the lettuce growers in the Salinas Valley and in the Santa Maria area of California that UFW represented a majority of the farm workers. The United Farm Workers sought to initiate an agreement for a recognition procedure. In addition to other negative responses, the growers refused the request of the Farm Workers. Accordingly, the workers struck and a boycott was conducted. After eight months of controversy a committee of growers agreed to meet with UFW. At that point the boycott was terminated. After another eight months of practically fruitless discussion, the United Farm Workers broke off negotiations, charging that the growers were not bargaining in good faith. Several growers did sign contracts, but the majority of the industry refused to do so and, after two years, still refuse to deal with the United Farm Workers. In the present situation, members of UFW have seen no alternative but to resume the lettuce boycott. Further complicating the problem is the fact that severe and repressive anti-labor legislation has already been enacted in Arizona and similar legislation is being sponsored in several other States.

As the Bishops of the United States said in their November 13, 1968, Statement on Farm Labor:

> We are aware that the small grower is often the victim of circumstances beyond his control, and that his sincere willingness to pay higher wages meets with obstacles which he cannot overcome without a realistic coordination of all his strengths. We urge him to examine his situation carefully in order to see that his so-called independence is unreal and could result in his vanishing from the American economy. We believe that this would be tragic for our country. To protect himself, his interests, and the interests of the farm workers, we plead with him to unite with his fellow farmers and growers in associations proper to themselves. This is their natural right and perhaps even their duty at the present moment of our history. At the same time we wish to note that throughout this century, our state and federal governments have done much to assist growers and farmers with their difficulties. The same, unfortunately, cannot be said for the men working in the fields.

Without strong, honest representation such as can be provided by the United Farm Workers, the plight of agricultural workers and their families will remain desperate. A fundamental issue of social justice is presented.

In these circumstances, the Committee on Social Development of the United States Catholic Conference recommends endorsement and support of the lettuce boycott and strongly urges that only "iceberg" lettuce clearly marked with the official United Farm Workers' label, the black Aztec eagle, be purchased. Our purpose in this is to bring about collective bargaining and a just settlement of the dispute.

In the name of justice, church agencies such as the USCC Committee on Social Development must speak out on controversial issues such as this one even with the knowledge that they might be misunderstood. Sensitive to the needs and the problems of both sides, these agencies must encourage dialogue by helping to create an atmosphere of charity and justice. It was in this spirit and for this purpose that the Second Vatican Council reaffirmed the traditional teaching of the Church with regard to the right of workers to organize and bargain collectively and, under certain conditions, to resort to the strike. These matters were treated by the Council in its Pastoral Constitution on the Church in the Modern World, which reads, in part, as follows:

> Among the basic rights of the human person must be counted the right of freely founding labor unions. These unions should be truly able to represent the workers and to contribute to the proper arrangement of economic life. Another such right is that of taking part freely in the activity of these unions without risk of reprisal. Through this sort of orderly participation, joined with an ongoing formation in economic and social matters, all will grow day by day in the awareness of their own function and responsibility. Thus they will be brought to feel that according to their own proper capacities and aptitudes they are associates in the whole task of economic and social development and in the attainment of the universal common good.
>
> When, however, socio-economic disputes arise, efforts must be made to come to a peaceful settlement. Recourse must always be had above all to sincere discussion between the parties. Even in present-day circumstances, however, the strike can still be a necessary, though ultimate, means for the defense of the workers' own rights, and the fulfillment of their just demands. As soon as possible, however, ways should be sought to resume negotiations and the discussion of reconciliation.

In supporting the efforts of the United Farm Workers to implement their right to organize and bargain collectively, we stress the fact that we are doing so in the spirit of the Council document referred to above and with sympathetic awareness of the problem faced by both parties. It is our earnest hope that ways can be found at the earliest possible date "to resume negotiations" and to bring about a "reconciliation" between the parties to the current dispute. We pledge our whole-hearted efforts to achieve this objective.

Resolution on Farm Labor

*USCC, Committee on Social
Development and World Peace
May 23, 1973*

Vatican II stated in the *Constitution on the Church in the Modern World* (par. 68):

> Among the basic rights of the human person is to be numbered the right of freely founding unions for working people. These should be able truly to represent them and to contribute to the organizing of economic life in the right way. Included is the right of freely taking part in the activity of these unions without risk of reprisal.

The social injustices which plague the nation's agricultural workers, and particularly the migrants, are well established. Major legislative efforts, federal and state, will be required to provide to agricultural workers the minimum labor standards now provided for most industrial workers. Real and lasting progress toward full participation in the American society can come, however, only when agricultural workers effectively organize their own trade union.

For these reasons we have been heartened by the successes of the United Farm Workers Union, AFL-CIO. In the last three years contracts, particularly in California, have indicated that unions of the workers' choice have a chance of taking root in the fields where much of the nation's food is grown.

The UFWU progress has been hampered by the lack of the legal protections which were enjoyed by the great industrial unions when they were beginning in the 1930's. However, there has been progress. Some of the California grower-employers have come to realize that a stable labor-management relationship can be built on collective bargaining.

Today, crashing destructively into these early hopeful developments has come the raid on the small and struggling United Farm Workers Union by leaders of the nation's largest union, the International Brotherhood of Teamsters. Making a common effort with the Teamsters, many growers in the table grape industry in California, who have had contracts with the UFWU for the past three years, have in recent weeks signed contracts with the Teamsters. Cynically, this raiding has come just a few months after the Supreme Court in California, in a 6-1 decision, found that the now-disputed lettuce contracts were executed through collusion of the lettuce growers and the Teamsters without any consultation with the workers.

This type of conduct on the part of the Teamsters is in violation of all canons of trade union ethics. The President of the AFL-CIO, George Meany, has termed it "positively disgraceful" and "union busting," the last the most derogatory term in the trade union lexicon.

In these circumstances, we call on the Teamsters Union and the growers to accept the request of the United Farm Workers Union to agree to a secret ballot, impartially supervised election to determine which union the farm workers prefer. The Committee on Social Development and World Peace of the United States Catholic Conference agrees with the bishops of California that the right of farm workers to organize and join a legitimate organization of their own choosing is the "dominant moral issue" in this dispute.

Until and unless justice and peace can be restored to the fields of California, we support and endorse the boycott of table grapes and iceberg (head) lettuce. We urge the purchase of table grapes and lettuce only if they clearly carry the Aztec black eagle label of the United Farm Workers Union, AFL-CIO. We urge men of good will to support this position in the name of social justice.

Resolution: Bishops' Committee on Farm Labor

NCCB, November 1974

We, the Catholic Bishops of the United States, reiterate the seriousness of the farm labor problem and believe the urgency for its solution is as grave as ever. It is a national scandal that at both the federal and state levels sufficient pressure is not being brought to bear on legislators to pass legislation that will be just to all parties. That legislation must assure the farm workers the right to elections by secret ballot of a union of their own choice. We therefore accept as a pastoral necessity that we be actively concerned in the solution of an evil that has gone on far too long.

Resolution on Farm Labor

NCCB, November 20, 1975

June 5, 1975 marked an important turning point in the history of farm labor relations in the United States. It was on that day that the California Agricultural Labor Relations Act was signed into law by Governor Edmund G. Brown, Jr. This is the first law ever enacted in any jurisdiction, federal or state, guaranteeing farm workers the right to determine, by secret ballot elections, which union, if any, they want to represent them. It is a good law and one that might well serve as a model for parallel legislation in other key agricultural states as well as at the congressional level in Washington. While it will not automatically resolve all of the problems involved in the farm labor dispute, it does provide the parties with a set of enforceable procedures through which they can begin, at long last, to settle their differences in an orderly manner. In short, it represents an historic step in the right direction.

We salute the innovative leadership of Governor Brown who set into motion the process which resulted in the enactment of this long overdue statute by an overwhelming vote of the California legislature and with the almost unanimous support of the parties involved. We sincerely congratulate all who participated in this process: members of the legislature, the many and varied grower organizations, the United Farm Workers of America, the Western Conference of Teamsters, and the technical advisors and consultants who helped to draft the statute.

We call upon all concerned—state officials, growers and union representatives—to cooperate with one another in implementing the spirit as well as the letter of the law. It would be a tragedy if the purpose of the law, which holds out such promise for the future of sound labor relations in the agricultural industry, were to be thwarted in practice, for whatever reason. If experience demonstrates that either the statute itself or its administration needs to be improved, we pledge our support to this end. The National Conference of Catholic Bishops stands prepared to cooperate with the parties to the fullest possible extent in their common effort to bring about a new era of peace and justice in the agricultural industry, not only in California but throughout the nation.

Resolution on Farah Manufacturing Company — Amalgamated Clothing Workers of America Labor Dispute

USCC, Committee on Social Development and World Peace November 1973

Vatican II stated in the *Constitution on the Church in the Modern World* (par. 68):

> Among the basic rights of the human person is to be numbered the right of freely founding unions for working people. These should be able truly to represent them and to contribute to the organizing of economic life in the right way. Included is the right of freely taking part in the activity of these unions without the risk of reprisal.

It is rare that the national Catholic bishops' conference would consider a specific labor dispute as being appropriate for comment by one of its committees. However, after the dispute between the Farah Manufacturing Company, Inc. and the Amalgamated Clothing Workers of America, AFL-CIO was called to the attention of the United States Catholic Conference Administrative Board on September 19, 1973, the Board directed our Committee to take appropriate action.

We have reviewed the findings and positions of the Bishop of El Paso, the Archbishop and Auxiliary Bishop of San Antonio, who are responsible for the dioceses in which the company is primarily located, and of the Bishops of the Southwest (USCC Region X), and the Texas Conference of Churches. In addition we have available a recently completed report by representatives of two divisions of the USCC*—the Division for Urban Affairs and the Division for the Spanish-speaking.

Based on these findings we judge:

—there is a lack of social justice and the workers organizing in the Amalgamated Clothing Workers of America deserve support of the Christian community and others of good will.

---

*Prior to this action of the Committee on Social Development and World Peace, consultations were held with ranking officials of the Farah Manufacturing Company and the Amalgamated Clothing Workers of America.

We add our Committee's support and endorsement of the strike and we urge a boycott of Farah products by all people of good will.

Farah Manufacturing Company has some nine plants in two states: five in El Paso, two in San Antonio, one in Victoria, Texas and one in Las Cruces, New Mexico. In addition, it has plants or sales offices, which do not import into the United States, in Belgium, Japan, and Hong Kong. It is one of the largest manufacturers of men's trousers employing, at the maximum, some 8,000 workers. Farah markets on a nationwide basis and, accordingly, the boycott is nationwide. The Amalgamated Clothing Workers is a nationwide organization of workers in the garment industry and is a member in good standing of the AFL-CIO.

Without recounting a more than three year history of charges and counter-charges, actions and counteractions, a few central facts are decisive for us:

—the company will not divulge the average pay of its workers, reported near the minimum permitted by law;

—the company will not divulge how many, if any, retirees benefit from its profit sharing retirement plan (reportedly few, if any, do);

—the company admittedly has no grievance procedures other than appeals to management; and,

—the company asserts there is no need for a union and that it will not even discuss negotiations with the union.

In view of the above, we concluded there is a lack of social justice for the Farah strikers. The circumstances of employment constitute a denial of human dignity.

We express our solidarity with the strikers and we urge all who are concerned to undertake the boycott of Farah trousers. We specifically commend and endorse the efforts of the Amalgamated Clothing Workers of America in this dispute, in the interests of social justice.

Our hope and prayer is that the parties to this labor dispute will promptly enter into good faith collective bargaining.

Minorities

In May 1976, the USCC issued a statement on elderly Americans entitled Society and the Aged: Toward Reconciliation. The bishops first identify the many problems facing the elderly and then call upon the Church—as individuals, families, communities, and public policy advocates—to address these problems.

The USCC does not attempt an exhaustive analysis of the problems of older citizens. It does, however, list the major problems as follows: the rise of a "mercy killing" mentality, along with death-with-dignity legislation; poverty, loneliness, and despair, fixed incomes, diminished by recession and inflation; mandatory retirement; inadequate medical, dental, and mental health care, and less than proper care in nursing homes; malnourishment; poor housing, and insufficient low-income housing; dangerous neighborhoods; fear of crime; discrimination against minorities; cut-backs in social security benefits, and inadequate pensions. The USCC then urges legislative action to alleviate these specific problems.

The bishops mention that the needs of the elderly will be adequately met only if the needs of all are met "through a national policy guaranteeing full employment, a decent income for those unable to work, equitable tax legislation, and comprehensive health care for all."

In the spring of 1977, the USCC issued a statement on the relationship between the Catholic Church in the U.S. and the American Indians. The bishops plan to work for justice in the following ways: acquire more knowledge of Indian needs, aspirations, and values; urge Catholic dioceses and organizations to improve their ministry to the Indians; urge Catholic educational institutions to promote programs and activities that will enable students at all levels to appreciate Indian history, culture, and spirituality; make church facilities adjacent to Indian lands and neighborhoods more available to Indians; develop Indian leadership within the church; and, finally, urge the government to adopt more just policies. In particular, the USCC favors the following policies:

> The speedy and equitable resolution of treaty and statute questions; protection of Indian land and resource rights; more adequate housing and delivery of social, education and health care services; and increased levels of funding and technical assistance necessary to aid Indians in achieving political and economic self-determination and full employment.

The bishops' statement on the handicapped was issued at their November meeting in 1978. They acknowledge the Church's failure to respond adequately to the needs of handicapped people. They urge the Church's leaders *and members to welcome the handicapped into their communities and to educate themselves "to appreciate fully the contribution handicapped people can make to the Church's spiritual life." The bishops believe that handicapped individuals have a special insight into the meaning of life because they live more than most in the shadow of the cross. The hierarchy concludes its statement by designating ministry to the handicapped as a special focus for action by the NCCB and the USCC.*

Society and the Aged: Toward Reconciliation

USCC, May 5, 1976

I. The Aged

1. America today faces a great paradox: It is an aging nation which worships the culture, values and appearance of youth. Instead of viewing old age as an achievement and a natural stage of life with its own merits, wisdom and beauty, American society all too often ignores, rejects and isolates the elderly.

2. In an increasingly mobile nation, where the single-generation family as well as the extended family is weakened, the elderly often find themselves cut off from their families and their communities; about 14 percent of elderly men and 41 percent of elderly women live alone or with nonrelatives. Even large numbers of elderly persons not lacking for material goods find themselves unwanted and out of place.

3. Society has come to take a negative view of the elderly. This can be seen in the increasing tendency of families to rely on institutions to care for their elderly members, and in repeated efforts by some government officials to cut services and benefits for the elderly in order to ease the burden of inflation on the rest of society.

4. Society's negative image of the elderly reinforces their own negative self-image. The result of this unfortunate process is a tragically wasted human resource. The elderly are denied their God-given right to develop their potential to the fullest at every stage of life; at the same time, society is denied the fruits of that development.

5. In rejecting the elderly we do more than perpetuate injustice: When we reject any stage of human life, we are in effect rejecting a part of ourselves and our connections with the human community. Perhaps we react to the elderly as we do because they are an unwanted reminder of our own mortality.

6. The Biblical commandment to "Honor your father and mother" (Deut. 5:16) reminds us that, above all else, the family ought to be a place of love, respect and caring for the aging members of society. But often this is not the case. Many elderly people are physically, culturally, psychologically and spiritually isolated from their families and the rest of society; equally as important, society has become isolated from this group which composes ten percent of its membership.

7. The break between generations is weakening our values as a nation and creating a form of discrimination—against the elderly—which parallels more widely recognized forms of discrimination against minorities, women, the poor or the unborn.

8. Such a wound demands healing. Such a separation calls for reconciliation. This requires a rethinking of personal attitudes in the light of gospel values. Our first task is to restore to the elderly the dignity and sense of worth which they deserve.

9. As religious people and followers of Jesus, who calls us to reconciliation and love, we must pledge ourselves, our communities, our influence and our prayers to bringing about this reconciliation between society and its elderly.

II. Human Rights and the Elderly

10. The elderly do not forfeit their claim to basic human rights because they are old. But a brief look at the plight of many elderly people shows that they are in fact being denied those rights. The reconciliation we seek begins with recognition of our responsibilities to the elderly to insure their dignity and worth so that they can enjoy their God-given rights. As Pope John has said:

> "Every man has the right to life, to bodily integrity, and to the means which are suitable for the proper development of life; these are primarily food, clothing, shelter, rest, medical care, and finally the necessary social services. Therefore, a human being also has the right to security in cases of sickness, inability to work, widowhood, old age, unemployment, or in any other case in which he is deprived of the means of subsistence through no fault of his own."
>
> (Pope John XXIII, *Peace on Earth*)

A. The Right to Life

11. The right to life is the most basic human right in the sense of being the pre-condition for realization of all the others. But the right to life of the elderly is under constant attack, both direct and indirect.

12. On one level, the elderly, along with the sick and the handicapped, are the targets of a "mercy killing" mentality which would dispose of the unwanted. Even well-meaning legislative efforts to cope with complex questions about when and when not to use extraordinary technological and therapeutic means to preserve life pose genuine dangers, particularly since some would place fateful decisions solely in the hands of physicians or the state.

13. A more subtle, although no less serious, threat to the right to life of the elderly is a social system which, by ignoring their poverty, loneliness and despair, denies them the means and sometimes the very will to live.

14. Sociologists tell us we are nearing a time when the elderly will be divided into the "Young-Old," age 55–75, and the "Old-Old," over 75. The "Young-Old" will be a relatively healthy group, capable of entering second careers and influencing social patterns. The "Old-Old" will feel more clearly that they are simply awaiting death. As President Kennedy once said: "It is not enough to add new years to life; our objective must be to add new life to those years."

15. The elderly have a right to "new life": not just to material survival, but to education, recreation, companionship, honest human emotions, and spiritual care and comfort.

16. Finally, in reflecting upon the right to life of the elderly, one must note that in America women live longer than men. There are 143 women over age 65 for every 100 men. To talk of the problems of the elderly, then, is to talk in particular of the problems of elderly women who in their declining years may feel more painfully than ever the burdens of society's discrimination against women.

B. The Right to a Decent Home

17. The elderly, often living on fixed incomes, are among those who suffer disproportionately from society's economic ills of recession and inflation. The costs of food, medical care and housing (including fuel) have risen much more sharply than overall consumer price increases; moreover, these areas take up some 70 percent of the income of the elderly, as opposed to less than 60 percent of the income of the non-aged.

18. Some 22 percent of the elderly have incomes below the 1971 federal poverty level and half have incomes below $5,000. Social Security and Supplemental Security Income payments, in these circumstances, remain inadequate to maintain a decent standard of living. Inflation eats away at the value of savings. Many of the elderly do not have pensions, and there are serious problems in existing pension plans.

C. The Right to a Job

19. Polls reveal that 85 percent of the American people are opposed to mandatory retirement ages, these often force able-bodied people out of their jobs when they still have much to offer and need the satisfaction of a mean-

ingful job. Older workers are frequently forced out of work by technological change and are handicapped in seeking new employment by discrimination on the basis of age. A recession at any time may force many older workers into premature retirement which can be spiritually and financially draining.

20. Even those elderly who are not seeking remuneration for work are under-utilized: Some two million elderly Americans willing to do volunteer work do not have such opportunities available.

D. The Right to Health Care

21. Health care is a basic right, but it is often regarded as an expensive luxury. Despite passage a decade ago of Medicare, millions of elderly people still lack adequate medical care.

22. The percentage of health care costs for the elderly paid by Medicare has dropped in recent years and will probably continue to drop. Medicare does not pay for preventive health care, which means that many elderly persons will develop health problems unnecessarily and will receive treatment only when their problems become serious.

23. In addition, Medicare does not pay for such necessities as prescription drugs, eyeglasses, hearing aids, dentures or dental care, all of which become extraordinarily expensive when measured against the income of most elderly persons.

24. Although only five percent of the elderly live in institutions, nursing home care is a serious problem. Well publicized scandals have arisen concerning the operations of some nursing homes, where patient care is sacrificed while operators amass huge profits. Large numbers of elderly people are institutionalized needlessly for want of simple services, such as visiting nurses or homemakers, which would help them remain in their homes.

25. Mental health care for the elderly is even more inadequate than physical health care. An estimated one-third of the elderly in mental hospitals are there because they have nowhere else to go. Physical illnesses such as diabetes, anemia, or simply over-medication may produce behavior patterns in the elderly which are mistaken for senility.

E. The Right to Eat

26. A 1971 Administration Task Force on Aging declared that the elderly are the most severely malnourished group in society. Poor nutrition is a major factor in the incidence of poor health among them.

27. The Food Stamp program, hot meals program and other efforts are a help to the elderly, but they still do not reach all those in need. The elderly are also threatened by new Food Stamp proposals. Some would increase the amount the elderly must pay for Food Stamps or create unreasonable assets limitations which would force them either to forfeit Food Stamps or sell their valuables, possibly their homes; other proposed regulations determining

Food Stamp benefit levels could result in a decrease in benefits for many of the elderly.

28. Inadequate income is not the only reason why many of the elderly have poor diets. Lack of proper kitchen facilities, nutrition education or simple lack of companionship and incentive to eat are also factors.

F. The Right to a Decent Home

29. America has a severe housing shortage which, like other economic problems affects the elderly more than most. Forty percent of the elderly live in homes which lack such facilities as central heating, hot water or inside toilets. (Seventy-seven percent of the elderly live in rural areas.)

30. Many elderly persons live in homes they own as the result of a lifetime of work, but are threatened with losing their homes because of waning physical strength, rising fuel and maintenance costs, and regressive property taxes.

31. Housing is particularly important to the elderly because they are often virtually trapped in their homes by lack of transportation and fear of crime.

32. Less than half of those over 65 are licensed to drive. Many, particularly those in rural areas, do not have access to mass transportation, which is often costly when it is available.

33. The elderly, particularly in urban areas, live in fear because of their particular vulnerability to such crimes as burglary and mugging, as well as "white-collar" crimes such as price-fixing and fraud.

G. The Right to Equal Treatment

34. Members of minority groups in America face special discrimination at all age levels. Minority elderly persons suffer discrimination on account of their race in addition to their age, their poverty, and often their sex.

35. A serious problem facing some minority elderly is a language barrier which may prevent them from obtaining medical and social services to which they are entitled. The same barrier may prevent them from participating in the social and recreational life of their communities and neighborhoods or the liturgical life of their churches.

III. The Role of the Church

36. The Church is many things—a community of faith, a community of individuals, and families and a voice in civil society. If the Church is to help reconcile society and the elderly it must act in all these roles. The elderly look to the Church for strength and assistance. They want the Church to be a community where they experience the comfort of the forgiving Lord, and the hope of the risen Lord. The elderly need the concern, joy and presence of a caring Christian community.

A. As Individuals

37. No institutional effort can be successful unless we examine our own individual attitudes and actions. We must ask ourselves how we treat the elderly in our families and communities.

38. Do we treat them with the respect and dignity which they deserve? Do we try to draw out the best in them and share ourselves with them? Do we carry our fair share of their financial support? Do we make an effort to try to understand and meet their special needs? Are we kind and patient?

B. As Families

39. The family is the basic unit of any community and is itself an expression of love. We cannot emphasize enough the critical role of the family in caring for their aging loved ones and keeping them in their midst as valuable, contributing members. The family is where the elderly feel most comfortable and accepted. We call on each family to weigh carefully its obligation to care for an elderly father or mother, uncle or aunt.

40. Should elderly family members require a form of institutionalization, the obligations of the family remain. Responsibility for their well-being cannot be left to health care professionals and social service agencies alone. Often, only relatives and friends can provide the love and personal attention that humanize the sometimes lonely experience of institutional care.

C. As a Community

41. We take pride in the fact that the Catholic community has always made special efforts to care for the elderly; but we also acknowledge with humility that there is much still to do.

42. One valuable task which can be performed at the parish level is simply to locate the "hidden" elderly in order to bring them into parish and community life and help them obtain community and government services to which they may be entitled but which they do not receive.

43. Parish structures offer many opportunities for leadership in helping the elderly: community dining rooms, "day care," home visits and telephone reassurance services; car pools and other transportation aids; recreation; continuing education programs.

44. We must not only help continue the education of the elderly. We must guarantee effective education of all age groups about the aging process, the rights of the elderly and their potential for more active and satisfying lives.

45. Catholic hospitals and other health care institutions have a special responsibility in meeting the needs of the elderly, as do all forms of Church social service agencies.

46. More coordination of services and outreach are needed in diocesan as well as local programs. There are special needs and opportunities in the areas

of low-cost housing, supervised housing, transportation and job training. Many dioceses have already sponsored low income housing programs for the elderly. We support these efforts and encourage wider participation in low income housing programs by other dioceses and religious orders.

47. The Church at all levels has a responsibility to seek out the elderly for their input into policy decisions and to provide them with opportunities for meaningful work, both as employees and volunteers.

48. The Church also must make provisions for retired priests and religious to live in a dignified manner. Special attention must be given to communities of religious women, which face particular financial hardship in caring for retired sisters. Adequate pension plans for all Church employees are essential.

D. As Public Policy Advocates

49. In this statement we have called on individuals, families, the Church, and community groups to assist the elderly in realizing their human rights and living decent lives. We also recognize, however, that some problems require the attention of society as a whole, through legislative and governmental action.

50. We must raise our voices clearly and effectively as advocates for the elderly on public policy matters. Elderly people cannot compete with well-financed interest groups for national resources; like other basically powerless groups, the elderly stand to lose the most in times of economic crisis.

51. Many of the needs of the elderly will only be met adequately when the needs of others are met through a national policy guaranteeing full employment, a decent income for those unable to work, equitable tax legislation and comprehensive health care for all. But a number of significant steps can be taken in the interim:

• Continued opposition to euthanasia and "death with dignity" legislation which gives undue power to the state or to physicians.

• A thorough review of the Social Security system to insure its continued stability.

• Continued opposition to cutbacks or ceilings on the Social Security cost-of-living index for the elderly which reflects actual increases in their living expenses.

• Reform of Medicare to provide coverage for preventive care, dental care, prescription drugs, devices such as eyeglasses and hearing aids and increased and more readily available home health care services to allow the elderly to avoid unnecessary institutionalization.

• Establishment of stricter standards for nursing homes and strict enforcement of those standards.

• Opposition to Food Stamp program changes which would penalize the elderly.

• Expanded nutrition, education, job training and recreation programs for the elderly.

• Special efforts to meet the transportation needs of the elderly.

• More low-income housing for the elderly. We strongly endorse continued congressional expansion and administration backing of the very successful Section 202 program. We further urge that the interest for Section 202 loans be set at the lowest possible rate.

• Continued reform of the pension system, and wider availability of pensions.

• A higher priority for mental health care for the elderly.

• An end to age discrimination in hiring and flexibility in setting retirement ages.

• Special attention to programs to reduce crime against the elderly.

IV. Toward Reconciliation

52. Healing the rupture between society and its elderly members requires a major effort to change attitudes as well as social structures. In undertaking this task we are not simply meeting the demands of charity and justice. We are accepting our own humanity, our link with past and future and, thereby, our link with the Creator. To do this is to add new life to the final stages of growth because Christ said, "I have come that they may have life and have it to the full." (John 10:10).

Statement of U.S. Catholic Bishops on American Indians

USCC, May 4, 1977

1. In this statement, we wish to share our reflections on the relationship of the Catholic Church in the United States with the American Indian peoples.

2. As American Catholics, we have learned only gradually and with difficulty that the building of one community can only be authentic if it is based upon respect for the distinctive traditions, customs, institutions and ways of life of its peoples. Indeed, we are only now beginning to understand that

unity which grows through dialogue and respect for diversity is far stronger and deeper than conformity forged by dominance.

3. We recall with gratitude the great dedication and sacrifice of the many priests, religious and lay persons, past and present, who have sought to share with the Indian people the Good News of Jesus Christ. They learned the Indian languages, and, insofar as they were able within their own cultural limits, they adapted themselves to Indian cultures. In the name of the Church, these missionaries also offered to the Indian communities their talents and knowledge of medicine and education.

4. Some who have worked with American Indians, however, recognize that efforts of the Church to promote the Gospel among Indian communities have at times been attempted in ways that actually failed to respect Indian cultures. We come to this statement with a keen awareness of our not infrequent failures to respect the inherent rights and cultural heritage of our American Indian brothers and sisters. We offer this reflection on our attitudes and actions in the spirit of reconciliation and with a stronger commitment to be more sensitive and just in our relationships with American Indians.

Faith and Culture

5. The Church, by its very nature, must always and everywhere proclaim and give witness to God's saving love revealed by Jesus Christ in the Holy Spirit. This is the center and foundation of the Church's mission—to proclaim that in Jesus Christ, the Incarnate Word, who died and rose from the dead, salvation is offered to all people as a gift of God's grace and mercy.[1]

6. This Good News of salvation is not bound by time or human structures. Christ's Gospel of love and redemption, addressed to all people, transcends national boundaries, cultural differences and divisions among peoples. It cannot be considered foreign anywhere on earth; nor can it be considered identical with any particular culture or heritage.[2] It is the common blessing of all.

7. But persons are vitally dependent upon the institutions of family and community that have been passed down to them. These institutions—political, social, economic and religious—shape their self-understanding and are necessary to their full development as persons. Indeed, the Second Vatican Council affirmed that persons can come to an authentic and full humanity only through those distinct cultures which form the basis and heritage of each human community.[3]

---

[1] Pope Paul VI, *Exhortation on Evangelization in the Modern World, 5,* 14–16, 26–27; Vatican II, *Decree on the Missionary Activity of the Church, 2*-4.

[2] Pope Paul VI, 20, 28; Vatican II, *Dogmatic Constitution on the Church,* 48; *Decree on the Missionary Activity of the Church,* 8.

[3] Vatican Council II, *The Church in the Modern World,* 53.

8. The Christian faith should celebrate and strengthen the many diverse cultures which are the product of human hope and aspiration. The Gospel message must take root and grow within each culture and each community. Faith finds expression in and through the particular values, customs and institutions of the people who hear it. It seeks to take flesh within each culture, within each nation, within each race, while remaining the prisoner of none. Pope Paul VI, in his recent statement on evangelization, stressed these themes in calling for "fidelity both to a message whose servants we are and to the people to whom we must transmit it."[4]

The Church and Justice

9. The Church is also required by the Gospel and by its tradition to promote and defend human rights and human dignity. Pope Paul VI has underscored the fact that "between evangelization and human advancement—development and liberation—there are in fact profound links. ... The necessity of ensuring fundamental human rights cannot be separated from this just liberation which is bound up with evangelization and which endeavors to secure structures safeguarding human freedoms." The Church, Pope Paul continued, "has the duty to proclaim the liberation of millions of human beings—the duty of assisting the birth of this liberation, of giving witness to it, of ensuring that it is complete. This is not foreign to evangelization."[5]

10. In all its activities the Church must seek to preach and act in ways that lead to greater justice for all people. Its ministry cannot neglect the violations of human rights resulting from racism, poverty, poor housing, inadequate education and health care, widespread apathy and indifference and a lack of freedom. These realities are fundamentally incompatible with our faith and the Church is required to oppose them. Pope Paul VI stressed the profound link between the Church's mission to preach the Gospel and action on behalf of justice: "How in fact can one proclaim the new commandment without promoting justice?"[6]

The American Experience

11. We, as American Catholics, should be especially sensitive to these aspects of the Church's mission. Over the centuries, peoples from every continent and heritage have joined in the formation of the United States. Each group to come has constructed its communities and established its institutions. Gradually, all Americans learned the lesson that to build a nation free and independent, a people must be prepared to engage in a never ending pro-

---

[4] Pope Paul VI, 4.
[5] Pope Paul VI, 31; 39; 30.
[6] Pope Paul VI, 29-36; Vatican Council II, *The Church in the Modern World*, 41.

cess of change and dialogue. Each group has experienced the tensions that arise between the legitimate cultural independence that people claim for themselves and the pressing need for true and fruitful dialogue with other groups.

12. Today, we Americans are called to reflect upon past injustices and to consider again the need for both unity and diversity, to become one nation built upon respect for the distinctive traditions and values of many peoples and cultures. Both respect for cultural diversity and dialogue between cultures are indispensable if the legitimate quest for cultural identity is to lead to human development and social progress and not simply perpetuate the bitter divisions of the past. The challenge of this effort is placed before the nation by Black Americans, by Spanish-speaking Americans, by the heirs of Europe's migrations and by the persevering voice of the oldest Americans, the American Indians.

American Indians

13. The American Indian peoples had developed rich and diverse cultures long before the first Europeans came to the American continent. Migrating across this great continent, they dispersed over thousands of years, from the coasts of the Pacific Northwest to the arid mesas of the Southwest, the vast grasslands of mid-America and the mountains and woodlands of the East. Adapting themselves to changing environments as they went, they developed over 200 distinct languages and a variety of carefully developed social, economic and political institutions to meet their needs.

14. But the arrival of later immigrants created conflicts not yet resolved. Indian ways of life were challenged; their very existence was continually threatened by newcomers who were their superiors in the arts of war. For the Indians, the saga of nation building in America has been a story filled with sorrow and death.

15. American Indians in the United States today comprise less than one percent of our total population. In all, they belong to more than 250 distinct tribes and bands.

16. Many tribes have retained a special trust status with the United States and continue to live on reservation lands held in trust for them by the federal government. Over the long years, however, many tribes have been deprived of their communal lands, and with them have partially or entirely lost the traditional vestiges of their culture, their languages, customs and ways of living.

17. During recent decades, increasing numbers of American Indians, especially the young people, have migrated to cities in search of jobs, shelter and social services which are sorely lacking on many reservations. Those who have chosen or been forced to migrate to cities in response to promises of employment and a better life have too often found only new frustrations and broken dreams. Many contend with a deep sense of uprootedness, trying to

maintain ties with their families and tribes while coping with the economic hardships and social prejudices, even racism, of urban society.

18. American Indians today are struggling against great obstacles to renew the special values of their unique heritage and to revitalize the ways of their ancestors. They are striving to achieve economic development and social justice without compromising their unique cultural identity. For some American Indian peoples the struggle is to retain rights to their land and resources; for some it is to gain employment and economic security; and for others, it is to obtain political power in order to set their own goals and to make decisions affecting their own futures. These goals, to be achieved within the framework of Indian culture and traditions, test the strength of the American ideal of liberty and justice for all. America must respond, not to atone for the wrongs of the past, for that in a sense is beyond our power, but to be faithful to our national commitment and to contribute to a truly human future for all.

The Role of the Church

19. As American Catholics, we have a special responsibility to examine our attitudes and actions in light of Jesus' command to love our neighbor and to proclaim the Gospel message and its implications for society. The Church is compelled, both through its institutions and through its individual members, to promote and defend the human rights and dignity of all people.

20. Accordingly, we recognize our own responsibility to join with our American Indian sisters and brothers in their ongoing struggle to secure justice. We realize that there is much that we can and must do within our Church and in society to make our support real. We must first of all increase our understanding of the present needs, aspirations and values of the American Indian peoples. This responsibility can only be carried out effectively in dialogue with American Indians.

21. We are encouraged in our efforts by the many hopeful initiatives that Catholic communities in various parts of the country have undertaken on behalf of American Indians. From the national level, the Campaign for Human Development, the National Conference of Catholic Charities and the Commission for Catholic Missions Among the Colored People and the Indians have provided support to many constructive local efforts.

22. For over 90 years, the Commission for Catholic Missions Among the Colored People and the Indians, together with the Bureau of Catholic Indian Missions, has had a particular responsibility to support efforts to advance the life of the Church among American Indian communities. The historical success of this work reflects the generosity of Catholics in the United States. We are particularly encouraged by the recent revitalization of these organizations and hope to see their efforts renewed and redoubled in the coming years. We should also support efforts to broaden the involvement of Indian peoples in the work of the Bureau of Catholic Indian Missions.

23. We note also the serious and sustained efforts in several dioceses to improve the Church's ministry among American Indians. In particular, the Bishops of Minnesota have offered their own reflection on the Church's relationship with American Indians in their statement, *A New Beginning*.

24. We recommend that other dioceses and Catholic organizations make similar efforts to improve their ministry with American Indians and we pledge our own efforts to cooperate with the American Indian people and the local Catholic churches in these endeavors.

25. One area which deserves our special attention is that of government policy and legislation. Perhaps no other group of people in the United States is so vitally affected by government policies and programs as are American Indians. We have a responsibility to examine these systems and policies in light of the Gospel and the Church's social teachings and to urge the adoption of more just policies and legislation affecting American Indians. It seems to us that such efforts must include advocacy of: the speedy and equitable resolution of treaty and statute questions; protection of Indian land and resource rights; more adequate housing and delivery of social, education and health care services; and increased levels of funding and technical assistance necessary to aid American Indians in achieving political and economic self-determination and full employment.

26. We understand that such efforts will mean little if they are not accompanied by honest reflection on the entire ministry of the Church with American Indians. We must examine the Church's liturgical expressions and social and educational services within Indian communities to ask if they indeed reflect an appreciation of Indian heritage and cultural values. We would encourage national and diocesan liturgical offices to provide assistance to Indian communities to incorporate their languages and prayer forms in the liturgy and other worship services. We urge Catholic educational institutions to examine their textbooks and curriculums and to promote programs and activities that will enable students at all levels to appreciate American Indian history, cultures and spirituality.

27. We also urge that Church property and facilities adjacent to Indian lands or located in the midst of urban Indian neighborhoods be made more available for use by Indian communities for such activities as religious celebrations, group meetings, programs for the elderly, day care centers and educational programs.

28. Perhaps the most important task before us is the development of Indian leadership—clerical, religious and lay—within the Church. This is necessary if the Church is to prosper in Indian communities. We are especially encouraged by the efforts of several dioceses to include American Indians in their permanent diaconate programs and hope that this effort is expanded. In addition, efforts should be made to insure that American Indians have representation and a voice in all decisions made by Church agencies and organizations affecting their communities.

29. Drawing on the two themes of faith and culture, and the Church and justice, and working with all others of good will, we hope to fashion a renewed commitment to serve Indian peoples. In turn, their participation in and challenge to our Christian community will strengthen our common witness to Jesus and the Gospel message.

Pastoral Statement On the Handicapped

USCC, November 15, 1978

The same Jesus who heard the cry for recognition from the handicapped of Judea and Samaria 2,000 years ago calls us, his followers, to embrace our responsibility to our own handicapped brothers and sisters in the United States. The Catholic Church pursues its mission by furthering the spiritual, intellectual, moral and physical development of the people it serves. As pastors of the church in America, we are committed to working for a deeper understanding of both the pain and the potential of our neighbors who are blind, deaf, mentally retarded, emotionally impaired, who have special learning problems, or who suffer from single or multiple physical handicaps—all those whom disability may set apart. We call upon people of good will to re-examine their attitudes toward their handicapped brothers and sisters and promote their well-being, acting with the sense of justice and the compassion that the Lord so clearly desires. Further, realizing the unique gifts handicapped individuals have to offer the church, we wish to address the need for their fuller integration into the Christian community and their fuller participation in its life.

Prejudice starts with the simple perception of difference, whether that difference is physical or psychological. Down through the ages, people have tended to interpret these differences in crude moral terms. "Our" group is not just different from "theirs"; it is better in some vague but compelling way. Few of us would admit to being prejudiced against handicapped people. We bear these people no ill will and do not knowingly seek to abrogate their rights. Yet handicapped people are visibly, sometimes bluntly different from the "norm," and we react to this difference. Even if we do not look down upon handicapped people, we tend all too often to think of them as somehow apart—not fully "one of us."

What the handicapped individual needs, first of all, is acceptance in this difference that can neither be denied nor overlooked. No act of charity or justice can be of lasting value to handicapped people unless it is informed by a sincere and understanding love that penetrates the wall of strangeness and affirms the common humanity underlying all distinction. Scripture teaches us that "any other commandment (is) summed in this sentence: 'You shall love your neighbor as yourself.'" In his wisdom, Jesus said, "as yourself." We must love others from the inside out, so to speak, accepting their difference from us in the same way that we accept our difference from them.

The Church's Response to the Handicapped Person

Concern for handicapped people was one of the prominent notes of Jesus' earthly ministry. When asked by John's disciples, "Are you he who is to come or are we to look for another?" Jesus responded with words recalling the prophecies of Isaiah. "Go and relate to John what you have heard and seen; the blind see, the lame walk, the lepers are cleansed, the deaf hear and the poor have the Gospel preached to them." Handicapped persons became witnesses for Christ, his healing of their bodies a sign of the spiritual healing he brought to all people. "Which is less trouble to say, 'Your sins are forgiven' or 'Stand up and walk?' To help you realize that the Son has authority on earth to forgive sins"—he then said to the paralyzed man—"Stand up! Roll up your mat and go home."

The church that Jesus founded would surely have been derelict had it failed to respond to his example in its attention to handicapped people. It remains faithful to its mission when its members become more and more a people of the Beatitudes, a people blessed in their meekness, their suffering, their thirst for righteousness. We all struggle with life. As we carry on this struggle in a spirit of mutual love, we build a community of interdependent people and discover the kingdom of God in our midst.

The church, through the response of its members to the needs of others and through its parishes, health-care institutions and social service agencies, has always attempted to show a pastoral concern for handicapped individuals. However, in a spirit of humble candor, we must acknowledge that at times we have responded to the needs of some of our handicapped people only after circumstances or public opinion have compelled us to do so. By every means possible, therefore, the church must continue to expand its healing ministry to these persons, helping them when necessary, working with them and raising its voice with them and with all members of society who are their advocates. Jesus revealed by his actions that service to and with people in need is a privilege and an opportunity as well as a duty. In extending our healing hands to others, we are healed ourselves.

On the most basic level, the church responds to handicapped individuals by defending their rights. Pope John XXIII's encyclical *Pacem In Terris* stresses the innate dignity of all men and women. "In an ordered and productive community, it is a fundamental principle that every human being is a 'person' ... (One) has rights and duties ... flowing directly and spontaneously from (one's) very nature. These rights are therefore universal, inviolable and inalienable."

The word "inalienable" reminds us that the principles on which our democracy is founded also guarantee certain rights to all Americans, regardless of their circumstances. The first of these, of course, is the right to life. We have spoken out on this issue on many occasions. We see defense of the right to life of handicapped persons as a matter of particular urgency, however, because the presence of handicapping conditions is not infrequently used as a rationale for abortion. Moreover, those severely handicapped babies who are permitted to be born are sometimes denied ordinary and usual medical procedures.

All too often, abortion and postnatal neglect are promoted by arguing that the handicapped infant will survive only to suffer a life of pain and deprivation. We find this reasoning appalling. Society's frequent indifference to the plight of handicapped citizens is a problem that cries aloud for solutions based on justice and conscience, not violence. All people have a clear duty to do what lies in their power to improve living conditions for handicapped people, rather than ignoring them or attempting to eliminate them as a burden not worth dealing with.

Defense of the right of life, then, implies the defense of other rights which enable the handicapped individual to achieve the fullest measure of personal development of which he or she is capable. These include the right to equal opportunity in education, in employment, in housing, as well as the right to free access to public accommodations, facilities and services. Those who must be institutionalized deserve decent, personalized care and human support as well as the pastoral services of the Christian community. Institutionalization will gradually become less necessary for some as the Christian community increases its awareness of disabled persons and builds a stronger and more integrated support system for them.

It is not enough merely to affirm the rights of handicapped people. We must actively work to make them real in the fabric of modern society. Recognizing that handicapped individuals have a claim to our respect because they share in the one redemption of Christ, and because they contribute to our society by their activity within it, the church must become an advocate for and with them. It must work to increase the public's sensitivity toward the needs of handicapped people and support their rightful demand for justice. Moreover, individuals and organizations at every level within the church should minister to handicapped persons by serving their personal and social needs. Many handicapped persons can function on their own as well as anyone in society. For others, aid would be welcome. All of us can visit the homebound, offer transportation to those who cannot drive, read to those who cannot read, speak out for those who have difficulty pleading their own case. In touching the lives of handicapped men, women and children in this way, we come closest to imitating Jesus' own example, which should be always before our eyes.

The Handicapped Person and the Ecclesial Community

Just as the church must do all in its power to help ensure handicapped people a secure place in the human community, so it must reach out to welcome gratefully those who seek to participate in the ecclesial community. The central meaning of Jesus' ministry is bound up with the fact that he sought the company of people who, for one reason or another, were forced to live on the fringe of society. These he made the special object of his attention, declaring that the last would be first and that the humble would be exalted in his Father's kingdom. The church finds its true identity when it fully integrates itself with these "marginal" people, including those who suffer from physical and psychological disabilities.

If handicapped people are to become equal partners in the Christian community, injustices must be eliminated and ignorance and apathy replaced by increased sensitivity and warm acceptance. The leaders and the general membership of the church must educate themselves to appreciate fully the contribution handicapped people can make to the church's spiritual life. Handicapped individuals bring with them a special insight into the meaning of life; for they live, more than the rest of us perhaps, in the shadow of the cross. And out of their experience they forge virtues like courage, patience, perseverance, compassion and sensitivity that should serve as an inspiration to all Christians.

In the case of many handicapped people, integration into the Christian community may require nothing more than issuing an invitation and pursuing it. For some others, however, full participation can only come about if the church exerts itself to devise innovative programs and techniques. At the very least, we must undertake forms of evangelization that speak to the particular needs of handicapped individuals, make those liturgical adaptations which promote their active participation and provide helps and services that reflect our loving concern for those with serious problems.

This concern should be extended also to the families and especially the parents of handicapped people.

No family is ever really prepared for the birth of a handicapped child. When such a child does come into the world, families often need strong support from their faith community. That support must remain firm with the passage of years. The path to independence for handicapped individuals can be difficult. Family members need to know that others stand with them, at least in spirit, as they help their children along this path.

The central importance of family members in the lives of all handicapped people, regardless of age, must never be underestimated. They lovingly foster the spiritual, mental and physical development of the handicapped person and are the primary teachers of religion and morality. Ministers working in the handicapped apostolate should treat them as a uniquely valuable resource for understanding the various needs of those they serve.

Full participation in the Christian community has another important aspect that must not be overlooked. When we think of handicapped people in relation to ministry, we tend automatically to think of doing something for them. We do not reflect that they can do something for us and with us. As noted above, handicapped people can, by their example, teach the non-handicapped much about strength and Christian acceptance. Moreover, they have the same duty as all members of the community to do the Lord's work in the world, according to their God-given talents and capacity. Because handicapped individuals may not be fully aware of the contribution they can make, church leaders should consult with them, offering suggestions on practical ways of serving.

Parish Level

For most Catholics the community of believers is embodied in the local parish. The parish is the door to participation for handicapped individuals, and it is the responsibility of the pastor and lay leaders to make sure that this door is always open. We noted above that the task, on occasion, may not be an easy one; involving some handicapped people in parish life may challenge the ingenuity and commitment of the entire congregation. Yet, in order to be loyal to its calling, to be truly pastoral, the parish must make sure it does not exclude any Catholic who wishes to take part in its activities.

If the participation of handicapped persons and their families is to be real and meaningful, the parish must prepare itself to receive them. This preparation might begin with a census aimed at identifying parishioners and those with no church affiliation who have significant disabilities. Parish leaders could then work with individuals and their families to determine what steps, if any, are needed to facilitate their participation in parish life.

It may be necessary at this initial stage to place considerable emphasis upon educating the members of the parish community on the rights and needs of local handicapped people. All too often, one hears that there are too few persons with disabilities in a given parish to warrant ramped entrances, special liturgies or education programs. Some say that these matters should be handled on the diocesan level. Although many parishes have severely limited resources, we encourage all to make the best effort their circumstances permit. No parishioner should ever be excluded on the basis of disability alone.

The most obvious obstacle to participation in parish activities faced by many handicapped people is the physical design of parish buildings. Structurally inaccessible buildings are at once a sign and a guarantee of their isolation from the community. Sometimes all that is required to remedy the situation is the installation of outside ramps and railings, increased lighting, minor modification of toilet facilities and, perhaps, the removal of a few pews and kneelers. In other cases, major alterations and redesign of equipment may be called for. Each parish must examine its own situation to determine the feasibility of such alterations. Mere cost must never be the exclusive consideration, however, since the provision of free access to religious functions for all interested people is a clear pastoral duty.

Whenever parishes contemplate new construction, they should make provision for the needs of handicapped individuals in their plans. If both new construction and the adaptation of present buildings are out of the question, the parish should devise other ways to reach its handicapped members. In cooperation with them, parish leaders may locate substitute facilities, for example, or make a concerted effort to serve at home those who cannot come to church.

It is essential that all forms of the liturgy be completely accessible to handicapped people, since they are the essence of the spiritual tie that binds the Christian community together. To exclude members of the parish from these celebrations of the life of the church, even by passive omission, is to deny the reality of that community. Accessibility involves far more than physical alterations to parish buildings. Realistic provision must be made for handicapped persons to participate fully in the eucharist and other liturgical celebrations such as the sacraments of reconciliation, confirmation and anointing of the sick. The experiences and needs of handicapped individuals vary, as do those of any group of people. For some with significant disabilities, special liturgies may be appropriate. Others will not require such liturgies, but will benefit if certain equipment and services are made available to them. Celebrating liturgies simultaneously in sign language enables the deaf person to enter more deeply into their spirit and meaning. Participation aids such as Mass books and hymnals in large print or Braille serve the same purpose for blind or partially sighted members.

Handicapped people can also a play a more active role in the liturgy if provided with proper aids and training. Blind parishioners can serve as lectors, for example, and deaf parishioners as special ministers of the eucharist. In this connection, we look forward to the day when more handicapped individuals are active in the full-time, professional service of the church, and we applaud recent decisions to accept qualified candidates for ordination or the religious life in spite of their significant disabilities.

Evangelization and catechesis for handicapped individuals must be geared in content and method to their particular situation. Specialized catechists should help them interpret the meaning of their lives and should give witness to Christ's presence in the local community in ways they can understand and appreciate. We hasten to add, however, that great care should be taken to avoid further isolation of handicapped people through these programs which, as far as possible, should be integrated with the normal catechetical activities of the parish. We have provided guidelines for the instruction of handicapped persons and for their participation in the liturgical life of the church in "Sharing the Light of Faith: National Catechetical Directory for Catholics of the United States."

Finally, parishes must be sensitive to the social needs of handicapped members. We have already touched on some ways in which Christians can express their concern for their handicapped brothers and sisters. These actions and others like them can help solve some of the handicapped individual's practical problems and dispel a sense of isolation. They also create an opportunity for handicapped and nonhandicapped people to join hands and break down the barriers that separate them. In such an interchange, it is often the handicapped person who gives the gift of most value.

Diocesan Level

Efforts to bring handicapped people into the parish community are more likely to be effective if the parishes are supported by offices operating at the diocesan level. At present, the social-service needs of handicapped individuals and their families are usually addressed by established diocesan agencies. The adequacy of this ministry should be re-evaluated in the light of present-day concerns and resources. Where it is found to be inadequate, the program should be strengthened to assure that specialized aid is provided to handicapped people. In those cases where there is no program at all, we urge that one be established.

The clergy, religious and laity engaged in this program should help the parish by developing policy and translating it into practical strategies for working with handicapped individuals. They should serve as advocates for handicapped people seeking help from other agencies. Finally, they should monitor public policy and generate multifaceted educational opportunities for those who minister to and with handicapped people.

Many opportunities for action at the diocesan level now exist with regard to public policy. Three pieces of federal legislation that promise significant benefits to handicapped individuals have been passed within the past few years; each calls for study and possible support.

We refer to the Rehabilitation Act of 1973, the rehabilitation amendments of 1974, and the Education for All Handicapped Children Act of 1975. Enforcement of the regulations implementing section 504 of the Rehabilitation Act, which forbids discrimination on the basis of handicapping conditions, is a matter of particular interest. In response to the rehabilitation amendments, the executive branch of the federal government has also taken recent action, sponsoring a White House Conference on Handicapped Individuals in 1977. This conference was attended by official state delegations, and there would be value in determining which of its recommendations are being applied in the state or states where a given diocese is located. Diocesan offices will also wish to keep abreast of general public policy and practice in their states.

Dioceses might make their most valuable contribution in the area of education. They should encourage and support training for all clergy, religious, seminarians and lay ministers, focusing special attention on those actually serving handicapped individuals, whether in parishes or some other setting. Religious education personnel could profit from guidance in adapting their curricula to the needs of handicapped learners, and Catholic elementary and secondary school teachers could be provided in-service training in how best to integrate handicapped students into programs of regular education. The diocesan office might also offer institutes for diocesan administrators who direct programs with an impact on handicapped persons.

The coordination of educational services within the dioceses should supplement the provision of direct educational aids. It is important to establish liaisons between facilities for handicapped people operating under Catholic auspices (special, residential and day schools; psychological services and the like) and usual Catholic school programs. Only in this way can the structural basis be laid for the integration, where feasible, of handicapped students into programs for the nonhandicapped. Moreover, in order to ensure handicapped individuals the widest possible range of educational opportunities, Catholic facilities should be encouraged to develop working relationships both among themselves and with private and public agencies serving the same population.

National Level

As the most visible expression of our commitment, we the bishops now designate ministry to handicapped people as a special focus for the National Conference of Catholic Bishops and the U.S. Catholic Conference. This represents a mandate to each office and secretariat, as it develops its plans and programs, to address the concerns of handicapped individuals. Appropriate offices should also serve as resource and referral centers to both parochial and diocesan bodies in matters relating to the needs of our handicapped brothers and sisters.

Concluding Remarks

Handicapped people are not looking for pity. They seek to serve the community and to enjoy their full baptismal rights as members of the church. Our interaction with them can and should be an affirmation of our faith. There can be no separate church for handicapped people. We are one flock that serves a single shepherd.

Our wholeness as individuals and as the people of God, we say again, lies

in openness, service and love. The bishops of the United States feel a concern
for handicapped individuals that goes beyond their spiritual welfare to en-
compass their total well-being. This concern should find expression at all
levels. Parishes should maintain their own programs of ministry with handicapped people, and dioceses should make every effort to establish offices that
coordinate this ministry and serve as resource and referral centers for parish
efforts. Finally, the National Conference of Catholic Bishops and the U.S.
Catholic Conference will be more vigilant in promoting ministry with handicapped persons throughout the structure of the church.

We look to the future with what we feel is a realistic optimism. The church
has a tradition of ministry to handicapped people, and this tradition will fuel
the stronger, more broadly based efforts called for by contemporary circumstances. We also have faith that our quest for justice, increasingly
enlisted on the side of handicapped individuals, will work powerfully in their
behalf. No one would deny that every man, woman and child has the right to
develop his or her potential to the fullest. With God's help and our own
determination, the day will come when that right is realized in the lives of all
handicapped people.

Race

Race Relations and Poverty, *issued by the bishops in 1966, supports legislation against racial discrimination and poverty, condemns discrimination
based on race, language, religion, or national origin as contrary to right
reason and Christian teaching, and encourages individuals, groups, and
government to mount a concentrated attack on poverty.*

*Particular recommendations to government include upgrading the quality
of education for the poor; making adult education available to all, but
especially to the poor; providing family assistance that encourages fathers to
remain in their homes; and promoting job opportunities and adequate housing. Unions are urged not to discriminate in admission procedures, and
private citizens and churches "to promote low-cost housing for the poor, to*

build well-planned public housing units and to rehabilitate run-down neighborhoods."

In 1968, the Catholic bishops return to the subject of discrimination in the midst of widespread urban unrest. The bishops reiterate their call for a cooperative response to economic and social injustice. They call upon everyone to "build bridges of justice, compassion, and understanding."

Race Relations and Poverty

NCCB, November 19, 1966

1. The pastoral concern of the Bishops of the United States goes to the poor in our midst, particularly to those who have felt the heavy burden of discrimination. This means, in our day, racial discrimination.

2. These are turbulent days, marked by severe social strains and civic clashes. We are grateful that much progress in civil rights legislation has been made in recent years. Laws have been passed to eliminate discrimination in our nation and to open voting to all. We urge the vigorous use of all legal means to assure their prompt implementation.

3. Comprehensive programs to eradicate poverty have been begun. We ask for strong and continuing support for them and constant efforts to improve them. However, the great task of changing the hearts of men on the subject of equal rights for all requires more than laws and programs. It needs above all a true sense of neighborliness, based upon a religiously inspired conviction that all men are equal before God and that all should be welcomed in our midst.

4. We note with sorrow that civil strife is an ever-present danger. There have been riots in our cities. Racial antagonism has been fostered and continues to be fostered under many emotionally charged and irrational slogans. Moreover we are still confronted with the depressing problems of poverty, joblessness, and urban and rural slums.

Suffering Minorities

5. As American citizens we deplore the fact that such conditions exist in a nation so endowed with wealth. As Christian leaders, we must repeat the con-

stant refrain of recent Popes, and of Vatican Council II, that material goods are held in stewardship for the welfare of all men. Destitution, and degrading, avoidable poverty hurt family life, blight the promise of youth, and lead to a bitter harvest of sickness, delinquency and crime.

6. The problem of poverty is inflicted particularly upon minority groups in our society. The Negro, the Spanish-speaking, and the Indian suffer inordinately under this burden. Nearly half the members of these groups live in poverty. Their unemployment rate is double the national average. They are far more likely than others to be condemned to urban or rural slums.

7. While there are many causes of poverty, most are connected with past or present discrimination. Hence we affirm once again, as we did in our statement of 1958 and our letter of 1963, and on many occasions in the pronouncements of Vatican Council II, that discrimination based on race, language, religion or national origins is contrary to right reason and to Christian teaching.

8. We are all the children of God. We share the same rights before God and man. All men of good will desire that the doors of opportunity be opened equally to all who are their brothers under one eternal Father.

9. These statements of principles are so clear and so widely accepted that it is not necessary to dwell upon them here. Our present concern is to reduce principles to action, ideals to programs. In light of these considerations we respectfully propose the following pastoral suggestions. While these are general in nature, it is our hope that they can be translated, in our cities and throughout our nation, into specific and workable social programs.

10. First, in the current discussion of racial tensions slogans have at times taken the place of reasonable dialogue. We ask that dialogue replace slogans. It would be tragic were our nation to suffer a deepening of the cleavages along racial or economic lines, with shouted epithets of hate replacing reasoned discourse.

11. Since the aggrieved in our nation are mostly the poor and the members of minority groups, it is the clear duty of those who have jobs and status to talk openly and freely to those who have been less fortunate. We must learn, and learn first-hand, what it is to be a poor Negro, a neglected Spanish-American or a disenfranchised Indian.

Beginning of Solution

12. Open discussion of these problems is the beginning of their solution. It is our hope that all our Catholic people will join with their Christian and Jewish brothers, and indeed with all men of good will, in common projects which affirm and realize the dignity of all men.

13. Second, we ask that a concentrated attack upon poverty be mounted upon many fronts. This is a complex problem and its solutions are equally

complex. There is work that can be done by individuals, by religious groups, and by the community organizations.

14. Other aspects of this problem require a strong governmental intervention at appropriate levels. We wish to suggest certain objectives that seem to us paramount at this time and which require adaptation to different places in their application.

15. Foremost among these is the quality of education given to the poor. The poorly educated child and the school drop-out face life with almost insuperable handicaps in our society. Communities should be concerned about the quality of teachers, schools, guidance programs, and the supplementary aids needed by all children.

16. Adult education is also a great necessity. Citizens in every city, and in our rural areas, should examine critically the type of education afforded to the poor at all age levels, and act decisively to make educational opportunities equal for all.

17. Next we should be concerned with the type and quality of assistance available to poor families. Where welfare relief is necessary, it should be given in a context that favors family stability and respects the human dignity of those who cannot earn their living. Such programs should help maintain the father in the home and be joined, where need be, with training facilities to enable the unemployed to secure gainful work. These programs should offer incentives to part-time or temporary employment, often refused today because of regulations that penalize such efforts.

18. A key concern is job opportunity. This problem has two main facets: realistic training joined with proper motivation and the willingness of employers to hire and promote without discrimination. Unions likewise should open their membership rolls to all without discrimination. We especially compliment those employers and unions which have agreed to take affirmative actions to secure a fully integrated working force. Such open attitudes best express the Christian response to racial discrimination.

Problem of Housing

19. Finally there is the problem of adequate housing. Millions of Americans live in overcrowded substandard homes. Under such conditions, it is difficult to promote sound family life, to encourage education or to bring about stable, peaceful neighborhoods.

20. Our citizens, our civic groups and our churches should be eager to use the opportunities they now have to promote low-cost housing for the poor, to build well planned public housing units and to rehabilitate rundown neighborhoods.

21. But this is only part of the task. As our nation becomes increasingly suburban, industry and service occupations are expanding far more rapidly in the suburbs that in our inner cities. We cannot hope to solve the problem

of joblessness in our cities if men and women are denied the opportunity of living near possible places where work is available.

22. While the issue of fair housing has been the source of grave tensions in some parts of our nation, conditions have noticeably improved in certain areas. We urge support for sound programs to assure equal housing opportunities for all, without discrimination based on race, creed or color. Here is a unique chance for responsible dialogue, for learning from successes and from failures, and thus constructuring harmonious communities in every part of our nation.

23. We ask these steps out of our pastoral concern for all who are in need. In this world, under God's providence, our nation has been cast into a position of world leadership. This stems in part from our economic and military power, but it is also a recognition of certain unique elements in our democracy. More than most peoples in recorded history, we have striven to make all men equal under law.

24. Today the world watches us anxiously, as it reads of racial struggles and tensions and learns about poverty in an affluent society. If men elsewhere become disillusioned with our democracy, they are offered the choice of another powerful system which also promises equality, but at the sacrifice of basic freedoms.

25. Ours is a fateful choice, one which can decide the destiny, not merely of this American nation, but possibly of the entire world. In this instance at least, what is morally right is a political imperative. Prayerfully we commend these thoughts to our Catholic people and to all our fellow citizens who share our hopes.

This statement was not signed individually.

The National Race Crisis

NCCB, April 25, 1968

1. In 1958, the Catholic bishops of the United States issued a statement on Discrimination and the Christian Conscience. In it they condemned racism in all its forms. They could not do otherwise, given what faith and reason clearly teach concerning the unity of the human family: "He has made of one all mankind to dwell upon the whole face of the earth ... that they should seek God" (Acts 17:26–27).

2. The bishops pointed out that full and equal justice must be given to all citizens, specifically those who are Negro. They urged that the religious community "seize the mantle of leadership from the agitator and the racist." They further pleaded: "It is vital that we must act now and act decisively."

3. The religious bodies of the United States did act in the years that followed. The 1963 National Conference on Religion and Race became a landmark of ecumenical social action. There is reassuring evidence that the ensuing religious involvement contributed greatly to the passage of national civil-rights legislation in 1964 and 1965.

4. Now—10 years later—it is evident that we did not do enough; we have much more to do. When the National Advisory Commission on Civil Disorders concluded last month that white racism was a key factor in creating and maintaining the explosive ghettoes of our cities, it became clear that we had failed to change the attitudes of many believers.

Needs

5. Despite 10 years of religious, civic, and governmental action, millions of our fellow Americans continue to be deprived of adequate education, job opportunity, housing, medical care, and welfare assistance, making it difficult, perhaps even impossible, for them to develop and maintain a sense of human dignity.

6. Catholics, like the rest of American society, must recognize their responsibility for allowing these conditions to persist. It would be futile to deny what the Commission on Civil Disorders has told America—a white segregationalist mentality is largely responsible for the present crisis.

7. Yet, we must not waste time beating our breasts or pointing an accusing finger at those whom we consider racists. In varying degree, we all share in the guilt.

8. We must recognize the fact that racist attitudes and consequent discrimination exist, not only in the hearts of men but in the fabric of their institutions. We must also commit our full energies to the task of eradicating

the effects of such racism on American society, so that all men can live in the image and likeness of God.

9. We must build bridges of justice, compassion, and understanding, and we must do so at once. As the Commission on Civil Disorders warned, we are moving rapidly in the opposite direction, toward two societies, "one black, one white: separate and unequal." We must enter into a full dialogue on matters of substantial interest with members of minority groups who suffer from discrimination and its effects.

Unfinished Business of the Catholic Community

10. There are certain tasks which we must acknowledge remain the unfinished business of the Catholic religious community. First among these is the total eradication of any elements of discrimination in our parishes, schools, hospitals, homes for the aged, and similar institutions. Second, there is the Christian duty to use our resources responsibly and generously in view of the urgent needs of the poor.

11. Other tasks may be performed better by a united front of the religious community. Here we pledge our continued cooperation with the National Council of Churches, the Synagogue Council of America, and with other religious groups. Effective action is demanded of us all in the midst of this crisis in American life.

12. It is to this task that the statement issued on April 14 by the spokesmen for the major religious traditions in the United States addressed itself when it called for: (1) coordinated efforts on the part of the American religious community to raise the substantial funds needed for the implementation of local programs; (2) continuing interfaith efforts to push for the enactment of critically needed legislation in the fields of employment, housing, health, and welfare which comprise what the late Martin Luther King, Jr., called the "Poor Man's Bill of Rights."

13. Within our own communion, we hereby direct the various departments, offices, and bureaus of the United States Catholic Conference, in collaboration with other interested Catholic organizations, to set up an Urban Task Force to coordinate all Catholic activities and to relate them to those of others working for the common goal of society, based on truth, justice, and love.

14. It is essential that similar programs be established within the Church on the provincial, diocesan, and local levels throughout the land.

Bridges to Be Built

15. Perhaps the most important single task confronting the religious community is that of building bridges of understanding, irrespective of political

boundaries or loyalties, which will link Americans of every color, city dwellers and suburbanites, factory workers and farmers, civil servants and professional people.

16. Many such programs are in existence in various parts of the country. We can all learn from the successes and failures of these experiments as we press forward in a massive and sustained effort to break down the cleavages and divisions which today embitter so many Americans.

Cooperative Effort

17. We also emphasize that there are areas of concern that are best handled by working with civic groups such as the National Urban Coalition and its local counterparts, and with organizations having deep roots in the Negro community.

18. We strongly urge Catholics of every color and ethnic group to ally themselves with these religious and civic programs as the most convincing way of demonstrating the love of neighbor which is the proof of love of God.

19. The Gospel of Christ and the good of the nation must motivate us to encourage, support, and identify with the efforts of the poor in their search for self-determination. It is chiefly through the attainment of control over one's personal and social destiny that destructive feelings of despair, frustration, and helplessness can be eliminated. These efforts require the help—free from all spirit of paternalism or condescension—not only of organizations and institutions, but of each and every believer.

20. No one pretends that the material resources of the religious community alone can possibly meet the complex needs of society. On the financial front, for example, our resources are necessarily limited; this pinpoints rather than diminishes our responsibility. The Commission on Civil Disorders called on all segments of society—governmental and private—to commit themselves to meeting the nation's needs in the present crisis.

21. We owe special attention to the following areas:

Education

22. Education is a basic need in our society, yet the schooling available to the poor is pitifully inadequate. We cannot break the vicious cycle of poverty producing poverty unless we achieve a breakthrough in our educational system. Quality education for the poor, and especially for minorities who are traditionally victims of discrimination, is a moral imperative if we are to give millions a realistic chance to achieve basic human dignity. Catholic school systems at all levels must redouble their efforts, in the face of changing social patterns and despite their own multiple problems, to meet the current social crisis. The crisis is of a magnitude and peril far transcending any which the Church in America or the nation has previously confronted.

Job Opportunity

23. Job opportunity is also essential to insuring self-respect and stable family life. We urge American business, the industrial community, management, and labor, to put every possible initiative, resource, and know-how into the fight against the problem of minority unemployment. But, if the private sector of the economy is unable to provide work for the unemployed members of the minority groups—particularly, at the moment, young Negroes—then it becomes the duty of government to intervene. It should step in with socially useful programs designed to put to work the skills and energies of the jobless or, as is often the need, to provide for the discovery and development of skills. While urging others to do their part, we pledge to do ours and will work towards increasing the effectiveness of ecumenical and community programs requiring fair employment practices.

Housing

24. Lack of decent housing adds pathetically to the burdens of millions of American families. Living conditions in many cities and rural communities are themselves an obstacle to wholesome family life. Housing segregation inevitably becomes an added barrier to employment, particularly as job opportunities open in the suburbs and decline in the cities. The problem is twofold: removing the barriers of segregation for those who prefer and can afford suburban living, and providing low-cost housing in the cities for those who cannot afford decent housing at the prevailing prices. Private efforts should receive the legislative and administrative support of government. In this connection, we strongly urge strict implementation, nationally and locally, of both the letter and the spirit of the recently enacted federal open-housing act. Wherever and however possible, the Catholic Church in America will work with other churches, with private groups including industry and labor, and with government to help provide housing for low income families.

Welfare Assistance

25. Finally, there is need for welfare assistance which respects dignity and privacy, for those who cannot secure adequate employment. The so-called "Man in the House" rule is a national scandal. It is absolutely intolerable that families are being broken up by its application. Every possible care should be taken that public or private assistance always be provided under conditions that respect the dignity of the person and the integrity of the families assisted. It is hoped that organized Catholic social services will lead the struggle for adequate and compassionate aid for those in need.

26. We list these needs with full awareness of the tremendous costs involved. It will take much time and even more sacrifice to implement programs needed to rebuild our society. But surely the richest nation in the world can afford a massive war on poverty.

Critical Questions Remain

27. Certain critical questions remain. When will we realize the degree of alienation and polarization that prevails in the nation today? When will we understand that civil protests could easily erupt into civil war? Must we rebuild on the scorched earth of our ruined and gutted cities, or will we begin to rebuild now with a heightened sense of justice and compassion for the suffering?

28. There is no place for complacency and inertia. The hour is late and the need is critical. Let us act while there is still time for collaborative peaceful solutions. We must show concern, we must give ground for hope. In the name of God, our Father—and we do not lightly invoke His name—let us prove to all men that we are truly aware that we are a single human family on the unity of which depends our best hope for our progress and our peace.

The Church's Response
To the Urban Crisis: A Report*

USCC, Social Action Department
April 25, 1968

Our nation is moving toward two societies, one black, one white—separate and unequal. Reaction to last summer's disorders has quickened the movement and deepened the division. Discrimination and segregation have long permeated much of American life; they now threaten the future of every American. (Report of the National Advisory Commission on Civil Disorders, March 3, 1968).

The Catholic Church, which comprises nearly one-quarter of American society, with institutions that deeply affect all phases of that society, can hardly consider itself immune to the criticism of this nation's racial attitudes contained in the above statement. But there is no time for breast-beating; from almost every city in the United States comes confirmation of this deep-

---

*Report published in connection with the issuance of the Bishops Statement on the National Race Crisis.

ing division along racial lines. There is no time for idle talk; positive action must be taken to heal this rift, to build solid bridges between white and black men and within the white and black communities themselves.

The Church, because of its divine mission and the human institutions at its disposal, has within its power to be a major force in reshaping American society into a truly democratic society in which all men are true equals, in which their lives can truly reflect the fact that they are created in the image and likeness of God.

The Social Action Department, USCC, has been asked to suggest specific steps which can be taken, and to point the direction in which future actions should be guided. We hope here to state some of the concrete principles which should guide these actions and to suggest some of the methods which should be employed to implement Church action in the areas of urban affairs and race relations.

Principles

1) The moral and doctrinal heresy called "racism" works through people and through institutions. The Church's efforts must be two-pronged: directed at both "personal racism"—combating it in the minds and hearts of its largely white membership—and at "institutional racism," cleansing its institutions and organizational life. The question must be asked of each diocese, each Parish, each Church agency or organization; "Does every aspect of its work support truly open, Christian behavior, or does it tend to reinforce the walls of separation and of white superiority?"

2) The black community is often poorly organized and unable to present a strong, united voice on matters affecting it or to wield effective political power. Political, organizational and economic independence were important elements in the earlier rapid integration of immigrant ethnic groups into the American society. The Church must now support the black community in its efforts to achieve organizational, political and economic power so necessary to break down existing patterns of dependency and frustration.

3) Corollaries to this are the duty of citizens of every ethnic and color group to work for their own improvement, plus the right of citizens of every color to self-determination within the broad and positive limits of constitutional law and their right to exert meaningful control over public decisions which affect them.

4) There is a crying need for communication on matters of substance between people of all colors. The Church, with its deep involvement in all aspects or metropolitan life, is in a unique position to develop such bonds as an effective means of bridging gaps between whites and blacks and between city-dwellers and suburbanites.

5) The Church in this country has traditionally been a Church of the poor but there are many ethnic groups only minimally represented among its membership because of historic circumstances. Negroes are proportionally

fewer in Catholicism than in society at large, and there are fewer than 200 black priests in America. The Church must direct the major portion of its efforts toward the white community, then, in order to develop within it the necessary "new will" of which the Commission on Civil Disorders spoke, and without which no reform of our society is possible.

6) This "white apostolate" will have an effect on the ghetto and its residents because that white society is deeply implicated in the ghetto.

7) Action on urban and racial matters must be framed in the context of interreligious cooperation.

8) There is much that we do *not* know about ourselves and about the Church's effect on society.

Action

In the light of these principles the Social Action Department urges the Bishops to lead the Church in undertaking a number of action programs. It goes without saying that none of the specific programs mentioned is a solution by itself; taken together, however, they would indicate the depth of the Church's interest and concern, and in conjunction with the efforts of others, would be a sizable contribution leading towards a solution of our present difficult position.

National Efforts

Interreligious Cooperation

It is to be hoped that the American Catholic Bishops will be able to join with the Synagogue Council of America and the National Council of Churches in a joint statement exposing racist attitudes in any form and pledging a massive effort on the part of religious groups in America to cleanse themselves and their institutions of every vestige of racist attitudes.

This joint statement should be followed by unified efforts on the part of the three faiths to utilize every available program in education, family life, leadership training, etc., to realize our potential to effect needed social change.

Many joint religious efforts are already under way. Catholic participation in these must be stepped up. Operation Connection, Project Equality and like employment programs, the Joint Strategy and Action Committee and similar programs need measurable Catholic support if they are to succeed.

Of special importance are ecumenical programs such as the Urban Training Center for Christian Mission. Almost every diocese will need priests specially trained in urban problems. Many are already attending the Center. We recommend formal Catholic participation in the work of the Center and broader financial support by the Church.

Catholic News Media

One of the chapters in the Report of the National Advisory Commission on Civil Disorders is entitled "The News Media and the Riots." Any attempt of the Catholic Church in the United States to collaborate in the elimination of racist attitudes and its effects must take into consideration the Catholic press as well as the efforts of diocesan Bureaus of Information and offices of radio and television.

The Catholic Church should first strive to support and become actively engaged in the proposed Institute of Urban Communications. As to support and involvement, a committee drawn from the Catholic Press Association, NCCM's Radio & Television Office, the National Catholic Office of Radio and Television, and the Bureau of Information should be formed immediately. Members of this committee would be a cross-section of Catholics concerned with all the news media. This committee first should build bridges with the Institute and solicit funds from Catholic communications centers in order to make a suitable grant to the Institute from the outset.

The Catholic Church, through its agencies dealing with the news media, should promote a deeper understanding among journalists and communicators of the problems of urban living. Rather than establish separate meetings and symposia, these communications offices, as well as the committee referred to above, should collaborate with other Catholic agencies in sponsorship of such meetings (e.g., with the USCC Social Action Department, the National Catholic Conference for Interracial Justice, schools, universities, etc.).

Educational Programs

In studying the ghetto schools the Comission found that "the greatest unused and undeveloped human resources in America are in our ghetto children for whom a bleak school record is becoming bleaker." Poor schools were found to be the "greatest source of grievance to resentment within the Negro community." Public schools cannot solve their problems of racial isolation if the private school complement does not cooperate closely with public school efforts of desegregation and improvement. Since Catholic schools represent 85% of the private schools in America, it is urgent that a national strategy be developed and implemented regarding basic crucial issues in our present educational dilemma.

The educational resources of the Church should be activated to assist in improving the education of black people and other minority groups handicapped by underprivilege, and in attacking the evil of segregationist attitudes.

Over 200 Catholic schools located in the ghettoes have closed their doors in the last two years. Not only must this trend be reversed but the Church must make every effort to provide the highest quality of education in such schools.

Her limited resources of money and personnel prohibit mass education in these areas; however, model schools should be developed and maintained. Catholic teachers must actively participate in and sponsor such programs as NDEA, Headstart, Neighborhood Youth Corp, Push-Up, and Upward Bound. They should be alert to guide drop-outs into the Job Corps.

Our educational authorities should immediately review existing literature relating to Negro heritage and the many contributions to American life. This material should be incorporated into the curricula. A serious review of all instructional material should be undertaken, in cooperation with publishers and Negro representatives, in order to insure that the Negroes' role in American life becomes an integral part of Catholic school curricula.

Church organizations, such as the National Councils of Men and Women, the Conference of Major Superiors of Men and Women, the Christian Family Movement and others must increase those activities aimed at promoting concepts of racial justice and equality among their members. While many of these organizations offer excellent programs and materials, they too often are rendered ineffective by lack of implementation at the local level and frequently smack of paternalism.

Health Programs

One weakness in the report of the Commission on Civil Disorders was the inadequate attention given to the widening gap in health care between the white and non-white population. The Negro has the highest infant and maternal death rates, suffers proportionately more acute and chronic illness and has a shorter life expectancy than the white race of this nation.

The poor health of the Negro, as of all poor, is both an expression and the result of the social and economic burdens imposed upon him. His health is inseparably connected with poor housing, unemployment and an inadequate education.

The Catholic Church has massive resources in the health field. Part of the national and local task forces, which will be referred to later in this report should be drawn from the Catholic Hospital Association and the U.S.C.C. Bureau of Health and Hospitals. This commission or committee should be given responsibility and authority to provide leadership and services to facilities, organizations and citizens, working to provide quality health care to poor and black communities.

The Urban Coalition

Although still in its formative stage, the National Urban Coalition is almost universally considered to be a significant hope for cities in crisis. It brings together leaders and decision makers who actually have the resources (political as well as financial) to direct a meaningful reordering of priorities in this country. The National Urban Coalition gives a prominent place to religious leaders. One of the Catholic participants should be the General Secretary of USCC, and he should be authorized to act decisively in the name of the hierarchy.

Legislative Goals

A recent analysis of the legislative goals of the National Urban Coalition, the National Conference on Automation, the Southern Christian Leadership Conference, the National Advisory Commission on Civil Disorders, and the President's messages to Congress indicate a striking consensus with regard to the kind of legislation needed in order to confront our urban problems. These goals can be summarized under jobs, housing, education, and welfare. They should be supported by Catholic agencies in company with Protestant and Jewish religious groups, and our staffs urged to assist in their passage.

A National Day of Penance and Atonement

The Report of the Commission on Civil Disorders hardly mentions the Churches. The fact that they are overlooked in a report that points out the chasms that separate whole bodies of people in this country, a fantastic degree of fear and hatred among our citizens, and rampant, deeply rooted racism might in itself be interpreted by many as an indication of the churches' failure to reach the majority of Americans with the basic principles of our Judeo-Christian heritage.

We suggest a National Day of Penance and Atonement for the three faiths. This should be undertaken without thought as to how it might affect our present problems but merely as a day of penance, fasting, and prayer in which the Church seeks atonement for the sins of its members in practicing, condoning, or failing to condemn white racist attitudes in all of their manifestations.

Diocesan Efforts

Much of what has been said regarding a national response can be said again of efforts at the diocesan level. Local urban coalitions are in the process of forming in most cities. The dioceses should actively assist in their formation and cooperate fully in their programs.

No amount of talk, study, or programming at the national level has any real meaning apart from the commitment, energy, and effort put in by men of good will in the neighborhoods and cities of this country. The Church's overall accomplishment will total little more than the combined effort of the dioceses. Nothing is more local than a ghetto! Each diocese should take firm, positive, action towards their elimination.

The passing and enforcing of local open housing ordinances; positive steps to integrate neighborhoods; increased ecumenical participation in that construction of integrated housing—all are but first steps in attacking the ghetto and its problems.

Finally every parish in this nation has a responsibility to act and to serve as leaven in our larger communities. While leaving to individual dioceses the task of urging specific programs the many existing efforts need to be commended and their number and effectiveness increased.

Credit unions and cooperatives, parish interracial councils, the "twinning" of suburban and innercity parishes are all commendable steps, the growing utilization of parish facilities as community facilities indicated the rapidly increasing awareness by parishes that they do not stand apart from the problems of the city but rather that they are.

Self-Help Programs in the Ghetto

All the above programs are those in which Church organization, Church resources and Church responsibility must, in order to be successful, be fully exercised.

However, residents of the black ghetto community have many needs which they and they alone can meet. Community organizations, the training of responsible leaders, economic development are vitally important if the black community is to break the bonds of dependency which have persisted for so many years.

Yet programs in these areas need help from the white community—help offered unselfishly, without conditions or restrictions—for it is only in the exercise of responsibility and power that one learns responsibility and the proper exercise of power. It is only through the attainment of effective control over one's own life that frustration—which breeds violence and despair—can be conquered.

While aid must come from outside the black community, sufficient aid will not come from government. Additional aid *must* come from private sources—foundations, individuals, organizations and churches.

An outstanding example of programs of this sort is the work of the Inter-religious Foundation for Community Organization, with headquarters in New York, which provides grants for community development in a number of cities across the nation. IFCO is now primarily supported by contributions from Protestant denominations. A strong interreligious commitment to IFCO and similar organizations will hasten the end of urban frustration and dependency.

Organization and Implementation

In order to implement these programs and to conduct the necessary research, communications and field services necessary for their success and for the development of new forms of action, two needs must be met: 1) a vehicle for national coordination and development of the Church's work must be established, and 2) some agencies and organizations now working in the field should receive additional support. In each case additional funding will be required.

The Church on both the national and diocesan levels urgently needs a means with which to coordinate its many services—charities, education, ecumenical affairs, press, lay organizations, health services and hospitals, student affairs—so that they can cooperate with social action programs to meet this urgent need for massive and unified action.

In order to do this it is *not* necessary to create a "super-agency" or to restructure each base of Church organization. It *is* necessary to draw together, at the proper time and in the proper place, these various aspects of Church activity which affect urban life in order to help them determine their needs and their strengths in the light of local situations and to assist them when and where they need assistance.

It is therefore recommended that an "Urban Task Force" be created, adequately funded and staffed with experts in all fields of Church life which touch on urban and racial affairs. This Task Force would coordinate the activities of the appropriate Church agencies and organizations at the national level, and would provide research, planning, communications and field service support necessary to carry out an effective program without wasteful overlapping and duplication of efforts.

This national Task Force should function in concert with local Task Forces in each diocese, each headed by a full-time, professionally qualified person, supported by the necessary staff. Local Task Forces would provide the necessary coordination within each diocese, would serve as a means of coordinating programs on an area-wide basis, and would provide communications between local, regional and national levels.

At all levels, Task Forces must seek to cooperate with other religious bodies and civic groups. They should seek to work closely with Urban Coalitions where they already exist and should support the creation of Urban Coalitions where they do not yet exist.

Nationally and locally, Task Force activities should be carried out by professional staffs, responsible to governing boards composed of the bishops or their representatives, all relevant Church agencies and organizations, and clerics and laymen involved in urban and racial affairs.

Such coordinating bodies cannot be recommended too strongly. The USCC Social Action Department was told time and again by those with whom it consulted in preparing this report that an urgent need exists for coordination, communication, research and planning, particularly—but not exclusively—at the national level.

As James Farmer, the former director of CORE and now Professor of Social Welfare at Lincoln University, recently noted we are just now becoming aware of "the complexity of the problems confronting us and ... the interrelatedness of their various parts. There follows logically the need for comprehensive and coordinated solutions."

Yet in our haste to act we must resist the temptation to plunge our resources into short-term programs of doubtful longterm value. Our actions must be based on long-range goals, and our resources must be allotted on the basis of priorities, determined in the light of these goals. Experience has shown that the Church's moral force and human and financial resources can be expected to have little immediate effect; but they can, through sustained effort, become a strong force in the creation of lasting conditions of social justice and economic and political equality in America.

Immediate creation of national and local Task Forces will enable all Church agencies and organizations to commit themselves to this cause without wastefully duplicating and diffusing their efforts, and to continue and strengthen their efforts through careful and sustained planning.

Adequate funding and staffing are absolute necessities, yet the need for immediate action, of necessity, raises short-term budgetary questions. Some of these problems could be overcome by utilizing at the national level the USCC Social Action Department as a nucleus around which to build. A number of agencies have indicated their willingness to provide professional and clerical staff on temporary loan until more permanent financial and staff arrangements can be made. It was in this manner that the Urban Coalition was able to begin its work within a matter of days after its organization.

Both nationally and locally, there exist many religious and civic organizations concerned with research, communications and action programs in the fields of urban and racial affairs. The Church and individual Christians should work in every way possible with these existing bodies and should support their work to the fullest possible extent.

The Report of the National Advisory Commission on Civil Disorders made clear the need for "a commitment to national action" which will require "new attitudes, new understanding, and above all, new will." It repeatedly stressed the need for communication among whites and between whites and blacks in order to reverse the divisive trend in American racial affairs. The Report made clear the fact long apparent to Negroes—that white attitudes and white actions are in great measure responsible for their condition.

There is no question that the Church can through education and action contribute significantly to creation of this new will. The nation should be confident that it will do so, that it will provide the active, moral, leadership required by the urgency of this crisis.

Said the Commission on Civil Disorders:

"There can be no higher priority for national action and no higher claim on the nation's conscience."

Adopted by the Bishops of the United States, April 25, 1968.

Statement on School Desegregation
Bishop Joseph L. Bernardin,
General Secretary

USCC, March 22, 1972

President Nixon's proposals for a busing "moratorium" and efforts relating to quality education for the disadvantaged are complex, and their full implications are by no means immediately clear. The U.S. Catholic Conference is studying the legislation put forward by the administration and expects to make its views known, in detail, at a later date. In the meantime, however, there are certain principles which form the basis for the Conference's approach to this entire matter and which, one hopes, will also be respected in the development of government policy.

The Catholic bishops of the United States have previously pointed out that the question of racial relations in our country is fundamentally a moral issue. This is as true in education as in any other area. The Conference trusts, therefore, that the moral dimensions of public policy will be at the fore in the continuing national debate over the best means to achieve quality education and equal opportunity for every child.

The Conference is committed to the principle of quality education and equal educational opportunity for every child in public as well as non-public schools, provided these schools conform with existing civil rights legislation. Raising the quality of education and guaranteeing equal educational opportunity, especially for the disadvantaged, are the duties of government. Thus, the Conference would naturally be in favor of any legislation which does, in fact, help to achieve these goals.

One cannot give a simple yes or no answer to the question of busing. In some cases, busing may be the only effective instrument by which justice in education can be secured for children of all races. For this reason, it would be a serious mistake to rule out busing entirely. Furthermore, the federal government obviously must take into consideration the effect of its policies and programs on good faith efforts now being made in various parts of the country to deal with the problems of racial separation and quality education in the schools. Caution should be exercised not to undermine the position of the many educators, public officials and private citizens who have been seeking to bring about equality in American education.

It is evident that busing is not the total solution to racial and educational problems in the nation's schools. It is also true that in particular situations busing may be an extreme and even counterproductive measure and should not, therefore, be employed indiscriminately.

As President Nixon has said, our nation's citizens, in taking a stand on busing in a particular situation, should be guided by right reasons. The best right reason is the right of every child to quality education.

Brothers and Sisters to Us: A Pastoral Letter on Racism

NCCB, November 14, 1979

Racism is an evil which endures in our society and in our Church. Despite apparent advances and even significant changes in the last two decades, the reality of racism remains. In large part it is only the external appearances which have changed.

In 1958 we spoke out against the blatant forms of racism that divided people through discriminatory laws and enforced segregation. We pointed out the moral evil that denied human persons their dignity as children of God and their God-given rights.[1] A decade later in a second pastoral letter we again underscored the continuing scandal of racism and called for decisive action to eradicate it from our society.[2]

We recognize and applaud the readiness of many Americans to make new strides forward in reducing and eliminating prejudice against minorities. We are convinced that the majority of Americans realize that racial discrimination is both unjust and unworthy of this nation.

We do not deny that changes have been made, that laws have been passed, that policies have been implemented. We do not deny that the ugly external features of racism which marred our society have in part been eliminated. But neither can it be denied that too often what has happened has been only a covering over, not a fundamental change. Today the sense of urgency has yielded to an apparent acceptance of the status quo. The climate of crisis engendered by demonstrations, protests, and confrontation has given way to a mood of indifference; and other issues occupy our attention.

---

[1] *Discrimination and Christian Conscience.* National Catholic Welfare Conference. 1958.
[2] *National Race Crisis.* National Conference of Catholic Bishops. 1968.

In response to this mood, we wish to call attention to the persistent presence of racism and in particular to the relationship between racial and economic justice. Racism and economic oppression are distinct but inter-related forces which dehumanize our society. Movement toward authentic justice demands a simultaneous attack on both evils. Our economic structures are undergoing fundamental changes which threaten to intensify social inequalities in our nation. We are entering an era characterized by limited resources, restricted job markets and dwindling revenues. In this atmosphere, the poor and racial minorities are being asked to bear the heaviest burden of the new economic pressures.

This new economic crisis reveals an unresolved racism that permeates our society's structures and resides in the hearts of many among the majority. Because it is less blatant, this subtle form of racism is in some respects even more dangerous—harder to combat and easier to ignore. Major segments of the population are being pushed to the margins of society in our nation. As economic pressures tighten, those people who are often Black, Hispanic, Native American and Asian—and always poor—slip further into the unending cycle of poverty, deprivation, ignorance, disease, and crime. Racial identity is for them an iron curtain barring the way to a decent life and livelihood. The economic pressures exacerbate racism, particularly where poor white people are competing with minorities for limited job opportunities. The Church must not be unmindful of these economic pressures. We must be sensitive to the unfortunate and unnecessary racial tension that results from this kind of economic need.

Mindful of its duty to be the advocate for those who hunger and thirst for justice's sake, the Church cannot remain silent about the racial injustices in society and in its own structures. Our concern over racism follows, as well, from our strong commitment to evangelization. Pope John Paul II has defined evangelization as bringing consciences, both individual and social, into conformity with the Gospel. We would betray our commitment to evangelize ourselves and our society were we not to voice strongly our condemnation of attitudes and practices so contrary to the Gospel. Therefore, as the bishops of the United States, we once again address our pastoral reflections on racism to our brothers and sisters of all races.

We do this, conscious of the fact that racism is only one form of discrimination that infects our society. Such discrimination belies both our civil and religious traditions. The United States of America rests on a constitutional heritage that recognizes the equality, dignity, and inalienable rights of all its citizens. Further, we are heirs of a religious teaching which proclaims that all men and women, as children of God, are brothers and sisters. Every form of discrimination against individuals and groups—whether because of race, ethnicity, religion, gender, economic status, or national or cultural origin—is a serious injustice which has severely weakened our social fabric and deprived our country of the unique contributions of many of our citizens. While cognizant of these broader concerns, we wish to draw attention here to the particular form of discrimination that is based on race.

The Sin of Racism

Racism is a sin: a sin that divides the human family, blots out the image of God among specific members of that family, and violates the fundamental human dignity of those called to be children of the same Father. Racism is the sin that says some human beings are inherently superior and others essentially inferior because of race. It is the sin that makes racial characteristics the determining factor for the exercise of human rights. It mocks the words of Jesus: "Treat others the way you would have them treat you."[3] Indeed, racism is more than a disregard for the words of Jesus; it is a denial of the truth of the dignity of each human being revealed by the mystery of the Incarnation.

In order to find the strength to overcome the evil of racism, we must look to Christ. In Christ Jesus "there does not exist among you Jew or Greek, slave or freeman, male or female. All are one in Christ Jesus."[4] As Pope John Paul II has said so clearly, "Our spirit is set in one direction, the only direction for our intellect, will and heart is—toward Christ our Redeemer, toward Christ, the Redeemer of [humanity.]"[5] It is in Christ, then, that the Church finds the central cause for its commitment to justice, and to the struggle for the human rights and dignity of all persons.

When we give in to our fears of the other because he or she is of a race different from ourselves, when we prejudge the motives of others precisely because they are of a different color, when we stereotype or ridicule the other because of racial characteristics and heritage, we fail to heed the command of the Prophet Amos: "Seek good and not evil, that you may live; then truly will the Lord ... be with you as your claim! ... Then let justice surge like water, and goodness like an unfailing stream."[6]

Today in our country men, women, and children are being denied opportunities for full participation and advancement in our society because of their race. The educational, legal, and financial systems, along with other structures and sectors of our society, impede people's progress and narrow their access because they are Black, Hispanic, Native American or Asian. Racism exists not only among whites, however. It also resides in the attitudes and behavior of some who are members of minority groups themselves.

The structures of our society are subtly racist, for these structures reflect the values which society upholds. They are geared to the success of the majority and the failure of the minority; and members of both groups give un-

---

[3] Matthew, 7:12.
[4] Galatians, 3:28.
[5] Redemptor Hominis, 7. Pope John Paul II. 1979.
[6] Amos, 5:14, 24.

witting approval by accepting things as they are. Perhaps no single individual is to blame. The sinfulness is often anonymous but nonetheless real. The sin is social in nature in that each of us, in varying degrees, is responsible. All of us in some measure are accomplices. As our recent pastoral letter on moral values states: "The absence of personal fault for an evil does not absolve one of all responsibility. We must seek to resist and undo injustices we have not caused, lest we become bystanders who tacitly endorse evil and so share in guilt for it."[7]

Racism Is a Fact

Because the Courts have eliminated statutory racial discrimination and Congress has enacted civil rights legislation, and because some minority people have achieved some measure of success, many people believe that racism is no longer a problem in American life. The continuing existence of racism becomes apparent, however, when we look beneath the surface of our national life: as, for example, in the case of unemployment figures. In the first quarter of 1979, 5% of white Americans were unemployed; but for Blacks the figure was 11.4%; for Hispanics, 8.3%; and for Native Americans on reservations, as high as 40%. The situation is even more disturbing when one realizes that 35% of Black youth, 19.1% of Hispanic youth, and an estimated 60% of Native American youth are unemployed.[8] Quite simply, this means that an alarming proportion of tomorrow's adults are cut off from gainful employment—an essential prerequisite of responsible adulthood. These are the same youths presently suffering the crippling effects of a segregated educational system which in many cases fails to enlighten the mind and free the spirit, which too often inculcates a conviction of inferiority and which frequently graduates persons who are ill prepared and inadequately trained. In addition, racism raises its ugly head in the violence that frequently surrounds attempts to achieve racial balance in education and housing.

With respect to family life, we recognize that decades of denied access to opportunities have been for minority families a crushing burden. Racial discrimination has only exacerbated the harmful relationship between poverty and family instability.

Racism is only too apparent in housing patterns in our major cities and suburbs. Witness the deterioration of inner cities as well as the segregation of many suburban areas by means of the unjust practices of social steering and blockbusting. Witness also the high proportion of Hispanics, Blacks, and Indians on welfare and the fact that the median income of nonwhite families is

---

[7] *To Live in Christ Jesus,* Page 25. National Conference of Catholic Bishops. 1976.
[8] Precise data on youth unemployment among Native Americans are not available. The 60% unemployment figure is an estimate by the U.S. Department of Labor.

only 63% of the average white family income. Moreover, the gap between the rich and the poor is widening, not decreasing.

Racism is apparent when we note that the population in our prisons consists disproportionately of minorities; that violent crime is the daily companion of a life of poverty and deprivation; and that the victims of such crimes are also disproportionately nonwhite and poor. Racism is also apparent in the attitudes and behavior of some law enforcement officials and the unequal availability of legal assistance.

Finally, racism is sometimes apparent in the growing sentiment that too much is being given to racial minorities by way of affirmative action programs or allocations to redress long-standing imbalances in minority representation, and government-funded programs for the disadvantaged. At times, protestations claiming that all persons should be treated equally reflect the desire to maintain a *status quo* that favors one race and social group at the expense of the poor and the nonwhite.

Racism obscures the evils of the past and denies the burdens that history has placed upon the shoulders of our Black, Hispanic, Native American, and Asian brothers and sisters. An honest look at the past makes plain the need for restitution wherever possible—makes evident the justice of restoration and redistribution.

A Look at the Past

Racism has been a part of the social fabric of America since the beginning of European colonization. Whether it be the tragic past of the Native Americans, the Mexicans, the Puerto Ricans, or the Blacks, the story is one of slavery, peonage, economic exploitation, brutal repression, and cultural neglect. All have suffered indignity; most have been uprooted, defrauded or dispossessed of their lands; and none has escaped one or another form of collective degradation by a powerful majority. Our history is littered with the debris of broken promises and treaties, as well as lynchings and massacres that almost destroyed the Indians, humiliated the Hispanics, and crushed the Blacks.

But despite this tragic history, the racial minorities of our country have survived and increased. Not only that, but each racial group has sunk its roots deep in the soil of our culture, thus helping to give to the United States its unique character and its diverse coloration. The contribution of each racial minority is distinctive and rich; each has become a source of internal strength for our nation. The history of all gives a witness to a truth absorbed by now into the collective consciousness of Americans: their struggle has been a pledge of liberty and a challenge to future greatness.

Racism Today

Crude and blatant expressions of racist sentiment though they occasionally exist are today considered bad form; but racism itself persists in a covert way. Under the guise of other motives, it is manifest in the tendency to stereotype and marginalize whole segments of the population whose presence is perceived as a threat. It is manifest also in the indifference that replaces open hatred. The minority poor are seen as the dross of a post-industrial society—without skills, without motivation, without incentive. They are expendable. Many times the new face of racism is the computer print-out, the graph of profits and losses, the pink slip, the nameless statistic. Today's racism flourishes in the triumph of private concern over public responsibility, individual success over social commitment, and personal fulfillment over authentic compassion. Christian ideals of justice must be brought to bear in both the private and the public sector in order that covert racism be eliminated wherever it exists.

The new forms of racism must be brought face-to-face with the figure of Christ. It is Christ's word that is the judgment of this world; it is Christ's cross that is the measure of our response; and it is Christ's face that is the composite of all persons but in a most significant way of today's poor, today's marginal people, today's minorities.

God's Judgment and Promise
The Voice of Scripture

The Christian response to the challenges of our times is to be found in the Good News of Jesus. The words which signaled the start of his public ministry must be the watchword for every Christian response to injustice, "He unrolled the scroll and found the passage where it was written: The spirit of the Lord is upon me; therefore, he has anointed me. He has sent me to bring glad tidings to the poor, to proclaim liberty to captives, recovery of sight to the blind and release to prisoners, to announce a year of favor from the Lord. Rolling up the scroll he gave it back ... and sat down. ... 'Today this Scripture passage is fulfilled in your hearing.' "[9]

God's word proclaims the oneness of the human family—from the first words of Genesis, to the "Come, Lord Jesus" of the Book of Revelation. God's word in Genesis announces that all men and women are created in God's image; not just *some* races and racial types, but *all* bear the imprint of the Creator and are enlivened by the breath of his one Spirit.

In proclaiming the liberation of Israel, God's word proclaims the liberation of all people from slavery. God's word further proclaims that all people are accountable to and for each other. This is the message of that great parable of the Final Judgment: "When the Son of Man comes in his glory, escorted by all the angels of heaven ... all the nations will be assembled before him. Then he will separate them into two groups. ... The king will say to those on his right: 'Come. You have my Father's blessing! ... For I was hungry and you gave me food, I was thirsty and you gave me drink. I was

---

[9] Luke, 4:17–21.

a stranger and you welcomed me. . . . I assure you, as often as you did it for one of my least brothers, you did it for me.' "[10]

God's word proclaims that the person "who listens to God's word but does not put it into practice is like a man who looks into a mirror at the face he was born with . . . then goes off and promptly forgets what he looked like."[11] We have forgotten that we "are strangers and aliens no longer. . . . (We) are fellow citizens of the saints and members of the household of God. (We) form a building which rises on the foundation of the apostles and prophets, with Christ Jesus himself as the capstone."[12]

The Voice of the Church

This is the mystery of our Church, that all men and women are brothers and sisters, all one in Christ, all bear the image of the Eternal God. The Church is truly universal, embracing all races, for it is to be "the visible sacrament of this saving unity."[13] The Church, moreover, follows the example of its founder and, "through her children, is one with men of every condition, but especially with the poor and the afflicted."[14]

This Church has a duty to proclaim the truth about the human being as disclosed in the truth about Jesus Christ. As our Holy Father Pope John Paul II has written: "On account of the mystery of the Redemption (every human being) is entrusted to the solicitude of the Church." The human being is "the primary and fundamental way for the Church."[15]

It is important to realize in the case of racism that we are dealing with a distortion at the very heart of human nature. The ultimate remedy against evils such as this will not come solely from human effort. What is needed is the recreation of the human being according to the image revealed in Jesus Christ. For he reveals in himself what each human being can and must become.

How great, therefore, is that sin of racism which weakens the Church's witness as the universal sign of unity among all peoples! How great the scandal given by racist Catholics who would make the Body of Christ, the Church, a sign of racial oppression! Yet all too often the Church in our country has been for many a "white Church," a racist institution.

Each of us as Catholics must acknowledge a share in the mistakes and sins of the past. Many of us have been prisoners of fear and prejudice. We have preached the Gospel while closing our eyes to the racism it condemned. We have allowed conformity to social pressures to replace compliance with social justice.

---

[10] Matthew, 25:31–40.
[11] James, 1:23–24.
[12] Ephesians, 2:19–20.
[13] *Dogmatic Constitution on the Church,* 9.
[14] *Decree on the Church's Missionary Activity,* 12.
[15] *Redemptor Hominis,* 13, 14.

But past mistakes must not hinder the Church's response to the challenges of the present. Worldwide, the Church today is not just European and American; it is also African, Asian, Indian, and Oceanic. It is western, eastern, northern and southern, black and also brown, white and also red and yellow. In our own country, one quarter of the Catholics are Spanish-speaking. A million Black Catholics make Catholicism one of the largest denominations among Black Americans today. Among our nation's original inhabitants, the Native Americans, the Church's presence is increasingly becoming developed and expressed within the cultures of the various Native American tribes.

It is a fact that Catholic dioceses and religious communities across the country for years have committed selected personnel and substantial funds to relieve oppression and to correct injustices and have striven to bring the Gospel to the diverse racial groups in our land. The Church has sought to aid the poor and downtrodden, who for the most part are also the victims of racial oppression. But this relationship has been and remains two-sided and reciprocal; for the initiative of racial minorities, clinging to their Catholic faith, has helped the Church to grow, adapt, and become truly Catholic and remarkably diverse. Today in our own land the face of Catholicism is truly the face of all humanity—a face of many colors, a countenance of many cultural forms.

Yet more is needed. The prophetic voice of the Church, which is to be heard in every generation and even to the ends of the earth, must not be muted—especially not by the counter witness of some of its own people. Let the Church speak out, not only in the assemblies of the bishops, but in every diocese and parish in the land, in every chapel and religious house, in every school, in every social service agency, and in every institution that bears the name Catholic. As Pope John Paul II has proclaimed, the Church must be aware of the threats to humanity and of all that opposes the endeavor to make life itself more human. The Church must strive to make every element of human life correspond to the true dignity of the human person.[16] And during his recent visit to this country, Pope John Paul II discussed the direct implications of this for the Church in the United States.

"It will always remain one of the glorious achievements of this nation that, when people looked toward America, they received together with freedom also a chance for their own advancement. This tradition must be honored also today. The freedom that was gained must be ratified each day by the firm rejection of whatever wounds, weakens or dishonors human life. And so I appeal to all who love freedom and justice to give a chance to all in need, to the poor and the powerless. Break open the hopeless cycles of poverty and ignorance that are still the lot of too many of our brothers and sisters; the hopeless cycles of prejudices that linger on despite enormous progress toward effective equality in education and employment; the cycles of despair

---

[16] *Redemptor Hominis,* 14.

in which are imprisoned all those that lack decent food, shelter or employment. . . ."[17]

Therefore, let the Church proclaim for all to hear that the sin of racism defiles the image of God and degrades the sacred dignity of humankind which has been revealed by the mystery of the Incarnation. Let all know that it is a terrible sin that mocks the cross of Christ and ridicules the Incarnation. For the brother and sister of our Brother Jesus Christ are brother and sister to us.

The Voice of the World

We find God's will for us not only in the word of Scripture and in the teaching of his Church but also in the issues and events of secular society. "The Church . . . recognizes that worthy elements are found in today's social movements, especially an evolution toward unity, a process of wholesome socialization and of association in civic and economic realms."[18] Thus spoke the Church in the Second Vatican Council. In that same Council the Church admonished its members, especially the laity, to work in the temporal sphere on behalf of justice and the unity of humankind.[19]

With this in mind, we wish to pay special tribute to those who have struggled and struggle today on behalf of civil rights and economic justice in our own country. Nor do we overlook the United Nations' Universal Declaration of Human Rights which still speaks to the conscience of the entire world and the several international covenants which demand the elimination of discrimination based on race. None of these, unfortunately, have been ratified by our country, whereas we in America should have been the first to do so. All have a duty to heed the voice of God speaking in these documents.

Our Response

Racism is not merely one sin among many, it is a radical evil dividing the human family and denying the new creation of a redeemed world. To struggle against it demands an equally radical transformation, in our own minds and hearts as well as in the structure of our society.

Conversion is the every present task of each Christian. In offering certain guidelines for this change of heart as it pertains to racism, we note that these are only first steps in what ought to be a continuing dialogue throughout the Catholic community and the nation at large. In this context we would urge that existing programs and plans, such as those dealing with family ministry, parish renewal, and evangelization, be used as vehicles for implementing the measures addressed here.

---

[17] Homily at Battery Park, New York. Pope John Paul II. October, 1979.

[18] *Pastoral Constitution on the Church in the Modern World,* 42.

[19] *Pastoral Constitution on the Church in the Modern World,* 43.

Our Personal Lives

To the extent that racial bias affects our personal attitudes and judgments, to the extent that we allow another's race to influence our relationship and limit our openness, to the extent that we see yet close our hearts to our brothers and sisters in need[20]—to that extent we are called to conversion and renewal in love and justice.

As individuals we should try to influence the attitudes of others by expressly rejecting racial stereotypes, racist slurs, racist jokes, and racist remarks. We should influence the members of our families, especially our children, to be sensitive to the authentic human values and cultural contributions of each racial grouping in our country.

We should become more sensitive ourselves and thereby sensitize our acquaintances by learning more about how social structures inhibit the economic, educational, and social advancement of the poor. We should make a personal commitment to join with others in political efforts to bring about changes on behalf of justice for those who are victims of such deprivation.

Our Church Community

The Church too must be constantly attentive to the Lord's voice as he calls on his people daily not to harden their hearts.[21] We urge that on all levels the Catholic Church in the United States examine its conscience regarding attitudes and behavior toward Blacks, Hispanics, Native Americans, and Asians. We urge consideration of the evil of racism as it exists in the local Church and reflection upon the means of combatting it. We urge scrupulous attention at every level to insure that minority representation goes beyond mere tokenism and involves authentic sharing in responsibility and decision making.

We encourage Catholics to join hands with members of other religious groups in the spirit of ecumenism to achieve the common objectives of justice and peace. During the struggle for legal recognition of racial justice, an important chapter in American history was written as religious groups, Catholic, Protestant, and Jewish, joined hands in support of a civil rights movement which found much of its initiative and inspiration within the Black Protestant Church. This type of cooperation should continue to serve as a model for our times.

All too often in the very places where Blacks, Hispanics, Native Americans, and Asians are numerous, the Church's officials and representatives, both clerical and lay, are predominantly white. Efforts to achieve racial balance in government, the media, the armed services, and other crucial areas of secular life should not only be initiated but surpassed in the institutions and programs of the Catholic Church.

---

[20] I John, 3:17.
[21] Psalms, 94:8.

Particular care should be taken to foster vocations among minority groups.[22] Training for the priesthood, the permanent diaconate, and religious life should not entail an abandonment of culture and traditions or a loss of racial identity but should seek ways in which such culture and traditions might contribute to that training. Special attention is required whenever it is necessary to correct racist attitudes or behavior among seminary staff and seminarians. Seminary education ought to include an awareness of the history and the contributions of minorities as well as an appreciation of the enrichment of the liturgical expression, especially at the local parish level, which can be found in their respective cultures.

We affirm the teaching of Vatican II on the liturgy by noting that "the liturgy is the summit toward which the activity of the Church is directed."[23] The Church must "respect and foster the spiritual ... gifts of the various races and peoples"[24] and encourage the incorporation of these gifts into the liturgy.

We see the value of fostering greater diversity of racial and minority group representation in the hierarchy. Furthermore, we call for the adoption of an effective affirmative action program in every diocese and religious institution.

We strongly urge that special attention be directed to the plight of undocumented workers and that every effort be made to remove the fear and prejudice of which they are victims.

We ask in particular that Catholic institutions such as schools, universities, social service agencies, and hospitals, where members of racial minorities are often employed in large numbers, review their policies to see that they faithfully conform to the Church's teaching on justice for workers and respect for their rights. We recommend that investment portfolios be examined in order to determine whether racist institutions and policies are inadvertently being supported; and that, wherever possible, the capital of religious groups be made available for new forms of alternative investment, such as cooperatives, land trusts, and housing for the poor. We further recommend that Catholic institutions avoid the services of agencies and industries which refuse to take affirmative action to achieve equal opportunity and that the Church itself always be a model as an equal opportunity employer.

We recommend that leadership training programs be established on the local level in order to encourage effective leadership among racial minorities on all levels of the Church, local as well as national.

In particular, we recommend the active spiritual and financial support of

---

22 Concern for vocations from minority groups and the preparation of priests to serve in a multi-cultural and multi-racial society has been previously expressed in *The Program for Priestly Formation*, which was developed and approved by the National Conference of Catholic Bishops, 1976.

23 *Constitution on the Sacred Liturgy*, 10.

24 *Constitution on the Sacred Ligurgy*, 37.

associations and institutions organized by Catholic Blacks, Hispanics, Native Americans, and Asians within the Church for the promotion of ministry to and by their respective communities. There is also need for more attention to finding ways in which minorities can work together across racial and cultural lines to avoid duplication and competition among themselves. There is also a need for cooperative efforts between racial minorities and other social action groups, such as labor and the women's movement.

Finally, we urgently recommend the continuation and expansion of Catholic schools in the inner cities and other disadvantaged areas. No other form of Christian ministry has been more widely acclaimed or desperately sought by leaders of various racial communities. For a century and a half the Church in the United States has been distinguished by its efforts to educate the poor and disadvantaged, many of whom are not of the Catholic Faith. That tradition continues today in—among other places—Catholic schools, where so many Blacks, Hispanics, Native Americans, and Asians receive a form of education and formation which constitutes a key to greater freedom and dignity. It would be tragic if today, in the face of crying need and even near despair, the Church, for centuries the teacher and the guardian of civilization, should withdraw from this work in our own society. No sacrifice can be so great, no price can be so high, no short-range goals can be so important as to warrant the lessening of our commitment to Catholic education in minority neighborhoods. More affluent parishes should be made aware of this need and of their opportunity to share resources with the poor and needy in a way that recognizes the dignity of both giver and receiver.

The World at Large

Individuals move on many levels in our complex society: each of us is called to speak and act in many different settings. In each case may we speak and act according to our competence and as the Gospel bids us. With this our prayer, we refrain from giving here detailed answers to complex questions on which we ourselves have no special competence. Instead, we propose several guidelines of a general nature.

The difficulties of these new times demand a new vision and a renewed courage to transform our society and achieve justice for all. We must fight for the dual goals of racial and economic justice with determination and creativity. Domestically, justice demands that we strive for authentic full employment, recognizing the special need for employment of those who, whether men or women, carry the principal responsibility for support of a family. Justice also demands that we strive for decent working conditions, adequate income, housing, education, and health care for all. Government at the national and local levels must be held accountable by all citizens for the essential services which all are entitled to receive. The private sector should work with various racial communities to insure that they receive a just share of the profits they have helped to create.

Globally, we live in an interdependent community of nations. Some are rich; some, poor. Some are high consumers of the world's resources; some eke out an existence on a near starvation level. As it happens, most of the rich, consuming nations are white and Christian; most the world's poor are of other races and religions.

Concerning our relationship to other nations, our Christian faith suggests several principles. First, racial difference should not interfere with our dealing justly and peacefully with all other nations. Secondly, those nations which possess more of the world's riches must, in justice, share with those who are in serious need. Finally, the private sector should be aware of its responsibility to promote racial justice, not subordination or exploitation, to promote genuine development in poor societies, not mere consumerism and materialism.

Conclusion

Our words here are an initial response to one of the major concerns which emerged during the consultation on social justice which was part of the U.S. Catholic participation in the national bicentennial. The dialogue must go on among the Catholics of our country. We have proposed guidelines and principles and as the bishops of the Catholic Conference in the United States, we must give the leadership to this effort by a commitment of our time, of personnel and of significant financial resources. Others must develop the programs and plan operations. There must be no turning back along the road of justice, no sighing for bygone times of privilege, no nostalgia for simple solutions from another age. For we are children of the age to come, when the first shall be last and the last first, when blessed are they who serve Christ the Lord in all His brothers and sisters, especially those who are poor and suffer injustice.

Rural America

In 1972, the USCC spoke out on problems of rural America in a message entitled Where Shall the People Live? Its main point is that legislation is needed to end discrimination against family farmers, farm workers, and the rural poor. The bishops especially favor legislation that would inhibit further expansion of great farm corporations, and thus contribute to preserving the family farm.

The USCC Committee on Social Development and World Peace issued a call for regulation of the strip mining industry in the autumn of 1976. The bishops explain that lack of regulation caused great damage to the environment in Appalachia and severe hardship to the people in the affected areas. They fear the same might happen in Western states, and therefore they make several recommendations to public policymakers.

The bishops acknowledge a particular responsibility to address the strip mining issue because of the moral problems involved: "Our tradition teaches us that we are stewards of God's gifts of creation, not the least of which are our abundant energy resources." To be responsible stewards, people must avoid mistreating the land, and see that the goods of the earth are distributed in ways that provide for the basic needs of all people.

Early in 1979, the USCC's Committee on Social Development and World Peace returned to a theme first developed by the entire body of American bishops in 1972: the preservation of the family farm. The Committee's statement specifies why and how the family farm can be preserved. It contains many recommendations which the Church, farmers, and government can adopt to promote the continued existence of the family farm.

Where Shall the People Live?

USCC, November 1972

The problems which today confront rural America are in many ways inseparably linked to those of urban America. Either the problems of America's rural areas and America's cities will be solved together or they will not be solved at all.

This statement is amply documented by the facts of contemporary rural and urban life. Rural poverty and urban poverty are closely related. Poverty experienced in farm communities drives many people into cities, where their presence notably contributes to urban ills. Today over 70 percent of the people in America live on less than two percent of the land. The results: air and water pollution, transportation congestion, increasing urban crime, housing shortages. Yet at the same time the movement of people from the countryside to cities is continuing, often under the pressure of forces which make neither social nor economic sense.

Each census finds fewer farmers and weaker communities. Nearly two-thirds of all the ill-housed in our nation are in rural America. Education, health benefits, and other services in rural America lag behind those available in urban America. Many communities in the countryside are dying due to declining population; the people left behind find it increasingly difficult to sustain already inadequate standards of living. At the same time agricultural conglomerates are expanding, raising the possibility of their taking over virtually all farming in the United States. Few Americans seem aware of this development, and fewer still are concerned with the fundamental question of its desirability.

In 1973 the National Catholic Rural Life Conference, which in 1968 became part of the United States Catholic Conference as its Division of Rural Life, marks its 50th anniversary. As a result of the vision of its founder, Archbishop Edwin O'Hara, and the hard work of leaders such as Monsignor Luigi Ligutti, it has played an important role in the history of the Catholic Church in the United States. However, many of the problems which brought this agency into existence not only continue to exist today but if anything are more acute than they were 50 years ago. The United States faces pressing challenges concerning population distribution, economic opportunity, and the conservation of natural resources. These are issues with significant moral and spiritual implications, which demand the serious attention of all Americans and, in particular, the nation's churches. In view of this we wish, on this 50th anniversary of the National Catholic Rural Life Conference, to address ourselves to some of the central questions which today confront rural

America—and all America—in the belief that the future of our nation's cities and suburbs, as well as its rural communities, will be determined in large measure by the answers which Americans give to them.

The Problem

Rooted in the pioneering efforts of rural leaders of the Church, the work of the National Catholic Rural Life Conference throughout its 50-year history has been directed to the spiritual, social and economic betterment of rural people. This commitment has been founded not only on the belief that rural Americans are entitled to the same material and cultural advantages as other Americans, but also on the conviction that the best interests of the entire nation are served when the needs and aspirations of rural America are met.

Today, however, the issue is not simply the well-being of farm people but their very existence as a people. In recent years hundreds of thousands of farm families have been forced off the land by low prices, soaring costs and high taxes. There are fewer than three million farms in the United States today, a decrease of more than 25 percent in a decade. It has been predicted that, if present trends continue, within 15 years about half of America's farmers, efficient though small, will quit the land, leaving production largely in the hands of big farms and corporations.

Some claim that the alleged efficiency of the large farm conglomerates— an efficiency which has never been proven—permits them to drive farm people from the land to the cities. In honesty, those who advance such claims should include in their cost accounting the vastly increased expenditures required to meet the needs of these new urban poor. They should include the social and human costs resulting from the needless shift of population from vacated farm homes to overcrowded cities and suburbs. They should include the ecological damage to soil, water and food produced by attitudes and practices that treat agriculture as an industrial venture rather than a biological enterprise.

Such trends in American agriculture, and the huge social costs that accompany them, should not be written off simply as inevitable consequences of technological progress. Technology is a factor in the situation but it need not have these results. At its heart this is a question of social policy to be weighed and decided by the American people. Agricultural technology could be used to produce more socially beneficial developments than those we have witnessed to date. It could, for example, be employed to strengthen the commercial family farm of moderate size which, up to now, has provided Americans with an abundance of food and fiber at very low cost without disruption of the God-given ecological balance in nature. It could provide farm families with a host of sorely needed social advantages without driving them off the land. It could foster the growth of rural industry and rural area development. It could bring increased cultural opportunities and expanded health facilities to the countryside.

The general failure of these benefits to materialize in rural America up to now is not the result of technological or social necessity, but of mistaken policy and practice. Laissez-faire and adaptive approaches to farm problems must now be repudiated and rejected. The laissez-faire approach allows harsh forces of uncontrolled competition to drive less prosperous farmers out of agriculture. The adaptive approach goes so far as to employ that powerful influence of government and educational institutions, including land grant universities, to accelerate the migration of families from the land. This should not be permitted to happen.

The Solution

In face of such powerful influences and interests the individual farmer is helpless. His "solitary voice," as Pope John XXIII said, "speaks to the winds." (*Mater et Magistra,* 146) It is essential for farmers to unite and cooperate, as the Pope emphasized in his great encyclical. In light of this there is critical need for the great farm organizations—the Farm Bureau, the Farmer's Union, the National Farmers Organization, the Grange—as well as commodity groups and farm workers, to set aside their differences and join in an effective united effort based on the positive contribution that each can make to rural America. Without such unity the efforts of farmers to secure fair prices and beneficial farm legislation are likely not to succeed in time to check the movement of people from the countryside to crowded cities. Unless they stand together, their voices will go unheard in the halls of government where decisions affecting their future are made.

Other forms of cooperation among farmers are also needed. "It is necessary that farmers form among themselves mutual aid societies; that they establish professional associations." (*Mater et Magistra,* 143) Many such organizations, of which cooperatives are a notable example, now exist. But they should exhibit a stronger Christian commitment to support the smaller producer and businessman. This is the view of Pope John, and has been the view of the National Catholic Rural Life Conference for five decades.

There is need, too, for farmers to join hands with other members of the rural community to work for common goals. Farm workers, for so long the most forgotten laboring men in America, are now seeking allies in their efforts to achieve a decent standard of living for themselves and their families. Rural small businessmen are dependent on the maintenance of a rural population base for their livelihood. All these, the people of rural America, must acknowledge their interdependence and join in efforts on behalf of the common good.

In recent years government has shown increased sensitivity to the needs of rural people and greater willingness to address those needs. In particular, Congress deserves commendation for the recent steps it has taken in this regard. At the same time, however, legislators and government officials must continue to examine the social and economic trends in rural America and evaluate their consequences for the nation. Our laws still embody many injustices which discriminate against family farmers, farm workers and the rural poor. For example, our tax laws still permit "write-off" advantages for those who invest in farming merely to offset profits from other sources and our labor relations and labor standards laws still exclude or extend only limited protections to farm workers. These, and all such injustices, should be remedied as soon as possible.

Prompt legislative action is required to assist family farmers and inhibit the further expansion of giant farm corporations. This should include prohibiting laws, effective limits on federal payments for land retirement and crop reduction, and even graduated land taxes. Although such legislation may be regarded as controversial by some, it is surely preferable to inaction, whose consequence would be to create in the United States the situation which today exists in some other countries, where ownership of the land has fallen into the hands of a few, leading to discontent among the landless and to angry demands for land reform. The current trend in land ownership is a serious social issue that demands the urgent attention of all Americans.

Appropriate legislative action to keep the land in the hands of those who work it will, however, be only a first step, albeit an essential one. It must be accompanied by continuing efforts on the part of public and private agencies and rural people themselves to ensure an adequate economic base for rural communities. Lacking such a base, the socially important objectives of widely diffused ownership of the land will not be realized. We feel that the wide ownership of land is vital to the future of America. In the words of Pope John, "Today more than ever the wider distribution of private ownership ought to be forcefully championed." (*Mater et Magistra,* 115)

Equitable prices for agricultural products are of first importance in creating and maintaining this base. Also needed are efforts to foster rural industry and develop common services in rural communities for preserving, processing and transporting farm products. (Cf. *Mater et Magistra,* 141) The rural economy could be further strengthened by other small industries, tourism, and the development of recreational facilities. Accomplishing these objectives will require the creation of closer, cooperative relationships among the rural communities.

Today, fortunately, more and more Americans are coming to realize that our nation, blessed with an abundance of land, must yet make better use of its green space so that migration from countryside to city will be greatly reduced, for the sake of both. The further congestion of urban areas can only complicate their problems while the problems of the countryside grow simultaneously more acute. The needs of rural Americans must be met—and met in rural America—by providing them with more opportunity for the management of their own economic affairs. Such opportunity can be guaranteed through increased ownership of property and through mutual self-help organizations such as cooperatives.

The Church can play a unique leadership role in promoting these changes in rural America. In spite of the decreasing population base, it must maintain and strengthen its ministry to farm and rural people and articulate the redeeming message of Christ in terms of the spiritual values inherent in their way of life. Through pastoral training in our seminaries and through programs of continuing education, it must educate priests to the socio-economic realities of rural America and prepare them to exercise a role of rural community leadership.

For half a century the National Catholic Rural Life Conference has sought to make its policies operative through diverse programs. It has long been an educator in rural values through workshops, lectures and literature. It has fostered the development of liturgy oriented to rural concerns. It has advocated government programs and policies which better meet the needs of rural people. Through diocesan rural life directors, it has sponsored many local-level programs and observances. In the South and Southwest, in Appalachia and overseas, it has cooperated in countless projects to encourage self-help efforts among the poor.

As the National Catholic Rural Life Conference marks its 50th anniversary we extend our congratulations and thanks to its board, staff and members for their efforts over the years. Problems of urbanization, farm production, and rural poverty continue to oppress people in our nation and abroad; and we shall continue to look to the Rural Life Conference for leadership in carrying out the mission of the Church in these areas. The ministry of the Church is a shared one, and it is through agencies such as the National Catholic Rural Life Conference that the People of God can most effectively participate in this shared responsibility. As we unite our intentions with those of the Rural Life Conference on this anniversary, we invite all people of good will to join with us in efforts to ensure that renewed commitment today will lead to a better, more just, more Christian world tomorrow.

Strip Mining: A Call for Regulation

USCC, Committee on Social
Development and World Peace
September 16, 1976

1. During the last several years we have witnessed in the United States a substantial increase in the practice of strip mining to obtain coal and other minerals. This has been due primarily to the rising demand for the development of our domestic energy resources.

2. The issues involved in the development of a just U.S. energy policy are many and complex. Our intention here is not to treat all the aspects and ramifications of such a policy, but rather to deal with the strip mining of coal. We feel that this is a particularly pressing issue deserving of our immediate attention.

3. In order to meet the demand for coal, the federal government is encouraging a rapid escalation of strip mining in Appalachia and in the western states. In many areas this practice has been virtually unregulated, causing severe damage to the environment and great hardship to the people in the surrounding communities.

4. In the mountains of Appalachia, flooding and landslides caused by unstable high walls and lands left barren from strip mining, have destroyed homes, property and roads and have accounted for the loss of many lives in the region. The exploitation of the rich coal and mineral resources especially in central Appalachia, has resulted in chronic unemployment and poverty for the people who live in the strip mined areas. The Bishops of Appalachia, in 1975, expressed their deep concern for the "powerlessness" of the people within the region to have control over their own lives and lands.

5. In the western states, without strict regulation, this development poses threats similar to those experienced by the people of Appalachia. Farmers and ranchers are confronting increased pressures to sell their lands to strip mining companies. Indian tribes, particularly those whose lands are held in trust by the federal government, have faced similar pressures. In addition, proposed strip mining operations and coal conversion plants will require vast amounts of water, a resource already scarce in many parts of the West.

6. The Church has a particular responsibility to address the moral questions involved in the issue of strip mining. Our Tradition teaches us that we are stewards of God's gifts of creation, not the least of which are our abundant energy resources. As responsible stewards we must take care to see that these gifts are distributed in ways that provide for the basic needs of all peo-

ple and that the development of these resources does not infringe on the basic human rights of people nor mistreat the land from which they come.

7. The Catholic Committee of Appalachia, the National Catholic Rural Life Conference, the Campaign for Human Development, as well as several dioceses and religious congregations, have worked diligently to apply Catholic social teaching to the complex problems associated with this issue and to serve the people and communities adversely affected by strip mining. We are greatly encouraged by their efforts and wish to join our voices with theirs in calling for a more just and responsible approach to the production and use of our coal and mineral resources.

8. Specifically, we feel that national regulatory legislation is urgently needed to promote the responsible development of our coal and mineral resources and to protect the people and lands affected by such production. Until such time as new national legislation is adopted, state laws should be strictly enforced. National legislation should at least:

- Prohibit strip mining of lands which cannot be returned to their original contour or productivity;
- Prohibit strip mining on prime agricultural lands;
- Protect the owner-operators of surface lands;
- Require and set strict guidelines for reclamation wherever strip mining is permitted;
- Provide for the reclamation of lands previously stripped and abandoned;
- Establish methods of determining priority uses for water and other resources needed for strip mining;
- Require public participation in determining whether individual sites should be strip mined;
- Require the coal industry to observe the laws of individual states regarding strip mining when these are stricter than federal law;
- Promote research and development of less damaging mining techniques;
- Preserve the option for individual states to enforce stricter mining and reclamation standards on non-federal lands than provided under federal law;
- Provide adequate funding of enforcement agencies to enable them to fully implement strict regulatory programs.

The Family Farm

*USCC, Committee on Social
Development and World Peace
February 14, 1979*

Introduction

The history of the Catholic Church in the United States is bound up with our great urban centers and the growth of organized labor. Nourished by the faith of countless immigrants who built city parishes and forged a living in the blackened factories of the Industrial Revolution, the Church fought for justice where the need was most pressing. The Lord in his goodness blessed this effort with spectacular success. Today's industrial worker would seem a marvel of prosperity to his forebears who crept in poverty through the streets of New York and Boston, and Catholics are proud of their part in fostering this transformation.

Yet the Church, in its social ministry, has never focused solely on urban problems. The society of the Bible was essentially an agricultural society. The question of who would manage the land, and for what ends, was central to the health of the nation. Many passages in the Old Testament that refer to Israel's covenant with God reflect this practical interest. We read in the Book of Proverbs, for example: "For the upright will dwell in the land, and the honest will dwell in it; but the wicked will be cut off from the land, the faithless will be rooted out of it" (2:21-2). In the same way, the custom of the Jubilee Year aimed to ensure that not even the humblest family was divorced forever from its ancestral fields. The New Testament continues this general theme. As the language of his parables shows, Jesus spoke out of a rural tradition, and his proclamation of justice for the poor has immediate application to rural life.

Scripture thus provided the basis for social action in town and country America. The founding of the National Catholic Rural Life Conference in 1923 merely formalized a concern that has expressed itself, undramatically perhaps, since Catholics helped settle the wilderness. That concern was reaffirmed most recently by the delegates to the 1976 conference, A Call to Action. Among the resolutions they approved was one seconding "those movements and organizations designed to preserve the land both as a gift from God and as a precious natural resource. The activities of [appropriate] offices and agencies will include support of legislation to stop the abuse of land speculation; exploitation of agricultural workers, including the undocumented alien; large agribusiness and concentrated land holdings; and will express continued support of the family farm."[1]

The Family Farm: Moral Implications

In referring to the family farm, the Call to Action delegates take a position that characterizes the Church as a whole. Pope John XXIII's encyclical, *Mater et Magistra*, which devotes entire sections to social justice in rural settings, gives defense of a family-based agriculture special emphasis. The Holy Father says: "However, those who hold [humanity] and the family in proper esteem ... surely look toward some form of agricultural enterprise, and particularly of the family type, which is modeled upon the [human] community wherein mutual relationships of members and the organizations of the enterprise itself are conformed to norms of justice and Christian teaching. And these [people] strive mightily that such organization of rural life be realized as far as circumstances permit" (142).

Pope John's endorsement of the family farm system finds a ready echo in American hearts. The family farm is one of our most pervasive cultural symbols. Statesmen since colonial times have heaped praise on the institution, and such landmark legislation as the Pre-Emption Act of 1841, the Homestead Act of 1862 and the Reclamation Act of 1902 has elevated its encouragement and preservation to the status of national policy.

Nevertheless, it is in a state of rapid decline. The number of farms in the United States peaked at some 6.8 million in the mid-1930s. Today there are less than 3 million. While the trend has been decelerating in recent years, we are still losing about 30,000 farms annually.[2] These statistics take on a human face when set beside a second set of figures. In the 59 years since 1920, the number of those living on farms has dropped 76 percent, from 32 million to about 8 million. No one knows how many families these people represent, but it is clear that in the middle years of the 20th century the family farm, so prominent in the American imagination, has been terribly weakened as an American institution.

The number of acres under cultivation has not fallen. Farms have simply grown much larger. The structure of American agriculture is a pyramid, with a great number of small, part-time farms at the bottom, a layer of substantial operations in the middle and a very few large farms at the top. Economic power in modern farming lies near the apex of the pyramid. In 1977, 69 percent of our farms (1,875,000) were small enterprises with gross incomes of

---

[1]The Call to Action Conference. Resolution #3, "The Church and the Rural Community," *Neighborhood*. Quoted in *A Call to Action: An Agenda for the Catholic Community/Resources for Parish and Diocesan Programs* (Washington, D.C.: National Conference of Catholic Bishops/United States Catholic Conference, 1977), pp. 102–103.

[2]There were 2.77 million farms in 1975, 2.74 million in 1976, 2.71 million in 1977, and 2.67 million in 1978. *Farm Numbers* (Washington, D.C.: Crop Reporting Board, U.S. Department of Agriculture, 1978), p. 1.

less than $20,000. Though they formed the majority, they accounted for only 11 percent of all agricultural sales. Twenty-five percent (669,000) earned between $20,000 and $100,000, and accounted for about 36 percent of agricultural sales. The largest six percent of our farms (162,000), those with gross incomes in excess of $100,000, sold a staggering 53 percent of the agricultural products in that year.[3]

Americans are receiving their food from fewer and fewer hands, and the pace of change is dramatic. A recent study estimates that by 1986 nearly all the agricultural products sold in this country may come from just 10 percent of the farms.[4] If this prediction proves true, it is hard to see much future for the family farm. Most of the operations in that 10 percent will still be controlled by families. They will be so large, however, and there will be so few of them, that traditional family farming as a significant element in our economic structure will be virtually a thing of the past.

The observation that many giant farms are family farms raises the question of definition. What is a family farm? Because conditions and crops vary so widely across the country, one cannot realistically assign an arbitrary size to the family operation. A family growing vegetables on irrigated land in California can make a living on 10 acres. At the other extreme, one large family can cultivate several thousand acres of wheat in North Dakota.

It is essential that the definition take into account the demands of social conscience. In *Gaudium et Spes*, the bishops of the Universal Church said: "By its very nature private property has a social quality deriving from the communal purpose of earthly goods. If this social quality is overlooked, property often becomes an occasion of greed and of serious disturbances" (71). We challenge the notion that the size of the family farm is limited only by the number of acres a farmer can cover with sophisticated machinery. For us, the family farm is a unit engaged in the production of food, fiber or timber which is owned or managed by a family or partnership of families that does all or most of the work of running it, which implies a personal relationship to the land, which is intended for transfer from generation to generation within the family, and which is small enough to allow for widespread ownership of agricultural land by resident farmers and to permit the responsible stewardship of natural resources.

In defending the family farm, then, we are primarily interested in those operations that fall into the small and moderate-sized range, where the family earns a substantial part of its income from agriculture. These two classes of farms face somewhat different problems, because the small farmer is almost always a part-time farmer. There is sufficient similarity between the groups to justify treating them together, however.

---

[3]Peter M. Emerson, *Public Policy and the Changing Structure of American Agriculture* (Washington, D.C.: Congressional Budget Office, 1978), p. 10.

[4]Leo V. Mayer, *Agricultural Financial Issues and Policy Alternatives Raised by the Farm Protest Movement of 1977–78*. A Congressional Research Service Report, March 10, 1978, p. 19.

Human Values Related to Family Farming

The twenty-fourth Psalm opens with these words: "The Lord's are the earth and its fullness; the world and those who dwell in it." Although it has been romanticized in American folklore, farm life can be hard. It confers no automatic nobility upon the individual; farmers face the same temptations to materialism and superficiality as the rest of us, and perhaps as often succumb. Nevertheless, those who see agriculture as more than an occupation feel that farmers are uniquely situated to realize the central truth the psalmist states. They live in close touch with the earth, cooperating with nature in the production of nature's gift of food. Dependent for their livelihood on forces they cannot control, farmers have their hand on the pulse of the created world and feel the rhythms running through all life, plant, animal and human. Once clarified by an acceptance of revealed religion, this inner knowledge can inspire a reverence for the land and the inhabitants of the land. Then farmers can become like the "little people" of the Bible, open in their humility to the ways of the Lord.

These values apply to the individual. We must not forget, however, that the farm is essentially a communal enterprise, providing a solid foundation for family life. While strong families thrive in all settings—urban, suburban and rural—the farm environment encourages the development of patience, self-reliance, a simplicity of outlook and the particular bond that comes when father and mother and children join in earning their common bread. This aspect of life on the land deserves special emphasis at a time when the Church in the United States is preparing for the Year of the Family in 1980.[5]

Mention of the farm mother raises an important consideration. To the popular mind, the American farmer is a man who preserves the family heritage by passing on his land to his sons. The woman is always quietly in the background. This image distorts reality. At least one-half the people on farms are women. Besides serving as wife and mother, many of them contribute heavily to the operation of the family business. In some cases, indeed, a woman is the head of the household; the "farmer himself" is really the farmer herself.

Our defense of the family farm is in part a defense of the private and family values it can foster. These values have had the firm backing of the Church. In *Mater et Magistra,* Pope John remarks: "Since everything that makes for [humanity's] dignity, perfection and development seems to be involved in agricultural labor, it is proper that [people] dedicate work of this kind to the most provident God who directs all events for the salvation of [humanity]" (149). It is interesting to note that secular society seems to be

---

[5]See *The Plan of Pastoral Action for Family Ministry: A Vision and Strategy* (Washington, D.C.: National Conference of Catholic Bishops/United States Catholic Conference, 1978). Among the developments that "can contribute to an erosion of the health and vitality of the family," the bishops list "the spread of giant agri-business at the expense of the small family farm" (p. 6).

adopting some of the same attitudes. The last decade has witnessed a "back to nature" movement, characterized by a reversal of migration patterns from rural areas, new commitments to the simple way of life and the establishment of group farming operations. These developments, though their depth is yet unproved, point to the power with which the land and rural ways still call to modern humanity.

The Family Farm and Food Production

Besides its implications for personal values, the small and moderate-sized family farm is the basis for a humane, responsible and effective national food production system. The alternative to this system is one dominated by large investor-owned corporations and massive farms. The possibility of a corporate takeover seems remote if we consider only the number of acres that publicly-held firms own. As yet, relatively few farms are in corporate hands, and most of the corporations in question are family businesses. It is not necessary to own farmland in order to control agricultural production, however. Many farmers sign sales contracts with large firms in which they agree to grow their crops to certain specifications and deliver them at a certain time. The company agrees in turn to buy the produce at the price the contract specifies.

Using the contract system and their holdings in agricultural land, investor-owned corporations are now extremely prominent in the production of poultry, sugar, citrus fruits and vegetables for processing, and have substantial interests in other commodities. The 1974 Census of Agriculture notes that they control over one-fourth of our total farm output. It is reasonable to believe, given the high price of land and the economic advantages to be gained, that the corporate share in agricultural production will grow at an even more rapid rate in the years ahead.[6]

The consequences of a massive transition to a corporate-controlled system of food production are already becoming apparent. Sensitive consumers are aware of the decline in nutrition and taste that corporate practices seem to impose, and have begun to protest the introduction of such innovations as the hard tomato bred to withstand machine picking. Of even greater concern is the potential for price manipulation in food marketing. The Church and the United States Congress have stated that every person, rich or poor, has a right to eat regardless of his or her ability to pay for food. What assurance is there that this right would be secure if our food supply came under the control of corporations?[7]

---

[6]V. James Rhodes and Leonard R. Kyle, "A Corporate Agriculture," *Who Will Control U.S. Agriculture?* Special Publication 28 (Urbana-Champaign: University of Illinois, 1973).
[7]For a fuller discussion of the implications of corporate control of agriculture, see Jim Hightower, "The Industrialization of Food," *The People's Land,* ed. Peter Barnes (Emmaus, Pa.: Rodale Press, 1975), pp. 81–85.

The Family Farm and Land Ownership

The family farm system is a system of land ownership. One of the strongest guarantees of human dignity and of democratic freedoms is the widespread personal ownership of productive property. The decline in the number of small businesses, including family farms, is a symptom of the erosion of this guarantee. According to calculations based on the 1974 census, 62,000 farmers own 24 percent of all privately-held land in the United States.

Statistics on farm consolidation can be somewhat misleading, however. Census data reveals that in 1974 about one-third of agricultural land was rented. The great bulk of this land is in small parcels. Non-farm investors of various kinds own it, ranging from the speculator to the heir no longer active in agriculture. While the concentration of ownership remains an important issue, it is a singularly difficult one to define, since large numbers of individuals still hold title to American farmland.

The problem, then, is not so much private ownership as farmer ownership. The ideal family farmer is the resident owner-operator, the man (or woman) whose land is his home and livelihood. The land is a gift from God, and the farmer should pass it on unimpaired to the next generation. The renter may not hold his lease five years from now. No matter how conscientious he may be, he cannot be expected to have the same feel for his farm as the person who sees it as the link that binds his family together in space and through time. Stewardship of our most basic natural resource depends heavily on maintaining the farm as a stable homestead.

This ideal is quickly slipping away. Agricultural land prices have tripled in some areas since 1970. In many cases, the only way a family can make a start in farming or control enough land to compete successfully is to rent part or all of its holdings. This sad reality leads us to acquiesce in the rental system for the present, but we strongly oppose it as a permanent feature of the agricultural economy. The future must provide opportunities for tenants to become owners. Farmers, consumers, the fabric of American culture in general will be the poorer in the absence of such opportunities.

The Church's Interest

In summary, concern for the individual and family values associated with farm life, for a family-based food production system, and for principles related to the ownership of land and the stewardship of natural resources converge to determine the Church's interest in the preservation of the family farm. It is primarily a moral interest. One cannot discuss the situation without dealing in practical ways with economic issues, and we address these issues in this document. Our primary prupose, however, is to treat the decline of the family farm, and suggest ways of halting or even reversing that decline, in the context of our commitment to social justice. In doing so, we join other Christian denominations that have already made formal statements on agricultural policy, including the United Presbyterian Church in the U.S.A., the Church of the Brethren, the United Methodist Church, the American Lutheran Church and the Lutheran Church in America.

The Decline of the Family Farm: Causes

Economic and Cultural Developments

The reasons for the precipitous decline of the family farm in this country are clear enough in outline. America flourished with the Industrial Revolution and the capitalist system that fueled it. Especially in the 20th century, the focus of economic activity has shifted from the small town with its light industry, limited services and surrounding farms to the city with its huge business and financial concerns. As the sphere of the agricultural sector narrowed and rural America stagnated, people inevitably were forced off the land. Lured by the hope of employment, they rushed to the growing metropolitan centers.

This economic shift has been compounded by a cultural shift to urban life and urban values. In literary image, the idyllic world of Tom Sawyer shrank and grew dark until, by a strange magic, it emerged as the dull, cramped Main Street of Carol Kennicott. Considering this atmosphere, where people espousing traditional rural ways were hicks and hayseeds, it is small wonder that Johnny left the land. Not only did he need a job, he was under psychological pressure to be modern, to go where the action was. To some extent, this set of attitudes still operates to alienate the rural resident from cultural roots.

The "Bigger Is Better" Philosophy

The American economy has evolved rapidly from one dependent on relatively small-scale structures to one based on national and multinational corporations. This development has spawned a certain orientation summed up in the phrase "bigger is better." We achieved unmatched material prosperity by adapting technology to ever larger production and distribution systems. As a result, the majority of Americans has uncritically accepted the idea that greater size equals greater economic efficiency and that greater economic efficiency alone spells progress. This belief stimulates a drive for expansion in all sectors of the economy as the keystone of our national pursuit of wealth.

The Industrialization of Agriculture

American farmers have been as deeply affected by the "bigger is better" philosophy as any other group, and the industrialization of agriculture has enabled them to put their ambitions into practice. Since the days of the horse-drawn reaper, machinery has progressively replaced labor in agricultural production. The increasing refinement of farming technology and the availability of abundant cheap energy have made it possible for a single farm family to cultivate more and more land, spurring a decline in the number of farms.

Of course, farm machinery is extremely expensive. These technological developments would have had little impact in the absence of capital to take advantage of them. Since World War II, the requisite capital has poured into agriculture from a variety of sources. Farmers themselves have generated much of it. Successful individuals used their profits and equity to buy machines and the additional land to utilize them efficiently. Other capital has come from non-farm people, the American or foreign investor who sees farmland as a sound buy, or wants to take advantage of the tax laws. Finally, corporations have invested in agriculture with the same motives as individuals or, in some cases, with the hope of increasing their profits through vertical integration.

Thus, the dynamics and even the spirit of our economic system have worked powerfully to bring about a growing consolidation of productive land in fewer and fewer farms. In 1954, 65 percent of all purchases of farmland involved complete farm units. Less than one-half as many transactions, 29 percent, were for farm enlargement. In 1977, 58 percent of the purchases were made for purposes of enlargement, while 29 percent represented the transfer of complete units.[8]

The economic patterns at work are self-perpetuating. It is generally recognized that the fully mechanized one-person farm produces food and fiber about as efficiently as large operations.[9] These bigger farms still enjoy competitive advantages, however, because they generate higher net incomes, they can buy and sell in volume and they have the financial base to withstand a bad year or two. As long as farmers see benefits in growth and as long as the technology and capital that facilitate growth are present, large farms can expand by swallowing small farms. The size factor, left to operate without modification, may well render the small or moderate-sized family farm an economic impossibility.

There are at least three things that could reverse this gloomy outlook. The first, government policy, is discussed below. The second is the depletion of worldwide supplies of oil. Large farms are highly energy-intensive. If petroleum products grow scarce and prices skyrocket, the profit margins of these operations might erode dramatically. In that case, the nation might be

---

[8]Larry A. Walker and John F. Jones, *Farm Real Estate Market Developments, February 1977 to February 1978* (Washington, D.C.: Economics, Statistics and Cooperatives Service, U.S. Department of Agriculture, 1978), p. 13.

[9]The classic study on this point is Warren R. Bailey, *The One-Man Farm*, ERS 519 (Washington, D.C.: Economic Research Service, U.S. Department of Agriculture, 1973). Both earlier and later studies confirm Bailey's findings. For a more recent analysis, see Bruce F. Hall and E. Philip LeVeen, "Farm Size and Economic Efficiency: The Case of California," *American Journal of Agricultural Economics*, Vol. 60, No. 4 (November 1978), 591, 597.

forced to adopt a "post-industrial agriculture" based on relatively small, labor-intensive, localized farms.

The third possibility is a change of heart among farmers. With characteristic zeal, Isaiah declares: "Woe to you who join house to house, who connect field with field, till no room remains, and you are left to dwell alone in the midst of the land!" (5:8). Our genuine concern for all farmers leads us to beg them not to crush one another by engaging in destructive competition.

Restricted Entry into Farming

The forces that encourage farm consolidation combine with other economic trends to deny access to families seeking to enter agriculture. The growth policies of large operators, the activities of foreign and domestic speculators and corporate investors, the pressure to develop farmland for residential or other uses, and general affluence and inflation all work to push up the price of land. As a result, would-be farmers need prohibitive amounts of capital; in the Midwest, they have to raise at minimum a quarter of a million dollars. It is no accident that the figures given above on farmland purchases show a great reduction in farming "starts."

Government Policy

Some would argue that government policy, especially on the federal level, is at least as important as market forces in speeding the decline of the family farm. Tax laws favor the larger operators or make it difficult to hold a farm together.[10] Federally-supported research through the land-grant university system has historically stimulated the spread of ever-bigger farms.[11] Department of Agriculture policy, in ways both subtle and blunt, has worked to the disadvantage of small family enterprises.[12] Finally, the economic benefits of federal commodity and insurance programs, which are based on volume of production, have gone disproportionately to large farms. In 1976, the top 17 percent of American farms in terms of sales received 60 percent of government payments.[13]

Other Causes

The wide abandonment of diversified agriculture has had a negative impact on family farming. The farmer who raises both corn and cattle is less vulnerable to market fluctuations than the one who specializes in corn only. Moreover, urban sprawl takes many acres of agricultural land out of produc-

---

[10]Emerson, p. 51.

[11]Emerson, p. 55.

[12]Emerson, p. 45. "In this section, six areas of public policy involvement that affect the structure of farming are examined. A major conclusion is that federal policy has on the whole discouraged small farm operations and led to greater concentration in farming."

[13]Mayer, p. 39.

tion each year, while the construction of the interstate highway system and the proliferation of electric transmission lines have made cultivation more difficult on thousands of farms. Credit policies tend to increase the advantages of large operators since, in general, the greater the size of the loan the less interest the lender charges. Though relatively minor in themselves, all these elements contribute to the truly desperate situation family farmers face in the America of the 1970s.

The Decline of the Family Farm: Consequences

Economic Considerations

As we have seen, many would defend the movement towards consolidation in agriculture as progress. From a certain perspective, it is progress. If bigger is better, American agriculture has immeasurably improved from its condition prior to World War II. The nation produces its food with much less labor, freeing people to work at other tasks. Output has risen dramatically even as the number of farms has fallen. Marketing and processing concerns find it easier and cheaper to deal with a relatively small group of big producers, resulting in economies of scale. The continuation of present trends seems to promise more benefits along these same lines.

Upon closer examination, however, the matter is not quite so simple. Some fundamental questions suggest themselves, even when we confine ourselves to economics. The family farm system produces an abundant food supply. Why alter it when there is no indication that total production would rise with increased consolidation?[14] The family farm system is already efficient. Why seek further economies which are likely to be marginal, if they materialize at all?[15] Finally, do economic gains in agriculture necessarily mean economic gains for the society as a whole? Can the industrial sector absorb those displaced from the land? It is hardly progress if farm families find distasteful, unproductive jobs or, worse, become statistics in employment offices or on the welfare rolls.

---

[14]Harold F. Briemyer and Barry L. Flinchbaugh, "A Dispersed, Open Market Agriculture," *Who Will Control U.S. Agriculture?* Special Publication 28 (Urbana-Champaign: University of Illinois, 1973), p. 4.

[15]Emerson, pp. 67-68. The author projects the probable consequences of decelerating, maintaining and accelerating the current trends towards farm consolidation between now and the year 2000. With respect to food prices, he says, "Therefore, accelerating the current trend would probably decrease retail food prices 3 to 5 percent, while slowing the current trend might increase food prices by 3 percent." Emerson makes no prediction on the impact of maintaining the current trend, but logic indicates that such a prediction would fall between the two extremes. In a footnote, he adds, "Other experts do not believe that retail food prices would differ under the alternative farm structures considered here. They argue that any economies of size realized by a shift towards larger farms would be offset as the processing and marketing of food is further transformed toward promotional instead of price-based competition."

The Common Good

While economic arguments and counterarguments have their place, they flow from a terribly narrow perspective. The Church has consistently held that the excellence of a society depends upon the extent to which it fosters justice and serves the common good. Even if one could demonstrate that some absolute economic gain could be realized from further concentration in the agricultural sector, that gain would not be worth the price paid in social terms. It would cost this country an important and universally-praised feature of its culture, and further limit the number of our people engaged in the production of basic necessities. It would increase the risk that control over our food production system would be forfeited to powerful corporate interests. It would all but destroy a system of widespread farm ownership by resident operators that is conducive to responsible stewardship. To suggest that such a prospect serves the common good is a mockery.

Stewardship

The question of stewardship is complex. We have noted that the owner-operator has incentives to preserve the health of the land that the renter cannot be expected to share. Speculators and corporations that farm suffer from the same disadvantage. They will make sure that their property is well managed in order to protect their investment. That personal love of the land, that commitment to the homestead is missing, however.

The owner-operator's motivation to practice good stewardship is a valuable asset to American agriculture. It should be fostered and encouraged wherever possible. This encouragement is necessary because, sad to say, many family farmers cultivate their land in a wasteful and imprudent way. Quick and easy farming techniques such as straightline plowing and concentration on a single crop have helped create a very serious erosion problem. Farmers have become partners with the forces of wind and water as they carry off our fertile topsoil.[16] In the same way, undue irrigation depletes underground aquifers, wasting precious water. Nature can renew both land and water over time, but it cannot rebuild as quickly as humanity takes away.

The use of chemical fertilizers and pesticides has greatly increased agricultural production, and most farmers would find it difficult to set them aside entirely. It is well-known, however, that the indiscriminate application of these substances wears out the land over a period of years. Chemicals also contribute to water pollution when they are borne as runoff into surface and subsurface water supplies; this problem is most severe where heavy use is linked with heavy irrigation. Diversified family farmers can reduce their

---

[16]Luther J. Carter, "Soil Erosion: The Problem Persists Despite the Billions Spent on It," *Science* (April 22, 1977). Reprinted in the *Congressional Record* (May 16, 1977), S 7677–79.

dependence on chemicals by employing organic fertilizers produced on the premises. Moreover, they can experiment with integrated pest management systems combining pesticides and biological controls, and make an effort to get by with as little irrigation as possible. Contrary to popular opinion, moving towards the adoption of organic farming methods does not appear to damage the farmer's competitive position.[17]

Stewardship also involves the conservation of scarce energy reserves. Fertilizers and pesticides are mostly petroleum-based. To the extent that farmers can replace these chemicals with organic and biological alternatives, they can help stretch the remaining supplies of fossil fuels. Generating energy on the farm from renewable sources (sun, wind, agricultural products) can serve the same purpose.

Some of these considerations apply to farm mechanization as well. Few would urge American farmers to abandon their machines. In our time, much of the backbreaking work of raising the country's food and fiber has been eliminated, and that is all to the good. Government support should be available for the purchase or rental of equipment that enables farmers to operate economically. Mechanization can be carried to harmful extremes, though. The labor of family members that contributes to the good of the whole has a legitimate place on the farm. If adequate funds were invested in machinery that left scope for voluntary family labor, farmers could cut back on their use of fuel.

Impact on Individuals

The continued decline of the family farm will have a direct impact on the lives of thousands, perhaps millions of people. Despite revolutionary changes in urban-rural migration patterns in this decade, about 600 nonmetropolitan counties are still losing population. For the most part, these counties have a large minority representation and an agricultural economy.[18] Besides documenting the ongoing travail of the small farmer, the statistics highlight a phenomenon that has only recently received widespread attention. Earlier in our history, thousands of Hispanic farmers were driven from their land. Now the number of farms owned by black people is falling at a frightening rate, presumably because members of minority groups are least able to withstand the economic pressures leading to farm failure. Black people represent 11.6 percent of the total population, and in 1970 black farmers represented nine percent of the farm population. By 1977, that percentage had been cut

---

[17]Sue Lukens, "On the Competitiveness of Organic Farms," *Ag World,* Vol. 5, No. 6 (June–July 1978), p. 18.

[18]Subcommittee on the City; Committee on Banking, Finance and Urban Affairs; U.S. House of Representatives, *Small Cities: How Can the Federal and State Governments Respond to Their Diverse Needs?* (Washington, D.C.: U.S. Government Printing Office, 1978), pp. 10–11.

to five.[19] The racial problems that beset America surface in the farm situation, as in so much else.

In the past, a high percentage of the families who left the farm came to the cities, exacerbating the conditions of unemployment and overcrowding they found. There is no reason to believe that farmers displaced in the future will not follow the same path. Once again, minority people are likely to suffer the most. The same lack of resources that renders them vulnerable in rural areas will make life with dignity difficult in our urban ghettoes.

Those who harvest much of the produce we eat, the migrant workers, are also largely members of minority groups. The Church has played a significant role in encouraging the unionization of these workers, but many of the injustices basic to the migrant system remain. The gradual disappearance of the family farm tends to perpetuate that system, since most migrants are employed by large growers or corporate enterprises. The small family farmer, by and large, can use family labor or local labor, obviating the need for the migrant "stream," with all its attendant evils.

Impact on Rural Communities

Farm residents and farm workers, as important as they are, make up only a small percentage of our nonmetropolitan population. In terms of human suffering, the broadest implications of the decline of the family farm lie in its effect on rural communities. Farm-related businesses—the feed store, the grain elevator, the machinery dealer—are important cogs in their towns' commercial structures. Moreover, the people on surrounding farms nourish the community with their trade and their support of local schools, churches, health facilities and civic activites. A famous study done in California over 30 years ago and partially replicated in 1977 confirms what common sense would suggest. The rural community serving as a trading center for many small farms is more vigorous both socially and economically than a town serving a few large farms.[20] The widespread failure of family farms poses a distinct danger to small towns all across America.

Conclusion

In a way, it seems superfluous to plead the case of the family farm, since it pleads its own case so well. We cannot believe that its further decline will benefit this country. That same decline, meanwhile, can mean significant losses in the social, cultural, political and environmental spheres, and can have very disturbing economic side-effects. Farmers themselves, the govern-

---

[19]*Farm Population of the United States: 1977 (Advance Report)*. Series P-27, No. 50 (Washington, D.C.: Bureau of the Census, U.S. Department of Commerce and Economics, Statistics and Cooperatives Service, U.S. Department of Agriculture, 1978).

[20]The Small Farm Viability Project, "The Small Farm in California: An Examination of Its Viability," *Center for Community Economic Development Newsletter* (February-March 1978), p. 14.

ment, even the Church must move immediately to defend the family farm system. They must act boldly and with vision. The industrialization of American agriculture has rightly been called a revolution. Now the nation needs a second revolution to contain the effects of the first within reasonable bounds.

Preserving the Family Farm: the Church's Role

Catholics, joining in the general mobility of society, have spread through all parts of nonmetropolitan America. In 1970, some seven million, or 15.5 percent of the total Catholic population, lived in rural counties.[21] This development, coupled with a heightened concern for all people in our small towns and open countryside, has prompted a growing rural involvement on the part of the Church. Sixteen years after the establishment of the National Catholic Rural Life Conference, Father William Howard Bishop founded the Glenmary Home Missioners, an order of priests and brothers dedicated solely to a rural apostolate. Many dioceses have launched programs in nonmetropolitan ministry, and the National Conference of Catholic Charities is encouraging its member agencies to place more emphasis on rural parishes in their allocation of services.

We have tried to show how, as it seeks to promote social justice, the Church naturally becomes a firm advocate of the family farm system and the values that systems upholds. The Church's role in the struggle to save the family farm may not be a decisive one. Nevertheless, it has a clear responsibility to minister to farmers in their need. While the good sense and creativity of church leaders on the local, diocesan and national levels will determine the precise form this ministry takes, we would like to point out a few areas where action would be especially helpful.

1. *In parishes and dioceses, hold up for praise the individual and family values traditionally associated with American agriculture. Educate people on the social, economic, cultural, political and environmental issues posed by the decline of the family farm.* The moral dimensions of agricultural trends must be clarified if Catholics are to rally in defense of the family farm. It is essential, first and foremost, that consumers understand the structure of the system by which their food is produced. They should also be knowledgeable on land issues, on the activities of agribusiness corporations, on the impact of governmental policies on agriculture, on the problems of minority farmers and on related questions. This education should by no means be restricted to parishes and dioceses in rural areas. The future of the family farm may well depend on the strength of the support it receives from urban dwellers.

2. *In parishes and dioceses, encourage or establish programs that help the family farmer to survive.* Such programs might include providing human ser-

---

[21]These figures represent unpublished data developed by the Glenmary Research Center, Washington, D.C.

vices and easing access to government assistance, supporting the formation of cooperatives and mutual-aid associations among farmers, and experimenting with direct farmer-to-consumer marketing systems (food buying clubs, roadside stands, farmers' markets in urban areas, and so on).

3. *On the diocesan level, ensure that a fair proportion of priests with special leadership abilities are trained for rural ministry and located in rural parishes.* In the past, rural ministry, which receives little attention in seminary curricula or continuing education programs, has often suffered for lack of adequate clerical leadership. Rural pastors will become even more effective if qualified sisters, brothers, deacons and lay people are recruited to assist them in guiding their parishes.

4. *On the diocesan level, help farm workers who wish to obtain farms of their own.* Through support of their efforts at unionization, the Church has ministered to farm workers within the prevailing system. Now is the time for a new initiative to aid them in escaping that system. Those who till the land should have the opportunity to own it.

5. *On the diocesan level, examine Catholic institutional land holdings to see if these holdings could be used in any way to stimulate family farming.* Small or beginning farmers, especially low-income people and members of minority groups, might be given preference when agricultural land is to be sold or leased, for example.

6. *On the diocesan level, consider putting resources into and/or encouraging farmers to invest acreage and money in land trusts that guarantee the use of the land in perpetuity for family farming.*

7. *On all levels, advocate and work for changes in public policy favorable to family farming.* Political action groups can be formed in parishes and dioceses to monitor current state and federal legislation and administrative action that has an impact on the agricultural sector. The information such groups gather can form the basis for advocacy. The United States Catholic Conference, the National Catholic Rural Life Conference and other national agencies are in a position to disseminate information on farming issues and to impress the Catholic viewpoint on legislators and government officials in Washington.

8. *On all levels, work in cooperation with other Christian denominations wherever possible.* The major Churches long have shared an interest in ministry to farmers and farm workers. This ministry, therefore, presents an excellent opportunity for witness to Christian unity. Moreover, because the issues involved touch so many people, ecumenical activities are more likely to be effective than those sponsored by a single denomination.

Preserving the Family Farm: the Farmer's Role

While the Church can lend its moral authority and, in some cases, its material resources to the effort to preserve the family farm, the major responsibility for reform falls upon farmers themselves and the governments that set agricultural policy. The determination farmers feel to defend their individual and group interests must lie at the core of any campaign in support of a family-based agriculture. They are the people most centrally concerned in the struggle, and they will bear the heaviest consequences of failure.

Farmers will be successful only to the degree that they recognize and accept their relationship to the economic system. Their pride in their independence is proverbial and, if one considers the operation of the farm in isolation, this independence is very real. Assuming that they hold title to the land they work, farmers are their own bosses. Subject only to the demands of the common good, they can manage their businesses as they wish.

They are often in debt, however, and must rely on private and public sources of credit to stay in farming. They may need the revenue from federal price support programs for the profit margin essential to survival. Moreover, depending on the size of their operation, they occupy a certain place in the hierarchy of American agriculture. For most family farmers, this position is a highly vulnerable one. As our discussion of the forces fueling farm consolidation indicates, the small farmer lives in danger of being driven out of business by the large farmer and, by the same logic, the large farmer is subject to extinction by corporate competition.

Finally, farmers must buy fertilizer, seed and machinery and must sell what they grow. When they view themselves in relation to the enclosing supply and marketing systems, their independence must seem elusive indeed. They have little choice but to buy from giant companies whose economic power dwarfs them. Just two firms accounted for 57 percent of all tractor sales in 1972, for example.[22] In the same way, unless they sell directly to local consumers, farmers usually deal with large handlers who are in a position to set prices to their own advantage.[23] If the farmers do not like what is offered, their only alternative is to make use of the federal government's reserve program. Their situation with respect to the companies that buy their products is analogous to the situation of industrial workers with respect to their employers. While the workers sell their labor, farmers sell their products. In the absence of the power that only determined collective action can provide, neither group has much control over its economic fate.

These are some of the harsh realities family farmers face in working towards a more promising future for themselves and their peers. Pope John XXIII had a particular concern for the powerlessness of the modern farmer. In *Mater et Magistra,* he wrote: "Nor may it be overlooked that ... farmers should join together in fellowships, especially when the family itself works the farm. ... They should strive jointly to set up mutual aid societies and professional associations. All these are very necessary either to keep rural dwellers abreast of scientific and technical progress, or to protect the prices of goods produced by their labor. Besides, acting in this manner, farmers are put on

---

[22]Jim Hightower, *Eat Your Heart Out* (New York: Crown, 1975), p. 140.
[23]Emerson, pp. 13-14.

the same footing as other classes of workers who, for the most part, join together in such fellowships. . . . For today it is unquestionably true that the solitary voice speaks, as they say, to the winds" (146).

Historically, farmers have lacked a group consciousness. Each individual has preferred to be the "solitary voice" ruling a separate kingdom. It seems to us that farmers caught in the subtle web of the economic system need a new independence—not an independence from one another but a spirit of common rebellion against those forces, physical and psychological, that threaten their way of life. We urge farmers and their representative organizations to take a wide range of actions to meet this challenge. These actions might include the following:

1. *Renounce the "bigger is better" philosophy that ultimately poses a danger to all family farmers.* If farmers themselves see agriculture simply in business terms and condone the "cannibalism" whereby one producer swallows up another's land, there is no hope of preserving the family farm as an American institution. Rather than seeking enlargement, farmers might adopt more economical methods (organic techniques; a diversified approach; use of smaller, more appropriate machinery) that enable them to obtain a profit adequate for decent family support with the land they have.

2. *Make individual efforts to help neighbors survive in farming.* A group of farmers could share labor and equipment instead of competing, for example.

3. *Form and loyally sustain bargaining cooperatives to offset the advantages that large producers enjoy in buying from supply firms and selling to marketing and processing firms.* As with industrial workers, farmers must take united action to gain essential economic leverage. They must be content with obtaining just prices, of course, and not seek to generate excessive profits at the expense of consumers. The collective bargaining process should always take the interests of farm workers into account.

4. *As a complementary strategy, encourage existing marketing cooperatives to cooperate, especially in the export trade.* If the consortium thus formed could gain control of a substantial slice of the market, it could compete successfully with the huge corporations dealing in grain and other commodities.

5. *Loyally support other mutual-aid organizations whose purpose is to cut production costs, provide managerial assistance, develop economical farming methods, establish direct farmer-to-consumer marketing systems and so on. Form new organizations if the existing ones no longer fulfill their roles as cooperative ventures.* In the past, a lack of member loyalty has routinely undermined the effectiveness of cooperatives. Successful cooperatives have sometimes abandoned the principles on which they were founded and adopted the methods of investor-owned business.

6. *Through national farm organizations, mount an intensive educational campaign to present the farmer's case to the consumer.* All Americans

should be aware of the implications of a shift from a family-based agriculture to an agriculture dominated by corporate interests.

7. *As individuals and through national farm organizations, advocate and work for public policy favorable to the family farmer.* Farmers should use all legal and peaceful means at their disposal to bring their point of view to the attention of government on the state and federal levels. National farm organizations are in a position to represent their members' interests before Congress and administration officials in Washington.

Preserving the Family Farm: the Role of Government

We hold to the principle of subsidiarity enunciated by Pope Pius XI in his encyclical, *Quadragesimo Anno*, and reaffirmed by Pope John XXIII.[24] In order to preserve citizen liberties, action to promote social justice should be taken at the lowest practical level within a society. Functions properly performed by individuals should not be given over to groups, functions properly performed by small groups should not be given over to large groups, and government should act only when it alone is competent to achieve the desired end. This is why we have reserved discussion of the role of government in preserving the family farm until last.

Government does have a legitimate and very important part to play, however. Pope John remarks: "Where, on the other hand, appropriate activity of the state is lacking or defective, commonwealths are apt to experience incurable disorders, and there occurs exploitation of the weak by the unscrupulous strong . . ." (*Mater et Magistra,* 58). As we have seen, government policy itself has contributed to the grave situation in which family farmers find themselves. Further, only government is powerful enough to temper the economic forces that lead inexorably to consolidation in the agricultural sector. Farmers complain about the weight of government regulation, and certainly regulation should never be imposed in such a way as to add to the burdens of the small operator. Some regulation is necessary, though, if the family farmer is to survive in the prevailing economic system.

In recent years, there have been salutary changes in state and federal government policy that respond to the needs of small and moderate-sized family farms. This movement towards reform must expand and grow stronger if the efforts of the Church and the farmer to defend a family-based agriculture are to succeed. We support government action that would:

1. *Structure federal commodity and insurance programs so that farmers who derive a substantial part of their support from agricultural sales can attain an annual income adequate to meet their families' needs.* "Income" should be defined to include revenue from both farm and non-farm sources. Commodity and insurance programs must be carefully designed and ad-

---

[24]See *Mater et Magistra,* 51–58.

ministered to preclude discrimination against women and members of minority groups.

2. *Structure federal commodity and insurance programs so that no farmer receives payments in excess of the amount required to provide an annual income adequate to meet his or her family's needs.* Programs now in force permit subsidies to the wealthy.

3. *Stimulate rural development so that farmers who need to supplement their agricultural incomes have the opportunity to find off-farm employment.* Ideally, all farm families with reasonable assets in capital and land should be able to support themselves from agriculture alone. The primary goal of government agricultural policy should be to make this ideal a reality. As long as farmers find it necessary to take off-farm jobs in order to stay on the land, however, these jobs should be available to them.

4. *Address the social needs of rural America so that farmers, especially low-income farmers, have better access to basic human services.* Families are more likely to remain in agriculture if adequate health care, housing assistance, special nutrition programs and other services are readily available.

5. *Structure production control programs in keeping with the interests of small and moderate-sized farmers.* These programs should be designed to eliminate loopholes that undermine their usefulness. Of course, production control should never be so stringent as to threaten the existence of sufficient reserves to keep prices within reasonable bounds and to satisfy the hunger of the poor at home and abroad. The United States has a continuing responsibility to give free food assistance to other nations when necessary, while helping these nations to move towards self-sufficiency in food production.

6. *Encourage the entrance of new families into farming, and improve the competitive position of existing small farmers, through grants or low-income loans, technical assistance and training, and preferential treatment in the sale or lease of government-controlled land (including "excess lands" made available through the provisions of the 1902 Reclamation Act).* Governments on the state and federal levels might also explore the feasibility of establishing land trusts under public auspices to serve the same purposes. Any program aimed at maintaining or increasing the number of family farmers must be carefully designed and administered to preclude discrimination against women and members of minority groups.

Particular attention should be paid to the needs of farm workers whose jobs may be taken by mechanization or, conceivably, by a resurgence of the family farm system. Government should help displaced workers to become farmers in their own right if they choose to do so or, failing that, should retrain them for other dignified and substantial employment.

7. *Continue and expand credit programs to help small and moderate-sized farmers retain control of their land under economic pressure.* While the simple extension of credit cannot solve farmers' long-term problems, it can help them to survive bad times or to stay in business while building up equity

in their holdings. Credit programs must be carefully designed and administered to preclude discrimintion against women and members of minority groups. Many black farmers in the South, for example, are at present denied participation in these programs because their land is "heirs' property."

8. *Change the overall thrust of agricultural research and information delivery to support family farmers.* More money might be devoted to developing ways of making optimal use of family labor; employing smaller, more appropriate machinery; generating energy from renewable sources; diversifying operations; and using organic techniques and integrated pest management systems. An equitable share of research funds should be allocated to the black land-grant colleges, and women and members of minority groups should be fairly represented in agencies providing agricultural services.

9. *Encourage the growth and effectiveness of bargaining cooperatives and other mutual-aid organizations for farmers, especially new and low-income farmers.*

10. *Encourage the development of direct farmer-to-consumer marketing systems.* Such a thrust implies placing a priority on fostering localized farming. By selling directly to local consumers, farmers can escape a large part of the charges they now pay for transportation, lowering their overall production costs and contributing to the conservation of fossil energy. Consumers, of course, benefit from the opportunity to buy fresh farm produce at prices unaffected by wholesalers, processors and retailers.

11. *Reform the tax laws that stimulate farm expansion, that favor large operations, that cut heavily into farm profits without regard for ability to pay and that encourage absentee ownership and speculation in agricultural land.* Tax policy on both the state and federal levels has a great impact on the structure of American agriculture.

(a) Tax savings associated with investment credits and accelerated depreciation allowances, available primarily to farmers and investors with high incomes, fuel farm expansion. A system of tax incentives should be devised that encourages maintaining farming operations at a moderate size.

(b) Property taxes can be crippling, especially when farmland is assessed at its potential development value. Agricultural land should be zoned for agricultural use and assessed according to its capacity for producing agricultural revenue. Moreover, property taxes on farms should be graduated to inhibit the consolidation of land holdings; the small landowner should be taxed at a lower rate than the big landowner.

(c) Tax rates on capital gains and provisions permitting the practice of "tax-loss" farming form a strong stimulus to outside investment and speculation. Applicable sections of the tax code should be revised to promote the prevalence of resident owner-operators in agriculture.

12. *Bar the purchase of agricultural land by large investor-owned corporations, especially those engaged in food processing and/or marketing.* Antitrust laws that bear on the activities of investor-owned business in the agricultural sector should be tightly enforced. Government action should prohibit advance sales contracts that have the effect of giving corporations strict control over food production.

13. *Preserve farmland.* Care should be taken now to ensure that America will always have sufficient agricultural land. Government should be very cautious in setting aside good farm and range land for recreational purposes or for designation as wilderness. Positive steps to maintain the land base might include agricultural zoning, directing development away from prime farmland and establishing effective land use commissions.

Conclusions

Those who propose a major new thrust for society must be prepared to count the costs, or risk having their proposals dismissed as idle dreaming. The most common measure of cost is hard economics. Is an all-out campaign to preserve the family farm really practical, or would it force unacceptable increases in taxes and food prices? We noted earlier that slowing the trend toward further consolidation in agriculture would affect prices only marginally, if at all. The impact of stopping or reversing that trend might be greater. How much greater is hard to judge. Establishing an organized system of direct farmer-to-consumer markets would result in sharply lower prices for produce, and the adoption of more economical farming methods would cut production costs. On the other hand, food prices would go up if farmers succeeded in obtaining more equitable returns through collective bargaining, and if linkages in the agribusiness chain of production, processing and marketing were loosened. In order to maintain a family-based agriculture, consumers might have to pay more at the supermarket, but the effect on any one individual would be small. We cannot imagine that the American people would resent the added cost if they knew it guaranteed family farmers a decent income.

The same is true of taxes. The bulk of the benefits under present farm programs go to large farmers, many of whom have incomes well above the level adequate to meet a family's needs. To some extent, therefore, we are calling for a redistribution rather than a broad expansion of federal payments. Some expansion would be necessary, though. At the same time, new programs aimed at helping families get started in farming or providing off-farm jobs would require funding. State and federal expenditures in the agricultural sector would certainly rise, and these increases might not be entirely offset by the savings in aid to displaced families and weakened rural communities that preservation of the family farm system would yield. Once again, however, each taxpayer's share in the additional financial burden could not be heavy.

There are more important considerations than debates over prices and taxes. We have tried to show that the continued decline of the family farm involves hidden social costs in restricted opportunities for farmers to own their land, in corporate control of the food system, in environmental deterioration, in the growing dependence of our culture on ever larger, more impersonal structures. We fear these costs more than the others because they threaten freedoms basic to the American experience and cloud the future.

Most of all, we seek justice. As servants of God, we defend the rights of farmers and consumers caught up in the whirling gears of an economic system that seems to have lost its human face. To preserve the family farm is to cherish a fading link with the earth and the earth's Creator. It reminds us that there are values that endure, even in the noise and rush and flashing change of modern civilization.

Television

For the first time in eighteen years, the bishops addressed the problem of censorship on September 10, 1975 in a statement entitled Family Viewing Policy of Television Networks *prepared by the USCC Administrative Board. The bishops responded to new guidelines created by networks for evening—and especially prime time—programming. Briefly stated, the networks decided to show material suitable for families during prime time and the hour immediately preceding. If programs shown in the "family viewing" period were unsuitable for younger family members, a "viewer advisory" would precede such shows. These advisories also would be used later in the evening if a program contained material that might be offensive to a significant portion of viewers.*

The family viewing policy represents an act of self-regulation on the part of the networks, which the bishops basically support. However, the bishops argue that even self-regulation must be an open, accountable, and cooperative process. They contend that the networks do not seriously consult either local broadcasters or the public about programming. In fact, neither was asked its opinion about introducing a distinction between family and adult programming. Effective self-regulation, the bishops continue, is thwarted because the broadcast industry is dominated by commercial in-

*terests. "American television is essentially concerned with the sale of con-
sumers to advertisers." In other words, the networks present those shows
that attract the most viewers and thus the most profits. Hence, most shows
contain shallow comedy, crime, violence, and sex.*

*To counteract the commercialism dominating the broadcast industry, the
bishops urge the viewing public to convince local station managers that it
really wants better programming. In particular, the bishops encourage
Catholics to cooperate with their fellow citizens in pursuing this objective.*

*Late in the summer of 1977, the USCC's Department of Communication
vigorously protested ABC's decision to broadcast "Soap," a television program described by the network management as "a satire on the daytime soap
operas, a comedic farce and . . . an adult character comedy with a continuing
story line that parallels real life. . . ." The USCC Department argues that
"Soap's" plot description "defines the principal characters solely in terms of
their sexual proclivities," and that "Soap's" obsession with sex "debases not
only the television medium but the humanity of the viewers."*

Statement on the Introduction Of the Family Viewing Period During Prime-Time by the Television Networks

*USCC, Administrative Board
September 10, 1975*

I. Introduction

With the 1975 Fall season the three television networks have introduced
their new policy of a "Family Viewing" period during prime-time programming hours.

In summary, the following guidelines will be observed by the networks.
The first hour of network entertainment programming in prime-time and the
immediately preceding hour are to be set aside as a "Family Viewing"
period. Secondly, in the occasional case when an entertainment program

broadcast during the "Family Viewing" period contains material which may be unsuitable for viewing by younger family members, a "viewer advisory" will be broadcast in audio and video form. Moreover, viewer advisories will also be employed during the later evening hours for any program containing material that might be disturbing to significant portions of the viewing audience. Finally, broadcasters will endeavor to inform publishers of television program listings of these programs that will contain "advisories." A responsible use of "advisories" in promotional material is also urged upon broadcasters.

This new network policy on family viewing is the result of conversations that the Chairman of the Federal Communications Commission had with network leaders in the early part of this year. The results of those negotiations were made public by the Commission in its "Report on the Broadcast of Violent, Indecent and Obscene Material" on February 19, 1975 (FCC 75-202,30159). The report, which was in response to Congressional directives on the subject, addresses the "specific positive action taken and planned by the Commission to protect children from excessive programming of violence and obscenity." The acceptance by the Commission of the "Family Viewing" concept constitutes the major element of this plan.

II. Presuppositions

Before evaluating this "Family Viewing" policy we wish to outline certain presuppositions which the United States Catholic Conference views as important and relevant to the question at hand.

(1) In our society today television is the single most formative influence in shaping people's attitudes and values. It is not only the power the medium itself possesses that supports this proposition. Of even greater significance is the cumulative effect upon an individual of his daily television experiences, frequently passive and uncritical, from early childhood until the evening of life. By the time they have completed high school, most children have spent more hours before a television set than they have in the classroom. The average adult also spends considerable time each day viewing television.

(2) Unquestionably, therefore, the *experience* of television is both an *ordinary* and *integral* part of American *home life* today. Hence it follows that any evaluation of the role that television plays in the American experience must focus on the actualities, first, of substantial daily viewing by the average American, and secondly, of the home environment in which the viewing is experienced. We are not dealing then with the occasional entertainment experience that a child or adult may have by going out of the home to see a movie. Much less are we dealing with the even rarer entertainment experience of a nightclub show.

(3) The Church respects the enormous potential that television has: for education; for providing full and accurate information so essential to enlightened public opinion; for building understanding and community

among men and nations; for preserving and, indeed, creating art; for providing entertainment and relaxation that re-create the human spirit and emotions.

In the face of this enormous potential broadcasters cannot view themselves as merely entertainers or technicians. Because social communications are so central to modern life the vocation of a broadcaster is a calling of high honor—and of heavy responsibility. The broadcaster, more than others, helps to shape the very ethos of the world in which we live.

(4) It should be noted as well that American broadcasters' responsibilities go far beyond the frontiers reached by their signals. They have a global responsibility because they belong to an industry that has established American international leadership in the technology, the content, and the style of contemporary mass communications. One example is enlightening: during 1974, of 1707 film entertainment programs shown on Brazilian television 1267 programs were of American origin; only ten were Brazilian productions. American broadcasters cannot therefore take a parochial or narrowly nationalistic view of their responsibilities. They must be increasingly sensitive to the cultural and moral imperatives of societies other than our own. The American people, sharing as they do a collective responsibility in our interdependent world, have every right and duty to protest whenever broadcasters may manifest indifference or insensitivity to the needs of their sisters and brothers across the world. In a word, the question of the broadcast of violent, indecent and obscene material has to be viewed from an international as well as a domestic perspective.

III. USCC Evaluation of the "Family Viewing" Policy

At the very outset of our evaluation of the FCC acceptance of the "Family Viewing" policy it seems important to state that if our opinion of the Commission's recommendations must be largely negative, it is not because we have failed to appreciate the most difficult task of the Commissioners.

The FCC report (page 3) quite rightly observes that "administrative actions regulating violent and sexual material must be reconciled with constitutional and statutory limitations on the Commission's authority to regulate program content." Not only do we support this observation but we would oppose any recommendation that would call for the direct involvement by government in the content area of programming. Section 326 of the Communications Act specifically prohibits the Commission from exercising the power of censorship. This prohibition must be maintained.

Opposition to *direct* governmental involvement in program content, however, does not call in question the role required of the Commission by the same Communications Act, namely, that it ensure that broadcast licensees operate in a manner consistent with the public interest. The *Red Lion* decision of the Supreme Court explicitly reminded broadcasters that they are "public trustees" with fiduciary responsibilities to their communities. We strongly support the Commission's policy that program service in the public interest is an essential part of every licensee's obligation.

Nor again, by opposing *direct* involvement by government, do we intend to cast any doubt on the obligation that Congress has to legislate effectively against the broadcast of violent, obscene or indecent material. Specifically, we support the Commission's legislative proposal that Congress amend Section 1464 of Title 18, United States Code, in order to remove the present uncertainty of the Commission as to whether it has statutory authority to proceed against the video depiction of obscene or indecent material. (*Report*, page 9).

In the light of the constraints placed on it by the Constitution and Section 326 of the Communications Act, the Commission understandably notes that it "walks a tightrope between saying too much and saying too little" when applying the public interest standard to programming. In the present instance, the Commission decided that "regulatory action to limit violent and sexually-oriented programming which is neither obscene nor indecent is less desirable than effective self-regulation." (*Report*, page 3). Hence the Chairman of the Commission met with broadcast industry leadership in the hope that he might "serve as a catalyst for the achievement of meaningful self-regulatory reform."

Although the effort of the Chairman is commendable, our judgment is that the results are unacceptable. Our reasons are as follows:

(1) *Self-regulation must be open, accountable and cooperative.*

The United States Catholic Conference has been, is and will continue to be firmly committed to the principle of voluntary self-regulation for all the communications media. We therefore share the Commission's conviction that broadcast self-regulation is the basic solution to the problems at hand. However, we strongly disagree with the Commission's apparent conviction that a few modifications in the status quo will enable the networks to achieve "meaningful self-regulatory reform" in the area of broadcast entertainment.

Self-regulation is not a unilateral activity performed behind closed doors by a few powerful individuals at the top. Self-regulation, to deserve the name, is an *open, accountable* and *cooperative* process, involving both broadcasters and the public they serve.

We are far from convinced that broadcast management is genuinely *open* to dialogue with the public or accountable to it. The very corporate structure of the networks, for example, is such a forbidding and complicated maze that it appears designed to guarantee that, insulated from public scrutiny, top management may, without fear of challenge or other encumbrance, pursue the uniquely important goal of maximizing profits. And yet, of all the communications media, broadcasting should be the one most open to dialogue with the public precisely because the airwaves belong to the public and broadcasters are public trustees with fiduciary responsibilities to their communities. The polished rhetoric of industry public relations releases is not dialogue but self-serving monologue. In spite of good intentions, the series of closed meetings which the Chairman of the Commission held with the inner circle of network top management strikes us as having little to do with openness to public dialogue, or public accountability. Even worse, it can only serve in effect to strengthen the claims currently being made by some broadcasters that the public does not really own the airwaves.

Neither will the quality of openness and accountability characterize industry self-regulation as long as the public is without ready access to reliable advance information about broadcast entertainment programming. This need for information is not satisfied by industry-generated publicity releases or advisories. Books, plays, records, movies, circuses, exhibits of all manner are also the object of publicity and promotion, but before buying, the interested consumer has critical evaluations of the product available to guide his or her choice. Since, apart from summer repeats, broadcast entertainment is essentially a one-time presentation, reliable advance program information would only be possible were networks and local stations to adopt and implement a policy of prescreening *all* entertainment programs for critical review. We are aware, of course, that the "rating-game" approach to television entertainment effectively precludes even the consideration of any prescreening policy that might, in effect, serve to restrict potential audiences. Without it the broadcast industry cannot justify claim to be open and accountable to the public it claims to serve. One might have expected that the Chairman of the Commission would have seen this as an important question to have posed to network top management.

Self-regulation is also a *cooperative* activity that should involve every local broadcaster. A frequent complaint of the local broadcaster is that he is rarely consulted or otherwise actively involved by the networks in the decision-making process with regard to network entertainment programming. To the best of our knowledge top network management did not invite the *prior* counsel of their affiliate stations on the subject of whether there ought to be a family-viewing period during prime time. Neither are we aware that the Commission sought the opinion of the affiliates in the matter. If the decision has been unilaterally taken by the networks and accepted by the Commission, it may be because, were it left to local affiliate management, who alone must bear the ultimate responsibility to the public, many of them might have rejected the idea on the grounds that their prime-time audience is a family audience. At the very least, they might have demanded stricter and more precise standards.

Self-regulation also involves *cooperation* on the part of the *viewing public*. No system will succeed unless it enjoys public confidence and support. Part of our complaint is that neither the networks nor the Commission made any effort to consult the public on whether it was indeed prepared to accept the introduction of a distinction between family-type and adult programming and, if so, under what conditions. We seriously doubt that the average parent would or should find it reasonable to insist that older children be excluded from watching television in their own home after certain time periods. By what mandate or legal title, parents might rightfully demand, can the Commission and the networks unilaterally decide that henceforth minor children are entitled to enjoy only a limited access to evening television entertainment? A more than lurking suspicion remains that the audience for prime-time television is after all not the general American public but older teenagers, young adults and the affluent who have the money to spend on the products advertised. In short, children, the poor and the aged are to be disenfranchised. How all of this relates to high-sounding network appeals to creativity and First Amendment guarantees or is to be reconciled with serving the public interest is difficult to perceive.

(2) *Commercialism—Core Problem*

And so we come to what must be acknowledged as the *core* obstacle to effective self-regulation in the broadcast industry—its complete domination by commercial interests. What American commercial television is all about is not primarily either information or entertainment, neither news nor culture. Its primary objective is to create a meeting place for consumers and advertisers. American television is essentially concerned with the sale of consumers to advertisers.

As long as this equation controls programming decisions, especially during prime-time when network competition is keenest, the central concern of broadcast mangement has to be to air that type of program which will deliver the greatest possible audience. And what kind of programming is this? Look at the record. Do we find serious dramatic works or programs that might challenge viewers to confront disturbing social issues or documentaries that might open American minds and hearts to understanding and compassion for the powerless at home and abroad? What has the average American viewer of prime-time entertainment programming learned about the global village, the interdependent world in which we are said to live—about Africa, Latin America, Asia, Oceania? The record will reveal that network management programming decisions have much more to do with appealing to the alleged lowest common denominator of audience interest, smart comedy, crime, violence and sex. Were the record otherwise, the Commission would never have been mandated by Congress to undertake its study.

(3) *Lessons Learned From Motion Picture Code and Rating Program*

On page five of the Commission's Report it is stated that "the Chairman raised the possibility of the adoption of a rating system similar to that used in the motion picture industry." We believe that some sobering conclusions might have emerged for the members of the Commission had they reflected on what has happened to American motion pictures since October 7, 1968, when the Motion Picture Association of America (MPAA) first announced the details of its new and expanded plan of movie-industry self-regulation.

The MPAA plan bore the title "The Motion Picture Code and Rating Program." We wish to emphasize that it was a *code* as well as a rating program. At the top of the document appears a section entitled "Declaration of Principles of the Code of Self-Regulation of the Motion Picture Association." A few excerpts from this section are of interest:

"This Code is designed to keep in close harmony with the mores, culture, the moral sense and change in our society.

"The objectives of the Code are:

1. To encourage artistic expression by expanding creative freedom; and

2. To assure that the freedom which encourages the artist remains responsible and sensitive to the standards of the larger society."

"We believe self-restraint, self-regulation, to be in the American tradition. The results of self-discipline are always imperfect because that is the nature of all things mortal. But this Code, and its administration, will make clear that freedom of expression does not mean toleration of license.
"The test of self-restraint—the rule of reason—lies in the treatment of a subject for the screen."

Under the second section of the MPAA document which is entitled "Standards for Production" there are eleven standards enunciated which will determine whether a motion picture will qualify for a Code Seal of approval. Those standards read as follows:

"—The basic dignity and value of human life shall be respected and upheld. Restraint shall be exercised in portraying the taking of life.

—Evil, sin, crime and wrong-doing shall not be justified.

—Special restraint shall be exercised in portraying criminal or anti-social activities in which minors participate or are involved.

—Detailed and protracted acts of brutality, cruelty, physical violence, torture and abuse shall not be presented.

—Indecent or undue exposure of the human body shall not be presented.

—Illicit sex relationships shall not be justified. Intimate sex scenes violating common standards of decency shall not be portrayed.

—Restraint and care shall be exercised in presentations dealing with sex aberrations.

—Obscene speech, gestures or movements shall not be presented.

—Undue profanity shall not be permitted.

—Religion shall not be demeaned.

—Words or symbols contemptuous of racial, religious or national groups shall not be used so as to incite bigotry or hatred.

—Excessive cruelty to animals shall not be portrayed and animals shall not be treated inhumanely."

The Motion Picture Code and Rating Program envisioned two distinct questions for its administration. The first question pertained to these Standards for Production; if the submitted motion picture conformed to the standards, it would be issued a Code Seal of Approval. If it did not qualify for a code seal, it could only be rated (X). For a Code-approved film a second question was then to be applied, namely, which of the first three ratings (G, M, or R) were to be applied.

The United States Catholic Conference and the National Council of Churches endorsed in principle this MPAA program "as being consistent with the rights and obligations of free speech and artistic expression, as well as with the duty of parents and society to safeguard the young in their growth to responsible adulthood." The Churches "relying on the good faith of the industry" gave "genuine and full support to this plan" and urged "its conscientious implementation on every level of production, distribution, and exhibition."

The Churches maintained their support of the MPAA plan for over two and a half years. Finally, on May 18, 1971, after a detailed statement of concern published a year previously, the Churches, because they could no longer in good conscience be party to a charade, withdrew their support.

How could a plan which had been welcomed with genuine enthusiasm only two and a half years previously have failed so miserably? The best of motivation and the highest good faith could not stand up to the pressures of commercial competition. Within a few short weeks of the introduction of the Code and Rating Plan, there began to emerge an attitude on the part of some film producers that "now that the kids are protected, anything goes." And in no short order, almost everything did go—including the standards for production, which, as noted previously, were to determine whether films qualified for the Code Seal of Approval. Although the MPAA has not formally advised the public, the Code is officially dead. All that remains is the rating aspect of the original plan.

One result of all this is that the theatrical motion picture as such has become a lost experience for the majority of Americans. For the industry, in spite of the occasional box-office successes that keep some of the Hollywood glitter going, the loss of the general audience has resulted in serious financial reverses for many producers and exhibitors across the industry. Perhaps, the worst consequence of all for American society is that too many of the creative community of producers, writers, directors and actors have been replaced by hacks whose artistic perception is limited to "exploit-the-audience-with-sex-and-violence."

Our purpose in this review is not to focus on the problems of the motion picture industry but to raise the question of why a reasonable person would be expected to accord greater confidence to effective self-regulation by the television networks than to the MPAA. To the credit of the MPAA it has involved itself in broad consultation with representatives of the public before introducing its Code and Rating Program and continued to collaborate with them in an effort to make the program work. Again, the film industry prescreens its product for public review and takes its chances at the box-office. As already noted, the broadcast industry's self-regulation is a closed shop and, short of the risk of challenge at license renewal time, is not otherwise accountable to the public. In fact, the networks do not even have to face that risk—except in the narrow area of their owned and operated stations.

We have no confidence that once the commercial broadcast industry as presently constituted is permitted without challenge to introduce what is in effect a rating system for programming, the identical excesses that have occurred in the motion picture medium will not be visited upon the American public—but this time not at the local theater but in the American home. In making this judgment we are not limiting our concern to the pressures of commercial competition presently experienced by the networks. We are also looking down the road when the networks will have to face the added competition from pay-television, video-cassettes, video-discs, and whatever else technological genius may develop.

(4) Greater Handicaps for Parents and Family Life

We have placed great emphasis upon television's role in American family life. We do not think that it is possible to exaggerate the centrality and importance of this role, especially at a time in our history when the very structure of family life is seriously threatened. We, therefore, commend the Commission when it states (*Report*, pages 7–8):

"Parents in our view, have—and should retain—the primary responsibility for their children's well-being. This traditional and revered principle . . . has been adversely affected by the corrosive processes of technological and social change in twentieth-century American life. Nevertheless, we believe that it deserves continuing affirmation."

"Television . . . also has some responsibilities in this area. . . . The Commission has sought to remind broadcasters of their responsibility to provide some measure of support to concerned parents."

However, we must also seriously fault the Commission for then making recommendations which, in the light of our foregoing observations, will only serve to create even greater handicaps for parents as they struggle not only to assure the well-being of their children, but also to preserve family life which is so essential to the well-being of this or any nation.

(5) *Specific Criticism of "Family Viewing" Plan*
Although it may seem unnecessary to comment on the specific recommendations that the FCC Report has proposed for the Fall 1975 television season, we will do so anyway with the understanding, however, that these criticisms are secondary to our already stated core concerns.

(a) Inspection of the report reveals that the 7:00–9:00 p.m. "Family Viewing" period, which appears to have been the initial FCC objective, will hold only in fact for the Eastern and Western time zones. For the Midwest it will mean a 6:00–8:00 p.m. period and for the Rocky Mountain time zone 5:00–7:00 p.m. Why? The Commission lamely acknowledges that the networks had informed it that "a standard based on a 9:00 p.m. local time would require prohibitively expensive separate program transmissions to each time zone." This concession to commercial considerations is incredible. It hardly demonstrates an honest commitment by the networks to American parents.

(b) The use of the so-called "advisory warnings," the second point in the FCC proposals, is an equally incredible concession. "Viewer advisories," the Report states, "will be broadcast in audio and video form *in the occasional case* when an entertainment program broadcast *during the "Family Viewing" period* contains material which may be unsuitable for viewing by younger family members." (Emphasis added.) Not only does this "advisory warning" concession open the door to abuse in order to attract larger audiences; there is something far more disturbing about it. It leads to the obvious conclusion that neither the Commission nor the networks are single-minded about keeping the "Family Viewing" period inviolate.

(c) The combination of "viewer advisories" and the "advance notice" to be given about such advisories clearly implies that a television *rating system,* almost as developed as that of the motion picture industry, is about to be foisted upon the American public without, however, it being candidly identified as a rating system and, of course, without any previous public debate as to the merits of same.

(d) Granted the advisory or rating system proposal, who is going to be making the necessary judgments as to material "which may be unsuitable for viewing by younger family members" or concerning programs, "in the later evening hours," which "contain material that might be disturbing to significant portions of the viewing audience?" The Commission report makes much of the "subjectivity" of these matters. But even if artistic and moral considerations were actually as subjective as the approach of the Commission would imply, there is no reason to conclude, as the Commission does in fact conclude, that such decisions must be left to the networks. This, of course, touches on the basic issue: despite the fervent rhetoric of the FCC report, the networks continue to be answerable to no one but themselves. In some respects the report of the Commission is an insult to the public's intelligence and inescapably lends credence to the suspicion that the main function of the FCC is after all to act as a buffer between the networks and public accountability.

(e) An integral part of the Commission's plan involves the incorporation of the "Family Viewing" period concept and the advisory warnings into the Television Code of the National Association of Broadcasters. It appears unnecessary to observe that the NAB as presently constituted has been neither organized for, nor is it capable of, taking on any serious representation role for the public interest. The NAB is a trade organization whose function is to argue for the interests of its members before the government and the public. Moreover, since no more than 60 percent of all stations belong to this voluntary organization, NAB cannot even speak for the entire industry. Nor, in fact, can it effectively discipline its members who choose not to abide by its Standards and Practices rules. Finally, the FCC has not yet secured agreement of the independent television stations to support the NAB TV Code's incorporation of "Family Viewing" despite the fact that the NAB voted to give independents a waiver on restrictions against sex and violence until September, 1977, for any programs under contract since last April.

IV. Conclusions

For all the reasons set forth in this statement the United States Catholic Conference finds the proposals contained in the FCC's report to be unacceptable. Our principal reason is that those proposals stand or fail upon effective self-regulation by the broadcast industry.

Effective self-regulation has to be an open, accountable, and cooperative process. Our judgment is that to date the networks have not demonstrated a commitment to such a process. Moreover, we seriously question whether such a commitment is even possible for the networks as long as no industry effort is undertaken to reduce the impact of commercial pressures upon their program decision-making.

In this connection, the "rating game" must be addressed specifically. A basic weakness of commercial broadcasting is that management is incapable of exercising responsible freedom in the program decision-making process because they are trapped in a rating thralldom.

If ratings objectively identified the needs of the public, they would be a true service both to broadcasters and the public they are to serve. We doubt anyone can make a case in favor of the rating organizations that would prove them to be providing a constructive service to the medium or the public. We, therefore, recommend that Congress investigate the program rating services which appear to exercise an inordinate influence upon television programming and which have thus far successfully resisted public scrutiny.

As for the broadcast industry we strongly urge all broadcast licensees, whether network affiliates or independents, whether members of the NAB or not, to reflect anew upon their responsibilities to the public they are licensed to serve and to examine how well they are meeting those responsibilities. We fully appreciate that service to the community by commercial broadcasters cannot be delivered without a profitable operation. Yet the profit motive can never justify programming that debases rather than builds community.

As for the viewing public, it must respond and demonstrate to local station management that it cares and is ready to work with management for the achievement of a program schedule that serves the community's needs. In particular, we encourage our Catholic people, under the leadership of their bishops and pastors, to take an active and affirmative role in working with their fellow citizens, especially on an interfaith basis, in pursuit of the same objectives. Neither networks nor advertisers, neither Hollywood nor government can influence station managers who have their communities strongly behind them.

For its part, the Federal Communications Commission must demonstrate that it is more concerned about how well the public interest is served by commercial broadcasters than how well it serves the interests of commercial broadcasters. In particular, a scrupulous enforcement of the spirit as well as the letter of the community ascertainment requirement is essential.

Moreover, recent efforts either to exempt certain broadcasters from the requirement to ascertain community problems or to reduce the requirements for others must be resisted by the Commission. The Commission must also fully support the right of the public to challenge license renewals. This requires that communities have access to all necessary information and be afforded adequate time to exercise the right to challenge.

Finally, the business community has a special responsibility for the quality of commercial broadcasting. It is their advertising dollars that either enhance or debase the medium. If all advertisers had been as sensitive to the broadcast needs of the American public, especially of the family, as some have been, this statement might not be necessary.

Statement on "Soap"

USCC, Department of Communication
August 10, 1977

At a June 29, 1977 meeting, the television board of directors of the National Association of Broadcasters passed a resolution that "calls on the Television Code Review Board to take positive, visible, affirmative steps to encourage industry and public awareness of both the spirit and letter of the code." Specifically, the television board resolved to "alter the language of the code ... to reassert in more specific terms the broadcasters' recognition of television as primarily a family medium."

The proposed introduction this fall into prime-time scheduling on the ABC television network of a new series entitled "SOAP" is in direct contradiction with the NAB board's action and television's traditional status as a family medium. It must be publicly challenged.

"SOAP" has been variously described by ABC network management as a satire on the daytime soap operas, a comedic farce, and most recently, an adult character comedy with a continuing story line that parallels real life. The characters, at least those identified in the network's July 15, 1977 closed-circuit address to affiliated stations in defense of the series against criticism, include a guilt-ridden adulteress, a confused homosexual, a hilarious hit man, a confessional seductress, and a self-sacrificing philanderer.

The subject matter of the series, we are told by ABC, is human imperfection and "human imperfection is the basis of all comedy and drama." Furthermore, the "socially redeeming aspect" of "SOAP" is "that no character in 'SOAP' is ever rewarded for immoral behavior. And in the final analysis, there will always be retribution for such behavior." The purpose, ABC management attests, is to make the viewer "laugh, enjoy and learn what not to do."

Such an apologia for a TV situation comedy, a traditionally mindless, escapist entertainment genre, in itself raises intriguing questions, beginning with the much abused concept of "adult." If by adult material and treatment were meant a mature analysis of the complex questions of human behavior or of the social inequities that challenge our society today, "SOAP" might be a welcome innovation. Unfortunately, it is all too evident from "SOAP's" plot description, which defines the principal characters solely in terms of their sexual proclivities, that the term "adult" really means a titillating obsession with sex. What is adult about promiscuity and sexual maladjustment?

Taking the ABC defense before its affiliates at its face value, one may also question several of the premises upon which it would appear to be based. Is a situation comedy a credible, much less appropriate, format for moral preachment, learning, that is, "what not to do?" Is, in fact, the basis of all comedy and drama "human imperfection?" Or is that basis not, rather, the paradox of the human condition which continually juxtaposes man's frailty with his aspirations and strivings for greatness? What are the aspirations of the cast of characters in "SOAP?"

Setting aside the not inconsequential question of the sporadic nature of audience viewing habits—occasional viewers may, after all, miss the moral conclusion ABC claims will be in episode nine or thereabouts—the network's argument that in "SOAP" no character "is ever rewarded for immoral behavior" as justification for the series' stated obsession with sex, debases not only the television medium but the humanity of the viewer.

Retribution does not change the quality of past behavior: immoral behavior is no less immoral because it is punished, and a television series that endlessly wallows in the depiction and discussion of such actions is not socially responsible because at the conclusion the characters involved are punished. From such arguments it would seem that ABC places small value on the human dignity of its viewers, much less on their intelligence.

Whether "SOAP" could be an adult character comedy acceptable for adults, however, is not the issue. The core question is whether such a series is consistent with television's traditional role of being a family entertainment medium.

ABC is scheduling "SOAP" for broadcast at 9:30 p.m. eastern time. This would normally mean 8:30 p.m. central time zone, and 7:30 p.m. mountain time zone. ABC has informed affiliates in these two zones that they, in the event of local public reaction, have the option to broadcast "SOAP" at 9:30 p.m.

Yet, a memorandum leaked to the press last week indicated that ABC-TV's original premise for considering "SOAP" was based on scheduling it as a "late night or late prime time (10:00 p.m.) presentation."

We flatly reject ABC's assumption that it has the authority to decide for its affiliates that *any* period within the prime-time evening hours can be arbitrarily set aside for restricted adult viewing. For affiliates to permit the network to make such a decision for them is clearly an abdication of their legal obligations as licensees.

Moreover, according to audience research figures, as many as 18 million children will be *de facto* in the television audience at 9:30 p.m. local time— all of them potential viewers of "SOAP."

These are factors which the management of every ABC affiliate must squarely face in deciding whether to air "SOAP." Evening television is family television. And this is no accident. It was only a generation ago that intense promotion by a young television industry wrested family viewing away from local motion-picture theatres throughout the nation. The result of this competition for the family audience has been the establishment by licensees of family-viewing franchises serving almost every community in the country.

The pattern of family viewing has also been the main attraction for national advertisers, particularly for what are called "consumer non-durable" advertisers. These—which include sellers of cereals, soaps and gas—account for 43 of the top 50 advertisers on the networks. Other family-oriented advertisers such as fast-food stores, supermarkets and softdrink bottlers account for a lion's share of local spot advertising. In short, family viewing is the financial base of the commercial television industry.

Thus, both the public interest and the financial base of the commercial television industry are at stake when a network begins to curtail or to tamper with the industry's traditional commitment to family viewing in the true sense of that phrase.

Many ABC affiliates are still undecided as to whether to clear the program in their communities. Some are in the process of sampling local public opinion in the matter. Others have announced already that they will not carry the series. One ABC affiliate called the new series "a new sewer;" another called it "a dirty joke. You don't walk into a stranger's living room and tell a dirty joke." The chairman of Westinghouse Broadcasting Company notified the network that its ABC-TV affiliated station in Baltimore would not televise the first two episodes of "SOAP." He said, "The impression left by the two pilots is that there is no limit to what 'SOAP' will be allowed to do. It would appear that the series intends to break new barriers with constantly increasing leering sensationalism under the guise of comedy and satire on an ever-expanding basis."

A concerned advertising agency executive, writing in a public letter to Catholics about "SOAP," said: "There is absolutely no involvement, association or relationship between Compton Advertising, any of its clients, or any of its employees in the production, advertising of, or sponsorship of 'SOAP.' There never has been." About advertisers who plan to run commercials in the "SOAP" series, he said: "Salaciousness has its own short-term rewards."

Short-term rewards. Is that what ABC's introduction of "SOAP" is all about? Speaking to the New York Security Analysts on July 15, the ABC president predicted that the current spectacular growth rate of network TV advertising will continue for the next several years. ABC's network president told the same group that ABC has $500 million, or 42-45 per cent of the dollar volume committed by the advertisers to the three networks for the 1977–78 season. He said that ABC has landed "virtually" every major advertiser. The ABC entertainment president boasted that his network will be "a strong number one. . . ."

Number one, in this context, refers exclusively to the ratings game and the economic rewards attendant upon holding that position against the competition. In its September 1975 statement on the family-viewing policy of the television networks, the U.S. Catholic Conference stated that "a basic weakness of commercial broadcasting is that management is incapable of exercising responsible freedom in the program decision-making process because they are trapped in a rating thralldom." The case of "SOAP" may well reinforce doubts that commercial broadcasting is capable of self-regulation as long as the ratings game remains unchallenged.

There is no question that the public will ultimately decide the fate of "SOAP" and the fate of commercial broadcasting. Indeed, the public showed certain reserve strengths not previously tested in the general action against increasing violence in television. Religious organizations, parent-teacher organizations, members of the American Medical Association, major American advertisers, leading advertising agencies, and government leaders joined forces to represent the public interest in reducing the level of violence on television. Today, similar action is needed to prevent this new debasement of the medium through a contempt for human beings.

The executive secretary of the Christian Life Commission of the Southern Baptist Convention, representing 35,000 congregations, wrote to the president of the ABC-TV network urging him "to cancel this morally reprehensible program." The Baptists said that "SOAP" is "an expression of contempt for healthy family life, decent morality and responsible sexual expression." They said, "ABC should not air this series at all."

At this juncture what are ABC's intentions? It seems apparent that ABC is making every effort to ensure that "SOAP" should be allowed to get into the fall starting gate. ABC has withdrawn the two episodes which it had promoted to advertisers and screened for affiliates. They are attempting to sanitize these two episodes. Certain segments will be re-shot, according to the network.

ABC seems to be running a shell game. Now you see it. Now you don't. Criticism based on the original "SOAP" episodes, which a number of Catholic officials have viewed, is now conveniently made to seem invalid. The network is doing them over. The simple fact is that there is a run-for-airdate under way.

What can be done?

The advertiser, the local station licensee and the public—each has the right to refuse this program.

The business community has a special responsibility for the quality of commercial broadcasting. It is their advertising dollars that either enhance or exploit the medium. If advertisers are sensitive to the broadcast needs of the American public, especially the needs of the family, they can refuse to place their advertising in the program on the grounds that they do not want to be associated with the presentation of the content matter in "SOAP."

Affiliates, too, in reflection anew upon their responsibilities to the public they are licensed by the federal government to serve, can exercise their right to reject "SOAP," as a service to their family-viewing audiences. Under the doctrine of public trusteeship the right of the licensee's public circumscribes the broadcaster's discretion regarding program content. We fully appreciate that service to the community by local broadcasters cannot be delivered without a profitable operation. Yet the profit motive can never justify programming that undermines rather than builds the community.

The network cannot, under the law, enforce its will upon station licensees. In this instance, ABC cannot require its affiliates to run "SOAP" no later than 9:30 p.m. local time. It is the licensee who must make the judgment as to *whether* and *when* to air any program.

Obviously, people have a right to switch channels. Moreover, the public can and should work with station management to achieve a program schedule that truly serves the community's needs.

We encourage our Catholic people, under the leadership of their bishops and pastors, to take an active and affirmative role, working with their fellow citizens on an interfaith basis wherever possible to accomplish this purpose.

In the opinion of the U.S. Catholic Conference "SOAP" should be removed from family television entertainment.

Appendix A
Foreign Policy

War and Peace:

1971

Military Conscription
Monsignor Marvin Bordelon, USCC Congressional Testimony submitted to the House Armed Services Committee.
March, 1971

Stop the Arms Race Now
Cardinal Krol Speaking for the American Bishops at the World Synod of Bishops.
October, 1971

1972

"Statement on Vietnam Escalation"
Bishop Joseph L. Bernardin, General Secretary, NCCB/USCC.
May 4, 1972

Pursuing Peace: Working for Justice, A Political/Legislative Focus
Most Rev. John J. Dougherty, submitted to the Platform Committees of the Democratic and Republican Parties.
Summer, 1972

1973

Just War and Pacifism: A Catholic Dialogue
Edited by James R. Jennings.
1973

On Trial: An American War
USCC, Office of International Justice and Peace.
1973

Northern Ireland
Joint Statement of the USCC, the National Council of Churches and the Synagogue Council of America, on Violence in Northern Ireland.
March 9, 1973

1974

Amnesty: A Work of Reconciliation
Rev. J. Bryan Hehir on behalf of the USCC. USCC Congressional Testimony submitted to the House Subcommittee on Courts, Civil Liberties, and the Administration of Justice.
March, 1974

1975
"Statement on Humanitarian Aid to Vietnam"
Archbishop Joseph L. Bernardin.
April 10, 1975

Indochina: To Heal the Wounds of War
Edward W. Doherty, USCC Congressional Testimony submitted to the Committee on International Relations of the U.S. House of Representatives.

1976
U.S. Foreign Policy: A Critique From Catholic Tradition
Archbishop Peter L. Gerety, Congressional Testimony submitted to the Foreign Relations Committee of the U.S. Senate.
January, 1976

Mideast Issues
Archbishop Joseph L. Bernardin.
"On Israel and the U.N.," September 3, 1975.
"On U.N. Vote on Zionism," November 11, 1975.
"Statement on Lebanon and the Middle East," January, 1976.

1977
Northern Ireland: A Religious Conflict
Office of International Justice and Peace, USCC.
September, 1977

1978
U.S. Defense Policy: Reflections From a Catholic Perspective
Background paper of Rev. J. Bryan Hehir, Associate Secretary of the Department of Social Development and World Peace, USCC.
January 11, 1978

Testimony of J. Bryan Hehir Before the Committee on Armed Services, U.S. House of Representatives, on the Fiscal Year 1979 Defense Authorization Bill.
April 18, 1978

Testimony of Edward W. Doherty before the Subcommittee on Arms Control, Oceans, and International Environment of the Senate Foreign Relations Committee, on the U.N. Special Session on Disarmament.
April 24, 1978

"Statement on Neutron Warheads"
Archbishop John Quinn.
April 27, 1978

Arms Export Policies—Ethical Choices
Office of International Justice and Peace, USCC.
October, 1978

1979
Testimony on SALT
John Cardinal Krol, Archbishop of Philadelphia, to the Senate Foreign Relations Committee on Ratification of the Strategic Arms Limitations Treaty.
September 6, 1979

The Nuclear Threat: Reading the Signs of the Times
Materials developed for the World Day of Peace, USCC.
December, 1979

Ratification of SALT II by the U.S. Senate
Letter of Most Rev. Thomas C. Kelly, O.P., General Secretary, NCCB/USCC, to the U.S. Senate, regarding Ratification of SALT II.
October 16, 1979

The Arms Race: Illusion of Security
U.S. Catholic Conference.
1979

Development of Peoples:

1967

Foreign Aid
Joint Testimony of the USCC, the National Council of Churches and the Commission on Social Action of Reform Judaism, presented to the Senate Committee on Foreign Relations, on the subject of Foreign Aid.
May 25, 1967

Foreign Aid
Interfaith Statement of the USCC, the National Council of Churches and the Commission on Social Action of Reform Judaism, presented to the House Committee on Foreign Affairs, on the subject of Foreign Aid.
June 12, 1967

1972

Economic Power in a Shrinking World
Most Rev. John J. Dougherty, USCC Congressional Testimony submitted to the Senate Subcommittee on Anti-Trust and Monopoly.
March, 1972

Justice in the World: A Primer for Teachers
Office of International Justice and Peace, USCC.
1972

1973

Statement on Proposed Reforms of U.S. Overseas Investment and Trade Policies for the 1970s
Most Rev. James S. Rausch, General Secretary, NCCB/USCC. USCC Congressional Testimony submitted to the House Foreign Affairs Committee.
June 15, 1973

1974

"Statement on I.D.A."
Most Rev. James S. Rausch.
February 14, 1974

A Linked and Limited World
Most Rev. James S. Rausch on behalf of the USCC. USCC Congressional Testimony submitted to the Senate Foreign Relations Committee.
April, 1974

"Statement on Food and Fertilizer for the Third World"
Most Rev. James S. Rausch. Letter to Secretaries Kissinger and Butz.
May 16, 1974

Testimony on the Challenge of Food and Population
Rev. J. Bryan Hehir, Associate Secretary, Department of Social Development and World Peace, USCC, before the Senate Ad Hoc Committee on the Rome Conference.
December 18, 1974

1975

Our Daily Bread, Vol. I
Coordinated by the Office of International Justice and Peace, USCC.
1975

Letter of Bishop James S. Rausch, General Secretary, NCCB/USCC, to the U.S. Senate, regarding Foreign Assistance Appropriations for Fiscal Year 1975 and the World Food Crisis.
March 14, 1975

Our Daily Bread, Vol. II
Coordinated by the Office of International Justice and Peace, USCC.
September, 1975

1976

U.S. Foreign Policy: A Critique From Catholic Tradition
Archbishop Peter L. Gerety, Congressional Testimony submitted to the Senate Foreign Relations Committee.
January, 1976

Right to Eat
Testimony of USCC by Most Rev. James S. Rausch, to the House International Relations Committee of the Subcommittee on International Resources, regarding the Right to Food Resolution, H. Con. Res. 393.
June 24, 1976

1977

Testimony on Public Law 480
Testimony of the Most Rev. Edwin R. Broderick, CRS, USCC, before the Senate Committee on Agriculture, Nutrition and Forestry, regarding Public Law 480 and the Provision of Agricultural Commodities.
March 4, 1977

Testimony on Public Law 480
Rev. J. Bryan Hehir, Associate Secretary, Department of Social Development and World Peace, before the Subcommittee on Foreign Agricultural Policy of the Committee on Agriculture, Nutrition and Forestry, U.S. Senate.
April 5, 1977

1978

Testimony on Foreign Assistance
Rev. J. Bryan Hehir, Associate Secretary, Department of Social Development and World Peace, USCC, before the Subcommittee on Foreign Operations of the House Appropriations Committee, regarding Fiscal Year 1979 Appropriations for Foreign Assistance.
April 6, 1978

Testimony on Food Assistance
Rev. J. Bryan Hehir, Associate Secretary, Department of Social Development and World Peace, USCC, before the Subcommittee on Foreign Assistance,

Senate Foreign Relations Committee, regarding the International Development
and Food Assistance Act of 1978.
April 28, 1978

1979

Testimony on the Trade Act
Mr. Henry Brodie, Advisor for International Economic Affairs, USCC. Before
the Subcommittee on Trade, House Ways and Means Committee, on the subject of the Trade Act of 1974.
June 25, 1979

Human Rights

1972

Every Man My Brother?
USCC, Office of International Justice and Peace.
1972

1973

U.N. Declaration on Human Rights
John Cardinal Dearden on behalf of the USCC. USCC Congressional
Testimony submitted to the House Foreign Affairs Committee.
September, 1973

"Human Rights in Bolivia"
USCC, Office of International Justice and Peace.
August 30, 1973

U.N. Sanctions Against Rhodesia
Archbishop Joseph L. Bernardin on behalf of the USCC. USCC Congressional
Testimony submitted to the U.S. Congress.
Fall, 1973

Human Rights: Reflections on a Twin Anniversary
Bishop James S. Rausch, General Secretary of USCC/NCCB. Address to the
National Council of Catholic Laity, New Orleans.
October 17, 1973

"Human Rights in Brazil"
Thomas Quigley, Division for Latin America, USCC. Testimony before the
House Subcommittee on International Organizations and Movements.
October 18, 1973

Human Rights: A Question of Conscience
Division of Justice and Peace, USCC.
June, 1974

The Universal Declaration of Human Rights
Division for Latin America, USCC.
1974

"Statement on Trade Status of the USSR"
Bishop James S. Rausch.
September 26, 1974

1975

Homily: The Red Mass
Most Rev. James S. Rausch, General Secretary, USCC/NCCB.
January 26, 1975

Statement on the United Nations and the Republic of South Africa
  Bishop James S. Rausch, General Secretary, USCC/NCCB.
  October 9, 1975

Human Rights—A Priority for Peace
  Office of International Justice and Peace, USCC.
  1975

Korea: Security vs. Human Rights
  Rev. J. Bryan Hehir, USCC Congressional Testimony submitted to the House
  Committee on International Relations.
  November, 1975

1976

U.S. Foreign Policy: A Critique From Catholic Tradition
  Archbishop Peter L. Gerety. Congressional Testimony submitted to the Senate
  Foreign Relations Committee.
  January, 1976

Letter of Most Rev. James S. Rausch, General Secretary, USCC, on Africa
  To the Honorable Henry A. Kissinger, regarding American Foreign Policy vis-
  a-vis Africa.
  April 7, 1976

"Statement on Human Rights Violations in Chile"
  Rev. J. Bryan Hehir, submitted to the Inter-American Commission on Human
  Rights.
  May 27, 1976

"Statement of Support for Bishop Donal Lamont of Rhodesia"
  NCCB, Executive Committee.
  September 23, 1976

The Panama Canal and Social Justice
  Margaret D. Wilde, Editor. Office of International Justice and Peace, USCC.
  October, 1976

"Repression of the Church in Argentina"
  Rev. J. Bryan Hehir on behalf of the USCC. Testimony before a House Sub-
  committee of the Committee on International Relations (September 29, 1976).
  October 14, 1976

1977

"Statement on Southern Africa"
  Archbishop Joseph L. Bernardin.
  March 24, 1977

Resolution on Haitian Refugees
  NCCB, Ad Hoc Committee on Migration and Tourism.
  May 2, 1977

"Testimony on the Panama Canal Treaty"
  John Cardinal Krol on behalf of the USCC (October 12, 1977). Testimony
  before the Senate Foreign Relations Committee.

1978

Human Rights/Human Needs: An Unfinished Agenda
  USCC, Office of International Justice and Peace.
  1978

"Human Rights Factors in U.S. Foreign Assistance"
Rev. J. Bryan Hehir. Testimony before the House Subcommittee on Foreign Relations (April 6, 1978).
May 4, 1978

1979
The Ratification of The Human Rights Treaties
Msgr. Francis J. Lally. Testimony before the Senate Committee on Foreign Relations.
November 19, 1979

Appendix B
Domestic Policy

Abortion

Fetal Experimentation
Joint Statement of Sr. Virginia Schwager, S.P. and Msgr. James McHugh.
April 10, 1973

Documentation on the Right to Life and Abortion.
NCCB/USCC.
1974

Documentation on The Right to Life and Abortion II.
NCCB/USCC.
1976

Respect Life Program, 1972 through 1979
NCCB, Respect Life Committee

Call to Action

1974
Liberty and Justice for All Discussion Guide
NCCB, Committee for the Bicentennial
1974

Hearings on Social Justice
Conducted by NCCB Committee for the Bicentennial, Washington, D.C.; San Antonio; St. Paul-Minneapolis; Atlanta; Sacramento; Newark; Maryknoll, New York. (7 volumes). USCC Office of Domestic Social Development.
1975-1976

Criminal Justice

1975

Handgun Control
Letter of Msgr. Francis J. Lally, USCC, to Cong. John Conyers, Jr., Chairman, House Subcommittee on Crime, on the subject of handgun control.
September 12, 1975

Handgun Control
Letter of Msgr. Francis J. Lally, USCC, to Cong. Peter W. Rodino, Jr., Chairman, House Judiciary Committee on the subject of handgun control.
December 2, 1975

1976

Handgun Control
Letter of Msgr. Francis J. Lally, USCC, to House Judiciary Committee, on the subject of handgun control.
January 29, 1976

Prison Construction
Letter of Dr. Barbara Stolz, USCC, to Cong. John Slack, Chairman, House Subcommittee on State, Justice, Commerce and Judiciary, regarding Prison Construction.
March 30, 1976

Handgun Legislation
Letter of Msgr. Francis J. Lally, USCC, to the House Judiciary Committee on the subject of Handgun Legislation.
April 6, 1976

Handgun Legislation
Letter of Msgr. Francis J. Lally, USCC, to the U.S. House of Representatives, on the Federal Firearms Act of 1976.
April 26, 1976

Prison Construction
Letter of Msgr. Francis J. Lally, USCC, to Chairman John Pastore, Senate Subcommittee on State Justice, Commerce and the Judiciary, regarding the Legal Services Corporation and Prison Construction.
May 17, 1976

1977

Statement on Capital Punishment
Archbishop Joseph L. Bernardin, President, NCCB/USCC.
January 26, 1977

Prison Construction
Letter of Msgr. Francis J. Lally, USCC, to Senator Hollings, Chairman, Senate Subcommittee on State, Justice, Commerce and the Judiciary, Committee on Appropriations, regarding Prison Construction and Alternatives to Incarceration.
April 29, 1977

Capital Punishment
Letter of Dr. Francis J. Butler, USCC, to Senator John L. McClellan, Chairman, Subcommittee on Criminal Laws and Procedures, U.S. Senate, regarding Capital Punishment.
May 17, 1977

Criminal Code Reform
Letter of Msgr. Francis J. Lally, USCC, to Senator John L. McClellan, Senate Subcommittee on Criminal Laws and Procedures, regarding the Criminal Code Act of 1977.
July 13, 1977

1978

Criminal Code Reform
Testimony of Most Rev. J. Francis Stafford, Auxiliary Bishop of Baltimore, on behalf of the USCC, before the House Subcommittee on Criminal Justice, regarding Revision of the Criminal Code.
April 11, 1978

Capital Punishment
Letter of Msgr. Francis J. Lally, USCC, to the Senate Committee on the Judiciary, regarding Capital Punishment.
May 15, 1978

Capital Punishment
Testimony of Most Rev. Ernest L. Unterkoefler, Bishop of Charleston, on behalf of the USCC, before the House Subcommittee on Criminal Justice, regarding Federal Procedures for the Imposition of the Death Penalty.
July 19, 1978

1979

Victims of Crime
Letter of Msgr. Francis J. Lally, USCC, to Cong. Robert Drinan, House Subcommittee on Criminal Justice, regarding the Victims of Crime Act of 1979.
February 22, 1979

Capital Punishment
Message of Archbishop John Quinn, President, NCCB/USCC, to Alabama Governor Forrest James, Opposing the Execution of John Lewis Evans.
April 5, 1979

Capital Punishment
Statement of Most Rev. Thomas C. Kelly, O.P., General Secretary, NCCB/USCC, on the Occasion of the Execution of John Spenkelink.
May 25, 1979

Economic and Other Human Needs

1966

Civil Rights
Joint Testimony of the National Catholic Welfare Conference, the National Council of Churches and the Synagogue Council of America, before Subcommittee No. 5, House Judiciary Committee, In Support of the Proposed Civil Rights Act of 1966.
May 18, 1966

Unemployment Insurance
Testimony of Msgr. George G. Higgins, On Behalf of the Social Action Department, National Catholic Welfare Conference, Before the Subcommittee of the Senate Finance Committee, on the subject of Improvements in Unemployment Insurance Programs.
July 18, 1966

Civil Rights

Joint Testimony of the National Catholic Welfare Conference, the National Council of Churches and the Synagogue Council of America, Before the Senate Judiciary Committee, In Support of the Proposed Civil Rights Act of 1966.
July 21, 1966

1967

Social Security

Joint Testimony of the USCC and the National Conference of Catholic Charities, Before the House Committee on Ways and Means, regarding the President's Proposal for Revisions in the Social Security System.
April 5, 1967

Social Security

Joint Testimony of the USCC and the National Conference of Catholic Charities, Before the Senate Finance Committee, regarding the Social Security Amendments of 1967.
September 18, 1967

Civil Rights

Joint Testimony of the USCC, the National Council of Churches and the Synagogue Council of America, Before the Subcommittee on Constitutional Rights of the Senate Judiciary Committee, in support of the Proposed Civil Rights Act of 1967.
August 8, 1967

1968

Guaranteed Employment Act

Joint Testimony of the USCC, National Council of Churches and the Synagogue Council of America, in support of the Guaranteed Employment Act of 1968.
May 8, 1968

Employment Practices

Statement of Rev. John McCarthy, Assistant Director, Division for Urban Life, USCC, Before the Federal Communications Commission, on the Matter of Requiring Broadcast Licensees to Show Nondiscrimination in Their Employment Practices.
September 5, 1968 and August 1, 1969

1969

Domestic Hunger

Statement of Rev. John McCarthy, Director, Division for Poverty, USCC, to the House Committee on Agriculture, regarding Hunger and Malnutrition in the United States.
April 24, 1969

Poverty Programs

Statement of Rev. John McCarthy, Division for Poverty, USCC, Before the House Education and Labor Committee, on the subject of Federal Anti-Poverty Programs.
May 1, 1969

Food Stamps

Joint Testimony of the USCC, the National Council of Churches and the Union of American Hebrew Congregations, Before the Senate Agriculture and Forestry Committee on the Food Stamp Act of 1969.
May 26, 1969

Voting Rights Act
Testimony of the Division for Poverty, USCC, to the House Judiciary Subcommittee, regarding the Extension of the Voting Rights Act of 1965.
July 7, 1969

Voting Rights Act
Testimony of Rev. John McCarthy, USCC, to Constitutional Rights Subcommittee, Senate Judiciary Committee, regarding the Extension of the Voting Rights Act of 1965.
August 4, 1969

Welfare Reform
Testimony of John E. Cosgrove, USCC, to the House Committee on Ways and Means, regarding Welfare Reform.
November 12, 1969

Consumer Protection
Statement of John E. Cosgrove, Director, Department of Social Development, USCC, regarding The Consumer Agricultural Food Protection Act of 1969, S. 2203.
1969

1970

Welfare Reform
Testimony of John E. Cosgrove, USCC, David M. Ackerman, National Council of Churches, and Rabbi Richard Hirsch, Union of American Hebrew Congregations, Before the Senate Finance Committee, regarding Welfare Reform.
August 31, 1970

1972

Welfare Reform
Testimony of John E. Cosgrove, Director, Department of Social Development, USCC, before the Senate Finance Committee, regarding the Family Assistance Plan.
January 28, 1972

Busing
Letter of Most Rev. Joseph L. Bernardin to the U.S. House of Representatives, regarding "Anti-Busing" Measures.
August 10, 1972

Social Justice: Political/Legislative Goals
Most Rev. Raymond J. Gallagher. Testimony submitted to the Platform Committees of the Democratic and Republican Parties.
Summer, 1972

1973

Income Maintenance
Letter of Sr. Virginia Schwager, S.P., USCC, to Cong. Wilbur Mills, Chairman, House Ways and Means Committee, regarding eligibility requirements under the Supplemental Security Income Program.
June 25, 1973

Income Maintenance
Letter of Francis J. Butler, USCC, to the House Ways and Means Committee regarding Increases in Social Security Benefits.
September 12, 1973

Social Services
 Letter of Sr. Virginia Schwager, S.P., USCC, to Sen. Russell Long, Chairman,
 Senate Finance Committee, regarding proposals for a Revenue Sharing Ap-
 proach to Federal Social Service Programs.
 November 7, 1973

Maternal and Child Nutrition
 Statement of Sr. Virginia Schwager, S.P., USCC, to the Senate Select Committee on Nutrition and Human Needs, on the Nutritional Inadequacy of Mothers
 and Children.
 December 7, 1973

1975

Federal Nutrition Programs
 Letter of Msgr. Francis J. Lally, USCC, to the U.S. Congress, regarding Im-
 provement of Federal Nutrition Programs.
 August 29, 1975

Food Stamps
 Joint Testimony of the Most Rev. Ignatius J. Strecker and Most Rev. Joseph B.
 Brunini, representing the USCC, before the Senate Subcommittee on
 Agricultural Research and General Legislation, regarding Reform of the Food
 Stamp Program.
 November 20, 1975

Full Employment
 Testimony of the Most Rev. Joseph A. McNicholas, representing the USCC,
 before the Congressional Joint Economic Committee.
 October 20, 1975

The Distribution and Human Costs of Unemployment
 Testimony of Archbishop Thomas A. Donnellan, Archbishop of Atlanta,
 before the Congressional Joint Economic Committee, Atlanta, Georgia.
 December 8, 1975

Full Employment and Economic Justice: A Resource Book
 USCC, Office of Domestic Social Development.
 1975

1976

Employment
 Letter of Msgr. Francis J. Lally, USCC, to the U.S. House of Representatives,
 on the subject of The Public Works Employment Act of 1975.
 January 28, 1976

Human Costs of Unemployment
 Msgr. Francis J. Lally, USCC. Testimony presented to the House Subcommit-
 tee on Employment Opportunities.
 March 2, 1976

The Full Employment and Balanced Growth Act of 1976
 Testimony of Bishop Eugene A. Marino, Auxiliary Bishop of Washington,
 D.C., before the House Subcommittee on Equal Opportunity.
 March 15, 1976

National Economic Policy: Costs of Unemployment and Inflation
 Testimony of Most Rev. James S. Rausch, General Secretary, NCCB/USCC,
 before the National Conference on Full Employment of the Congressional Joint
 Economic Committee.
 March 18, 1976

Testimony on the Federal Food Stamp Program
Msgr. Francis J. Lally, USCC. Testimony presented to the House Committee on Agriculture.
March 23, 1976

Federal Food Stamp Program
Letter of Msgr. Francis J. Lally, USCC, to the U.S. Senate, regarding the Food Stamp Program.
March 31, 1976

Our Daily Bread, Vol. III
Coordinated by the Office of Domestic Social Development.
April, 1976

Food Stamp Legislation
Letter of Msgr. Francis J. Lally, USCC, to the U.S. Senate, regarding the Federal Food Stamp Bill.
April 4, 1976

Full Employment
Letter of Msgr. Francis J. Lally, USCC, to Cong. Dominick V. Daniels, Chairman, House Subcommittee on Manpower, Compensation, Health and Safety, regarding The Full Employment and Balanced Growth Act of 1976.
April 26, 1976

Full Employment
Letter of Most Rev. James S. Rausch, General Secretary, NCCB/USCC, to the U.S. House of Representatives, regarding The Full Employment and Balanced Growth Act of 1976.
May 12, 1976

Food Stamp Legislation
Letter of Dr. Francis J. Butler, USCC, to House Committee on Agriculture, regarding Food Stamp Revisions.
May 12, 1976

Employment
Letter of Most Rev. James S. Rausch, General Secretary, NCCB/USCC, to the President of the United States, on the subject of The Public Works Employment Act of 1976.
June 29, 1976

Public Employment
Letter of Msgr. Francis J. Lally, USCC, to the U.S. Congress, regarding Overriding the Veto of the Public Works Employment Act of 1976.
July 16, 1976

1977

Welfare Reform
Letter of Msgr. Francis J. Lally, USCC, to Hon. Joseph A. Califano, Jr., Secretary, HEW, regarding Welfare Reform.
February 24, 1977

U.S. Food Policy: Its Moral Implications and Its Domestic and International Dimensions
Testimony by Most Rev. Maurice Dingman, Bishop of Des Moines, Iowa, before the Senate Committee on Agriculture, Nutrition and Forestry.
February 24, 1977

Proposals for Economic Stimulus
Testimony of Msgr. Francis J. Lally, Secretary, Department of Social Development and World Peace, USCC, before the Senate Budget Committee.
March 2, 1977

Unemployment and Government Action to Combat Joblessness
Testimony of Msgr. Francis J. Lally, Secretary, Department of Social Development and World Peace, USCC, before the Subcommittee on Employment Opportunities, U.S. House of Representatives.
March 2, 1977

Grain Reserves
Testimony of Bishop James S. Rausch, General Secretary, NCCB/USCC, before the Senate Subcommittee on Nutrition.
March 14, 1977

Full Employment
Letter of Msgr. Francis J. Lally, USCC, to the President of the United States and the Council of Economic Advisors, regarding the issue of Full Employment.
March 16, 1977

Grain Reserves
Letter of Most Rev. Thomas C. Kelly, O.P., General Secretary, NCCB/USCC, to the President of the United States, regarding the Wheat Surplus.
August 26, 1977

Full Employment
Address of Bishop Thomas C. Kelly, O.P., General Secretary, NCCB/USCC, to the Full Employment Action Council.
September 8, 1977

Welfare Reform
Testimony of the Most Rev. Peter L. Gerety, Archbishop of Newark, on behalf of the USCC, Before the House Welfare Reform Subcommittee, regarding the Better Jobs and Income Act.
October 31, 1977

1978

Full Employment
Testimony of Most Rev. Eugene A. Marino, SSJ, Auxiliary Bishop of Washington, D.C., on behalf of the USCC, Before the House Subcommittee on Employment Opportunities, regarding the Full Employment and Balanced Growth Act.
January 31, 1978

Full Employment
Letter of Msgr. Francis J. Lally, USCC, to the U.S. House of Representatives, regarding the Full Employment and Balanced Growth Act.
March 3, 1978

Welfare Reform
Statement of the U.S. Catholic Conference and the National Conference of Catholic Charities, to the Senate Subcommittee on Public Assistance, regarding Welfare Reform Proposals.
May 12, 1978

Federal Spending Priorities
Joint Letter of Bishop Thomas C. Kelly, O.P., USCC, Rabbi Daniel Polish, Synagogue Council of America and Clare Randall, National Council of

Churches to the President of the United States, regarding the Federal Budget of 1980.
December 8, 1978

1979

Federal Spending Priorities
Letter of Most Rev. Thomas C. Kelly, O.P., USCC, to the U.S. Senate, regarding Proposed Federal Budget Cuts.
April 20, 1979

Welfare Reform
Testimony of USCC before the House Subcommittee on Public Assistance and Unemployment Compensation, regarding Welfare Reform Proposals.
June 27, 1979

Youth Employment
Testimony of Most Rev. Thomas C. Kelly, O.P., General Secretary, NCCB/USCC, before the House Subcommittee on Employment Opportunities.
July 18, 1979

Energy Crisis
Joint Response by the USCC, the National Council of Churches and the American Jewish Committee, to the President's Address on the Energy Crisis.
August 2, 1979

Women and Poverty
Resource book on Women and Poverty for parish and social action groups, edited by Barbara Stolz, Ph.D., USCC.
November, 1979

Education

1977

Elementary, Secondary Education Act
Testimony of Rev. Patrick Farrell, USCC Representative for Elementary and Secondary Schools, before the House Subcommittee on Elementary, Secondary and Vocational Education, regarding ESEA.
October, 1977

Federal Department of Education
Testimony of Msgr. Wilfrid Paradis, on behalf of the USCC Committee on Education, before the Senate Committee on Governmental Affairs, regarding the Cabinet Level Education Department.
March 21, 1978

Family Life

1970

Family Planning
Testimony of Rev. James T. McHugh, USCC, Before the Committee on Interstate and Foreign Commerce, of the U.S. House of Representatives, regarding Family Planning.
August 7, 1970

1977

White House Conference on Families
> Letter of Msgr. Francis J. Lally, USCC, to the Vice President of the United States, regarding the White House Conference on Families.
> December 15, 1977

1978

White House Conference on Families
> Testimony of Msgr. Francis J. Lally, Chairman, Catholic Coordinating Committee for the White House Conference on Families, before the Senate Subcommittee on Child and Human Development.
> February 2, 1978

White House Conference on Families
> Letter of Msgr. Francis J. Lally, USCC, to Sen. Alan Cranston, Chairman of the Senate Subcommittee on Child and Human Development, regarding the White House Conference on Families.
> July 24, 1978

1979

Domestic Violence
> Resource publication on the issue of Violence Within the Family, edited by Barbara Stolz, Ph.D., USCC.
> November, 1979

Health

1971

National Health Insurance
> Statement of the USCC before the House Ways and Means Committee, regarding National Health Insurance, by Msgr. Harrold Murray and Sr. M. Maurita Sengelaub, USCC, and Msgr. Lawrence J. Corcoran, National Conference of Catholic Charities.
> October 29, 1971

1973

Medicare
> Letter of Sr. Virginia Schwager, S.P., USCC, to Senator Edmund Muskie, regarding Proposed Changes in Cost Sharing Provisions of the Medicare Program.
> March 7, 1973

Medicaid
> Letter of Sr. Virginia Schwager, S.P., USCC, to the Social Rehabilitation Service of the Department of Health, Education and Welfare, regarding Determination of Eligibility Procedures for Medicaid.
> March 12, 1973

Handicapped
> Statement of Sr. Virginia Schwager, S.P., USCC, on the Enactment of the Vocational Rehabilitation Act.
> March 16, 1973

Emergency Medical Services
> Letter of Sr. Virginia Schwager, S.P., USCC, to Senator Edward Kennedy, Chairman, Senate Subcommittee on Health, regarding the Emergency Medical Services Act of 1973.
> March 19, 1973

Conscience Clause Legislation
Letter of Sr. Virginia Schwager, S.P., USCC, to Congressman Paul Rogers, Chairman, House Subcommittee on Public Health and the Environment, regarding the Public Health Service Act and the Protection of Conscientious Convictions of Hospitals and Health Care Personnel.
April 3, 1973

Medicare
Letter of Sr. Virginia Schwager, S.P., USCC, to the Senate Committee on Aging, regarding Cost Sharing Provisions in the Medicare Program.
April 9, 1973

Health Funding
Letter of Sr. Virginia Schwager, S.P., USCC, to the Health Services and Mental Health Administration, regarding Changes in Federal Health Services Funding.
May 23, 1973

Medicaid
Letter of Sr. Virginia Schwager, S.P., USCC, to the Social and Rehabilitation Service of the Department of Health, Education and Welfare, regarding Cost Sharing Proposals for the Medicaid Program.
July 18, 1973

Alcohol Abuse and Treatment
Letter of Sr. Virginia Schwager, S.P., USCC, to the House Committee on Interstate and Foreign Commerce, regarding the Comprehensive Alcohol Abuse and Alcoholism Prevention, Treatment and Rehabilitation Act Amendments of 1973.
July 30, 1973

Health Maintenance Organizations
Letter of Sr. Virginia Schwager, S.P., USCC, to Senator Harrison Williams, Chairman, Senate Committee on Labor and Public Welfare, regarding the subject of Health Maintenance Organizations.
October 4, 1973

Conscience Clause
Letter of Sr. Virginia Schwager, S.P., USCC, to Senator Frank Church, regarding "Conscience Clause" Legislation Under the Medicare and Medicaid Programs.
November 26, 1973

Prescription Drugs
Letter of Sr. Virginia Schwager, S.P., USCC, to Senator Edward M. Kennedy, Chairman, Senate Subcommittee on Health, on the subject of the High Costs of Brand Name Prescription Drugs.
December 11, 1973

Emergency Medical Services
Letter of Sr. Virginia Schwager, S.P., USCC, to Senator Alan Cranston, regarding the Emergency Medical Services Systems Development Act of 1973.
March 10, 1973

Medicare
Letter of Sr. Virginia Schwager, S.P., USCC, to Senator Frank Church, Special Committee on Aging, regarding Cost Sharing Provisions in the Medicare Program.
June 14, 1973

1974

National Health Insurance
Statement of the USCC, the Catholic Hospital Association, and the National Conference of Catholic Charities, regarding National Health Insurance. Testimony presented to the House Committee on Ways and Means.
July 2, 1974

1975

Health Education
Testimony of the USCC presented to the House Public Health and Environment Subcommittee, regarding Health Education and Promotion Legislation.
November 19, 1975

1976

Medicare
Testimony by the USCC, the Catholic Hospital Association and the National Conference of Catholic Charities, Before the Health Subcommittee of the House Ways and Means Committee, regarding Medicare Improvements.
February 11, 1976

1977

DNA Research
Statement of the NCCB Bishops' Committee on Human Values, regarding Recombinant DNA Research.
May 2, 1977

National Health Insurance
Joint testimony of Msgr. Lawrence J. Corcoran, Executive Director of the National Conference of Catholic Charities and Dr. Francis J. Butler, Associate Secretary, Department of Social Development and World Peace, USCC, Before the Honorable Joseph A. Califano, Jr., Secretary of HEW, regarding National Health Insurance.
October 4, 1977

1978

National Health Insurance
Testimony of Msgr. Francis J. Lally, Secretary of the Department of Social Development and World Peace, USCC, Before the Senate Subcommittee on Health, regarding National Health Insurance.
October 10, 1978

1979

National Health Insurance
Letter of Dr. Francis J. Butler, Associate Secretary, Department of Social Development and World Peace, USCC, to Senator Russell Long, Chairman, Senate Finance Committee, regarding Hearings on National Health Insurance Legislation.
July 17, 1979

Housing

1967

Fair Housing
Joint Testimony of the USCC, the National Council of Churches, and the Synagogue Council of America, Before the Senate Housing and Urban Affairs Subcommittee, In Support of the Fair Housing Act of 1967.
August 23, 1967

1973

Low-Income Housing
Testimony of John E. Cosgrove, Director, Division for Urban Affairs, USCC, Before the Senate Committee on Banking, Housing and Urban Affairs, regarding A Proposed Moratorium on Subsidized Housing Programs.
April 13, 1973

1975

Redlining
Letter of Msgr. Francis J. Lally, USCC, to the U.S. Congress, regarding the Home Mortgage Disclosure Act and the Practice of "Redlining."
August 28, 1975

Redlining
Letter of Msgr. Francis J. Lally, USCC, to Cong. Ferdinand St. Germain, Chairman, House Subcommittee on Financial Institutions, regarding the subject of "Redlining."
September 26, 1975

1976

Low-Income Housing
Letter of Msgr. Francis J. Lally, USCC, to the U.S. House of Representatives, regarding Housing for Low-Income Families.
May 11, 1976

Low-Income Housing
Letter of Msgr. Francis J. Lally, USCC, to the Congressional Conference Committee on Housing Authorization Act and Its Provisions for Low-Income Families.
June 10, 1976

Low-Income Housing
Letter of Most Rev. James S. Rausch, USCC, to the President of the United States, regarding the Housing Authorization Act of 1976.
July 23, 1976

1977

Low-Income Housing
Letter of Msgr. Francis J. Lally, USCC, to the U.S. Senate, regarding Low and Moderate Income Housing and Community Development.
April 22, 1977

Low-Income Housing
Letter of Msgr. Francis J. Lally, USCC, to the U.S. Senate, urging support for the Amendment to the First Concurrent Budget Resolution.
April 22, 1977

1979

Housing for the Elderly and Handicapped
Testimony of the USCC Before the House Subcommittee on Housing and Community Development, regarding Housing for the Elderly and Handicapped.
March 30, 1979

Fair Housing
Letter of Bishop Thomas C. Kelly, O.P., USCC, to the Secretary of Housing and Urban Development, regarding the Fair Housing Amendments Act of 1979.
July 23, 1979

Human Rights

1979

Rights of Institutionalized Persons

Letter of Msgr. Francis J. Lally, USCC, to Cong. Robert Kastenmeier, Chairman, House Subcommittee on Courts, Civil Liberties and the Administration of Justice, regarding the Rights of Institutionalized Persons.
February 21, 1979

Letter of Msgr. Francis J. Lally, USCC, to Senator Birch Bayh, Chairman, Senate Committee on the Judiciary, regarding the Rights of Institutionalized Persons.
April 5, 1979

Immigrants

1968

Aliens

Testimony of Rev. John McCarthy, Social Action Department, USCC, Before the Select Committee on Western Hemisphere Migration, on the subject of Green Card Commuter Laborers.
March 1, 1968

1969

Aliens

Testimony of Rev. John McCarthy, Director of the Division for Poverty, USCC, to the Special Subcommittee on Labor of the House Committee on Education and Labor, regarding the Employment of Certain Aliens in Circumstances Which Destroy the Rights of Workers to Organize and Bargain Collectively.
August 18, 1969

1974

Undocumented Persons

Letter of Most Rev. James S. Rausch, USCC, to Senator James Eastland, Chairman, Senate Committee on the Judiciary, regarding Hearings on the Illegal Aliens Bill.
December 4, 1974

1975

Aliens

Testimony of Msgr. George G. Higgins, USCC, Before the House Subcommittee on Immigration, Citizenship and International Law, regarding Illegal Aliens.
March 13, 1975

Critique by Most Rev. James S. Rausch, General Secretary, NCCB/USCC, on the subject of the Illegal Alien Bill.
August 20, 1975

1976

Immigration Laws

Testimony of Most Rev. Robert Sanchez of Santa Fe on behalf of the USCC, Before the Senate Subcommittee on Immigration and Naturalization, regarding Proposed Legislation to Reform the U.S. Immigration Laws.
April 1, 1976

1977

Reaction to President Carter's Immigration Proposal, by Most Rev. Thomas C. Kelly, O.P., General Secretary, NCCB/USCC.
August 5, 1977

Labor

1967

Agricultural Workers and the NLRB
Testimony of Rev. John McCarthy, Social Action Department, USCC, Before the Senate Subcommittee on Migratory Labor, on the subject of Extending Provisions of the NLRB to Cover Agricultural Workers.
July 12, 1967

1970

Unemployment Compensation
Letter of Most Rev. Joseph L. Bernardin, USCC, to Sen. Russell Long, Chairman, Senate Finance Committee, regarding Unemployment Compensation Law as it Applies to Farmworkers.
February 20, 1970

1971

Child Labor
Testimony of Stephen E. Bossi, on behalf of the National Catholic Rural Life Conference and the USCC, Before the House Subcommittee on Agricultural Labor, regarding The Agricultural Child Labor Act of 1971.
September 21, 1971

Workmen's Compensation
Testimony of John E. Cosgrove, Director, Department of Social Development, USCC, Before the National Commission on State Workmen's Compensation Laws.
December 13, 1971

1972

United Farm Workers
Letter of the USCC Department of Social Development to President Richard M. Nixon, regarding NLRB Action to Enjoin the Boycott of the United Farm Workers of America.
March 27, 1972

1975

Child Labor
Letter of Msgr. Francis J. Lally, USCC to the House Committee on Education and Labor, regarding Child Labor and the Fair Labor Standards Act.
April 24, 1975

1977

Labor Law Reform
Testimony of Msgr. George G. Higgins, Before the House Subcommittee on Labor Management Relations, on the subject of Labor Law Reform.
July 28, 1977

Teacher Organizations
    Statement of the USCC Subcommittee on Teacher Organizations, regarding
    Teacher Organizations in Catholic Schools.
    September 15, 1977

Population

1970
Testimony of Rev. James T. McHugh, USCC, Before the House Interstate and
    Foreign Commerce Committee Regarding Population Proposals.
    August 7, 1970

1971
Testimony of Msgr. James T. McHugh, USCC, Before the Commission on Popu-
    lation Growth and the American Future.
    April 14, 1971

Testimony of Msgr. James T. McHugh, USCC, Before the Senate Subcommittee
    on Human Resources, on the subject of Population Stabilization.
    November 3, 1971

Privacy

Statement of Most Rev. Mark Hurley, Moderator of the Secretariat for Human
    Values, Bishops' Committee for Ecumenical and Interreligious Affairs, NCCB.

Pornography

1970
Statement of Rev. John McLaughlin S.J. and W.R. Consedine Before House
    Subcommittee No. 3 of the Committee on the Judiciary regarding Legislative
    Measures to Control Dissemination of Sexually-oriented Materials.
    January 28, 1970

Regional Planning

1972
Testimony of John E. Cosgrove, USCC Before the House Public Works Committee
    Regarding Regional Planning.
    April 19, 1972

Rural America

1973
Migrant Health
    Statement of the USCC, on Migrant Health.
    March 8, 1973

1977
Surface Mining
    Letter of Dr. Francis J. Butler, Associate Secretary, Department of Social
    Development and World Peace, USCC, to the House Interior Subcommittee on
    Energy and the Environment, regarding the Surface Mining Control and
    Reclamation Act of 1977.
    March 24, 1977

Surface Mining
Letter of Dr. Francis J. Butler, Associate Secretary, Department of Social Development and World Peace, USCC, to the Senate Subcommittee on Public Lands and Resources, regarding the Surface Mining Control and Reclamation Act of 1977.
March 24, 1977

Surface Mining
Letter of Dr. Francis J. Butler, USCC, to the Congressional Conference Committee, regarding the Surface Mining Control and Reclamation Act of 1977.
June 10, 1977

1979

Land Reclamation
Letter of Dr. Francis J. Butler, USCC, to Senator Frank Church, Chairman Senate Subcommittee on Energy Research and Development, regarding Land Reclamation.
April 4, 1979

Farm Entry Assistance Act
Letter of Dr. Francis J. Butler, USCC, to Senator Herman Talmadge, Chairman, Senate Committee on Agriculture, Nutrition and Forestry, regarding Hearings on S. 582, the Farm Entry Assistance Act.
April 17, 1979

Rural Development
Testimony of the Most Rev. George H. Speltz, representing the USCC, Before the House Subcommittee on Family Farms and Rural Development, regarding Rural Development.
April 25, 1979

Land Reclamation Act
Letter of Bishop Thomas C. Kelly, O.P., NCCB/USCC General Secretary, to the U.S. Senate, regarding the Reclamation Reform Act of 1979.
July 16, 1979

Farmland Protection Act
Letter of Dr. Francis J. Butler, USCC, to Senator Roger Jepsen, regarding the Farmland Protection Act.
September 12, 1979

Structure of American Agriculture
Testimony of Most Rev. Murorice J. Digman, representing the USCC Before hearings conducted by The Department of Agriculture regarding The Structure of American Agriculture.
December 4, 1979

Taxes

Tax Reform

1969

Testimony of W.R. Consedine, General Counsel, USCC Before the House Committee on Ways and Means regarding Tax Reform Studies.
April 1, 1969

Testimony of W.R. Consedine, General Counsel, USCC Before the Commmittee on Finance, U.S. Senate on Tas Reform Proposals.
September 17, 1969

Tax Exemption

1972

Testimony of Most Rev. Joseph L. Bernardin, General Secretary, NCCB/USCC, Before House Ways and Means Committee regarding Taxes, the Churches, Public Witness.
May 9, 1972

Testimony of Most Rev. Joseph L. Bernardin, General Secretary, NCCB/USCC, Before the House Ways and Means Committee, regarding Taxes, the Churches, Public Witness.
June, 1972

Television

1973

Statement of Most Rev. James S. Rausch, General Secretary, NCCB/USCC, regarding a television episode of "Maude."
August, 1973

1976

Statement of Most Rev. James S. Rausch, General Secretary, NCCB/USCC, regarding Television Advertising of Contraceptives.
March, 1976

1979

Statement of Most Rev. Thomas C. Kelly, O.P., General Secretary, NCCB/USCC, Criticizing Broadcast Deregulation. *N.C. News.*
June 27, 1979

Appendix C
Encyclicals, Synod and Conciliar Documents

Abbott, Walter M. and Msgr. Joseph Gallagher, eds. *The Documents of Vatican II.* New York: Guild Press, 1966.

Gilson, Etienne, ed. *The Church Speaks to the Modern World: The Social Teachings of Leo XIII.* Garden City, N.Y.: Doubleday & Co., 1954.

McLlaughlin, T., C.S.B., ed. *The Church and the Reconstruction of the Modern World: The Social Encyclicals of Pius XI.* Garden City, N.Y.: Doubleday & Co., 1957.

Pope John XXIII. *Mater et Magistra.* Washington: NCWC, 1961.

_____. *Pacem in Terris.* Washington: NCWC, 1963.

Pope Paul VI. *A Call to Action: Apostolic Letters.* Washington: USCC, 1971.

_____. *On the Development of Peoples, Populorum Progressio.* Washington: USCC, 1967.

_____. *On Evangelization in the Modern World, Evangelii Nuntiandi.* Washington: USCC, 1976.

Pope John Paul II. *Redemptor Hominis.* Washington: USCC, 1979.

Roman Synod of Bishops. *Justice in the World.* Washington: USCC, 1972.

Synod Bishops, 1974. Washington: USCC, 1975.

Index

Editors

J. Brian Benestad, Ph.D., is assistant professor of political theory and social ethics at the University of Scranton.

Francis J. Butler, who holds a doctorate in sacred theology, served the U.S. Catholic Conference as associate secretary for domestic social development for five years. He is currently president of FADICA (Foundations and Donors Interested in Catholic Activities), an international association of private foundations.

NOTES

NOTES

NOTES